INTRODUCTION TO Computer Programming in Visual Basic 6.0

ROBERT J. SPEAR

Prince George's Community College
and
University of Maryland

TIMOTHY M. SPEAR

Independent Consultant

INTRODUCTION TO
Computer Programming in
Visual Basic 6.0

ROBERT J. SPEAR
Prince George's Community College
and
University of Maryland

TIMOTHY M. SPEAR
Independent Consultant

THE DRYDEN PRESS
A Division of Harcourt College Publishers

Fort Worth Philadelphia San Diego New York Orlando Austin San Antonio
Toronto Montreal London Sydney Tokyo

Publisher Mike Roche
Executive Editor Christina A. Martin
Developmental Editor Larry Crowder
Project Editor Claudia Gravier
Art Director Van Mua
Production Manager Cindy Young

ISBN: 0-03-026391-3
Library of Congress Catalog Card Number: 99–62185

Address for Domestic Orders
Harcourt Inc., 6277 Sea Harbor Drive, Orlando, FL 32887-6777
800-782-4479

Address for International Orders
International Customer Service
Harcourt Inc., 6277 Sea Harbor Drive, Orlando, FL 32887-6777
407-345-3800
(fax) 407-345-4060
(e-mail) hbintl@harcourtcollege.com

Address for Editorial Correspondence
Harcourt College Publishers, 301 Commerce Street, Suite 3700, Fort Worth, TX 76102

Web Site Address
http://www.harcourtcollege.com

Harcourt College Publishers will provide complimentary supplements or supplement packages to those adopters qualified under our adoption policy. Please contact your sales representative to learn how you qualify. If as an adopter or potential user you receive supplements you do not need, please return them to your sales representative or send them to: Attn: Returns Department, Troy Warehouse, 465 South Lincoln Drive, Troy, MO 63379.

Printed in the United States of America

9 0 1 2 3 4 5 6 7 8 751 9 8 7 6 5 4 3 2 1

Harcourt College Publishers

To Mary Helen and Dionne

THE DRYDEN PRESS SERIES IN INFORMATION SYSTEMS

Adams
First Steps Series
Word 97
Excel 97
Access 97
PowerPoint 97

Coorough
Getting Started with Multimedia

Fenrich
Practical Guidelines for Creating Instructional Multimedia Applications

Fuller/Manning
Getting Started with the Internet

Gordon and Gordon
Information Systems: A Management Approach
Second Edition

Gray, King, McLean, and Watson
Management of Information Systems
Second Edition

Harris
Systems Analysis and Design: A Project Approach
Second Edition

Larsen/Marold
Using Microsoft Works 4.0 for Windows 95: An Introduction to Computing

Laudon and Laudon
Information Systems: A Problem-Solving Approach
(A CD-ROM interactive version)

Licker
Management Information Systems: A Strategic Leadership Approach

Lorents and Morgan
Database Systems: Concepts, Management, and Applications

Martin
Discovering Microsoft Office 97

Martin/Parker
PC Concepts

Mason
Using Microsoft Access 97 in Business

Mason
Using Microsoft Excel 97 in Business

Millspaugh
Object-Oriented Programming with C++

Morley
Getting Started with Computers
Second Edition

Morley
Getting Started: Web Page Design with Microsoft Front Page 97

Parker
Understanding Computers: Today and Tomorrow
'98 Edition

Parker
Understanding Networking and the Internet

Spear
Introduction to Computer Programming in Visual Basic 4.0

Spear
Visual Basic 3.0: A Brief Introduction
Visual Basic 4.0: A Brief Introduction

Sullivan
The New Computer User
Second Edition

Martin and Parker
Mastering Today's Software Series

Texts available in any combination of the following:
Windows 98
Windows NT Workstation 4
Windows 95
Windows 3.1
Disk Operating System 6.0 (DOS 6.0)
Disk Operating System 5.0 (DOS 5.0)
Microsoft Office 97 Professional Edition
Microsoft Office for Windows 95 Professional Edition
Word 97
Word 7.0 for Windows 95
Word 6.0 for Windows
Corel WordPerfect 7.0 for Windows 95
WordPerfect 6.1 for Windows
WordPerfect 6.0 for Windows
WordPerfect 5.1
Excel 97
Excel 7.0 for Windows 95
Excel 5.0 for Windows
Lotus 1-2-3 97
Lotus 1-2-3 for Windows (5.0)
Lotus 1-2-3 for Windows (4.01)
Lotus 1-2-3 (2.4)
Lotus 1-2-3 (2.2/2.3)
Quattro Pro 4.0
Quattro Pro 6.0 for Windows
Access 97
Access 7.0 for Windows 95
Access 2.0 for Windows
Paradox 5.0 for Windows
Paradox 4.0
dBASE 5 for Windows
dBASE IV (1.5/2.0)
dBASE III PLUS
PowerPoint 97
PowerPoint 7.0 for Windows 95
A Beginner's Guide to QBASIC
A Beginner's Guide to BASIC
Netscape Navigator 4.0
Internet Explorer 4.0

PREFACE

Welcome to Visual Basic 6.0 Professional Edition and to the world of computer programming! This textbook, in conjunction with Windows 95/98/NT and Visual Basic 6.0 software, will teach you the fundamentals of applications computer programming in a Windows environment. It will allow you to create powerful, graphical applications for school, home, or business; and, by the time you complete the semester, you will have developed solid skills as an intermediate-level computer programmer.

Goals

This textbook has two principal goals:

- Development of sound, fundamental skills in graphical interface design and in structured computer programming. Modern information system designs emphasize the graphical interface (what the user sees on the screen while the program is running). The logic—largely unseen by the user—that stands behind the graphical interface provides most of the functionality of an application and must be carefully designed in a structured, modular fashion. Both elements are important, not only to satisfy the specifications for an application, but also to serve such other worthwhile goals as readability, maintainability, and reusability.
- Introducing Visual Basic to users of this textbook.

The vehicle for achieving both goals is Microsoft Corporation's state-of-the-art programming language, Visual Basic 6.0 Professional Edition. Our objective is to cover all of the fundamentals well, while leaving more advanced topics to other textbooks and to the trade publications.

Audience

This book is written for university and community-college students who are interested in learning Windows-based, business-oriented computer programming. Since graphical designs are becoming ever more important, the chosen language is one that emphasizes graphical design. The book assumes no previous knowledge of computer programming. A beginners class would be expected to cover all or most of the text in one semester.

We anticipate that most readers will be business students who need exposure to at least one computer-programming language, or information systems students who are studying Visual Basic as only one of many computer-related courses.

Some students may have had a previous course in computer programming in a procedure-oriented language such as Pascal or COBOL or even earlier versions of BASIC, but have not been exposed to computer programming for Windows-based applications. Students with some previous programming experience may be able to proceed more quickly through Parts One and Two, but should pay special attention to the sections dealing with the graphical interface and with event-driven programming, which may be new concepts.

Hardware/Software Assumptions

The only requirement for using this textbook is a computer equipped with Windows 95/98/NT and Microsoft Visual Basic 6.0 (any edition).

Organization

Part One, "Getting Started," provides a background for Visual Basic and an introduction to the Visual Basic Design Environment. Part Two, comprising Chapters Two through Five, discusses programming fundamentals. In these chapters the student learns how to design a graphical interface and the basics of writing Visual Basic code. Variables, constants, arrays, and control structures (sequence, selection, iteration) are all covered, in addition to the various standard graphical VB objects (controls). Part Three (Chapters Six through Nine) focuses on the Graphical Users Interface (GUI) and on the coding techniques needed to make that interface most effective. Part Four (Chapters Ten through Thirteen) covers databases and traditional files and includes a brief introduction to class libraries, ActiveX controls, Web-based applications, and other concepts needed for commercial "production" program development.

Within each chapter, a consistent outline is followed. Learning objectives for the chapter are stated first. There follows a list of keywords introduced in that chapter. The body of the chapter mimics the seven-step programming process:

- During the first step, "Understanding the Problem," the student is guided in running that chapter's application and noticing its new features. (The student files on the Dryden Web site include the executable file for each chapter's main application.)
- In the second step, "Design a Solution," the new features necessary for the chapter's application are discussed in detail.
- The third step, "Develop an Algorithm," is devoted to program logic. Beginning with Chapter Three, this includes the Hierarchy Table as well as pseudocode for individual procedures.
- Step 4, "Design the GUI," contains all of the property settings needed for the graphical interface.
- Step 5 presents the complete coding for the program and any needed explanations.
- Step 6, as appropriate, discusses testing and debugging of the program.
- Finally, Step 7 describes documentation that must be completed.

Following these seven steps, the chapter concludes with a chapter summary and two programming assignments.

Pedagogical Features

The basic pedagogical approach is for the instructor, the students, and the textbook to develop Visual Basic applications together. At the beginning, starting with Chapter Two, the student is given very careful step-by-step instructions in building an application. The text includes all of the property settings and instructions for building the graphical user interface (GUI) and all of the program code. Each chapter explains the graphical controls, properties, events, and methods, as well as the code needed for that application. The student is encouraged to build the application while going through the text. We ourselves use these materials in teaching: each chapter becomes the basis for a week's worth of class lectures and labs. As the chapters progress, the hand-holding becomes less pervasive. That is, the student is slowly weaned from the extremely detailed instructions at the beginning of the book. In the later chapters, the student is expected to figure out more of the material without our assistance.

We have found that students learn well and quickly from this project-oriented approach. Students tend to be near-term goal-oriented: Therefore, they may not want to learn everything there is to know about a particular topic, just because their textbook or their teacher tells them that they will need this information at some unspecified future date. Students pay close attention to learning those aspects of a topic needed to do today's assignment. For this reason, the text focuses on just those pieces of Visual Basic that the student needs for the application then under discussion.

In our courses, at the conclusion of each chapter, students are expected to turn in a disk containing the student's version of that chapter's main application, which we have completed together during lab time, as well as one of the two programming assignments from the end of the chapter, which students have completed on their own time. As to the main application in each chapter, students learn from implementing it even though they are just copying: They experiment with variations; they ask questions to try to understand what's really going on; they make mistakes and have to debug them. Students have given overwhelmingly positive feedback to this learning modality.

Ancillary Materials

The Instructor's Manual includes the following:

- A model course syllabus for a one-semester, first course in computer programming
- A model course syllabus for a one-semester course, for students studying Visual Basic as a second programming language
- Definitions of the keywords in each chapter
- The outline of topics in each chapter, with space left for the instructor's own notes
- Test questions (true/false and multiple choice)
- Programming exams

The Instructor's Manual and self-extracting, executable files for the student and for the instructor are available online at www.dryden.com/infosys/spear2/. STUDENT.EXE contains all of the executables for the main applications in each chapter. INSTRUCT.EXE contains source code for the main applications in each chapter and for sample solutions to the programming assignments.

Acknowledgments

Writing this text has been an exciting, enjoyable, collaborative experience for the father–son coauthors. But we were far from alone in completing this project.

First and most importantly, we wish to thank Christina A. Martin, executive editor and Larry Crowder, development editor. Their advice and counsel has been with us from beginning to end. We would also like to acknowledge other luminaries in the Dryden team: Cindy Young, production manager; Van Mua, art director; Linda Blundell, permissions editor; and Claudia Gravier, project editor. In getting a textbook from the mind of the original authors into the hands of the students, every job is important and challenging. We thank all of those who contributed directly and who facilitated the process.

As students in Bob Spear's classes, Bob Vanaman, Cary Algood, and Penny Thompson wrote computer programs that inspired some of the chapter projects and end-of-chapter programming exercises. Over the last several years, students in CIS 214 at Prince George's Community College and in BMGT 302 at the University of Maryland class tested all of these programs and materials. We believe that their comments and suggestions improved immeasurably the learning effectiveness of the final product.

Outside reviewers also suggested worthwhile changes, deletions, and additions. These include Denise McGinnis, Mesa State College; Vida Momenian, Prince George's Community College; Paula Tennison, DeVry Institute of Technology; Dennis C. Hipp, Guilford Technical Community College; and Viswanath Venkatesh, University of Maryland.

Finally, we would like to thank our wives, Mary Helen Spear (Bob's wife and Tim's mother) and Dionne Spear (Tim's wife and Bob's daughter-in-law) for their patience and support throughout the long authoring and revision process.

Robert J. Spear
Timothy M. Spear
May 1999

BRIEF CONTENTS

Preface ix

PART ONE **GETTING STARTED 1**

Chapter One Introduction: *Simple Application* 3

PART TWO **PROGRAMMING FUNDAMENTALS 25**

Chapter Two A First Program: Form, Controls, and Code: *Application: Hello, World* 27
Chapter Three Elements of VB's Programming Language: *Application: Simple Calculator* 49
Chapter Four Control Arrays and For/Next Loops: *Application: Colorful Backdrop* 77
Chapter Five Debugging, Multiple Forms, Graphical Controls: *Application: Shapes* 95

PART THREE **PROGRAMMING THE FRONT-END: THE GRAPHICAL USER INTERFACE 123**

Chapter Six Do Loops, Functions, Arrays of Variables: *Application: Finance (Version 1)* 125
Chapter Seven General Procedures, Case Construct, Error Traps: *Application: Finance (Version 2)* 147
Chapter Eight Math, Simulations, Function Procedures: *Application: Math Magic* 171
Chapter Nine Menus and MDI Forms: *Application: Finance (Version 3)* 191

PART FOUR **PROGRAMMING THE BACK-END: DATABASES, ACTIVEX, AND THE WEB 217**

Chapter Ten Databases and Data Control (Viewable): *Application: Class Scheduling (Version 1)* 219
Chapter Eleven Data Control (Updatable): *Application: Class Scheduling (Version 2)* 247
Chapter Twelve Advanced Concepts: *Applications: Class Scheduling (Versions 3 & 4) and Cool Visuals* 277
Chapter Thirteen Traditional Files: *Application: State Information* 315

APPENDIX A **ASCII Codes 337**

GLOSSARY **339**

INDEX **353**

DETAILED CONTENTS

Preface ix

PART ONE GETTING STARTED 1

Chapter One Introduction: *Simple Application* 3

A Quick Historical Review: How We Got to Visual Basic 4
Introducing the "Simple" Application 9
  Run the "Simple" Application 10
The Visual Basic Integrated Development Environment 12
  Title Bar 12
  Menu Bar 13
    File Menu 13
      New Project 13
      Open Project 13
      Save Project 14
      Save Project As 14
      Save <Filename> 14
      Save <Filename> As 14
      Print 15
      Make <ProjectName> EXE File 15
      Exit 15
    Edit Menu 15
    View Menu 15
    Project Menu, Format Menu, and Debug Menu 18
    Run Menu 18
    Query Menu and Diagram Menu 18
    Tools Menu 18
    Add-Ins Menu and Windows Menu 19
    Help Menu 19
Experiment with the "Simple" Application 19
Summary 22
Programming Assignment 22
  Pet Rock 22

PART TWO PROGRAMMING FUNDAMENTALS 25

Chapter Two A First Program: Form, Controls, and Code: *Application: Hello, World* 27

Introducing the "Hello, World" Application 28
Building the "Hello, World" Project 29
  Step 1. Understand the Problem. 29
  Step 2. Design Your Solution. 29
    Object Names 30
  Step 3. Develop Your Logic. 31
  Step 4. Build Your GUI. 32
  Step 5. Write the VB Code Associated with Each Form and Control. 38
    Program Constants 38
  Step 6. Test and Debug Your Program. 44
  Step 7. Complete the Program Documentation. 44
Revised "Hello, World" Project 44
Summary 45
Programming Assignments 45
  My Resume 45
  Knock-Knock Joke 46

Chapter Three **Elements of VB's Programming Language: *Application: Simple Calculator*** 49
Variables 50
Assignments 51
Expressions 52
Data Types 53
Introducing the Simple Calculator Project 54
Step 1. Understand the Problem. 55
Step 2. Design Your Solution. 56
Step 3. Develop Your Logic. 57
cmd0, cmd1, cmd2, cmd3, cmd4, cmd5, cmd6, cmd7, cmd8, and cmd9 57
cmdAdd and cmdSubtract 57
cmdEqual 58
cmdClear 58
Hierachy Table + Pseudocode 58
Control Structures 59
Step 4. Build Your GUI. 61
Step 5. Write the VB Code. 63
Option Explicit 64
Scope of Variables, Constants, and Procedures 64
Hungarian Notation 66
Command Button Click Event Procedures 67
cmd0 . . . cmd9 67
cmdAdd and cmdSubtract 67
cmdEqual 69
Relational Expressions 69
If Statements 71
cmdClear 72
Step 6. Test and Debug Your Program. 72
Step 7. Complete the Program Documentation. 73
Summary 73
Programming Assignments 73
Movie Theater Tickets 73
Football Scoreboard 75

Chapter Four **Control Arrays and For/Next Loops: *Application: Colorful Backdrop*** 77
Visual Basic Help 77
VB Menu Bar—Help Pull-Down Menu 78
Help Screen's Menu Bar 79
File Menu 79
Edit Menu 79
Help Screen's Button Bar 80
Reference Lists 80
Context-Sensitive Help 81
Help System Working Examples 82
Introducing the Colorful Backdrop Application 83
Step 1. Understand the Problem. 83
Step 2. Design Your Solution. 85
Control Arrays 85
Looping 86
For/Next Loops 86
Assigning the Background Color and Displaying the Color Code 88
Keyboard Input 88
Step 3. Develop Your Logic—Hierarchy Table and Pseudocode. 89
Step 4. Build the Graphical User Interface (GUI). 89
Step 5. Write the VB Code. 91
Step 6. Test and Debug Your Program. 91
Step 7. Complete the Program Documentation. 92

Summary 92
Programming Assignments 92
Improved Simple Calculator 92
Olympic Scoring 93

Chapter Five **Debugging, Multiple Forms, Graphical Controls: *Application: Shapes*** 95
Introducing Shapes 96
Step 1. Understand the Problem. 96
Step 2. Design a Solution. 97
Incorporating a Second Form in a Project 97
Twips—and Left, Top, Width, and Height Properties 97
The Shape Control 98
The TextBox Control and the Notion of "Focus" 99
Scope and Visibility of Form-level versus Procedure-level Variables 100
Step 3. Develop Your Logic. 101
Step 4. Build Your GUI. 102
The Project Explorer Window 102
frmShapes1 102
frmShapes2 103
Identifying the Start Up Form 104
Step 5. Write the VB Code. 104
Private Sub cmdExit_Click 105
Private Sub Form_Load (for frmShapes1) 105
Private Sub txtName_Change 106
Private Sub and Shape_Click (Index As Integer) 106
Rnd function 106
Private Sub Form_Load (for frmShapes2)—Locating the Form on the Screen 107
Private Sub cmdOk_Click () 107
Step 6. Test and Debug Your Program. 107
Syntax Errors 108
Runtime Errors 108
Logic Errors 110
Debug Facility 111
Summary of Menu Selections, Toolbar Icons, and Shortcut Keys 115
Step 7. Complete the Program Documentation. 118
A Variation on Shapes 118
Timer Control 118
Summary 119
Programming Assignments 120
Busy Box 120
Layout 120

PART THREE **PROGRAMMING THE FRONT-END: THE GRAPHICAL USER INTERFACE** 123

Chapter Six **Do Loops, Functions, Arrays of Variables: *Application: Finance (Version 1)*** 125
Introducing the Finance Project 125
Step 1. Understand the Problem. 128
Step 2. Design a Solution. 128
Array of Simple Variables 129
Frames and Option Buttons 130
Step 3. Develop an Algorithm. 131
Hierarchy Table 131
Event Procedures 132
Command Button Click Event Procedures Pseudocode 132
InputBox Function 133
Do Loop Construct 133
Mod Operator 135

Boolean expressions and variables 135
MsgBox Function 136
VB's Library of Symbolic Constants 136
Object Browser 137
Format Function 137
DDB, SYD, and SLN Depreciation Functions 138
FV and PV Functions; Pmt, NPer, and Rate Functions 140
Step 4. Build Your GUI. 140
Step 5. Write the VB Code. 141
Step 6. Test and Debug. 144
Step 7. Complete the Program Documentation. 145
Summary 145
Programming Assignments 145
Lotto 145
Revised Finance1 146

Chapter Seven **General Procedures, Case Construct, Error Traps:** ***Application: Finance (Version 2)*** **147**
Introducing the Finance Project (Version 2) 147
Step 1. Understand the Problem. 148
Step 2. Design a Solution. 148
Reusable Code 148
Static Versus Dynamic Variables 149
Step 3. Develop an Algorithm. 150
Hierarchy Table and Pseudocode 150
Case Structure 151
Parallel Arrays of Variables and Controls 153
Procedure Calls 154
Scope of General Procedures 155
Parameter Passing 156
Error Traps 160
Step 4. Build Your GUI. 164
Step 5. Write the VB Code. 165
cmdFinance Click Event Procedure 165
Depreciation General Procedure 166
Step 6. Test and Debug. 168
Step 7. Complete the Program Documentation. 168
Summary of Naming Conventions for Variables 168
Summary 169
Programming Assignments 169
QBColors Revisited 169
Revised Finance2 170

Chapter Eight **Math, Simulations, Function Procedures:** ***Application: Math Magic*** **171**
Introducing Math Magic 171
Step 1. Understand the Problem. 172
Step 2. Design a Solution. 175
Rnd Function and Randomize Statement 175
Computer Simulation 177
Other Mathematical Functions 178
Function Procedures 180
Step 3. Develop an Algorithm. 181
Hierarchy Table and Pseudocode 181
Window State Option Buttons 181
Form Color Option Buttons 181
General Procedures 182
Public Sub Primes() 183
Public Sub Fibonacci() 184

Public Sub Guess() 184
Step 4. Build Your GUI. 185
Step 5. Write the VB Code. 185
FrmMagic—filename frmMAGIC.FRM—Code 186
Step 6. Test and Debug. 188
Step 7. Complete the Program Documentation. 188
Summary 188
Programming Assignments 189
New Math 189
Randomly Selected Student Groups 189

Chapter Nine **Menus and MDI Forms: *Application: Finance (Version 3)*** **191**
Introducing Finance (Version 3) 192
Step 1. Understand the Problem. 194
Step 2. Design a Solution. 194
Menu Control 194
MDI Form 199
Image Control 205
Icon Property 207
Splash Screen 207
Picture Box Control and Toolbar 207
MousePointer Property 208
Step 3. Develop Your Logic. 208
Step 4. Build Your GUI. 208
Step 5. Write the VB Code. 209
mdiFinance—mdiFinance.frm (MDI Form) 209
frmLoan—frmLoan.frm (Child Form) 211
frmFutureValue—frmFuture.frm (Child Form) 212
frmDepreciation— frmDepreciation.frm (Child Form) 213
frmAbout—frmAbout.frm (Form) 214
Step 6. Test and Debug. 214
Step 7. Complete the Program Documentation. 215
Make EXE Command 215
Summary 215
Programming Assignments 215
Visual Basic Elements 215
Math Magic (MDI Version) 216

PART FOUR **PROGRAMMING THE BACK-END: DATABASES, ActiveX, AND THE WEB** **217**

Chapter Ten **Databases and Data Control (Viewable): *Application: Class Scheduling (Version 1)*** **219**
Files and Databases 220
Traditional File Structures 220
Databases 220
COLLEGE.MDB 220
Database Management Systems (DBMS) 224
Introducing the Class Scheduling Project (Version 1) 225
Step 1. Understand the Problem. 225
Step 2. Design a Solution. 226
Visual Basic's Data Control 227
Step 3. Develop Your Logic. 233
Step 4. Build Your GUI. 234
Step 5. Write the VB Code. 236
Step 6. Test and Debug Your Program. 237

Step 7. Complete the Program Documentation. 237
Displaying the Schedule of Classes 237
Step 1. Understand the Problem. 237
Table Join Operations and Embedded SQL 238
Step 2. Design a Solution. / Step 4. Build Your GUI. 239
Reposition Event and Refresh Method 240
App (Application) Object 240
Right Function and IIf (Immediate If) Function 241
Step 3. Develop Your Logic. / Step 5. Write the VB Code. 241
Step 6. Test and Debug Your Program. 243
Step 7. Complete the Program Documentation. 243
Summary 243
Programming Assignments 243
Courses and Section Display 243
Publishers Display 244

Chapter Eleven **Data Control (Updatable): *Application: Class Scheduling (Version 2)*** **247**
Intermediate-Level Visual Basic Programming 248
Introducing Version 2 of the Class Scheduling Application 248
Step 1. Understand the Problem. 248
Step 2. Design a Solution. 250
Review of Data Access Objects Terminology 250
Modifying a Table with AddNew, Edit, and Update Methods 251
Delete Method 252
Toggle AddEdit 252
DataChanged and EditMode Properties 253
Protecting a Database from Accidental Corruption 254
1. ReadOnly Property 254
2. TextBoxes Superimposed on Labels 255
3. Validate Event 255
4. Snapshots 256
Summary Comments Concerning Database Access 256
Common Dialog Control 257
ListBox, ComboBox, DBList, DBCombo, and MS Flex Grid Controls 262
List Box Control 262
ComboBox Control 264
Data-Bound List (DBList), Data-Bound ComboBox (DBCombo), and MS Flex Grid Controls 265
DBList Control 265
DBCombo Control 265
MS Flex Grid Control 265
Focus and TabIndex 267
CheckBox Control 268
Step 3. Develop Your Logic. 269
Step 4. Build Your GUI. 270
Step 5. Write the VB Code. 271
Step 6. Test and Debug Your Program. 273
Step 7. Complete the Program Documentation. 274
Summary 274
Programming Assignments 275
Bookstore Database 275
College Database—Updating the Schedule of Classes 276

Chapter Twelve **Advanced Concepts: *Applications: Class Scheduling (Versions 3 & 4) and Cool Visuals*** **277**
Advanced Concepts 278

Introducing the Visual Data Manager and the Faculty3.vbp Project 279
Using the Visual Data Manager to Create a Table, an Index, and Records 279
Creating a New Table 279
Creating an Index for a Table 281
Adding/Deleting/Modifying Records 282
Using the Visual Data Manager to Create a Database Application 283
Introducing the Data Form Wizard and the Faculty4.vbp Project 284
Introducing the VB Application Wizard and the Schedule3.vbp Project 288
Class Scheduling Application (Version 3) 288
Standard Modules and Public Variables 288
Class Module 289
TreeView and ListView Controls 289
VB Application Wizard 290
Windows API Calls 296
Finishing the Schedule3.vbp project 297
Introducing the Cool Visuals project 297
Cool Visuals Learning Objectives 301
Cool Visuals—New Code, Graphics, and Controls 301
User-Defined Data Types 301
User-Defined Data Types Representing a Record Layout 303
Graphics Methods versus Graphical Controls 304
Horizontal and Vertical Scrollbars 306
Windows API Calls 306
"ClassLines"—Class Modules and Standard Modules 306
Object Linking and Embedding (OLE) 307
Clipboard object 308
Tag Property 308
Package and Deployment Wizard 309
Summary 311
Programming Assignments 313
Completed Class Scheduling Application (Version 4) 313
Wine Inventory Valuation 313

Chapter Thirteen **Traditional Files: *Application: State Information* 315**
Introducing the State Information Project 316
Step 1. Understand the Problem. 316
Step 2. Design a Solution. 317
Sequential Data Files 317
Open Statement 318
Write # Statement 318
Input # Statement 319
Close Statement 319
Kill Statement 319
EOF() Function 319
Line Input # Statement and Input() Function 320
User-Defined Type (UDT) to Represent a Record 321
With/End With Statements 322
Sorting a Table 323
Mouse Movements 325
Step 3. Develop an Algorithm. 326
Step 4. Build Your GUI. 326
Step 5. Write the VB Code. 327
Step 6. Test and Debug. 329
Step 7. Complete the Program Documentation. 329
Introducing Random Data Files 329
FreeFile Function 330
Summary 331

Programming Assignments 331
- Flags 331
- Basketball 333
- Paradigm for a Random Data File 334
- Personnel 335

Appendix A **ASCII Codes** **337**

Glossary 339

Index 353

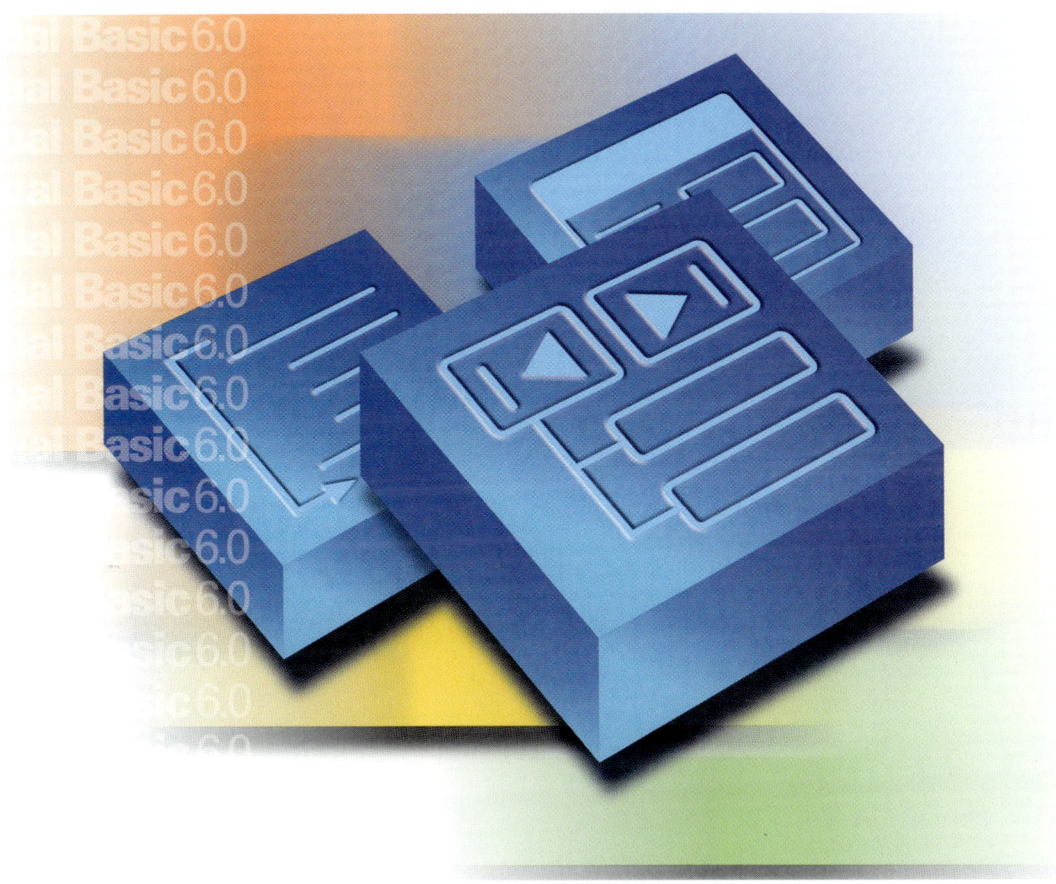

PART ONE

GETTING STARTED

CHAPTER ONE

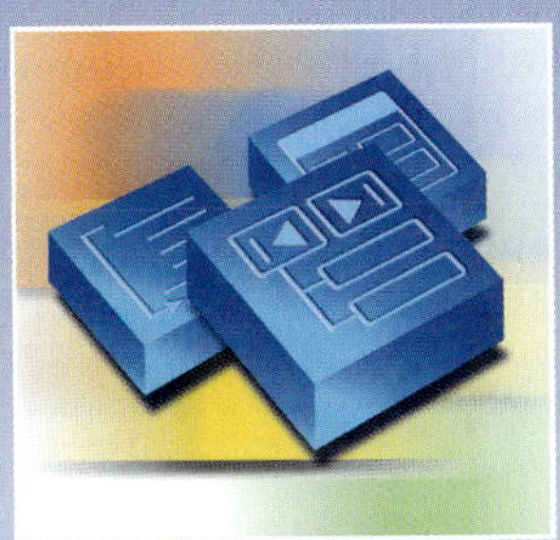

INTRODUCTION
Simple Application

LEARNING OBJECTIVES

Upon completion of Chapter One, you will be able to:

- Define machine, assembly, and higher-level language; assembler, compiler, and interpreter; and source, object, linker, and executable program.
- Define graphical user interface, window, and object-oriented programming.
- Define variable, local and global variables, and information hiding.
- Define structured programming, module, function, and procedure.
- Start up Visual Basic, Open a project, Save a form, Save a project, Print a project, Run a project, and Exit Visual Basic.
- Describe the parts of the Visual Basic [design] screen, including the Title Bar, Menu Bar, Toolbar, Toolbox Window, Project Explorer Window, Properties Window, and Form Window.
- Open, Maximize, Minimize, Restore, Move, Resize, and Close a window.
- Define these Visual Basic terms: object, form, control, property, event, method, and procedure.
- Use the Visual Basic pull-down menus.
- Use the following Toolbar icons:

open a project

save the project

go to Properties window

start, break, stop execution of a program

Keywords

Application
Assembly language
Assembler
Break time
Compiler
Computer program
Control
Design time
Event
Executable program
Form
Function
Global variable
Graphical user interface (GUI)

Higher-level language
Icon
Immediate Window
Information hiding
Instantiation
Interpreter
Linker program
Local variable
Machine language
Macro
Menu bar
Method
Module
Object
Object-oriented programming (OOP)
Object program
Procedure
Program
Project
Project Explorer Window
Properties Window
Property
Run time
Source program
Structured programming
Syntax
Syntax error
Title bar
Toolbar
Toolbox
Variable
Variable declaration
Window

A QUICK HISTORICAL REVIEW: HOW WE GOT TO VISUAL BASIC

This book will teach you fundamental techniques of computer programming in Visual Basic, Microsoft Corporation's language for building visually engaging computer applications for a Windows environment. Before we get started on Visual Basic itself, a little history and a few definitions are needed.

A **computer program** is a set of instructions that tells a computer what to do. The computer itself is only able to execute instructions written in a cryptic code called **machine language.** In this language, each instruction, consisting entirely of ones and zeros, causes a very small step within the program to take place. Naturally, human beings find machine language onerous to write and maintain. If we had to write all of our programs in machine language, very likely programmers would still be trying to get the first payroll program working correctly, and certainly we would never have been able to write a program complex enough to guide a spaceship to the moon.

In the late 1940s, symbolic code was developed, and then the first assembly languages began to appear around 1950. One statement (or instruction) written by a programmer in an **assembly language** is equivalent to one machine language statement. For example, an assembly language instruction might look like this:

```
mov  NameOut, NameIn
```

meaning "move (copy) the contents of NameIn to NameOut."

In this example, NameIn and NameOut are variables. Technically, a **variable** is a symbolic reference to an address in memory. That is, in the main memory of the computer, NameIn refers to a particular memory location where somebody's name has been stored. The notion of a variable is central to all computer programming. As a practical matter, we use variables about the same way we used them in algebra: A variable contains a particular value, and over the course of program execution, that value can change. Assembly language programming is still a long way from writing in English, and each assembly language statement is still nothing more than a single, tiny step within the overall program; but clearly this assembly language statement is far easier to compose than the corresponding machine language statement of ones and zeros. After the programmer writes the whole program (called the **source program**) in assembly language, a special purpose program called an **assembler** translates the source program into machine language, and the resulting code is known as the **object program.** In most cases, the object program must still be linked with some prewritten sections of standardized machine code (such as the instructions for accessing a disk drive or for controlling the printer) in order to produce the finished product, which is an **executable program.**

An assembly language, like machine language, is unique to a specific computer processor or, at best, to a family of processors. Thus the assembly language for IBM 360/370 series machines is unlike the assembly language for IBM personal computers, which is again totally unlike the assembly language for Macintosh computers.

Although assembly language is exceedingly tedious compared to later inventions, some organizations still write programs in an assembly language, either because they believe they can achieve extra efficiency in the executable program, or because they have a large number of old assembly programs and a staff of assembly programmers, and inertia precludes a rapid changeover to a newer way of programming.

The first higher-level programming language, FORTRAN, was invented by Jim Backus at IBM in 1954. A higher-level language contains **syntax** (vocabulary and grammar rules) more akin to English or to the domain for which the higher-level language was designed. (FORTRAN, meaning "FORmula TRANslation," was designed for scientists, engineers, and mathematicians, and so its vocabulary reflects the world of trigonometry and calculus.) In addition, many statements in the higher-level language are **macro** statements: That is, a single statement in the source language represents many statements in the corresponding machine language. Hence, programs written in a **higher-level language** are both more intelligible and shorter than the corresponding assembly or machine language programs. FORTRAN also introduced other important high-level concepts, such as arithmetic expressions and formatted input/output.

A special translator program is needed to convert a source program written in a higher-level language into machine language. These translators come in two varieties, compilers and interpreters: A **compiler** works like an assembler, translating the entire source language program into a machine language object program; then a **linker program** adds the necessary input/output (I/O) routines to convert the object program into an executable program. By contrast, an **interpreter** translates only a single source language statement into machine language and then immediately executes that statement. For purposes of program development, an interpreter is more convenient, because the programmer can run (execute) a program that is only partly developed or even a program containing syntax errors (violations of the rules of the programming language). The interpreter just runs until it finds a syntax error or until it finishes executing the code that has been written so far, and then it stops and gives immediate feedback to the programmer. However, the interpreter must translate each source language statement each time the statement is executed, and so it is far less efficient than a compiler in terms of running the executable program. Furthermore, after the compiler and linker do their jobs, the executable program is complete unto itself, and the compiler and linker are no longer needed. By contrast, an interpreter must always be present.

Some languages, such as BASIC, lend themselves well to an interpreter. Others, such as COBOL, must always be compiled. One of the distinct advantages of Visual Basic is that it offers both an interpreter and a partial compiler.

Following FORTRAN, dozens of higher-level languages came into existence. Among the most important to our understanding of the background, purposes, and concepts of Visual Basic were COBOL, BASIC, Pascal, C, and C++.

COBOL (COmmon Business-Oriented Language), introduced in 1960 by a government/industry committee headed by Grace Hopper, was intended to provide a standardized computer programming language for business applications on all models of computers. With the advent of COBOL, commercial and government users would no longer be trapped into allegiance to a single manufacturer's hardware by having to invest heavily in that manufacturer's proprietary business programming language. Subsequently, standardization across different hardware vendors became a prime objective of higher-level languages. COBOL was also the first self-documenting language, meaning that COBOL programs include their own documentation and explanation, so that other programmers are able to read and make modifications to the program after the original programmer is no longer involved. This too remains an important concept today. COBOL has been updated a number of times, and the current standard, COBOL-85, remains the principal business programming language on mainframe computers. Although several microcomputer implementations of COBOL have been produced, the language has not become popular in the PC world. Thus, businesses that are converting mainframe applications to microcomputers need a business programming language more attuned to the PC environment. COBOL is not dead, because mainframes are not dead (and are not going to leave us anytime soon), but COBOL is not the answer for most microcomputer applications.

BASIC (Beginners All-purpose Symbolic Instruction Code) was invented at Dartmouth College by Professors John Kemeny and Thomas Kurtz in 1964. A subset and simplification of FORTRAN, Dartmouth BASIC used easy-to-understand commands to execute relatively simple programming tasks on a GE time-sharing computer system, and so it freed students and faculty who needed computer support from having to depend on and wait for overburdened professional programmers. When the microcomputer revolution began in 1975, manufacturers wanted a programming language that home hobbyists could learn and use, rather than a language requiring professional programmers. Thus, BASIC was adopted by microcomputer manufacturers and was included for free with most microcomputer systems. Unfortunately, the language was not standardized. Over 100 separate versions of BASIC (often called street-BASIC dialects) came into existence, some widely divergent from the original Dartmouth BASIC model. Because it was easy and unsophisticated, BASIC also got a reputation as a toy language, not useful for serious programming. But BASIC was responsible for the initial programming experiences of literally millions of people, including many who subsequently made their careers in the computer software field.

One of the significant problems with early BASIC programs (and with early FORTRAN and COBOL programs, one might add) was the complete lack of any internal program structure. The original BASIC used a line number to identify each separate statement. Simple variables did not have to be declared, and the names of variables were limited to two characters, making it difficult to remember what each variable stood for. And nothing was indented or modularized, so each statement seemed to stand alone. The resultant programs were criticized as "spaghetti code," because following the logic was like following individual strands in a bowl of spaghetti. For example, consider this program:

```
10 PRINT "PRIME NUMBERS FROM 1 TO 50"
20 PRINT 2,3,
30 N=1
40 N=N+2
50 IF N>50 THEN STOP
60 X=1
70 X=X+2
80 IF INT(N/X)=N/X THEN GOTO 40
90 IF X<SQR(N) THEN GOTO 70
100 PRINT N,
110 GOTO 40
120 END
```

Pascal, an outgrowth of an earlier language called ALGOL, was developed by the Swiss software scientist Nicholas Wirth in the late 1960s and officially published in 1971; its purpose was to teach novice programmers new highly structured, modularized, and disciplined programming techniques called **structured programming.** Pascal programs include **variable declarations:** Every variable must be specifically declared by the programmer, along with the type of data it will contain—unlike the BASIC and FORTRAN practice of just introducing new variables on the fly. Pascal programs are divided into a main program, which controls the overall program flow, and subprograms—user-written functions and procedures—which are called by the main program when they are needed. Each subprogram (also called a **module**) is complete unto itself, including its own **local variables,** whose existence is unknown to other modules of the program. This demonstrates the principle of **information hiding,** which holds that a higher-level (or calling) module only needs the results produced by a lower-level (called) module; the higher-level module does not need to know about the internal operations of the lower-level module. Each module of a Pascal program has one entry point (at the beginning) and one exit point (at the end). The only variables shared between subprograms or between the main program and a subprogram are those specifically passed as parameters from one to the other and those declared as **global variables** in the main program. Using global variables and using GOTO statements, though supported by Pascal's formal rules, are strongly discouraged.

Because of the excellent discipline that it instills in students, Pascal has been widely adopted as a first programming language in computer science curricula. But because Pascal programs often execute slowly, and because standard Pascal handles large-volume input/output rather poorly (a major consideration for businesses), Pascal has had little popularity in the business world.

Pascal's academically successful design principles affected later developments in other programming languages, especially BASIC. True BASIC (from Drs. Kemeny and Kurtz), Turbo BASIC (from Borland International), and most especially QuickBASIC (from Microsoft), all introduced in the 1980s, implemented most of Pascal's design concepts and facilitated structured programming, while retaining the simple, easy-to-use and understand, English-like vocabulary and statement syntax of earlier versions of BASIC. QuickBASIC became relatively popular as a serious programming language in the business community. In terms of the vocabulary and programming language syntax, Visual Basic is just the next development of QuickBASIC. Programmers already familiar with an earlier BASIC dialect will find much in Visual Basic that is familiar.

C was invented by a Bell Labs team headed by Dennis Ritchie in 1972 and published for public use by Kernighan and Ritchie in 1978. C has features of both an assembly language and a higher-level language (and so it is often termed a midlevel language). Though less structured than Pascal, it is far more structured than traditional assembly languages. Its vocabulary and syntax are cryptic in the extreme, making C programs difficult to read and decipher, but facilitating the creation of new C programs by accomplished C programmers. C programs often take longer to write than would the same program in a higher-level language; but, by using the assembly-like features of C, the C program may run more efficiently than a comparable program written in another language. Because it formed the basis of the UNIX operating system and was also standardized on most microprocessors, C became immensely popular for developing commercial computer software for personal computers. Many of the software application packages that you use every day—word processors, spreadsheets, data managers, personal organizers, etc.—were probably written in C.

Bjarne Stroustrup, also at Bell Labs, developed C++ in the early 1980s as an object-oriented version of the C language. The notion of **object-oriented**

programming (OOP) is this: The real world around us is filled with objects, which are more than pieces of raw data. As an example, consider a chair: the notion of a chair includes a function (something on which to sit), inherent characteristics or properties (legs, seat, back), optional features (arms, seat cushion, upholstery), and variable features (construction materials, place and date of manufacture, style, color). When we ask Junior to go upstairs and get another chair for an extra person at the dinner table (notice how many objects—Junior, chair, person, dinner, and table—are involved in that request), we do not need to specify all of the functions and properties of a chair, since these are implied in the term itself (although we may identify a specific chair, that is, a specific instance or **instantiation** of the notion of a chair). Similarly, in computer programming we often want to store and manipulate information about objects, without having to describe fully all of the properties and functions associated with that object. An object, in the sense of object-oriented programming, is a computerized representation or abstraction of a real-world entity. The definition of the object includes its properties (characteristics, attributes, or features), the events to which it can respond, and the operations or methods the object is able to perform. In languages such as C++, the programmer can create an object as an instantiation of a class of objects (think of a specific chair as an instantiation of the object class chair), tailor or specify the properties of the object, assign operational capabilities to the object, and then make duplicate copies of the object or pass the object to other programs. As an example, a programmer might create a new object class called "Switch." The properties of Switch include its value ("on" or "off"), its image (a wall switch, a lamp switch, or a radio push button), and its color (perhaps brown, cream, or white). Switch might respond to a mouse click that turns the switch on or off. Having the object class, the programmer might then insert MySwitch and YourSwitch, two actual switches in a program, that is, two instantiations of the object class Switch.

Like C++, Visual Basic is an object-oriented language. Visual Basic has quite a few objects built in, each of which has its own characteristics (properties) and functionality (events to which it can respond and methods it can perform). These objects can be tailored to the needs of a specific program by modifying the property settings and by choosing among the available events and methods. Visual Basic also permits the programmer to define new classes of objects and to store these objects in an object library, where any program can use them.

Microsoft Corporation's **Windows** provides a "graphical operating environment," consisting, first of all, of graphical images and functions that correspond to textual commands in the underlying operating system (originally MS-DOS). Some of the functions of Windows are used directly by PC end-users, such as clicking (pressing the left mouse button while pointing to an object) on an **icon** (a small picture) representing an application program in order to execute that program. Other Windows functions are used by PC programmers to create and manipulate graphical objects and images in application programs that run in the Windows environment. Introduced in 1985, Windows gained popularity gradually until Windows 3.1 was released in 1992, after which Windows sales really took off. The newest version of Windows, launched in 1998, is Windows 98, which is both an operating system (replacing MS-DOS) and a graphical operating environment. Today, well over half of the PCs in the United States run Windows.

Until the invention of Visual Basic, programmers who wished to write Windows-based applications were pretty much limited to C and, more recently, C++. Although these languages are reasonably well-suited to this task, especially when used in conjunction with Microsoft's Software Development Kit (SDK), they still require too many hours of effort and too much programmer sophistication to produce even simple application programs. There are not enough C/C++-trained programmers, nor enough programming hours available, to satisfy the burgeoning demand for graphical, Windows-based computer applications.

And that's where Visual Basic comes in. First available in 1989, Visual Basic is Microsoft's answer to the need for an application development tool for programs that run under Microsoft Windows and take advantage of the graphical Windows environment. The first two versions of Visual Basic were exciting in potential but limited in actual capacity. Version 3.0, released in 1993, was a full-fledged professional programming language. Version 6.0, released in 1998, offers additional features and functionality for both novice and experienced professional programmers. Visual Basic 6.0 is sold commercially in three versions: the Learning Edition, the Professional Edition, and the Enterprise Edition. The Learning Edition provides an excellent environment for learning the language and for developing single-office, single-user applications. The Professional Edition contains more sophisticated objects and functionality, especially for accessing remote databases and for creating complete database applications. The Enterprise Edition offers additional tools for robust client/server applications, for programs used by many concurrent users, and for maintaining multiple versions of Visual Basic programs. This textbook is based on the Visual Basic 6.0 Professional Edition.

Among professional programmers—over half of whom now include this programming language in their programming repertoire—Visual Basic (VB) has four principal commercial uses:

1. VB is a Rapid Application Development (RAD) tool. It allows a company/individual to quickly develop new computer applications that incorporate graphical features and have the look and "feel" of Windows packages produced by the big players in this market—packages such as Excel, Quattro Pro, Word, WordPerfect, Quicken, and Paradox, produced by companies such as Microsoft, IBM, and Corel.
2. VB provides the "front end" user interface to database applications in any environment: a local database, a remote database on a local or wide area network, or a database housed on the World Wide Web.
3. Visual Basic for Applications, a subset of Visual Basic, is excellent for tailoring your Windows-based application package (such as Excel or Access) for a particular use (switching between budget years in a spreadsheet display, for example).
4. VB is a prototyping tool. Many developers use other, perhaps more powerful languages (Java, C++, COBOL, Oracle, etc.) for full-blown applications; but they use Visual Basic to prototype a model of a proposed application before undertaking the actual development.

VB applications work best on standalone PCs and in small local area networks and in conjunction with relatively small databases. Finally, VB is most effective when speed during program execution is not of the essence, since the graphics features require heavy use of memory, the CPU, and the video card in your computer. Although VB 6.0 executes more quickly and more capably than earlier releases of the language, many professional programmers still believe that large VB applications tend to degrade performance and can overwhelm the processing capability of a network. Nevertheless, the professional programming community has agreed that, for thousands of computer applications and businesses, Visual Basic provides a viable and cost-effective solution.

INTRODUCTING THE "SIMPLE" APPLICATION

As the name implies, the "Simple" application is exceedingly simple, but we will use it to see some of the elements of a Visual Basic program running in the Windows 98 environment. We will also use it to look at the components of the Visual Basic Integrated Development Environment—what you see on the screen when you are creating your own Visual Basic application.

This Simple application contains two objects: a **form** titled "Simple" and a single **control** (a Command Button) with the initial caption, "This is a control—Click Me!" When the user clicks the mouse on the Command Button, the message "And this is a form" is printed directly on the form, while the caption of the Command Button changes to "EXIT." When the user clicks a second time on the Command Button, the program stops running.

Run the "Simple" Application

Before you do anything else, you should see this program in operation. In fact, we suggest that throughout this textbook you run each completed application as we introduce it. Watching it run for real gives you much more information than just reading our narrative description.

1. If your computer is not already in Windows 95, 98, or NT, you will need to get there. The method of getting into Windows varies from school to school, depending on locally defined options and menus. If the method of starting the Windows program is not obvious, ask your instructor or lab assistant to show you how to do it. You will need to start from Windows 95/98/NT for everything we do in this book.
2. In many instances in this text, you will need to know and see the *filename extension* (also called the *file type*) of each file you are working on in a Visual Basic program. However, Windows 95/98/NT does not automatically display file extensions unless you tell it specifically to do so. To force Windows to display file extensions, run Windows Explorer. Then select View | Folder Options (in Windows 98) or View | Options (in Windows 95/NT). A dialog box will appear. Click on the View tab at the top of this dialog box. You will find a checkbox with the caption "Hide file extensions for known file types". This box must be clear (unchecked). If the checkbox has a check in it, click the checkbox in order to uncheck it. Then click OK at the bottom of the dialog box (see Figure 1.07, page 14). The options you select in Windows Explorer affect the way files are displayed in all Windows programs, including Visual Basic. [Note: Options selected in this way only remain in effect until someone else changes them, or until the Windows default options are reset. In many student labs, the default options are automatically reset each day. Therefore, if you are not on your own computer when you perform this procedure, you will probably need to perform this same procedure every time you sit down at a computer to work on Visual Basic.] [Also note: Although VB 6.0 runs under Windows 95, 98, or NT, from this point forward we will only mention Windows 98. All of the screen captures in the text were made with Visual Basic 6.0 Professional Edition installed under a Windows 98 system. If you are running Windows 95 or NT, or if you are using VB 6.0's Learning or Enterprise Edition, some of the screens in this text may appear slightly different on your machine.]
3. Install the VB Student Demos on your computer (if they have not already been installed). To do this, download the file "VB Demos.exe" from the World Wide Web site at http://www.dryden.com/infosys/spear2, or copy this file from a network drive at your school, or from a disk given to you by your instructor. In any case, put this file into a folder called "C:\VB Student Demos", and then execute (run) this file. VB Demos.exe is a self-extracting executable file, which contains compressed versions of all of the student files referenced in this text. When the file is executed, it will create a folder for each chapter of

the book, and it will decompress the files associated with each chapter and place them in the appropriate folder. Throughout this text, we will assume that the demo files are on your hard drive in a folder called "C:\VB Student Demos". [Note: In previous versions of Windows, *folders* were called *directories*. Microsoft's Visual Basic documentation uses both terms interchangeably.]

4. To run the "Simple" program from the Windows 98 opening screen, click Start | Run. Click the Browse button, and navigate in the dialog box until you find and select "C:\VB Student Demos\Chap01\Simple.exe". Click OK to clear the Browse dialog, and OK again to begin execution of the program.

Experiment with running this program until you are comfortable with how it works and all of the options you can use with it (see Figure 1.01).

- Notice that you can click the Control Menu Icon (the little icon on the left side of the Title Bar) to obtain a drop-down list containing these selections: Restore, Move, Size, Minimize, Maximize, and Close. This drop-down list is called the Control Menu (Figure 1.02).
- The Move selection lets you use the arrow keys (up, down, left, right) to reposition the window in which the application is running, but actually it's easier to click and hold down the left mouse button on the Title Bar and then drag the window to a new position.
- Similarly, the Size selection in the Control Menu lets you use the arrow keys to change the height or the width of the application window, but you will find it easier to use the mouse directly: Just point to a border of the application, and when the mouse pointer is a double-headed arrow, drag the border to make the window larger or smaller as you see fit.
- Selecting the Minimize option in the Control Menu is the same as clicking the Minimize Button, that is, the third button from the right on the right side of the Title Bar. This option reduces the application to an icon and title on the Task Bar at the bottom of the screen. The program is still running, but you won't see it do anything as long as it remains minimized. To restore an application window that is minimized, click the icon once to resurrect the Control Menu (now a "pop-up" list rather than a "drop-down" list), and select the Restore option; or alternatively, just double-click the icon.
- Choosing Maximize in the Control Menu is the same as clicking the Maximize Button, the second button on the right side of the Title Bar. This makes the application fill up the whole screen. It also changes the Maximize Button to the Restore Button, which will resize the application back to a window rather than full-screen.

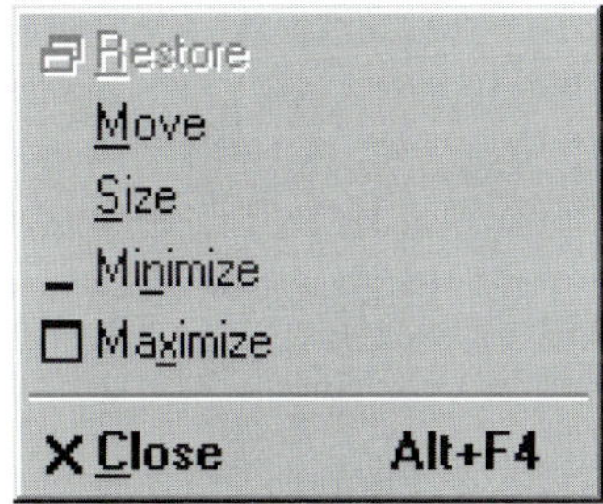

FIGURE 1.02 *Windows control menu*

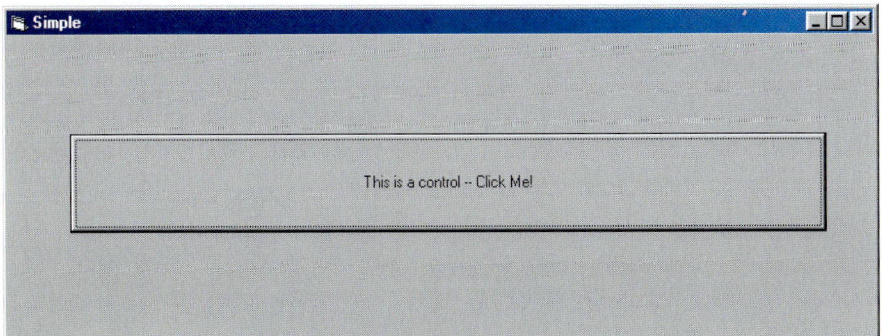

FIGURE 1.01 *Running the Simple application*

- The Close option in the Control Menu closes (exits or quits) the application; you can also close an application by double-clicking the Control Menu Icon or by pressing Alt-F4 (that is, pressing the F4 function key while holding down the Alt key).

Except for the rare occasions in which the Control Menu or some of its selections are intentionally disabled by the programmer, the techniques discussed here for running, moving, sizing, maximizing, minimizing, restoring, and closing a window are the same for all Microsoft Windows application programs, for Visual Basic itself, and for all of the windows within Visual Basic.

THE VISUAL BASIC INTEGRATED DEVELOPMENT ENVIRONMENT

Our next step is to load the Visual Basic software into memory and begin to become familiar with the Visual Basic Integrated Development Environment (IDE). We assume that Visual Basic for Windows is already installed on your computer. If Visual Basic (VB) is a Desktop icon on the Windows 98 opening screen, just double-click the icon to load VB. If VB is not a Desktop icon, click the Start Button, point to Programs, find Visual Basic in the pop-up list, and click it. The opening screen in Visual Basic will look approximately like Figure 1.03.

A user can modify the specific location of some parts of the Visual Basic design screen, and can also close or hide some of the windows on the design screen. Therefore, your screen may not look exactly like this, although you can make it look like this if you so choose.

Title Bar

The **Title Bar** (Figure 1.04) contains the name of the program, "Microsoft Visual Basic," and the notation "[design]," indicating that Visual Basic (VB) is in the design mode. You will use the design mode to design the graphical user interface and to write your VB program. The Title Bar also contains the now-familiar Control Menu Icon on the left, and the Minimize, Maximize, and Close Buttons on the right.

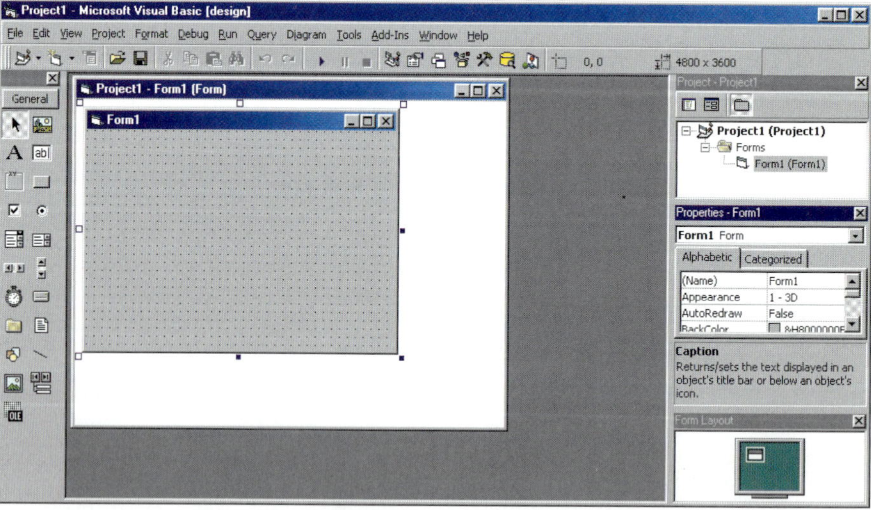

FIGURE 1.03 *Visual Basic opening screen*

FIGURE 1.04 *Visual Basic Title Bar*

Menu Bar

The **Menu Bar** (Figure 1.05) activates a series of pull-down menus, whose selections cover the commands and options you will need as a Visual Basic programmer. Don't be overwhelmed by the number of selections: We will only introduce the ones you need here for the Simple project; others will be covered as they are needed in later chapters.

Notice that each selection in the Menu Bar has an underlined letter: File, Edit, View, Project, Format, Debug, Run, Query, Diagram, Tools, Add-Ins, Window, and Help. A pull-down menu from the Menu Bar can be accessed by clicking on the menu with the mouse or by pressing the underlined letter while holding down the Alt key.

File Menu

The first group of selections in the File pull-down menu (Figure 1.06) relate to a Visual Basic Project. The term **project** in Visual Basic is synonymous with the term **application** or **program.** A VB project is stored on disk as a series of files. One of these files is the "project" file itself, with the extension "VBP" (meaning Visual Basic Project); this file serves only to tell VB the names and locations of all of the other files that make up the application. As a minimum, each project will also have one "form" file, with the extension "FRM"; a form file contains one window that will be seen by the user when the program runs, plus all of the code (Visual Basic statements) that are associated with that form. The first several applications in this book have only one form, but later applications will show you how to create applications with multiple forms.

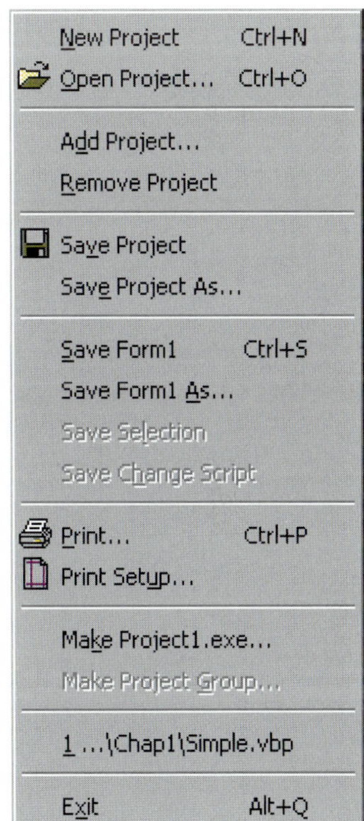

FIGURE 1.06 *File pull down menu items*

New Project New Project starts a new VB project. If you are currently working on a project, and changes have been made since the last time you saved it, VB prompts you to save the current project before starting a new one. Every new project starts only with a blank "Form1."

Open Project Open Project opens an existing VB project. If you are currently working on a project, and changes have been made since the last time you saved it, VB prompts you to save the current project before opening a different one. VB then displays the "Open Project" dialog box. Dialog boxes are used throughout the Windows environment, in order to force the user to take some action or to provide some information to Windows or to a Windows application. When a dialog box appears, the user must respond to it before Windows will do anything else. (As you will discover in Chapter Two, Visual Basic allows you to create dialog boxes yourself.) In this case, the "Open Project" dialog box lists all files in the current drive/directory that have the extension "VBP." You can change the drive or directory and then click on the appropriate filename, or you can type in the drive, directory, and filename yourself. Then double-click the filename or click the OK Command Button. VB loads the selected VBP file, whose contents tell VB the names of all of the other files that are components of the project. VB then loads all of those component files as well.

File Edit View Project Format Debug Run Query Diagram Tools Add-Ins Window Help

FIGURE 1.05 *Visual Basic Menu Bar*

Save Project Save Project saves the current VBP and FRM files. If a form in the project has not yet been named, VB activates the "Save File As" Dialog Box to prompt you for a name for that FRM file (with the default name FORM1.FRM). If the project has not yet been named, VB activates the "Save Project As" Dialog Box to prompt you for a name for the VBP file (with the default name PROJECT1.VBP). [Hint: Always change the default names FORM1.FRM and PROJECT1.VBP to something else. If you don't, you may accidentally overwrite an existing FORM1.FRM or PROJECT1.VBP.] The Dialog Box also allows you to select the folder (directory) in which the project will be saved, or to create a new folder for this project (highly recommended). [Note: Windows 95/98/NT has an option that allows you to view or to hide filename extensions, like the extensions VBP and FRM mentioned here. As a programmer, you will normally want to see these extensions, because they indicate which software created the files. If you do not see filename extensions in Visual Basic, Windows Explorer, or My Computer, then you will want to turn this option on. Here's how: Open My Computer or Windows Explorer, Select View | Folder Options in Windows 98, or View | Options in Windows 95or NT, then click the View tab. Unclick the checkbox (that is, click the checkbox to remove the checkmark) which reads "Hide file extensions for known file types", and then click OK. (See Figure 1.07)

Save Project As Save Project As saves the current VBP file under a new name and/or in a different drive/directory. [Beware! This is a dangerous command, because it does not save existing FRM files in the new drive/directory that you specify for the VBP file.]

Save <Filename> Save <Filename> saves the current FRM file. If the current form has not yet been named, VB activates the "Save <Filename> As" Dialog Box to prompt you for the name of the FRM file.

Save <Filename> As Save <Filename> As saves the current FRM file under a new name and/or in a new drive/directory.

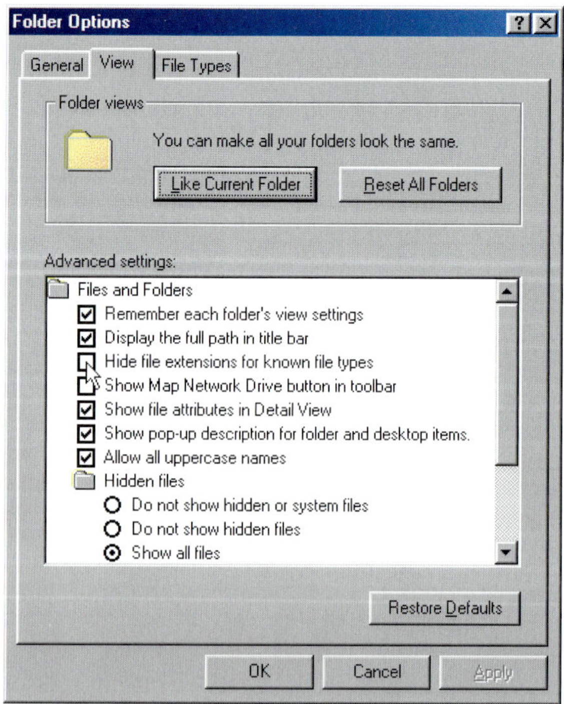

FIGURE 1.07 *Windows Folder Options*

Print Print allows you to print a hard copy of a form (the graphical image, provided you have a printer that can handle graphics), the form text (a text file that describes the form), or the code (Visual Basic statements). Your instructor may require that you print out and hand these things in when you submit a project.

Make <ProjectName> EXE File Make <ProjectName> EXE File converts your project into an executable program file, with the extension "EXE." An EXE file can be run directly from Windows Explorer or My Computer without loading Visual Basic.

Under the *Make EXE File* selection is a listing of the most recently saved VB projects. Clicking one of these projects is a shortcut to opening it with the *Open Project* selection.

Exit The last selection in the File Menu is used to *Exit* Visual Basic. Again, if the current project or components have changed since the last save operation, you will be prompted to save any changes before exiting Visual Basic.

Edit Menu

You are not likely to need the Edit Menu in Chapter One. We will explain its features in the course of Chapter Two.

View Menu

The View Menu (Figure 1.08) is used to open or switch to the various windows in the Visual Basic IDE. Important selections for your first few projects include *Code*, *Object*, *Properties*, *Toolbox*, and *Toolbar*. We will describe each of these below. For now, notice that you can open each of these windows by selecting it from the View Menu. Try opening and closing each of these windows, as follows:

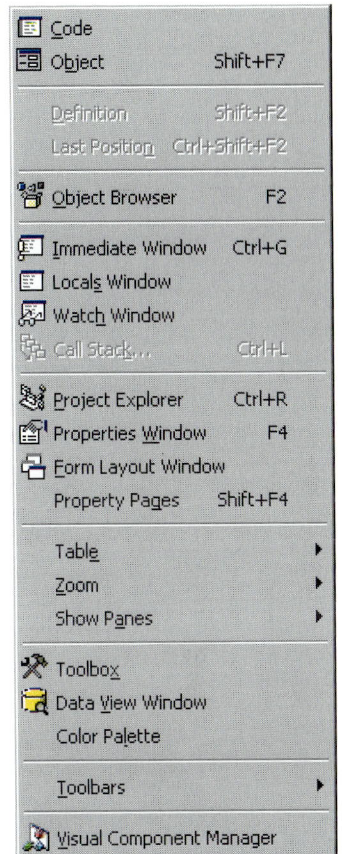

FIGURE 1.08
View pull-down menu items

- Open or switch to the *Code Window* by selecting View | Code or by pressing the F7 function key. Then close the Code Window by double-clicking its Control Menu Icon (upper left corner of the window), or by clicking the Control Menu Icon and selecting Close from the drop-down list, or by clicking the X icon on the right side of the window's Title Bar, or by pressing Alt-F4.
- Similarly, open or switch to, and then close, the *Object (Form)*, *Properties*, and *Toolbox* windows. The Object Window is opened by selecting View | Object or by pressing Shift-F7; the Properties Window by selecting View | Properties or by pressing F4; and the Toolbox Window by selecting View | Toolbox.
- Notice that, if a window is visible somewhere on the desktop, you can also switch to that window by clicking anywhere within it. One window will always be selected (called the Active Window). You can tell which is the Active Window because its Title Bar will be highlighted. Whenever you press Alt-F4, the Active Window is the one that gets closed. (If Visual Basic's Main Menu is selected, then Alt-F4 will exit VB altogether.)

Now let's examine each of the windows available from the View Menu.

The fundamental building block of a Visual Basic program is the form, and by default when you start a new VB project, VB gives you an empty Form1. When a VB application runs, the form is the screen image that the user sees. When you design a VB application, your first activity will be to position and size Form1, rename it, change the Caption from "Form1" to the name of your application, and then place graphical tools, called *controls*, on it. See Figure 1.09 for an example.

When a form file is saved, it actually consists of two principal pieces: the graphical user interface (that is, the form with all of its controls) and Visual Basic code, or Visual Basic language statements. Most of the code is written in blocks

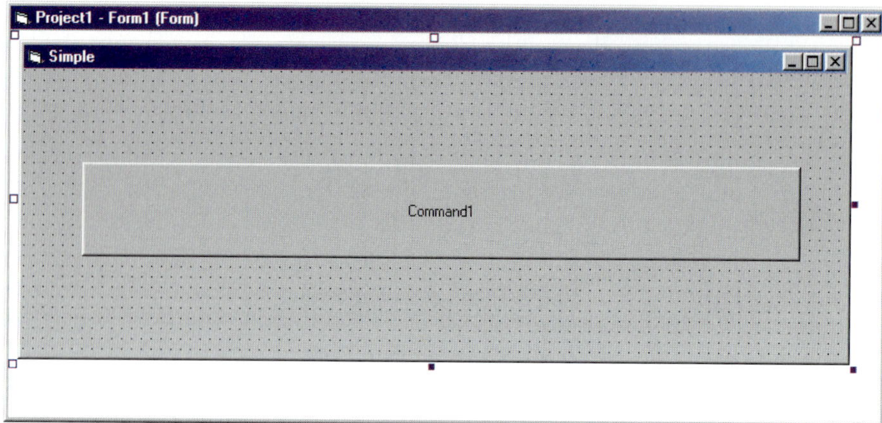

FIGURE 1.09 *Form1 with a control (a command button) placed on it*

called event procedures, such as Figure 1.10. An event **procedure** is a set of VB language statements whose execution is triggered by some event, usually something the user initiates, like clicking the mouse on a certain part of the form. When you write a Visual Basic program, you will first design the **graphical user interface (GUI),** and then you will write the code associated with that GUI design. During the development process, you will often need to switch back and forth between the GUI and the code. You do this by selecting View | Form (or Shift-F7) to see and work on the GUI, and by selecting View | Code (or F7) to see and work on the statements in your program.

The **Properties Window** shows the properties (characteristics) of the currently selected graphical object. Customarily, the Properties Window is kept partially visible in the lower right corner of the screen. If the Properties Window is not visible, you can open it by selecting View | Properties or by pressing F4. You can also expand the number of properties visible at one time by closing the Project Window above it or by dragging the border between the Properties Window and the Project Window. Properties are listed alphabetically, and you can scroll through the list.

A form has 51 properties, which you can use to tailor the form to your project's needs. Take a look right now at the properties of a form (Figures 1-11a and 1-11b). Don't study them; just read through them so that you have a sense of what is meant by the term *form properties*. To accomplish this, click anywhere on Form1, which makes Form1 the selected object, and then open the Properties Window. Notice the vertical scroll bar along the right side of the Properties Window. You can use the scroll bar to read through all of the properties of a form that

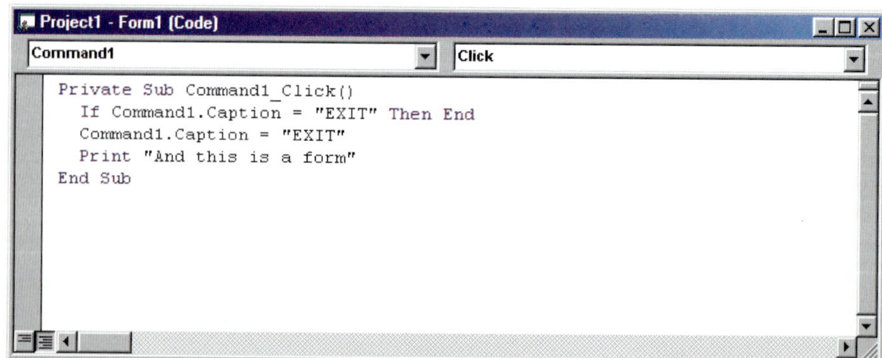

FIGURE 1.10 *Code window showing the event code*

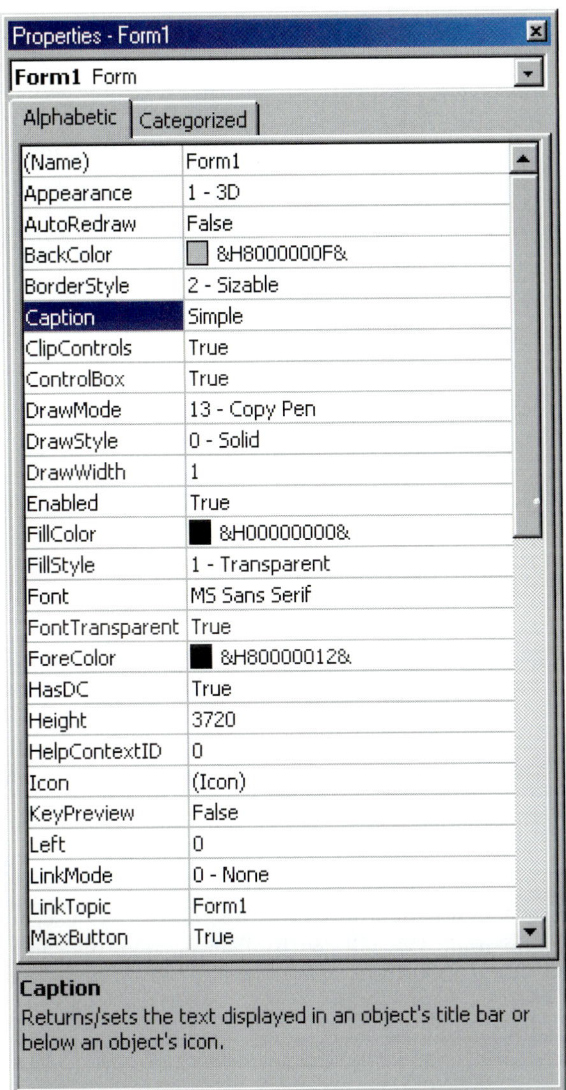

FIGURE 1.11a *Form properties window (part 1)*

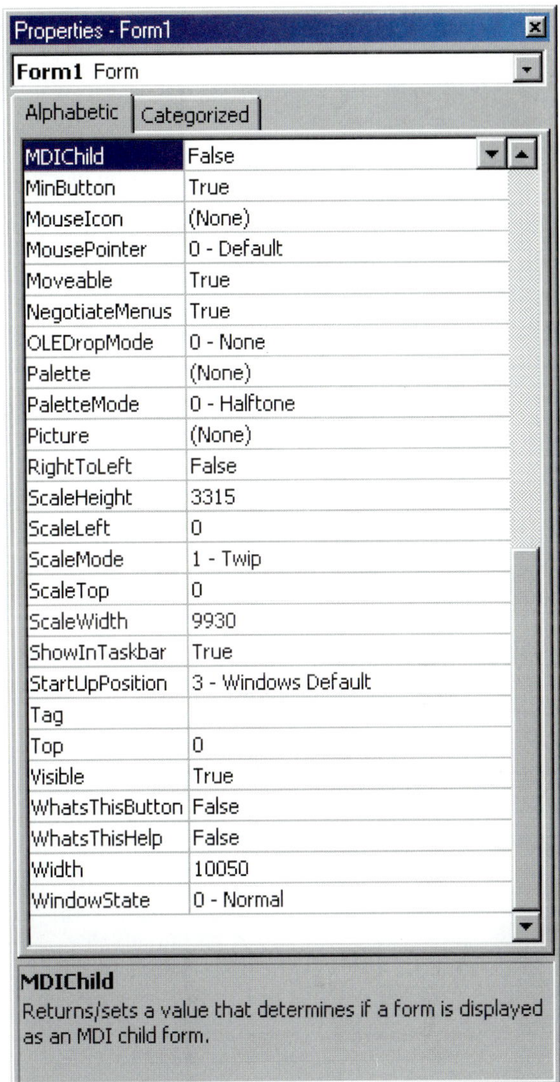

FIGURE 1.11b *Form properties window (part 2)*

are available to you at the time you design a VB application (called **design time**). Each **property** has a value, or setting. At initiation, VB assigns a value to each property, called its default value, that is, the value of that property if you do nothing to change it.

The Toolbox Window contains icons representing controls, which you will be able to use in designing a Visual Basic form (see Figure 1.12). (In addition, the top left icon represents the Mouse Pointer.) We will show you how to use each of these controls in the course of this text. Like a form, each control has an associated list of properties. By arranging controls on a form and modifying their property settings, you customize the form to the specifications of your project. The Toolbox shown here is the one that comes with the VB 6.0 Professional edition. If you have a different edition, your display could include more or different controls, and additional controls are available from a number of vendors.

The Toolbox Window is usually visible along the left-hand side of the screen. If it is not visible, select View | Toolbox to make it so, and move it wherever you would like it to appear.

Note that all of the windows discussed here—Object (Form), Code, Properties, and Toolbox—can be moved, resized, or closed, the same as any window

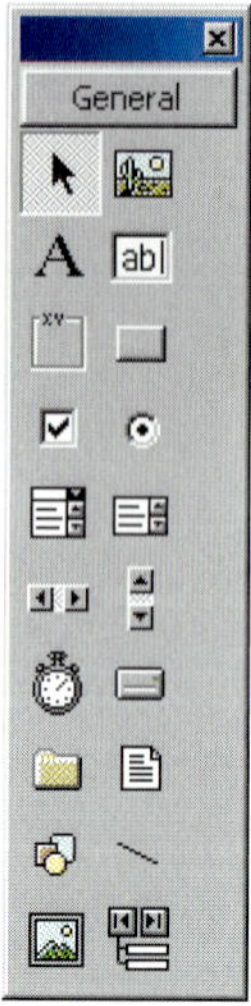

FIGURE 1.12
Standard Toolbox window

within Microsoft Windows, using the techniques described earlier when running the Simple project.

The **Toolbar** (Figure 1.13), immediately beneath the Menu Bar, contains a set of icons that represent the most frequently used menu selections. (If you don't see the Toolbar on the screen, click View | Toolbar to turn on the display.) Again, don't be overwhelmed—we will only use a few of these icons in Chapter One, and you never really need to memorize them, since you can always access the same features from the menus. Here are the first six icons you should learn and their corresponding menu equivalents:

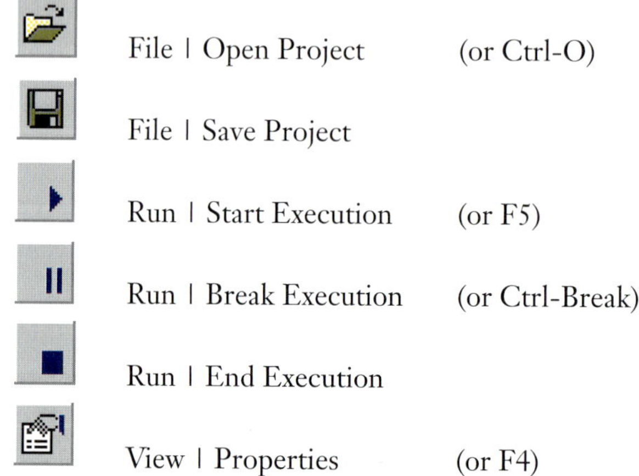

File | Open Project (or Ctrl-O)

File | Save Project

Run | Start Execution (or F5)

Run | Break Execution (or Ctrl-Break)

Run | End Execution

View | Properties (or F4)

Project Menu, Format Menu, and Debug Menu

These menus are not needed in this chapter.

Run Menu

Toolbar icons match the principal functions of this menu and are easier to use, so you won't normally need this menu at all. We will use Toolbar icons in this chapter to start and end program execution.

Query Menu and Diagram Menu

These menus are not needed in this chapter.

Tools Menu

The only selection you will need for now in this menu is Options, the last selection in the drop-down list. When you click the Options selection, VB presents a dialog bog with six tabs (Editor, Editor Format, General, Docking, Environment, and Advanced). We are interested now in the Editor tab, which allows you to change certain screen and language settings that affect all of your Visual Basic programs.

Right now, click on Tools | Options, and select the Editor tab (see Figure 1.14). Look at the "Require Variable Declaration" checkbox, which should be checked. If it is not already checked, then click it. By forcing you to declare all of your variables (a concept we discuss later), this action will prevent you from making many programming mistakes.

Next, look at the "Tab Width" textbox (see Figure 1.14 again), and set the tab width to 2. Then click OK at the bottom of the dialog box.

13 *Visual Basic Icon bar*

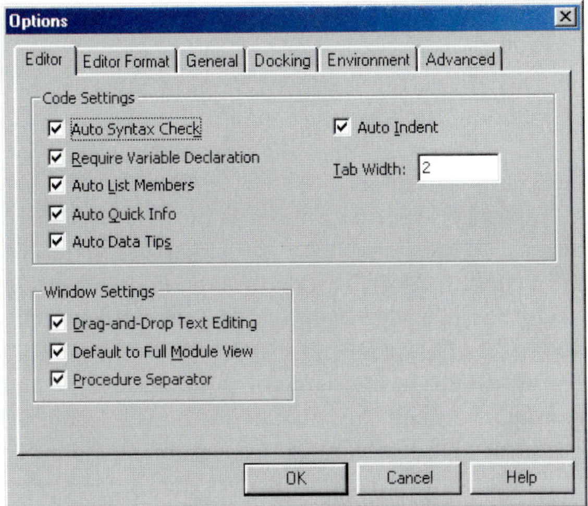

FIGURE 1.14 *Visual Basic Options—The Editor Tab*

The options that you have changed are in effect for your current Visual Basic session, and they will be saved for future sessions when you exit Visual Basic—provided you have *write privileges* on the disk from which Windows is loaded. If you cannot change these settings permanently (for example, if you load VB from a network in a computer lab in which you and your instructor do not control the settings), then you will need to change these two options every time you enter the Visual Basic IDE.

FIGURE 1.15
Visual Basic Help pull-down menu items

Add-Ins Menu and Windows Menu

These menus are not needed in this chapter.

Help Menu

You will really enjoy the on-line Help facility available in Visual Basic. First, context-sensitive help (that is, help pertaining to whatever Visual Basic component you are currently working on) is always available by pressing the F1 function key. You can also browse or navigate through the Help menus to find information on any aspect of Visual Basic.

From the Help Menu (Figure 1.15), choose "Contents." Then click on the + to the left of "MSDN Library Visual Studio 6.0." Then click the + to the left of "Visual Basic Documentation." And then click "Visual Basic Start Page." The topics on the Visual Basic Start Page provide a quick tour of Visual Basic's main features and can help you get started in building your own Visual Basic applications.

We will delve into Visual Basic Help more deeply in Chapter Four.

EXPERIMENT WITH THE "SIMPLE" APPLICATION

Open the Simple Project, as follows:

1. Click on the Open Project icon.

2. If you get a "Save changes to Form1.frm?" Dialog Box, answer "No."
3. Change the folder to Chap01.

4. Select Simple.vbp.
5. Select OK.

View the Project Window, the form, and the form properties:

1. Click on View | Project Explorer.
2. The **Project Explorer Window** (upper right side of screen) will say "Project—Simple" in its Title Bar. Under the parent item "Simple (Simple.vbp)" you should see a child item called "Forms", and under "Forms" you should see a lower-level child item called "frmSimple (Simple.frm)". If you do not see these child items, then click the + sign to the left of the parent item in order to see its child items. Click on the name of the only form in this project, "frmSimple (Simple.frm)". When the name of a form is selected, all three icons on the Project Explorer Window's tiny menu bar are enabled (that is, available to be clicked). Click on the middle icon, called "View Object". Alternatively, press Shift + F7.
3. Press F4 or click on the Properties Window icon.

4. Scroll through the form properties using the vertical scroll bar.

View the properties of the control (the Command Button):

1. Click on the Command Button (the object that reads, "This is a control—Click Me!"
2. Click on the Properties Window icon.

3. Scroll through the Command Button's properties using the vertical scroll bar.

View the code associated with the Command Button. Any of the following methods will display the Code Window for the Command Button:

Method 1
- Press F7 or click on the View Code icon in the Project Explorer Window

- Select Command1 from the object drop-down list, OR

Method 2
- Click on the Command Button
- Press F7, OR

Method 3
- Double-click the Command Button.

Because this little project has only the one form, you could have made all of these selections directly from the View Menu at the top of the Visual Basic screen. The selections are View | Code, View | Object, View | Project Explorer, and View | Properties Window. However, most programmers quickly adapt to clicking on the icons rather than the Menu Bar selections, since the icons usually save a few mouse clicks.

Run the Simple Project from the design environment, as follows:

1. Note that Visual Basic's Title Bar reads, "Simple—Microsoft Visual Basic [design]." This indicates that you are looking at the Simple Project in the design time environment.
2. Click on the Run icon.

3. Note that the Title Bar now reads, "Simple—Microsoft Visual Basic [run]," and that the program is running, which is referred to as runtime. Also note that the Form Layout, Properties, and Toolbox windows disappear, and that the **Immediate Window** appears under the Form Window. VB will not accept input from the Immediate Window while in Run mode (try typing something in the Immediate Window to verify that this cannot be done).
4. Click on the Break icon.

5. Note that the Title Bar now reads, "Simple—Microsoft Visual Basic [break]," and that the program is not running—actually, it is suspended, referred to as break mode or break time. Note also that you can now type something into the Immediate Window. If the form is no longer visible, you will find it on the Windows 98 Taskbar at the bottom of the screen, where you can click on it to make it visible while in break mode.
6. Click on the Run | Continue icon again.

7. Note that the Title Bar again reads, "Simple—Microsoft Visual Basic [run]", and that the program is again running.
8. Click the Command Button. Its caption will change from "This is a control—Click Me!" to "Exit", and the message "And this is a form" will appear on the form.
9. To stop execution of the program, click the Command Button again, or click on the End icon on the Toolbar.

10. After you exit the Simple program, note that you have returned to the design environment.

Make some changes to the design. For example, relocate the Command Button by dragging it with the mouse to a new location on the form, and change the Caption property of the form or of the Command Button through the Properties Window. These changes will not be saved on your disk unless you tell Visual Basic to save them. If you do wish to save them, choose File | Save Project, or click on the Save icon:

To obtain a printed copy of this project:

1. Select File | Print . . .
2. In the Print Dialog Box, the Check Boxes in the middle allow you to designate which things you want to print:
   - Form Image—that is, the visual image of the GUI itself.

- Form As Text—the properties of the form and all of the controls on that form. Only the properties that have been changed from their default settings are printed.
- Code—the Visual Basic statements attached to the form.

3. Click OK.

Exit Visual Basic:

1. Click on File | Exit from Visual Basic's Menu Bar, or double-click the Control Menu Icon (top left corner of VB), or click the Control Menu Icon once and select Close from the Control Menu's dropdown menu, or click the Close (X) button (top right corner of VB), or select the Menu Bar and then press Alt-F4.
2. If Visual Basic asks whether you want to save changes to SIMPLE.FRM and/or SIMPLE.VBP, click on "No," unless of course you wish to save any changes you have made to the application.
3. You will be returned to the Windows 98 opening screen.

SUMMARY

Visual Basic is a modern, general purpose, Windows-based programming language that will allow you to create graphical, event-driven applications for your microcomputer. It is a successor to earlier versions of BASIC as well as to structured languages such as Pascal. Unlike these earlier procedure-oriented languages, however, applications written in Visual Basic are driven by external events, often initiated by the user, such as mouse clicks.

A Visual Basic **application** consists of the **graphical user interface (GUI)** and the **program code.** The programmer draws the GUI on the screen using a set of VB **objects** (**forms** and **controls**). VB code is written in procedures attached to the objects. Associated with every object is a set of **properties, events,** and **methods. Properties** represent programmable characteristics of each object, such as size, location, shape, and color. **Events** are things that can happen to an object during program execution and to which the program can respond if the programmer writes code for that particular event. **Methods** are Visual Basic statements that affect an object.

The Visual Basic **Integrated Development Environment** includes all of the tools you will need to write complete VB applications: the **Menu, Toolbar, Toolbox, Form, Project Explorer, Form Layout, Immediate,** and **Properties** windows.

PROGRAMMING ASSIGNMENT

Pet Rock

See what the completed Pet Rock application should look like by running PetRock.exe from the Windows 98 Start | Run menu. Find this program in the folder "C:\VB Student Demos\Chap01". Click the large Command Button captioned "Please turn me over". Then click the Command Button again to end the program. Now create this application yourself, as follows.

Start a new project. Change the name of the Form1 object to "frmPetRock". (The Name property of any object in Visual Basic 6.0 is the first property listed for that object in the Properties Window.) Change the caption property of frmPetRock from "Form1" to "Pet Rock". Save the form on your floppy disk (or wherever your instructor tells you to save it) as "PetRock.frm", and save the project as "PetRock.vbp".

Draw a large Command Button on the form (almost as large as the form itself). You do this by clicking on the Command Button icon in the Toolbox (on the left of the Integrated Development Environment (IDE) design screen), moving the cursor (mousepointer) onto the form, clicking and holding down the left mouse button inside the form near the top left corner of the form, dragging down and to the right until the outline of the Command Button nearly fills the form, and then releasing the mouse button.

Change the name of the Command Button from "Command1" to "cmdRock". Then change the caption property of cmdRock from "Command1" to "Please turn me over". Since you have now completed the design of the graphical user interface (GUI), save the project again by clicking the Save icon on the Toolbar.

Select (click on) cmdRock. Double-click cmdRock or press the F7 function key. This will open the Code Window for the Command Button, showing only the header declaration and the End Sub statement. Type the code so that the completed procedure looks exactly like this:

```
Private Sub cmdRock_Click()
   If cmdRock.Caption = "Thank You" Then End
   cmdRock.Caption = "Thank You"
End Sub
```

Run the program to make sure that it works correctly. Then save the project again.

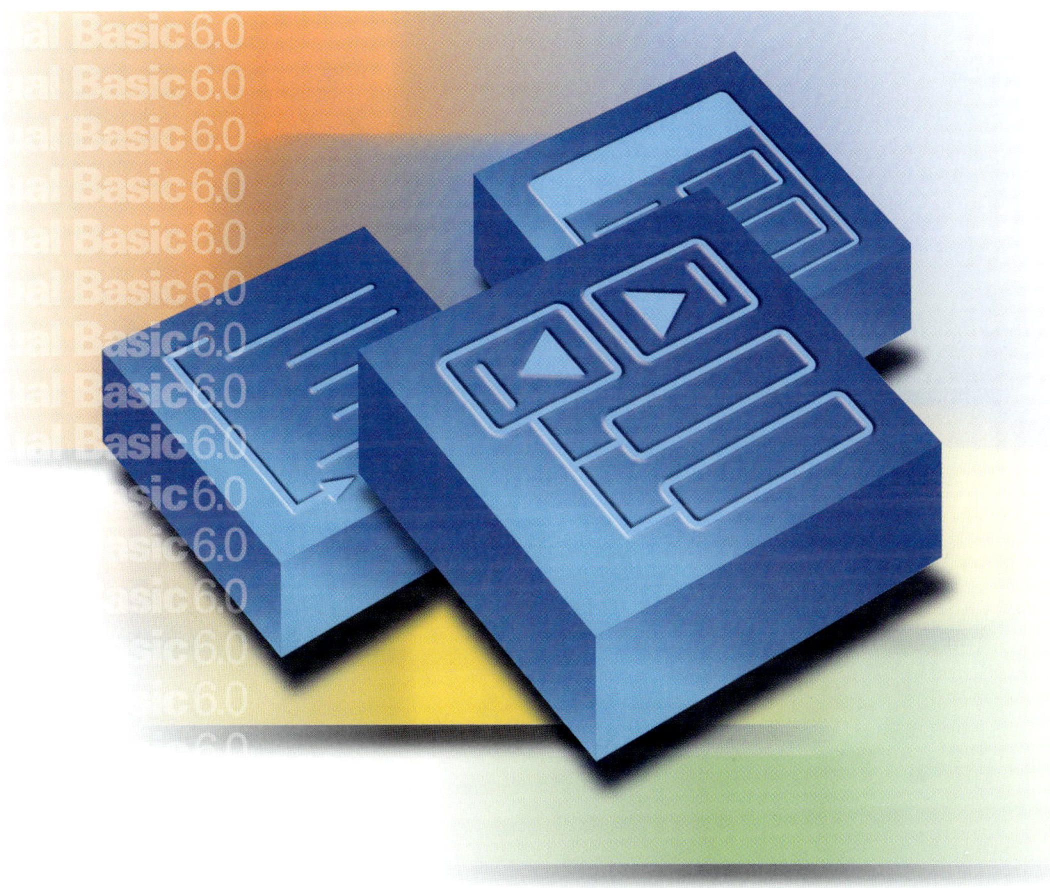

PART TWO

PROGRAMMING FUNDAMENTALS

CHAPTER TWO

A FIRST PROGRAM: FORM, CONTROLS AND CODE

Application: Hello, World

LEARNING OBJECTIVES

Upon completion of Chapter Two, you will be able to

- Create a complete, simple Visual Basic application, including the form, the controls, the FRM file, and the VBP file.
- Use the following controls from the Toolbox (that is, create, position, reposition, resize, delete, and set properties for these controls):

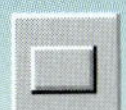
Command Button

Label

- Use the Cls and Print methods, Const declaration, Assignment statement, and MsgBox statement.
- Set properties at run time.

Keywords

Alignment property
Assignment statement
BackColor property
Caption property
Click event
Cls method
Command Button control
Const declaration
Control object
Dynamic Link Library
Enabled property
Font object
Font.Size property
Form object
General object
Handles
Label control
MsgBox statement
Name property
Print method
Sub/End Sub statement
Visible property

INTRODUCING THE "HELLO, WORLD" APPLICATION

This first application introduces you to the principal elements of Visual Basic. A single form (a window in the middle of your screen) contains three Command Buttons and a Label (Figure 2.01). Command Buttons are also sometimes called push buttons, because they look like they can be pushed, and graphically they appear to be depressed whenever you click on them with the mouse while the program is running. A Label contains whatever text (called the "caption") the programmer initially places there; the caption can be changed by the program (but not by the user) while the program is running. The background of the form starts out pale yellow; the Blue and Red buttons are both visible and enabled; and the Label at the bottom reads "Try the Blue or the Red Button."

When the Blue button is clicked, the background color changes to a light blue, the message "Hello, Blue World" is printed on the form, the Blue button is disabled, the Red button is enabled, and the Label changes to "Now try the Red Button, or Exit"; similarly when the Red button is clicked, the message "Hello, Red World" is printed on the form while the background color switches to red, the Red button is disabled, the Blue button is enabled, and the Label changes to "Now try the Blue Button, or Exit." Initially, the Exit button is not visible; clicking either the Red or the Blue button makes the Exit button visible. When the Exit button is clicked, a message box displays a concluding message, "Goodbye, World," while the background color changes back to pale yellow.

Before doing anything else, try running the "Hello, World" program. As explained in Chapter One, the Hello.exe program file will be found in the folder "C:\VB Student Demos\Chap02." Run the program from the Windows 98 Start | Run menu.

FIGURE 2.01 *Running Hello World Application*

BUILDING THE "HELLO, WORLD" PROJECT

Successful Visual Basic programming requires that you follow a proven, step-by-step methodology. Although you may find some of these steps cumbersome and unnecessary at first, especially when writing your first few, very simple programs, in the long run you will become a more efficient and effective programmer if you follow this methodology rigorously.

1. Understand the problem.
2. Design your solution.
3. Develop your logic.
4. Build your graphical user interface (GUI).
5. Write the Visual Basic code associated with each form and control.
6. Test and debug your program.
7. Complete the program documentation.

STEP 1. Understand the Problem.

The "Hello, World" Project is so simple that the first step requires little explanation. But when you try your own first application, such as one of the Programming Assignments listed at the end of Chapter Two, your first step must be that of gaining a complete understanding of the task at hand. Read the specifications carefully to see whether anything is unclear, and get answers from your instructor before you proceed. Most importantly, make sure you understand what results the program is supposed to produce—only when you know the desired results will you be able to judge whether your program has achieved them.

Go back now and reread the paragraph entitled, "Introducing the 'Hello, World' Application." Before creating the application yourself, you must be sure that you know what it is supposed to do.

STEP 2. Design Your Solution.

For each demonstration application in this textbook, step 2 has also been done for you. But when you are given one of the lab assignments or when you strike out on your own project, you must design tentative solutions, consider their strengths and weaknesses, select the most promising solution, and then refine it. Many programmers find it most efficient to do their preliminary design work on paper, long before they turn on the computer. Students who plunge right into the computerized solution to the first part of the problem before thinking about the entirety of the problem, the ramifications of each part of the solution, and the interrelationships of the parts often end up wasting a lot of time re-creating or fixing their initial solution. Also, their final product usually looks like a house built as a series of ill-thought-out additions rather than like a house designed by an architect following an overall plan.

- Start with a blank sheet of paper, preferably graph paper, held in the "Landscape" direction. Sketch the "Hello, World" form (see Figure 2.02). The form should appear centered on the page, about the size and shape of an index card. Above the top of the form, write "Hello, World," which will be the caption in the title bar of the form. Draw the three Command Buttons horizontally, across the lower middle of the form, and label them "Blue," "Red," and "Exit." Leave enough room on the form above these Command Buttons to print the message "Hello, Blue World" or "Hello, Red World" in large type. Put another rectangular box, centered near the bottom of the form, about three inches wide and one half inch tall (this will become a Label).

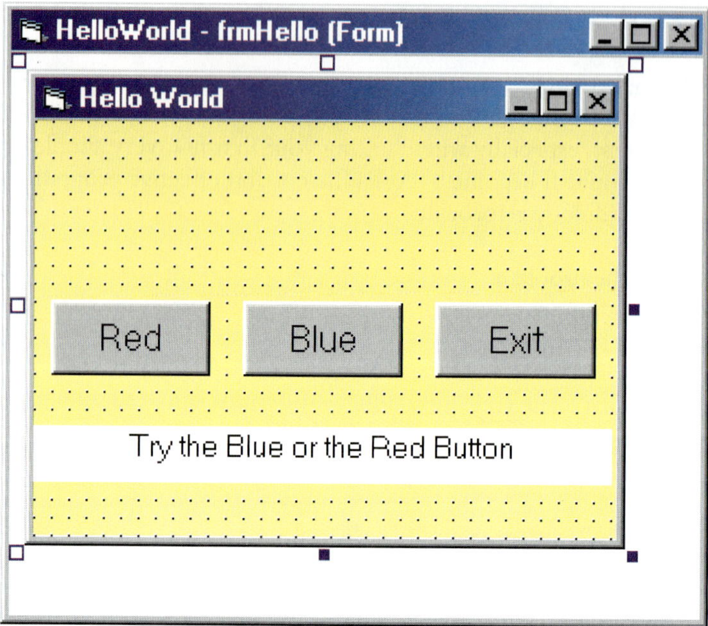

FIGURE 2.02 *Hello World Form at design time*

Object Names

At this point in the design phase of a VB application, we usually make up names and captions for the form and controls. Here they are for this application:

OBJECT	NAME	CAPTION
form	frmHello	Hello, World
Command Button	cmdBlue	Blue
Command Button	cmdRed	Red
Command Button	cmdExit	Exit
label	lbl	Try the Blue or the Red Button

Some VB programmers like to design their forms right on the screen rather than doing them on paper first. They have discovered that they can draw, erase, and revise the look of their screens more quickly and easily in Visual Basic than they can on paper. As a matter of fact, some non-VB programmers use Visual Basic as a means of helping them prototype a proposed screen design before actually implementing the design in another language. It's not necessarily wrong to do your screen design work on the computer, but you should be careful to think through the entire design and especially to develop your logic (step 3 as follows) before locking into a particular screen design and before writing any code. Do not invest your time implementing a preliminary design. You should be certain the finished design will work, because then you will have to implement it only once.

You do not always need to provide a new name for every object. Here are some rules to follow:

- Always provide your own name for a form. Since human beings are prone to error, we should take steps to minimize the risk of harming ourselves; leaving Form1 with its default name is dangerous, since at some point you may save two Form1s in the same directory, and the second will overwrite the first.
- Generally, a control should be given a meaningful name if you plan on referring to the control anywhere else in your program. This includes a control whose

purpose is to trigger some action, like a Command Button, or a control whose properties may be needed or changed during execution of the program (run time). The exception might be the case in which only one of a certain type of control appears on a form. In such a case, you are not likely to confuse the name of that control with any other control name on that form; therefore, you do not need to change the name.

- Finally, when you invent object names, use words that both identify the object class and distinguish this object from others of the same class on this form. We use the convention of a three-character abbreviation of the object class as a prefix to a meaningful name. Thus, cmdBlue identifies a Command Button (cmd), and distinguishes this button from all others on this form (Blue). But lbl is sufficient to identify the only Label on the form.

STEP 3. Develop Your Logic.

The initial settings of the form and controls are the starting point of your program logic. Although they aren't part of the execution logic, writing down these initial settings is a good idea, because it reminds you of the starting point from which subsequent actions take place. The following initial settings are derived from the description of the "Hello, World" application:

cmdExit is not visible
Large font size for the form

In accordance with the description of the application, you know that several things must happen when the user clicks on each of the Command Buttons. (When the user clicks on an object, a *click event* occurs, provided that the object is one that responds to a mouse click. If the program is supposed to do something when the click event happens, the programmer puts the actions in a *click-event procedure.* During program execution, we say that clicking the mouse on an object "fires" or "triggers" or "executes" or "calls" the associated procedure: these terms are all synonymous.) Therefore, this application will include a click-event procedure for each Command Button. On a sheet of paper, write down what actions your program must take when each click event occurs.

```
cmdBlue_Click procedure:
    clear the screen (to wipe out any previous message)
    change the background color of the form to blue
    print the message, "Hello, Blue World"
    disable cmdBlue
    enable cmdRed
    make cmdExit visible
    change the Label caption to "Now try the Red Button, or Exit"
cmdRed_Click procedure:
    clear the screen (to wipe out any previous message)
    change the background color of the form to red
    print the message, "Hello, Red World"
    disable cmdRed
    enable cmdBlue
    make cmdExit visible
    change the Label caption to "Now try the Blue Button, or Exit"
```

cmdExit_Click procedure:

clear the screen (to wipe out any previous message)

change the background color of the form to yellow

use a message box to display, "Goodbye, World"

end the program

Admittedly, you might not think of all of these actions the first time you consider the problem. For example, you might not discover the necessity of clearing a previous message from the screen until after you write the program and test it, and you might not notice that both the cmdBlue_Click procedure and the cmdRed_Click procedure must make cmdExit visible. But the process of thinking about your program logic, even if less than perfect, will help you write correct programs later.

STEP 4. Build Your GUI.

(Before you start, remember to select Tools | Options, Editor tab, Require Variable Declarations, and set Tab Width to 2, if these options have not been permanently changed on your computer.) Then follow these steps:

1. Start a new Visual Basic project—From the Menu Bar, select File | New Project.
2. Use the mouse to change the size and location of the form to approximate the form that you saw when running the application—roughly the shape of a large index card centered on the screen.
3. Open the Properties Window by pressing F4 or clicking on the icon below. Note that properties are listed in alphabetical order, except for the (Name) property, which is always listed first.

4. Make the form's initial background color yellow (see Figure 2.03):
   - Click on BackColor. (Scroll the list of properties if BackColor isn't visible.)
   - In the property "settings" box, that is, the area to the right of the property name, click on the down-arrow. A window will appear with two tabs, called "Palette" and "System". Select the "Palette" tab. A color palette will appear.
   - Click on the pastel (light) yellow square (the form will become the color you select).
5. Change the settings of the Caption and Name properties. In each case, choose the property, then type in the settings box:
   - (Name) frmHello
   - Caption Hello, World

Sometimes your screen will not look exactly the same as our Figure, which is intended to highlight a particular Window or part of a Window. On your screen that Window may be a different size or shape, or partially or completely hidden by other items on the desktop.

You should notice that in the Properties Window and elsewhere, Visual Basic identifies colors by a hexadecimal numeric code (such as &H80FFFF&), rather than by the English word that means that color (such as Yellow). (A number written in hexadecimal form begins with "&H". Most color codes are also very large integers, which must be stored in Visual Basic in a special type of data called a *long integer*, signified by "&" at the end of the number.) Few of us are any good at remembering which hexadecimal long integer is the code for which color. In the Properties Window, Visual Basic solves this problem for us by giving us a color

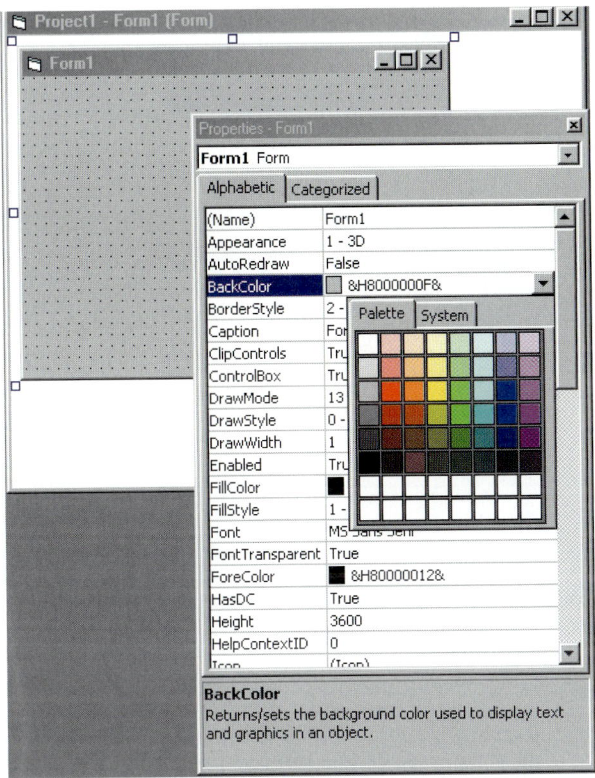

FIGURE 2.03 *Setting the form's BackColor*

palette from which to choose the desired color. Based on our selection, Visual Basic then assigns the appropriate hexadecimal number in the settings box.

The first control we will use is called a Command Button. To draw this control on your form, click on the Command Button icon in the Toolbox:

Then move the mouse back over the form. The mousepointer changes from an arrow pointing northwest to a set of crosshairs. Position the crosshairs where you want the top left corner of the Blue Command Button to appear on the form. Click and hold the mouse button, drag down and to the right until the Command Button outline is the size you want it to be, and then release the mouse button. The Command Button will appear within the rectangle you have described (see Figure 2.04).

By default, the caption and the name of your first Command Button are Command1 (we will change them later). Note the tiny squares (called handles) at the corners and along the sides of Command1. These handles mean that Command1 is currently selected. When an object is selected, you can reposition or resize it, and the Properties Window lists the properties pertaining to that object:

- To reposition: Click and hold the mouse button with the mousepointer in the middle of the control, then move in any direction. An outline of the control follows your mouse movements. When you release the mouse button, the control is moved to the new location.
- To resize: Position the mouse pointer over any handle. When the mousepointer changes to a double-headed arrow, click and drag to make the control image taller, shorter, wider, narrower. The handles in the middle of each side of the

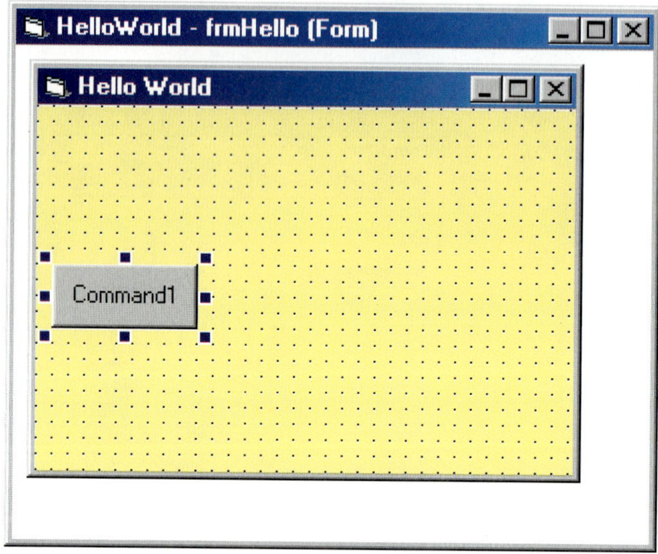

FIGURE 2.04 *Adding command buttons to the form*

control can be used to resize the control in one dimension. The handles at the corners of the control can be used to resize the control in two dimensions simultaneously.

- Open the Properties Window (see Figure 2.05): The properties listed are those available at design time (that is, while designing a VB application) for a Command Button.
- Click on the form, but outside the Command Button. You have now selected the form, so the handles around Command1 disappear, and if you open the Properties Window, the form properties are listed.

Draw two more Command Buttons on the form in similar fashion. Move and size them so that all three Command Buttons are the same size and all are aligned left to right across the middle of frmHello. (Figure 2.06).

Click on Command1, and set these properties:

Name	cmdBlue
Caption	Blue
Font.Size	12 (select Font, click on elipses, then select 12 from the dialog box)

For Command2, set these properties:

Name	cmdRed
Caption	Red
Font.Size	12

For Command3, set these properties:

Name	cmdExit
Caption	Exit
Font.Size	12
Visible	False (Note: Changing the Visible property has no visible effect except at runtime.)

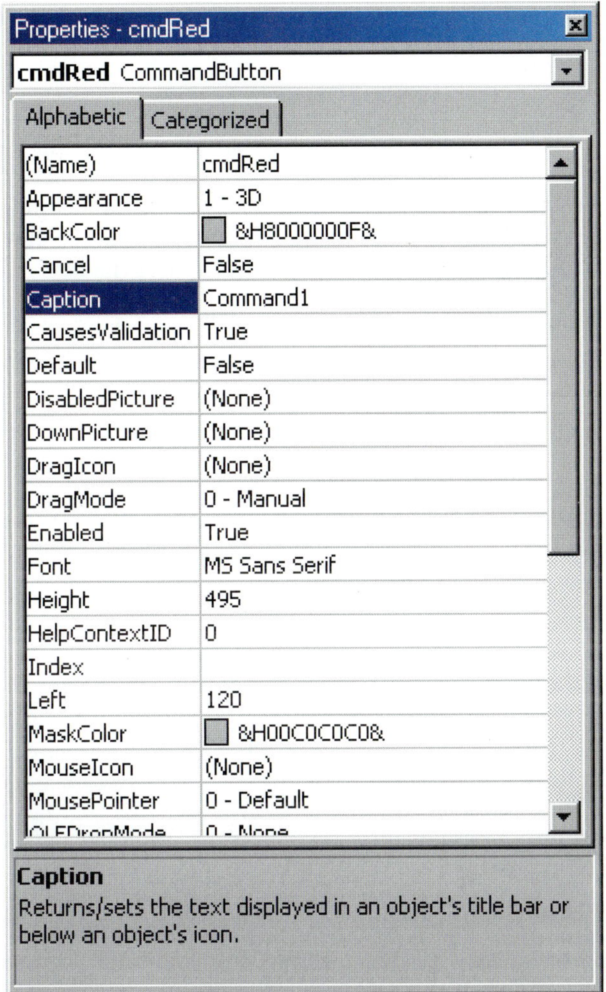

FIGURE 2.05 *Command Button property window*

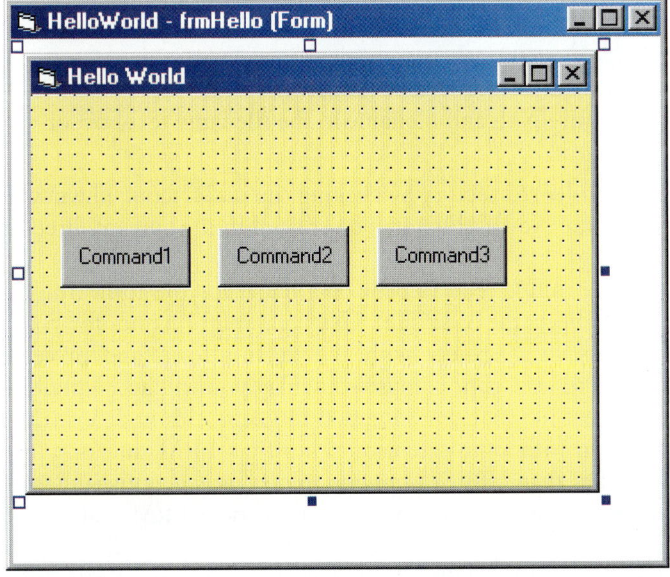

FIGURE 2.06 *Three command buttons across frmHello*

Now place a Label on the form:

1. Click on the Label icon.

2. Position and size the Label using the same techniques you employed for the Command Buttons. The Label should be about three inches wide and one half inch high, centered near the bottom of the form.
3. Set these properties for the Label:

Name	lbl
Alignment	2-Center (just type 2, or select 2-Center from the drop-down list)
Caption	Try the Blue or the Red Button

Change the Font.Size of the form to 18:

- First click on the form, but not on any control inside the form.
- Press F4 to open the Properties Window.
- Click on the Font property (also an object in its own right).
- Click on the ellipsis (. . .) on the right side of the Font property's settings box. An elipsis always opens a dialog box.
- In the Font Dialog Box, change Size to 18. (A form's Font settings carry over to controls subsequently placed on the form. For this reason, we waited until the rest of the GUI was complete before changing the form's Font Size.)

After all of the property settings are complete, frmHello should appear as in Figure 2.07.

Save your project by clicking on the icon.

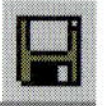

First, you should choose the directory (folder) where the project will be saved. By default, VB chooses VB's own directory. You can pick a different directory.

1. Double-click the directory name, to pick a lower level directory.
2. Click the to pick the parent directory, from which you can again move up or down one directory level at a time.
3. Type in the entire path and filename in the filename text box; or
4. Create a new folder/directory by clicking the icon. The new folder, with the default name New Folder, will be created in the current directory.

The Dialog Box prompts you to provide a name for the form (the FRM file) as well as for the project (the VBP file). Use meaningful names for your forms and projects. Never save a project with the default form and project names of Form1.frm and Project1.vbp, because some day you will accidentally overwrite a form file or project file that you intended to keep. Although Visual Basic allows you to save a form with a file extension other than FRM, and/or a project with a file extension other than VBP, it is unwise to do this, since Visual Basic will subsequently only automatically recognize forms of type FRM and projects of type VBP. In the present example, in response to the prompts, call your form frmMyHello and your project MyHello. Visual Basic will save your form under the name frmMyHello.frm (Figure 2.08) and your project under the name MyHello.vbp.

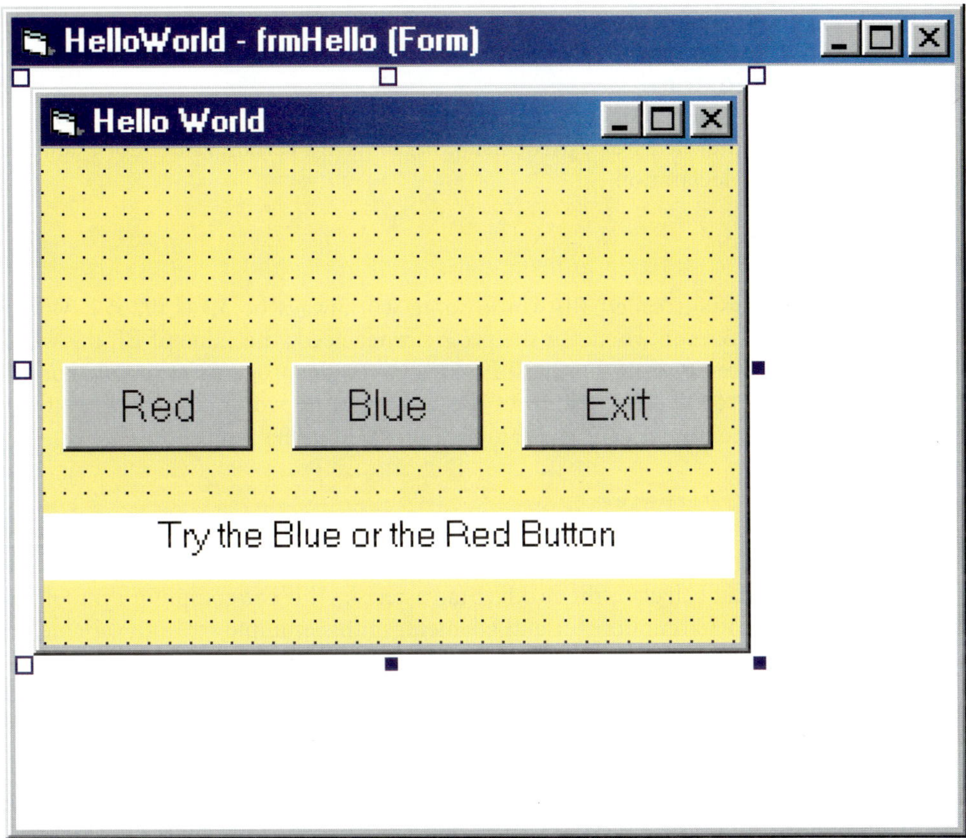

FIGURE 2.07 *Completed frmHello at design time*

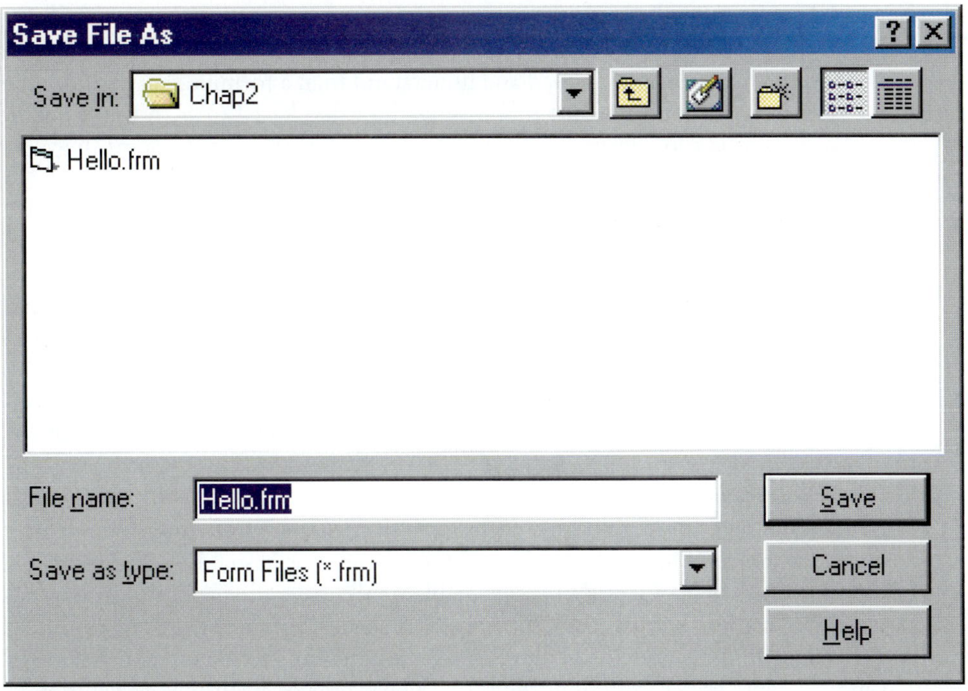

FIGURE 2.08 *Saving the file frmHello*

STEP 5. Write the VB Code Associated with Each Form and Control.

Program Constants

Constants in a computer program are data objects whose values do not change. The programmer declares a particular word to have a certain value. For example, the following declaration

```
Const PI = 3.141592654
```

declares a constant called PI, whose value will always be 3.141592654. When writing the program, whenever the programmer needs the value of PI, the word PI is used instead of the value 3.141592654. When the program is compiled or interpreted, the computer substitutes the value for the word, so that it can then carry out the computation. For example, the programmer may write:

```
Circumference = PI * Diameter
```

The computer substitutes 3.141592654 for PI and, provided it also has a value for Diameter, it can calculate the product (an asterisk [*] is the computer symbol for multiplication). Circumference and Diameter in this example are both variables, a topic that we will treat in Chapter Three.

Some other constants are equally obvious: DAYSINWEEK is always 7, the color WHITE on a PC is always &HFFFFFF&, and DUESOUTH is always 180 degrees. Other constants may change over time, but not in the course of the execution of your program, so these can be program constants as well. SALESTAXRATE, for example, is constant at least as long as the legislature is not in session.

We use constants in computer programs for three main reasons:

1. To avoid mistakes. We might accidentally mistype the value of the numeric code for yellow, but we are less likely to misspell the word PI or YELLOW. When we assign a value to a word as a constant, we only need to be careful of typing the value correctly once.
2. To make our programs more understandable. A formula that includes the word PI may be easier to read and understand than a formula that includes the numeric value. A statement that assigns the value YELLOW to the property BackColor is a lot clearer to the reader than a statement that assigns the value &HFFFF&.
3. To facilitate program maintenance when the value of a constant does in fact change. For example, if a retail sales program uses the state sales tax rate several places in the program, and then the legislature raises the rate from 5 percent to 5.5 percent, the maintenance programmer may be hard pressed to find every instance of .05 in the program, verify that the original programmer at each point meant to be calculating the sales tax, and then change the value to .055. It would be much easier and more sure to change the value of the constant SALESTAXRATE from .05 to .055 in the declarations portion of the program.

In Visual Basic, a constant can be declared in the *declarations* portion of the *general* object of a form. The general object of a form contains Visual Basic declarations, functions, and procedures that are available to all of the other objects and procedures that are part of that form. The declarations portion of the general object, as the name implies, contains only declarations: statements about constants and variables that apply throughout the form. The syntax of a constant declaration in the declarations portion of the general object of a form is:

```
Const CONSTANTNAME = constantvalue
```

where CONSTANTNAME is the single word you will use to invoke the constant, and constantvalue is the value that you want Visual Basic to substitute for CONSTANTNAME when your program runs. CONSTANTNAME must start with an alphabetic character (hereafter called an alpha) and must be fewer than 256 characters long. Alphas and numeric digits and some other special characters are permitted, but many special characters are not permitted. Do yourself a favor: Limit yourself to alphas and numerics. Also, by convention among programmers in many languages, CONSTANTNAME is usually written in all capital letters. In this way, in program listings you will be able to find constants readily. In our present application, we use constant declarations for the three background colors of the form. After these declarations are made, the programmer need not remember or look up the numeric code corresponding to each color.

The Environment option "Require Variable Declarations" causes the declaration "Option Explicit" to appear in the declarations portion of the general object of a form. As explained previously (and discussed again in Chapter Three), we will always use an Option Explicit statement in our programs to prevent ourselves from making foolish errors concerning accidental variables. Even though this first application has no variables, we will still include the Option Explicit statement, just so you get used to seeing it.

After all of this explanation, we can create the declarations portion of the general object, as follows (see Figure 2.09):

- Double-click frmHello to open the Code Window, or select View | Code from the Menu Bar, or press F7.
- Click the down-arrow symbol next to the Object drop-down list.
- Click on (general).
- The "(declarations)" portion is identified in the Proc (event procedure) drop-down list. Type in these declarations (Option Explicit should already be there; type it in if it is not.):

```
Option Explicit
'Note: We used soft, pastel colors for this application
```

HelloWorld - frmHello (Code)

(General) | (Declarations)

```
Option Explicit
'Note: We used soft, pastel colors for this application
Const BLUE = &HFFFF80
Const RED = &H8080FF
Const YELLOW = &H80FFFF
```

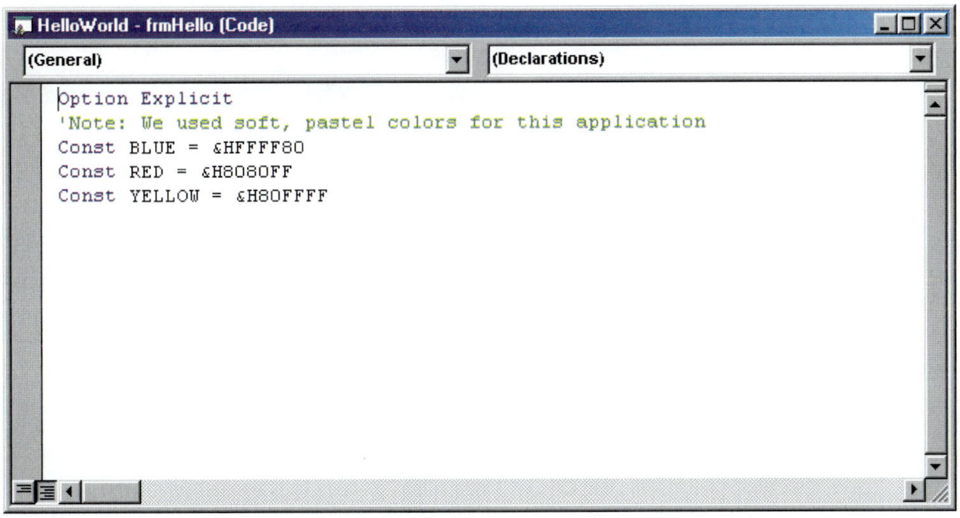

FIGURE 2.09 *The declarations portion of form frmHello*

```
Const BLUE = &HFFFF80
Const RED = &H8080FF
Const YELLOW = &H80FFFF
```

Save your project by clicking on

Using the logic that we developed in step 3 above, our task now is to write the Visual Basic statements that implement the logic associated with the three Command Buttons on frmHello.

Each Visual Basic object is able to respond to about a dozen different events, mostly mouse actions and keystrokes. To get a feel for the different possibilities, open the Code Window, and choose "Form" from the Object drop-down list. Now scroll through the Proc drop-down list (Figure 2.10).

Each event procedure represents some event that Windows traps while the program is running and to which your program could respond. In the "Hello, World" Project, the only events we wish to trap are mouse clicks on the three Command Buttons. Therefore, we now want to open the click event procedure for cmdBlue:

- From the Object drop-down list, choose cmdBlue.
- The click event procedure (Private Sub cmdBlue_Click()) is chosen by Visual Basic as the default procedure, because this is the procedure most often invoked for a Command Button by a Visual Basic programmer.
- Scroll through the other event procedures in the Proc drop-down list for cmdBlue, just to see what other events can be trapped by a Command Button. Then return to the click event in order to write the code that belongs there.

Type the code as shown in Figure 2.11. Notice in Figure 2.11 the color scheme used by Visual Basic to distinguish portions of the code: Visual Basic keywords (words that have a special meaning to VB) appear in blue. Comments appear in green (there aren't any comments in this procedure, but if there were, a comment, initiated by an apostrophe, would be in green). If VB detects a syntax error (a mistake in forming the statement) while you are typing in the code, the erroneous line will be highlighted in red along with an error message.

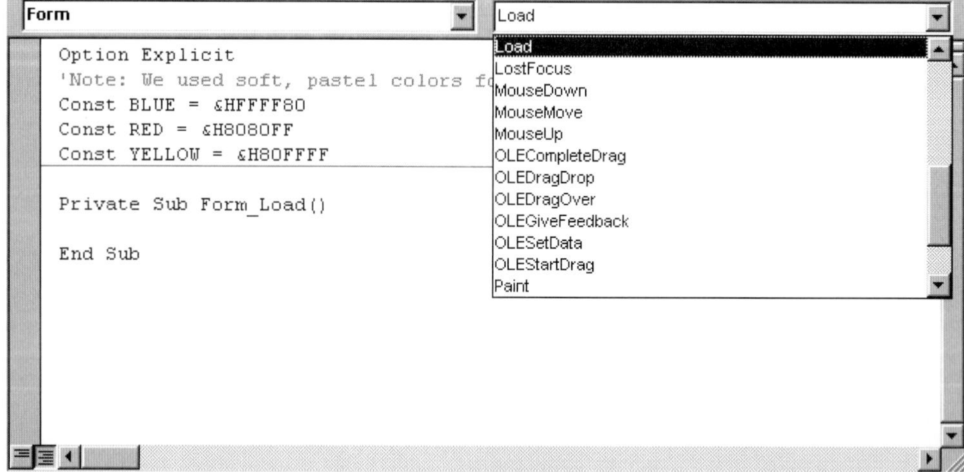

FIGURE 2.10 *Some of the available events for a form*

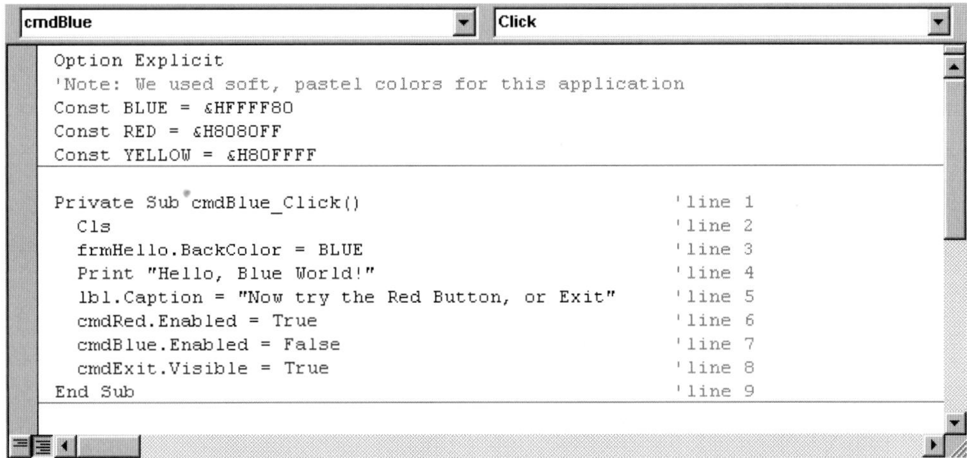


```
Option Explicit
'Note: We used soft, pastel colors for this application
Const BLUE = &HFFFF80
Const RED = &H8080FF
Const YELLOW = &H80FFFF

Private Sub cmdBlue_Click()                               'line 1
  Cls                                                     'line 2
  frmHello.BackColor = BLUE                               'line 3
  Print "Hello, Blue World!"                              'line 4
  lbl.Caption = "Now try the Red Button, or Exit"         'line 5
  cmdRed.Enabled = True                                   'line 6
  cmdBlue.Enabled = False                                 'line 7
  cmdExit.Visible = True                                  'line 8
End Sub                                                   'line 9
```

FIGURE 2.11 *Code window for cmdBlue*

Explanations of each line of code in this procedure follow:

```
Private Sub cmdBlue_Click()     'line 1
```

Every event procedure in Visual Basic begins with a heading line consisting of the words Private Sub, the procedure name, and parentheses. The procedure name consists of the object name (cmdBlue in this case), an underscore character, and the name of the event to be trapped.

A comment in Visual Basic starts with an apostrophe ('). Everything in a line of code following an apostrophe is meant for human rather than computer consumption and is ignored by Visual Basic. We used comments to provide line numbers keyed to these explanations. Obviously, the comments are not needed in your program.

```
frmHello.Cls     'line 2
```

Cls means "clear screen," a misnomer, since actually what it does is clear any text written directly on a form—it does not clear the whole screen, nor does it affect any controls that appear on the form. Cls is a Visual Basic method associated with the form object. A method is an action or statement that is associated with an object. In this case, the form object has the ability to erase messages written on itself. A method in Visual Basic is written in the general format

object.method

In many cases, the object need not be mentioned, since only one object can possibly be intended by the programmer.

```
frmHello.BackColor = BLUE     'line 3
```

This line assigns the constant value of BLUE (that is, &HFFFF80) to the BackColor property of frmHello. This line of code demonstrates the general form of the assignment statement in Visual Basic:

target = expression

In this case, frmHello.BackColor is the target of the assignment, or, to state it a different way, the expression becomes a single value that is assigned as the new value of the target, replacing whatever other value was there previously. When referring to the property of an object, the Visual Basic syntax is

object.property

As with methods, the object may sometimes be assumed, as long as Visual Basic will not be confused as to which object is intended.

```
frmHello.Print "Hello, Blue World!"    'line 4
```

Print is another method associated with the form object. Its action is to print a value on the form, starting at the top left of the form. In this case, the value to be printed is a string, which is enclosed in quotation marks.

Again, the name of the object could be omitted, since Visual Basic will assume that the programmer intends to apply the Print method to the current form.

```
lbl.Caption = "Now try the Red Button, or Exit"    'line 5
```

In this assignment statement, the caption property of the object lbl is given a new setting, another string enclosed in quotes.

```
cmdBlue.Enabled = False    'line 6
```

When *True*, the enabled property allows the user to click on the Command Button. The default value of the enabled property is True. When this property is set to *False*, the Command Button is "disabled": its appearance is dimmed, and clicking on the object has no effect.

With cmdBlue disabled, the user is forced to choose among the remaining Command Buttons.

```
cmdRed.Enabled = True    'line 7
```

If the user had previously clicked on cmdRed, the click event procedure for that button would have resulted in the Red button being disabled. This statement enables the Red button again. If cmdRed had already been enabled, this assignment statement would have no effect.

```
cmdExit.Visible = True    'line 8
```

When the program starts running, the Exit button is not visible, and clicking on the form in the location where the invisible button resides has no effect. We now want to make cmdExit visible.

```
End Sub    'line 9
```

The End Sub statement is the final statement in every procedure.

From the Object drop-down list, now choose the cmdRed object. The click event procedure for cmdRed is a mirror image of the procedure for cmdBlue (Because the code in Sub cmdRed_Click is so similar to the code in Sub cmdBlue_Click, you could use the Copy and Paste features from the Edit menu. These features will be covered more extensively in Chapter Three.):

```
Private Sub cmdRed_Click()
Cls
frmHello.BackColor = RED
Print "Hello, Red World!"
lbl.Caption = "Now try the Blue Button, or Exit"
cmdRed.Enabled = False
cmdBlue.Enabled = True
cmdExit.Visible = True
End Sub
```

Note that in this procedure, frmHello is omitted as the object in both the Cls and the Print method statements. The default object for these methods is the current form, so the form does not need to be stated explicitly.

We still need to create the code for the third Command Button, cmdExit. Here is another way to open the Code Window on a particular event procedure, which is especially convenient if you are currently looking at the form:

- Start by viewing the form—either click anywhere on the form if you can see it, or click on View Form from the Project Window.
- Click on the Exit button to select it (the familiar handles will appear around the Command Button).
- Double-click on the Exit button. The Code Window will appear, showing the click event procedure for this button.

Type in the following code:

```
Private Sub cmdExit_Click()
Cls
frmHello.BackColor = YELLOW
MsgBox "Goodbye, World!", 48, "Soooooo-Long"
End
End Sub
```

The new statement in this procedure is the MsgBox statement. This statement generates a Dialog Box containing a message. A Dialog Box is a rectangular graphical object that appears on the screen during program execution and demands a response from the user before anything else in the program is permitted to occur. Since you ran the "Hello, World" program earlier, you have already seen what this statement does, but now you can see the syntax:

MsgBox <message> [, style, title]

Following the reserved word MsgBox, the message itself is a string enclosed in quotes. The rest of the statement is optional (which is indicated here by brackets []). The style is a number that could have a variety of meanings, the most common of which is the numeric code for an icon, in this case the information symbol . The title, if present, appears in the Title Bar of the MsgBox Dialog Box; if the title is omitted in the MsgBox statement, then the name of the project (the name recognized by VB) appears in the Title Bar of the MsgBox Dialog Box.

Save your project by clicking on the icon.

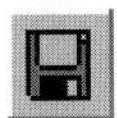

STEP 6. Test and Debug Your Program.

Run your completed application by selecting Run | Start from the Menu Bar or by clicking on the run icon.

Any syntax errors, violations of the rules of Visual Basic, will be discovered by Visual Basic when it tries to run your program.

Logic errors are harder to find. For this first application, just compare your output to that produced by the HELLO.EXE file that was given to you. You should be able to correct any errors by carefully following the instructions given to you above.

Debugging a program, that is, finding and fixing the errors in a program, is a whole subject unto itself. We will delve into it much more deeply in later chapters. Even though we treat it lightly in this first program, you should be aware that this is a most important phase of computer program development.

If you find any errors in your program, and after you have fixed them, save your project again. In future chapters, we won't remind you to save your project regularly, so you must remember to do it yourself.

STEP 7. Complete the Program Documentation.

Most programs need additional documentation other than the program itself, even though, if you follow the guidelines in this textbook, your Visual Basic programs are going to be fully intelligible and self-explanatory! Your program is not complete until you complete step 7.

Program documentation comes in two varieties, internal and external. Internal documentation occurs within the program itself, usually in the form of comments in the program code, and sometimes also in the form of "Help" modules that explain program functions and features to users. External documentation may include such things as a user's manual or computer operator's manual, as well as technical guides such as flowcharts for programmers who may have to update your program at a later date.

For this project, the only additional documentation your program needs is some personal identification. Open the project, and open the Code Window for the (declarations) portion of the (general) object. Insert these comment lines (after the Option Explicit statement):

```
'Project Name:    MYHELLO.VBP
'Written by:     <insert your name>
'Original date:    <insert today's date>
['Revision date:    <insert revision date, if any>]
'Adapted from Spear & Spear
'Form MYHELLO.FRM
```

REVISED "HELLO, WORLD" PROJECT

Visual Basic includes a number of "symbolic constants" built into the software, which we will discuss at greater length later. For now, we can just look at the results from using symbolic constants for the three colors in the "Hello, World" project, in lieu of the constant declarations which we asked you to type into the program.

We declared the constants YELLOW, BLUE, and RED in this program, and we assigned our own numeric values to these constants, in order to achieve a soft, pastel appearance. VB has built-in constants for these (and several other) colors, but those colors are vibrant, even glaring. However, you can see how such constants are used, by revising your program as follows:

- Delete the three constant declarations.
- In the command button click event procedures, use the symbolic constants vbYellow, vbRed, and vbBlue instead of YELLOW, RED, and BLUE, respectively.
- Using the palette for the form's BackColor property at design time, make the BackColor a vibrant yellow.
- Save the revised form as "frmMyHelloRev.frm" and the project as "MyHelloRev.vbp".

Your revised project should look like ours, to be found at C:\VB Student Demos\Chap02\HelloRev.exe.

SUMMARY

A simple Visual Basic Project can contain one **form object,** which can be sized and positioned as the programmer wishes. Two commonly used **control objects** that can be placed on a form are the **Label** and the **Command Button.** All Visual Basic objects have properties, events, and methods. A Label identifies objects on the form or provides other directions or information to the user. A Command Button is usually associated with a **Click-event procedure,** in which program code causes some action to take place.

A **form** has 51 properties at design time; the form properties introduced in this application are **BackColor, Caption, Font.Size,** and **Name.** Many properties of a form are also properties of certain controls that can be placed on the form. The chapter introduced these properties for controls: **Alignment, Enabled,** and **Visible.** The project included the **Cls** and **Print** methods, both associated with a form, and the **Assignment** statement, the most common statement in Visual Basic. Two other statements, **MsgBox** and the **Const declaration,** were also introduced.

PROGRAMMING ASSIGNMENTS

My Resume

Start a new project, and caption the form "My Resume." Put a Label at the top center of the form, captioned with your name in a large, bold font, centered. Arrange Command Buttons on the form with the captions "Career Objective," "Education," "Experience," "Honors," "Contact Info," and "Exit" (Figure 2.12). Name the form "frmResume" and save it as "frmResume.frm". Then save the project as "Resume.vbp".

When each Command Button is clicked, a message box with the appropriate information should appear. "Career Objective," "Education," "Experience," and "Honors" are self-explanatory. Contact information should include your address and phone number and should indicate the best time to call as well as your availability for employment. When the "Exit" button is clicked, repeat your phone number in a message box, and then exit the program. If you wish to include line

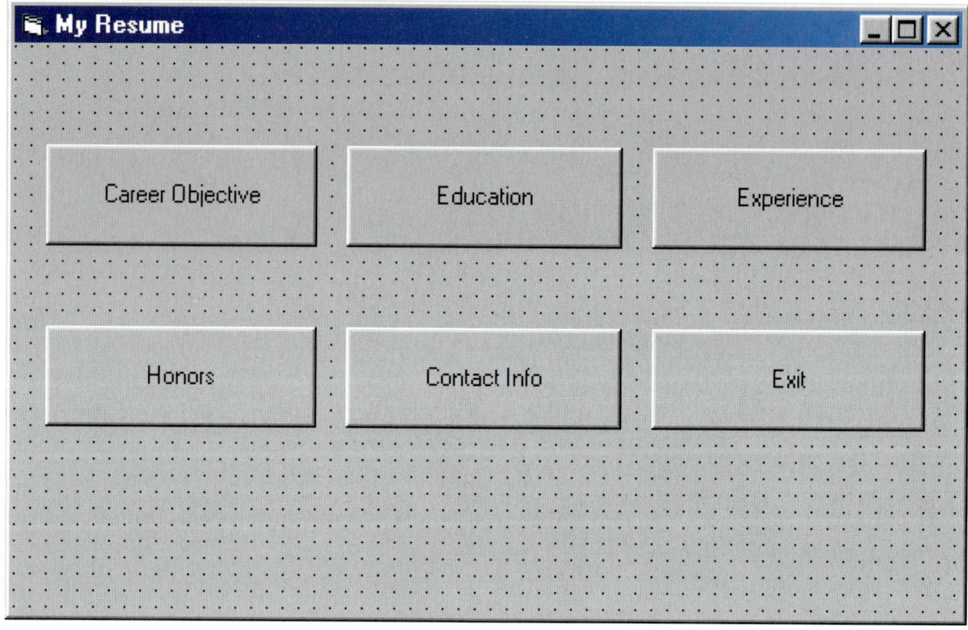

FIGURE 2.12 *frmResume at design time*

breaks in the middle of a message, follow this model (Chr$(13) causes a carriage return):

```
MsgBox "First Line" & Chr$(13) & "Second Line"
```

Use soothing background colors for the form, with a different color when each Command Button is clicked. When the user clicks OK to clear the message box, set the form's color back to its original color.

Knock-Knock Joke

Start a new project, and caption the form "Knock-Knock Joke." Put one Command Button on the form with the caption "Click Me." Set the background color of the form to yellow.

When the user clicks the Command Button, change the form's BackColor property to green and display a Message Box with the words "Knock-knock."

When the user clicks "OK," change the form's BackColor property to yellow, print "Knock-knock." on the form, and display a Message Box with the words "Who's There?"

When the user clicks "OK," change the form's BackColor property to green, print "Knock-knock." on the form, print "Who's there?" on the form, and display a Message Box with the word "BOO!"

When the user clicks "OK," change the form's BackColor property to yellow; print "Knock-knock," "Who's there?" and "BOO!" on the form; and display a Message Box with the words "Boo Who?"

When the user clicks "OK," change the form's BackColor property to green; print "Knock-knock," "Who's there?" "BOO!" and "Boo Who?" on the form; and display a Message Box with the words "Well, you don't have to cry about it!" (See Figure 2.13.)

When the user clicks "OK," change the form's BackColor property to yellow and display a Message Box with the words "That's all, Folks."

When the user clicks "OK," end the program.

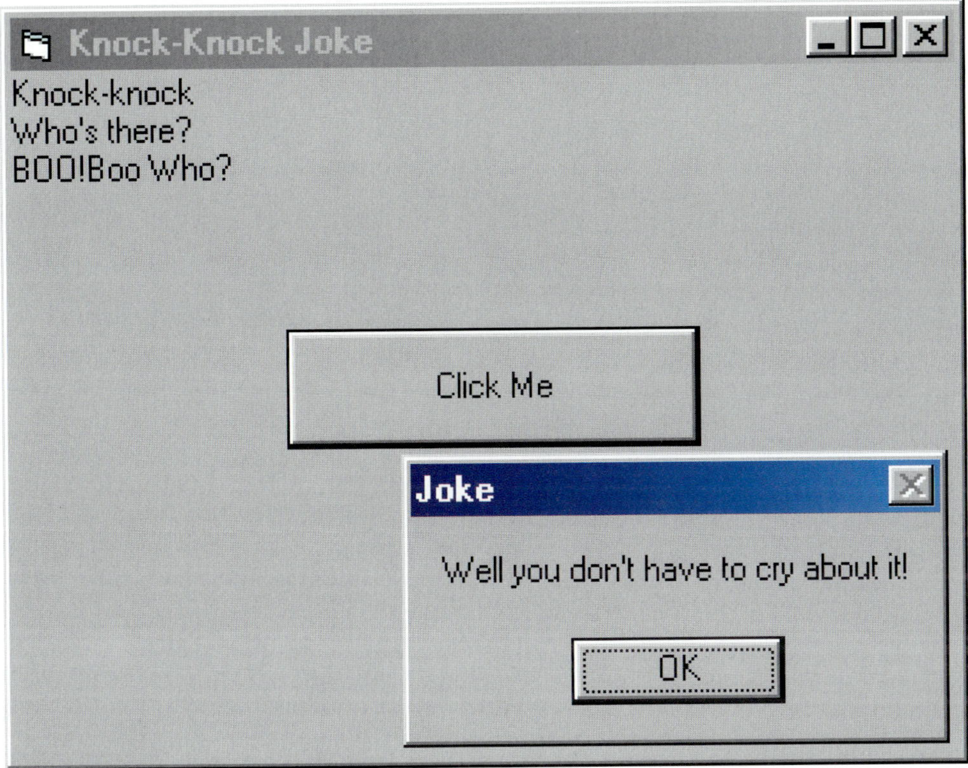

FIGURE 2.13 *Knock-knock joke at run time*

CHAPTER THREE

ELEMENTS OF THE VISUAL BASIC PROGRAMMING LANGUAGE

Application: Simple Calculator

LEARNING OBJECTIVES

Upon completion of Chapter Three, the student will be able to

- Identify the principal elements of the Visual Basic programming language.
- Understand the notion of variables, variable types, and variable scope.
- Apply Hungarian notation to the naming of objects and variables.
- Define structured programming and apply the three permitted control structures: sequence, selection, and iteration.
- Display the components of a project in a Hierarchy Table and the program logic in pseudocode.

Keywords

Argument
Arithmetic expression
Arithmetic operator
Boolean data type
Bug
Byte data type
Clipboard object
Control structures
Copy command
Currency data type
Cut command
Date data type
Dim statement
Dimension
Double data type
Expression
Hierarchy Table
Hungarian notation
If/Then
If/Then/Else
Integer data type
Iteration control structure
Line continuation character
Long data type
Next sequential instruction
Object data type
Paste command
Private command
Pseudocode
Public declaration
Relational expression
Relational operator
Scope
Selection control structure
Sequence control structure
Single data type
Str function
String data type
Type declaration character
Val function
Variant data type

VARIABLES

The notion of a variable is central to computerized data processing and to the very idea of a computer program. We think of a variable as something that can have a value that can change in the course of the execution of a program. From a logical standpoint, a variable is thus contrasted both with a constant and with a literal.

Constants were described in Chapter Two. A constant has a name and a permanently assigned value, which can never change. A literal is an explicitly stated value in a program, which can obviously never change (5 always means exactly 5). A variable may have one value at one time during program execution and a different value at a later time. A simple variable can have only one value at a time: Any new value completely replaces the previous value.

Consider the following snippet of code:

```
Private Sub Snippet()
   Const X = 5
   Dim Y
   Y = X
   Print Y,
   Y = X + X
   Print Y,
   Y = X * 2 + X ^ 2
   Print Y,
   Y = Y + 1
   Print Y
End Sub
```

The output from executing this procedure would be:

```
5    10    35    36
```

In this procedure, X is a constant. The value assigned to X in the Const declaration is the literal 5. Later in this code, 2 is also a literal. The declaration

```
Dim Y
```

dimensions or declares Y as a variable, so Y is able to take on different values while the program is running.

As mentioned in Chapter One, the formal definition of a variable is that it is a symbolic reference to an address in memory. In other words, the programmer makes up a name (in this case Y, the variable name) and declares (with the Dim statement) that Y shall henceforth be understood within the Snippet procedure to be a variable. Visual Basic assigns a specific memory address for storing the contents of the variable Y. The name Y and Y's memory address are placed in a look-up table of all of the variables in the Snippet procedure, which VB creates and maintains. Subsequently, throughout the Snippet procedure, whenever the program includes a reference to the variable Y, the Visual Basic compiler or interpreter uses the look-up table and substitutes the actual memory address where the contents of Y are stored for the symbolic reference Y in the source program. In this way, the programmer is relieved of the tedious task of keeping track of all of the memory addresses where variables are stored, and yet the machine is able to find those addresses during program execution.

The name that you give to a variable is entirely up to you, within the following simple guidelines:

- The length of the variable name is 1 to 255 characters.
- Use only alphabetic and numeric characters. Certain special characters, such as an underscore character (_), may also be part of a variable name, but it's easier and less confusing just to avoid special characters altogether.
- The first character of the name must be alphabetic.
- The name may not include any spaces.
- The name may not be exactly the same as a Visual Basic keyword, that is, a word that already has some special meaning to the Visual Basic compiler, such as a property (BackColor, Font) or a statement (MsgBox).

Visual Basic is not case sensitive—that is, you can use upper or lower case or a combination of upper and lower case for everything you type in your program. VB will change keywords to its own special scheme—both upper/lower case and color. When you type a variable name with a different case than that used in the variable's declaration, VB will change it automatically to conform to the declaration. For example, in Sub Snippet earlier, if you typed

```
Print y
```

in the very last line, VB would change "y" to "Y" to conform to the Dim Y statement above.

ASSIGNMENTS

An assignment statement is any Visual Basic statement of the form

```
variable = expression
```

Assignment statements occur in Visual Basic more often than any other type of statement. Even though the operator is an equals sign, an assignment statement is not an algebraic equation, as the examples below will show you.

Note that, in an assignment statement, only a variable can appear to the left of the equals sign (=). (In Chapter Two, we had property variables, such as frmHello.BackColor, on the left of the equal sign, rather than data variables, such as Y in this example.) An assignment statement is just that: It assigns the value of the **expression** on the right side of the equals sign to the variable on the left side of the equals sign. We could not have a statement in the Snippet procedure such as

```
X = Y
```

because X is a constant and cannot take on a new value, nor could we have the statement

```
Y + 4 = X
```

because only a single variable to the left of the equals sign can receive the value resulting from the expression on the right; an expression on the left is illegal. As final proof that an assignment statement is quite different from an algebraic equation, consider the Snippet procedure statement

```
Y = Y + 1
```

If we were writing an equation, this statement would be obviously invalid, but it is perfectly legal in Visual Basic. VB starts by evaluating the expression on the right, that is, Y (35 at that point) + 1, giving the result 36; VB then assigns this result to the variable on the left, at which point 36 replaces the previous value of Y.

EXPRESSIONS

An **arithmetic expression** may contain any combination of variables, constants, and numeric literals, separated by **arithmetic operators.** The arithmetic operators recognized by Visual Basic are

+	addition
–	subtraction/negation
*	multiplication
/	floating-point division (quotient may include a fractional part)
\	integer division (quotient is an integer)
Mod	result is the remainder of integer division
^	exponentiation

When an expression contains more than one operator, you must know in what order the operations will be performed. VB follows the same rules as algebra.

- Operations inside parentheses are performed before operations that are not enclosed in parentheses.
- Exponentiation has the highest order of precedence among arithmetic operations.
- Multiplication and division are next.
- Addition and subtraction are last.
- When more than one operation on the same level occurs in an expression, then those operations are performed in order from left to right.

Here is an example of an assignment statement, in which a lengthy expression is assigned to the variable Y:

```
           Y = 10 - 3 ^ 2 + (10 - 2) / (1 + 1) ^ 3 * 2
order of ops:           7        3         8        1    5  2  4  6
```

And here are the results after each separate operation:

After op 1: Y = 10 – 3 ^ 2 + 8 / (1 + 1) ^ 3 * 2
After op 2: Y = 10 – 3 ^ 2 + 8 / 2 ^ 3 * 2
After op 3: Y = 10 – 9 + 8 / 2 ^ 3 * 2
After op 4: Y = 10 – 9 + 8 / 8 * 2
After op 5: Y = 10 – 9 + 1 * 2
After op 6: Y = 10 – 9 + 2
After op 7: Y = 1 + 2
After op 8: Y = 3

More examples of expressions, assuming X = 5 and Y = 3 prior to evaluating each expression:

EXPRESSION	RESULT
Y + (–X)	–2
X * X/(Y + 2)	5
X * X/Y	8.333333
X * X\Y	8
X * X Mod Y	1
72/2/3/(Y –1) * (–X + 4)	–6
Y ^ 2 * 2/(3 + X/(–1) – 1)	–6
16/2 ^ (–4)	256

DATA TYPES

Every piece of data (whether a variable, a constant, or a literal) in a computer is stored as a series of 1s and 0s. A single memory address contains one byte or character of data, represented as a series of eight binary digits. These data values are coded differently, depending on the type of data being stored. To access and interpret the data values stored in the computer's memory or on a disk properly, Visual Basic needs to know what type of data is stored in particular memory locations.

For example, let's assume that a memory location contains a data value coded as

```
0011 0100
```

If Visual Basic is instructed to treat this data value as a pure binary number, then its value is

$$\begin{aligned} & 0*2^7 + 0*2^6 + 1*2^5 + 1*2^4 + 0*2^3 + 1*2^2 + 0*2^1 + 0*2^0 \\ = & \ 0 \quad + 0 \quad + 32 \quad + 16 \quad + 0 \quad + 4 \quad + 0 \quad + 0 \\ = & \ 52 \end{aligned}$$

but if Visual Basic interprets this data value as an ASCII code (that is, character data), then its value is the digit (not the number) "4." (See the table of ASCII codes, Appendix A.)

Visual Basic supports the following data types: **Byte, Boolean, Integer, Long, Single, Double, Currency, Date, Object, String,** and **Variant.** Each uses its own unique internal coding scheme and takes up differing amounts of storage. When the programmer declares a variable, the data type can be declared either by appending a **type declaration character** to the variable name or by using an "As *Vartype*" clause. We prefer the "As Vartype" syntax, because it is clearer to the reader, for example,

```
Dim ClassSize As Integer
Dim InterestRate As Single
Dim Salary As Currency
```

Here is the whole list of data types and characteristics:

DATA TYPE	TYPE DECLARATION CHARACTER	STORAGE SIZE (IN BYTES)	DESCRIPTION
Byte	None	1	Whole numbers from 0 to 255
Boolean	None	2	True or False
Integer	%	2	Whole numbers from –32768 to +32767
Long	&	4	Whole numbers up to +/– 2 billion (approx.)
Single	!	4	Single precision floating point numbers—approximately 7 digits of precision, with up to 38 zeros or up to 45 decimal places
Double	#	8	Double precision floating point numbers—about 15 digits of precision with up to 308 zeros or 324 decimal places
Currency	@	8	Scaled integer—19 digits of precision, including 4 decimal places
Date	None	8	January 1, 100 to December 31, 9999
Object	None	4	Any object reference
String	$	1 byte per character	Character data, from 0 to about 2 billion characters maximum (some storage over head is also needed)
Variant	None	16 bytes for a number, or 22 bytes & length of string	Any kind of data

If you do not assign a data type when declaring a variable, Visual Basic assigns *variant* as the default data type. For example, in the snippet procedure above,

```
Dim Y As Variant
```

would have had the same effect as

```
Dim Y
```

However, programming with variants, though easy and apparently convenient, is rarely a good idea. First, in terms of program execution efficiency, variants greatly slow down the whole process because VB has the additional burden of keeping track of the type of data each variant currently holds before it can operate on that data. Furthermore, the programmer may inadvertently change the kind of data held by a variant with unintended results. And thirdly, subsequent program maintenance is more difficult if the programmer cannot be sure of the kind of data held by each variable at all times. Thus, for the sake of program efficiency, clarity, and correctness, professional programmers avoid using variables of type variant, and we will avoid using them in this book.

INTRODUCING THE SIMPLE CALCULATOR PROJECT

This project provides a very simple version of an adding machine. It can only perform addition or subtraction, one problem at a time, and it only accepts whole numbers. The only way to enter numbers is by clicking on the Command Buttons with the mouse (you could also use the tab key to place the focus on a desired Command Button, and then press enter—but this is the same as clicking on the

Command Button with the mouse); you cannot enter numbers by pressing the digit keys on the keyboard. Try running the program "CALC.EXE" (Figure 3.01), and experiment with a few problems until you are sure you understand what it does.

Now let's build the project. In the course of this project, you will learn how to declare and use several variables, you will become acquainted with some new functions (Str and Val), and you will see how the scope of a variable is used. You will also see how to develop a project's Hierarchy Table and associated pseudocode, tools that will provide invaluable assistance in developing your own Visual Basic projects later on.

STEP 1. Understand the Problem.

As with the "Hello, World" project in Chapter Two, this step is relatively simple. Make sure that you understand what each Command Button on the Simple Calculator is supposed to do. Run the program again. You can be sure you understand it if you can tell what the program will do when you click on each Command Button, before the time that you actually click on it.

This calculator uses what is called infix notation. That is, the order of events to perform addition is as follows:

- the user enters the first operand
- the user clicks on the addition operator (+)
- the user enters the second operand
- the user clicks on the equal operator (=)
- the program calculates the sum of the first and second operands and displays the result
- the user clicks on the clear button

With infix notation, the arithmetic operator (plus or minus) is inserted between the first and second operands. This also implies that, when the operator is selected, the operation cannot be performed yet, because the second operand has not yet been entered. Rather, the first operand and the operation to be performed must be stored temporarily for later use after the second operand is entered. We will use variables to store these two pieces of information.

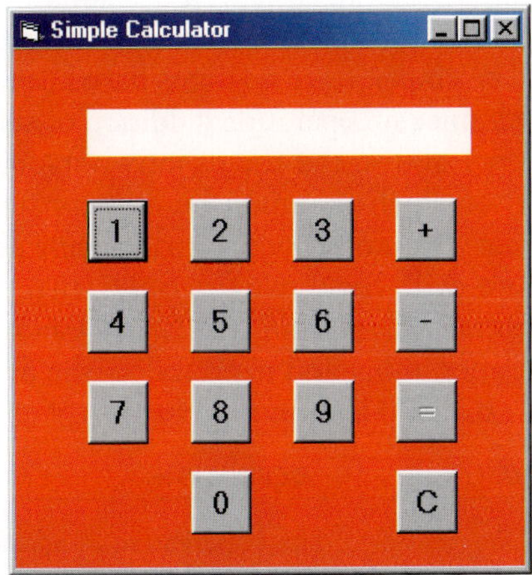

FIGURE 3.01 *Running the simple calculator program*

STEP 2. Design Your Solution.

As in "Hello, World," sketch out the design of the "Simple Calculator" form on a piece of paper or on the screen. There are 14 Command Buttons (for the digits 0 through 9; the operators +, –, and =; and clear) and a label (to display input numbers as well as the result).

Decide on the size and shape of your calculator and on the arrangement of the Command Buttons. The numeric keypad on a calculator usually (but not always) appears in one of two configurations: either like a telephone keypad, starting with "1" in the upper left corner, or like the numeric keypad on a computer keyboard, starting with "7" in the upper left corner. "0," clear, and the three operator keys can be sized and arranged as you see fit. Figures 3.02, 3.03, and 3.04 offer several suggestions.

Your program will need to do something whenever any of the Command Buttons is clicked. Therefore, all of these buttons should be named. The label will be referenced throughout the code, and so it should be named as well, even though we have only the one label. Naming even this one label is a good practice, because perhaps a future addition to this program will result in another label being added, at which point we would want to distinguish between them by more meaningful terms than the default names of Label1 and Label2. Here is a list of names and captions for all of the objects in this project:

OBJECT	NAME	CAPTION
form	frmCalc	Simple Calculator
Command Button	cmd0	0
Command Button	cmd1	1
Command Button	cmd2	2
Command Button	cmd3	3
Command Button	cmd4	4
Command Button	cmd5	5
Command Button	cmd6	6
Command Button	cmd7	7
Command Button	cmd8	8
Command Button	cmd9	9
Command Button	cmdAdd	+
Command Button	cmdSubtract	–
Command Button	cmdEqual	=
Command Button	cmdClear	C
Label	lblNum	blank

As with a real calculator, all of the Command Buttons should be the same size. Initially, lblNum should be empty, since no digits have been entered yet, and cmdEqual should be disabled, since no operation (addition or subtraction) is pending.

As explained in Step 1 above, the use of infix notation means that the first operand and the identity of which operation (addition or subtraction) is to be performed subsequently must be stored temporarily while the second operand is being entered. Thus we will have two variables that will be used by the cmdAdd_Click, cmdSubtract_Click, and cmdEqual_Click procedures (the prefixes to these variable names, mlng and mstr, follow the principles of Hungarian notation, which will be explained later in this chapter).

VARIABLENAME	VARTYPE	DEFINITION
mlngOperand1	Long	first operand in an addition or subtraction problem
mstrOpCode	String*1	a one-byte string containing "+" or "–", which will indicate which operation is to be performed

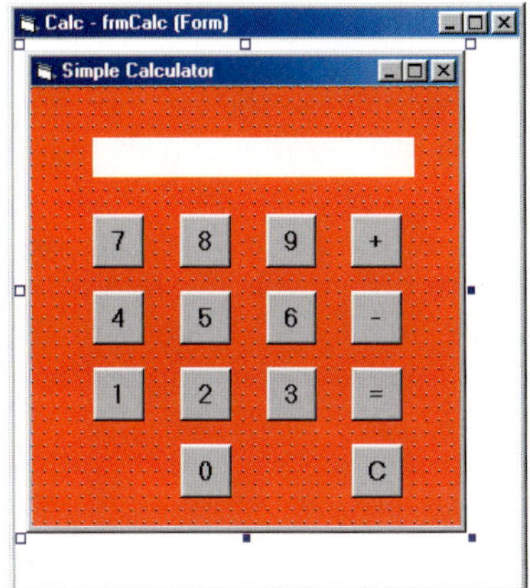

FIGURE 3.02 *Simple calculator with the buttons arranged like a numeric keypad*

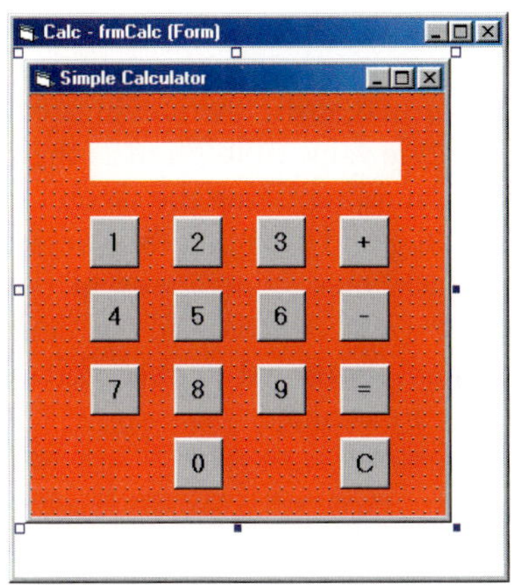

FIGURE 3.03 *Simple calculator with the buttons arranged like a telephone keypad*

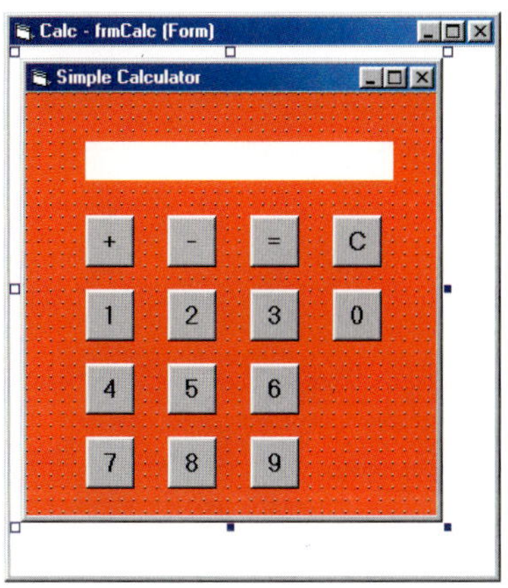

FIGURE 3.04 *Simple calculator with the buttons arranged like we felt like it*

The cmdAdd and cmdSubtract click event procedures will assign values to these variables. The cmdEqual click event procedure will use these variables in calculating the result.

STEP 3. Develop Your Logic.

All of the logic for this program occurs in the click event procedures for the Command Buttons.

cmd0, cmd1, cmd2, cmd3, cmd4, cmd5, cmd6, cmd7, cmd8, and cmd9

lblNum.caption initially contains an empty string (“ ”). When a digit is clicked, that digit is concatenated onto the right side of previously entered digits in lblNum. Concatenation is an operation that applies to strings. It differs from addition in that the characters of the strings are placed side-by-side (rather than being added), and the result is also a string (rather than a number). VB recognizes both + and & as concatenation operators. For example:

Concatenation:	“2” + “3” results in the string “23”
Concatenation:	“2” & “3” results in the string “23”
Addition:	2 + 3 results in the number 5

To avoid confusion, the & concatenation operator is preferred when the intention is to combine string data.

cmdAdd and cmdSubtract

When cmdAdd is clicked, the operation to be performed subsequently is set to addition—this fact must be stored in a variable that is available to the cmd Equal_Click procedure. The numeric value of lblNum must also be stored for subsequent use by the cmdEqual_Click procedure, and then lblNum must be reinitialized to an empty string.

Similarly, when cmdSubtract is clicked, the operation to be performed later is set to subtraction, the numeric value of lblNum must be stored, and lblNum must be set to an empty string.

cmdEqual

When cmdEqual is clicked, the previously stored operation (addition or subtraction) is performed, using the previously stored numeric value as the first operand and the numeric value of lblNum as the second operand. The answer is then displayed in lblNum, replacing the second operand.

By enabling and disabling the operators (+, –, =), the program forces the user to perform arithmetic operations in the appropriate order. When cmdAdd or cmdSubtract is clicked, cmdAdd and cmdSubtract are disabled while cmdEqual is enabled; when cmdEqual is clicked, cmdEqual is disabled while cmdAdd and cmdSubtract are enabled.

cmdClear

Whenever cmdClear is clicked, initial settings are restored: lblNum is set to an empty string, cmdEqual is disabled, and cmdAdd and cmdSubtract are enabled.

Hierachy Table + Pseudocode

The Simple Calculator project is still sufficiently simple that we can describe the logic in narrative paragraphs, as we have done above. However, as you study computer programming further, you will very quickly get to the point where narrative exposition is insufficient to state clearly the complexity of your logic and the interrelationships of project components. We need a tool to help us develop an algorithm—the step-by-step solution to a logical problem. Such an algorithm development tool would allow us to express program logic succinctly, but with precision, clarity, and completeness—while not worrying about the syntax rules of the particular programming language we are using. Computer scientists have developed a number of such tools over the years, including flowcharts, structure charts, Warnier-Orr diagrams, input-process-output (IPO) charts, and pseudocode. Of these, pseudocode has become the most common. Greatly influenced by the disciplined programming techniques of Pascal, and sometimes called "structured English", **pseudocode** displays the logic of a program in step-by-step fashion, using hanging indentation so that related steps are visually grouped together.

Traditional pseudocode, however, supports traditional computer programming in procedural languages—COBOL, FORTRAN, Pascal, and the like. Visual Basic programs are event-driven, the sequence of events being determined by the user through mouse clicks and menu selections and the like, rather than being predetermined by the programmer. Therefore, some aspects of traditional pseudocode need to be modified for application to Visual Basic.

Another algorithm development tool starts by breaking a project down into major components, and major components into subcomponents, and displaying all of these major and minor components in a format that looks something like the outline for a book or a table of contents. This "hierarchy chart" or "**hierarchy table**" technique lends itself well to a succinct identification of the components (forms, modules, procedures, and functions) of even the most complicated Visual Basic project. Pseudocode (or some other technique) can then be used to describe the internal logic of each Visual Basic component.

Throughout this book, we will use the combination of a hierarchy table plus pseudocode to document the logic of each Visual Basic project, that is, step 3 of program development. You are strongly encouraged to use these same techniques in accomplishing end-of-chapter programming assignments or your own VB programs.

Figure 3.05 is the hierarchy table for the "Simple Calculator" project.

```
HIERARCHY TABLE-SIMPLE CALCULATOR

Project: Calc(Calc.vbp)
Form:     frmCalc (frmCalc.frm)
          Form variables:
             mstrOpCode-one byte string containing "+" or" "-, indicating addition or subtraction
             mlngOperand1-holds the first operand
          Click Event procedures:
             cmd0, cmd1, cmd2, cmd3, cmd4, cmd5, cmd6, cmd7, cmd8, cmd9
             cmdAdd, cmdSubtract, cmdClear, cmdEqual
```

FIGURE 3.05 *Hierarchy Table—Simple Calculator*

The first few projects that we introduce in this text contain only a single form and its associated event-procedures. This makes the hierarchy table exceedingly simple, consisting of the project name on top, the name of the single form on the middle level, and the event-procedures underneath the form name. Later, this paradigm can be expanded to as many entries as are necessary to display all of the components of a project and the functional/logical interrelationships among them. Further details of the hierarchy table technique will be demonstrated later as the complexity of subsequent projects warrants.

For a Visual Basic program, pseudocode is developed to portray the logic flow within each procedure. In each case, the pseudocode begins with the name of procedure, and the logic proceeds with each step-by-step action until the end of the procedure is reached.

The most oft-occurring statement in pseudocode is the assignment statement. The conventional notation for an assignment operation is a left-pointing arrow, with the name of the variable, object, or property receiving the assignment to the left of the arrow, and the value to be assigned on the right side of the arrow.

Control Structures Since the late 1960s, programmers have followed principles of program logic design known collectively as structured programming, based on pioneering work by the Dutch computer scientist Edsgar Dijkstra. According to structured programming guidelines, programmers must limit themselves to three control structures: sequence, selection, and iteration. The term **control structure** refers to the ways in which computer program statements can be combined.

The **sequence structure** is the natural flow of computer program logic, one statement after another:

- Statement 1
- Statement 2
- Statement 3

Based on the **next sequential instruction** feature of all digital computers, computer program statements will always be executed in the order that they appear in the program, unless the program directs otherwise. In a VB program, this natural sequence applies to the order of execution of statements within a procedure.

The **selection structure** allows the program to choose whether or not to execute a process, or which of two processes to execute, depending on the answer to a yes/no type of question. The following pseudocode pattern shows one of these selection structures, called the **If/Then** structure:

If <conditional expression> Then Statement

An example of If/Then logic is this: "If it is raining outside, then I will take my umbrella." Note that the conditional expression (question or decision) is a yes/no type ("Is it raining?"), and the single action (taking an umbrella) is performed only when the answer is "yes." When the answer is "no," no action is performed.

Another selection structure, in which one chooses which of two processes to execute, is called the **If/Then/Else** structure and is shown by this pseudocode pattern:

If <conditional expression> Then Statement 1 Else Statement 2

An example of If/Then/Else logic might be this: "If winter comes early this year, then we plan on spending the Christmas holidays on the ski slopes in Colorado, else we plan on spending the holidays on the beach in Florida." Note that the question is still a yes/no type, but in this selection structure we are choosing between two mutually exclusive courses of action. If the answer is "yes," we will go to Colorado (and not to Florida); if the answer is "no," we will visit Florida (and not Colorado).

The selection control structure is often shown in block form, like this:

```
If <conditional expression> Then
    Statement 1
Else
    Statement 2
Endif
```

The reason for the block form is to accommodate the possibility that Statement 1 and/or Statement 2 may actually be several statements.

An important characteristic of both selection structures is that the program logic continues with the next sequential instruction following the conclusion of the selection structure. As demonstrated in the following pseudocode segment, statement 1 is executed first, then the selection structure results in execution of either statement 2 or statement 3, after which the program continues with statement 4:

```
Statement 1
If <conditional expression> Then
    Statement 2
Else
    Statement 3
Endif
Statement 4
```

The third control structure in structured programming is called **iteration,** that is, performing some action repetitively, also called *looping.* Several varieties of iterative loops can be implemented. We will show this control structure in Chapter Four.

With this brief introduction to pseudocode techniques, we can now present the pseudocode for the click event procedures in the Simple Calculator project (Figure 3.06). Compare the pseudocode to the narrative description of the logic up above. With the exception of the cmdEqual_Click procedure, the only control structure in this project is sequence. In the cmdEqual_Click procedure, two If/Then selection structures are also employed

```
PSEUDOCODE-SIMPLE CALCULATOR

Event procedure: Sub cmd0_Click
   Concatenate "0" onto the right side of lblNum
[Similar event procs for cmd1, cmd2, cmd3, cmd4, cmd5, cmd6, cmd7, cmd8, cmd9]

Event procedure: Sub cmdAdd_Click
   Assign: mstrOpCode ←"+"
   Assign: mlngOperand1 ← Val(lblNum)
   Clear lblNum
   Enable cmdEqual
   Disable cmdAdd and cmd Subtract

Event procedure: Sub cmdSubtract_Click
   Assign: mstrOpCode ←"-"
   Assign: mlngOperand1 ← Val(lblNum)
   Clear lblNum
   Enable cmdEqual
   Disable cmdAdd and cmd Subtract

Event procedure: Sub cmdClear_Click
   Clear lblNum
   Disable cmdEqual
   Enable cmdAdd and cmd Subtract

Event Procedure: Sub cmdEqual_Click
   IF (mstrOpCode = "+")
      True: Assign: lAnswer ← mlngOperand1 + lblNum
   END IF
   IF (mstrOpCode = "-")
      True: Assign: lAnswer ← mlngOperand1 - lblNum
   END IF
   Assign: lblNum ← lAnswer
   Disable cmdEqual
   Enable cmdAdd and cmd Subtract
```

FIGURE 3.06 *Pseudocode—Simple Calculator*

STEP 4. Build Your GUI.

Start a new Visual Basic Project. Size the form to the appropriate size and shape of the calculator you wish to design. Then set these properties:

Name	frmCalc
BackColor	take your pick
Caption	Simple Calculator

Put a label across the form, centered left to right, near the top; this will be used to display the input numbers and the calculated result. Then set these properties:

Name	lblNum
BackColor	White, the default, looks fine, but you can change it if you wish
ForeColor	If you want the displayed digits to appear in some color other than black, select your choice of ForeColor. (A light ForeColor, like yellow, requires a dark contrasting BackColor, like black.)

Caption	Blank out this field
Alignment	1-Right aligned
Font	Click the Font property. Then click the ellipsis (...). This presents a dialog box with various choices related to the font. In the Size box, select 12.

Put a Command Button on the form. Size and shape it for a digit on the numeric keypad. Move it to the proper location for the digit "1." Then set these properties:

Name	cmd1
Caption	1
Font	As above, change the font size to about 12.

Since all of the digits should be the same size and shape (except perhaps "0") and have analogous captions and names, it will save time and effort if we can just copy the design of cmd1 to use for all of the other digit keys. To do this, VB uses Windows' editing facilities of Copy, Cut, and Paste, available from the keyboard or from the Edit Menu. When an item, whether text or graphics, is selected, that item can be copied to a Windows memory region known as the **Clipboard.** In the **Cut** mode, the item is copied to the Clipboard and then deleted from its original location; in the **Copy** mode, the item is copied to the Clipboard but also remains in its original location. In the **Paste** mode, whatever is in the Clipboard is inserted into the currently selected object: In Visual Basic, if the Clipboard contains a copy of a control, then the Clipboard contents can be pasted onto a form; if the Clipboard contains text (VB code), then this text can be pasted into another procedure. We will use both the graphics and the text versions of Copy and Paste in this project.

For now, we wish to make nine copies of the cmd1 control and arrange them on our calculator form. Follow these steps:

- Select (click on) cmd1. (You know a control is selected when handles—tiny squares—surround it).
- Copy the selected object to the Clipboard. This can be done either by pressing Ctrl-C (the Control and C keys, simultaneously), or by clicking on Edit | Copy.
- Notice that cmd1 is no longer selected, that is, the handles around cmd1 disappeared. Instead, the form itself is now selected, and handles surround the form.
- To paste another copy of cmd1 on the form, press Ctrl-V or click on Edit | Paste.
- Visual Basic notes that you already have an object named cmd1 on this form. VB displays a dialog box asking whether you want to create a control array. For now, the answer is "No" (we will discuss control arrays in Chapter Four) (see Figure 3.07).
- VB places another Command Button in the top left corner of the form. The name of this object is Command1 (the default name assigned by VB, since Command1 is not currently in use). The caption, however, is 1, which was copied from cmd1.
- You need eight more copies of cmd1. To obtain them, repeat the Edit | Paste operation, answering "No" each time VB asks whether you want to create a control array. Each copy of cmd1 will be placed in the top left corner, on top of the previous copy. In other words, although you cannot see them on the form, you now have nine Command Buttons stacked on top of each other in the top left corner of the form.
- Select each Command Button and drag it into its appropriate position.

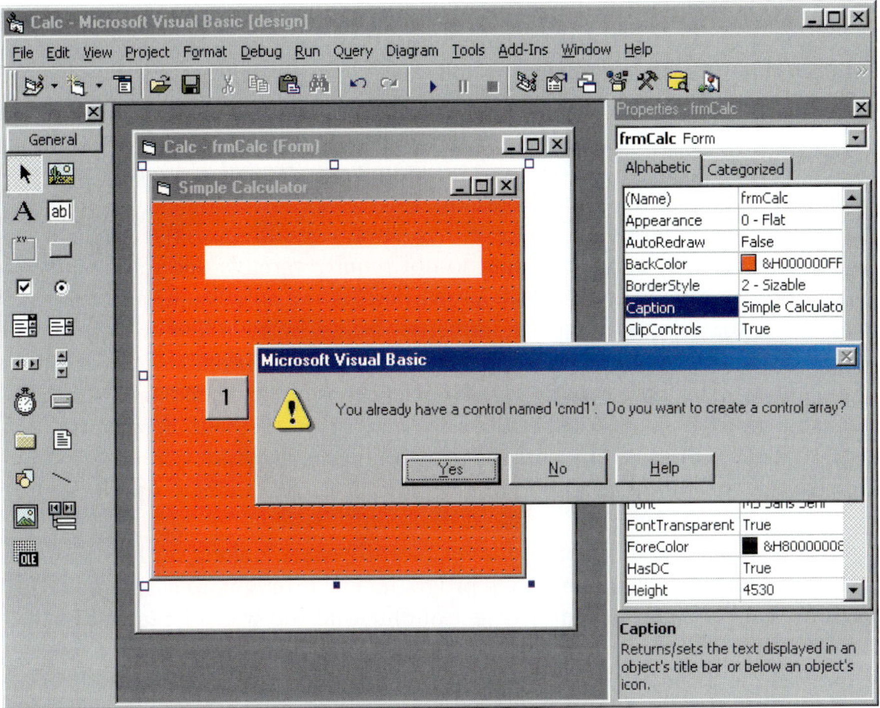

FIGURE 3.07 *Prompt to create a control array for cmd1*

Although the caption on each Command Button is "1," the names of the controls are different. Visual Basic assigned the name Command1 to the first copy, Command2 to the next copy, and so on. You now want to change both the caption and the name of each of the copies of cmd1. To accomplish this, select each control in turn, and change its name and caption in the Properties Window. You can select each Command Button in turn either by clicking on the control in the form and then returning to the Properties Window, or alternatively you can use the object pull-down list at the top of the Properties Window and select the next Command Button from there. Either way, when you get done, your form should have ten Command Buttons named cmd0, cmd1, cmd2, . . . , cmd9, and the corresponding captions should be 0, 1, 2, . . . , 9.

Next, add the Command Buttons for addition (+), subtraction (–), calculation (=), and clear (C). Probably you will want to make these buttons all the same size and shape (in our textbook version, we made four more copies of cmd1). You could put a new Command Button on the form, size and shape it for one of the operators as you wish, and then follow the same procedure you used earlier to copy this control to the Clipboard and place copies of it on the form for the remaining Command Buttons. Remember to set the captions and names (cmdAdd, cmdSubtract, cmdEqual, and cmdClear).

From the File Menu, choose Save Project. Save the form as MYCALC.FRM and the project as MYCALC.VBP.

STEP 5. Write the VB Code.

In the (declarations) portion of the (general) object of frmCalc, insert this code:

```
Option Explicit    'always!
'our program will handle integers up to 9 digits long:
Dim mlngOperand1 As Long
'declare a one-byte string to hold + or - sign:
Dim mstrOpCode As String * 1
```

Option Explicit

The Option Explicit statement forces the programmer to declare explicitly every variable. Without this statement, variables can be accidentally created "on the fly" simply by including a new variable name in a statement. If you follow the practice of naming variables on the fly, that is, if you do not use the Option Explicit statement, your chances of making serious programming errors that are not caught by the Visual Basic compiler increase greatly.

Most programming languages either always require variable declarations (COBOL, Pascal, C), or permit but do not require variable declarations (FORTRAN, earlier versions of BASIC). Visual Basic is the only language the authors are aware of that permits the programmer to decide, by including or omitting the Option Explicit statement, whether or not variable declarations will be required.

The fact is that requiring variable declarations is a tremendous asset to the programmer. It not only adds to clarity and helps to make a program self-documenting, but it also prevents the programmer from making much-too-easy-to-make but very-difficult-to-find misspellings of variable names, which can lead to disastrous results.

For example, a student programmer recently came looking for help in locating a **bug** (a mistake) in a rather long program. The program executed and terminated normally but produced incorrect output, and the student claimed to have spent many fruitless hours looking for the bug. The program included a long list of variables, one of which was AcctRec, and in one of the many procedures in the program he had accidentally spelled it AccttRec. Because he failed to use Option Explicit, Visual Basic assumed that AccttRec was simply a new variable introduced without being declared. As soon as the professor inserted "Option Explicit" in the program, VB immediately highlighted AccttRec with the error message, "Variable not defined." Identifying and fixing this problem should have taken only seconds right from the beginning.

In brief, the Option Explicit statement is the single most powerful feature that raises Visual Basic from the level of a home hobbyist's toy to the level of a serious, commercially viable programming tool. Always use it.

As explained earlier, you can ask Visual Basic to insert the Option Explicit statement automatically in the (declarations) portion of the (general) object of every form you create. From the VB Menu Bar, choose Tools | Options, and on the Editor tab, make sure that the Require Variable Declarations checkbox is checked. Now, to make this setting permanent for every future VB session, exit Visual Basic normally (choose File | Exit), and then reload Visual Basic. Note that Option Explicit appears in the (general) object of the form.

Scope of Variables, Constants, and Procedures

Another important feature of Visual Basic is its ability to limit the **scope** of a variable, constant, or procedure declaration, that is, the portion of a program in which the variable/constant/procedure exists and is recognized. By limiting the effective scope of a declaration to the specific context in which it is designed to occur, another variable/constant/procedure that exists in a different part of the program but happens to have the same name will be treated as a separate and distinct entity by Visual Basic. This idea is also important in commercial programming, where it is often desirable to reuse a procedure or form written by someone else. Variables and constants and procedures declared within a form are not recognized outside that form (with one exception, explained later). Hence it is safe to incorporate code from another program (provided, again, that Option Explicit was used in its creation).

Visual Basic recognizes three levels of visibility or scope: global or public, form/module level, and local.

- **Public** variables/constants/procedures are effective globally, that is, throughout a Visual Basic project. This concept is only important in projects with multiple forms or modules, which we haven't seen yet. We will revisit this concept later.
- Form/module-level variables are declared with a **Private** or **Dim statement** in the declarations portion of the general object of a form or module. In the present instance, we have two form-level variables, mlngOperand1 and mstrOpCode. These variables are visible to all procedures that are part of frmCalc. Of course, since this project has only the one form, mlngOperand1 and mstrOpCode are visible throughout the project. But suffice it to say that, if we added a second form to this project, procedures attached to that second form would have no knowledge of the private variables mlngOperand1 and mstrOpCode.
- Local declarations occur within a procedure and are always private to that procedure. In frmCalc, as you will see below, we will create local variables for lngOperand2 and for the calculated lngAnswer within the cmdEqual_Click procedure. Local variables declared with the Dim statement and local constants come into existence every time the procedure in which they occur is executed and are visible only within that procedure. Normally, such variables and constants go out of existence as soon as the procedure is finished executing, that is, upon End Sub.

In Figure 3.08:

- Any code in the whole VB project can reference the global variable X and the constant PI.
- Code that is part of Form1 can reference X, PI, and the form-level variables A and B.
- Code that is part of Form2 can reference X, PI, and the form-level variables C and D.

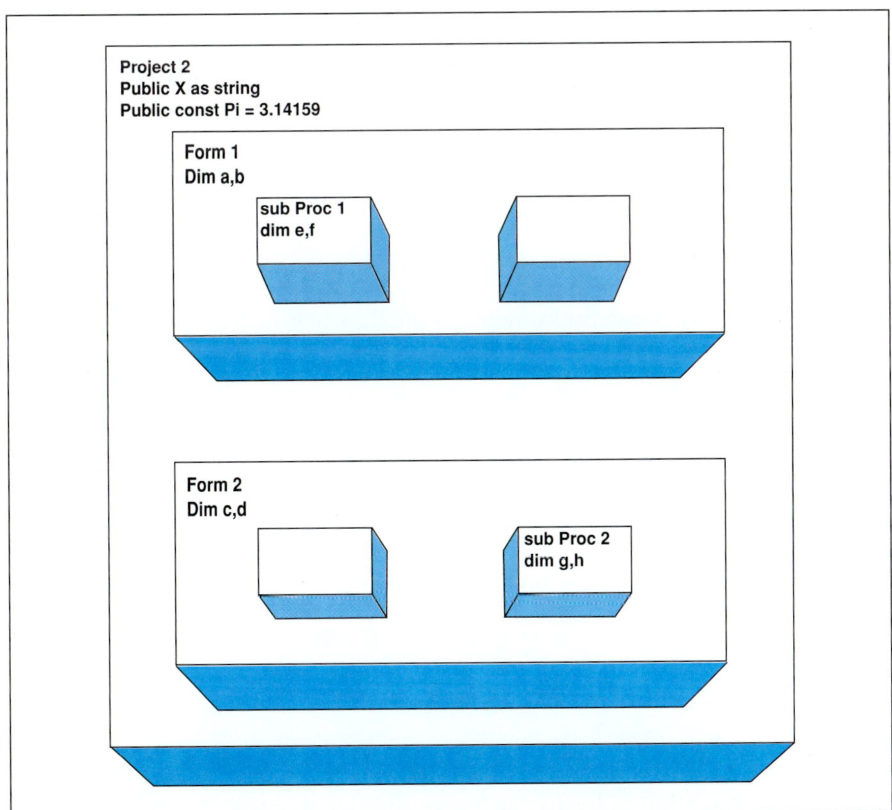

FIGURE 3.08 *Scope*

- Code that is part of procedure Proc1 can reference X, PI, A, B, E, and F.
- Code that is part of procedure Proc2 can reference X, PI, C, D, G, and H.

Hungarian Notation

A significant problem in many programming languages stems from confusion concerning the programmer-supplied names given to objects and variables. In the statement

```
X = Y
```

is either X or Y a variable, constant, object, or function? If a variable, what type of variable (integer, string, single, etc.) is it? Certainly, the program will be easier to interpret and to maintain if the name itself suggests something about what it represents.

Many professional programmers and programming organizations have adopted a set of naming conventions known in the industry as **Hungarian notation.** The practice started with C programmers, expanded to C++, and then spread through practitioners in other languages, including Visual Basic. Microsoft has published conventions for naming objects and variables in Visual Basic, following the principles of Hungarian notation. (You can read the entire document in the Help files if you like: In VB, select Help | Contents. Within the Help screen, select MSDN Library Visual Studio 6.0 | Visual Basic Documentation | Using Visual Basic | Programmer's Guide (All Editions) | Visual Basic Coding Conventions.) We have found that these standards are logical and easily comprehensible, and also are becoming an accepted practice in industry. Therefore, we have decided to follow them in this text and to recommend them strongly for your own programs.

The name of every Visual Basic object will include a three-character, lowercase prefix, which indicates the class of the object. The rest of the object name will be of mixed case, with a capital letter marking the beginning of each word. The prefixes and objects introduced so far are these:

frm	Form
cmd	Command Button
lbl	Label

For a variable, a lowercase prefix indicates the data type or purpose:

bln	Boolean
byt	Byte
int	Integer
lng	Long Integer
str	String
sng	Single (floating point number)
dbl	Double
cur	Currency
dtm	Date/Time
vnt	Variant

A form-level (module-level) variable has an additional prefix, the letter m. In the Simple Calculator project, for example, the following variable names are used:

mlngOperand1	module-level long integer
mstrOpCode	module-level string
lngOperand2	local (procedure-level) long integer
lngAnswer	local long integer

Command Button Click Event Procedures

cmd0...cmd9 As each digit is clicked, your program's task is to concatenate that digit on to the string of previously entered digits visible in the calculator's display window, that is, lblNum. For cmd0, the click event procedure should read:

```
Private Sub cmd0_Click()
    lblNum.Caption = lblNum.Caption & "0"
End Sub
```

In other words, when the digit "0" is clicked, we want this digit to be appended on the right to any digits already in lblNum. The contents of a label are given by the Caption property, so we want to append "0" to the existing caption, and assign the result back to the caption.

Actually, every control has one property that is most often referenced by programmers and is therefore the assumed property in a Visual Basic statement when no other property is mentioned. For a label, this property is the caption property. Therefore, the above statement can be shortened to:

```
lblNum = lblNum & "0"
```

The statement constructed for cmd0 should also be inserted in the click event procedures for cmd1, cmd2, . . . , cmd9, of course changing the digit to be appended in each case. The easiest way to accomplish this is by using the copy and paste features again. Follow these steps:

- Open the code window for the cmd0_Click() procedure: Either double-click cmd0 on the form, or choose View | Project from the Menu Bar, then click on View Code, and finally select cmd0 from the object drop-down list.
- Type this statement in the cmd0_Click procedure:

```
lblNum = lblNum & "0"
```

- Highlight the statement with the mouse and then press Ctrl-C or Edit | Copy to place this statement in the Clipboard.
- Click the object drop-down list, and choose cmd1.
- Paste the Clipboard contents into the cmd1_Click procedure.
- Change "0" to "1."
- Repeat these steps for cmd2 through cmd9.

cmdAdd and cmdSubtract mlngOperand1 and mstrOpCode must be captured and stored for later use. The program must assign mstrOpCode as either "+" or "–," depending on whether we are in cmdAdd_Click or cmdSubtract_Click. In either case, mlngOperand1 must be assigned the numeric value of the string in lblNum, and lblNum must then be reinitialized to an empty string, cmdEqual must be enabled, and cmdAdd and cmdSubtract must be disabled. All of these actions are assignment statements, which as mentioned above, are the most common type of statement in Visual Basic.

Select cmdAdd from the Object drop-down list, and type in this procedure:

```
Private Sub cmdAdd_Click()
      mstrOpCode = "+"
      mlngOperand1 = Val (lblNum)
      lblNum = ""
      cmdEqual.Enabled = True
      cmdAdd.Enabled = False
      cmdSubtract.Enabled = False
End Sub
```

Explanations of each line of code follow:

```
mstrOpCode = "+"
```

The operation to be performed later is addition.

```
mlngOperand1 = Val(lblNum)
```

Val is a function that has a string or a variant **argument** (the item in parentheses following a function's name is called the function's argument). Remember that lblNum.caption is a string, and you cannot use a string to perform arithmetic. Later, we will perform addition; hence we must convert lblNum into a number. Val returns or gives back the numeric equivalent of the argument, up to the first nonnumeric character. For example, in the statement

X = 4 + Val("123 Main Street, Scottsdale, Arizona")

X would be assigned the value of 4 + 123, or 127. In the present case, lblNum consists of a string of digits, and mlngOperand1 will be assigned the numeric equivalent. By the way, if the argument of Val is a null or empty string or if the first character is not numeric, then Val returns 0.

```
lblNum = ""
```

After the value of lblNum has been assigned to mlngOperand1, lblNum must be set back to an empty string so that it is ready to receive the second number in the addition problem.

```
cmdEqual.Enabled = True
cmdAdd.Enabled = False
cmdSubtract.Enabled = False
```

The program toggles between calculating a result (cmdEqual) and starting another problem (cmdAdd and cmdSubtract). Calculating the result is enabled only after half the problem has been entered, at which point cmdAdd and cmdSubtract are disabled, since an addition or subtraction operation is already pending.

Copy the code in Private Sub cmdAdd_Click() to the Clipboard (but don't copy the header or the End Sub statement), and paste it into cmdSubtract_Click. Only the first line needs to be modified—"–" rather than "+." The result should be as follows:

```
Private Sub cmdSubtract_Click()
   mstrOpCode = "-"
   mlngOperand1 = Val(lblNum)
   lblNum = ""
```

```
    cmdEqual.Enabled = True
    cmdAdd.Enabled = False
    cmdSubtract.Enabled = False
End Sub
```

cmdEqual In this procedure, you must compute and display the answer, and then reset the Command Buttons. As suggested above, local variables will be declared to hold the second operand and the calculated answer. The answer will then be displayed.

Type the procedure as shown. Long lines of code may be typed all on one line (even if you cannot see the entire line across one screen width). Alternatively, a long VB logical line may be broken into two or more physical lines by using a **line continuation character** at the end of the line to be continued. The line continuation character in Visual Basic is a space followed by an underscore (_) as the last two characters on a line. (You may not use this technique, however, to break apart a word or to continue a quoted string.)

```
Private Sub cmdEqual_Click()
    Dim lngOperand2 As Long
    Dim lngAnswer As Long
    lngOperand2 = Val(lblNum)
    If mstrOpCode = "+" Then lngAnswer = mlngOperand1 + _
        lngOperand2
    If mstrOpCode = "-" Then lngAnswer = mlngOperand1 - _
        lngOperand2
    lblNum= Str(lngAnswer)
    cmdAdd.Enabled = True
    cmdSubtract.Enabled = True
    cmdEqual.Enabled = False
End Sub
```

Line-by-line explanations follow.

Dim lngOperand2 As Long

This long integer will hold the second operand in the addition or subtraction problem, converted from the string in lblNum.caption.

Dim lngAnswer As Long

This long integer will hold the answer.

lngOperand2 = Val(lblNum)

As before, the Val function is used to convert lblNum.caption into a numeric value, which is then assigned to lngOperand2.

Relational Expressions

If mstrOpCode = "+" Then lngAnswer = mlngOperand1 + lngOperand2
If mstrOpCode = "-" Then lngAnswer = mlngOperand1 - lngOperand2

These two If statements contain **relational expressions** (underlined here), which merit a somewhat detailed discussion. The syntax of each If statement follows this paradigm:

If relational expression Then statement

A relational expression usually has the form

<string/arithmetic expression> relational operator <string/arithmetic expression>

The expressions on either side of the **relational operator** must both be strings or both be numerics. Each can be any combination of variables, literals, and constants. The following are relational operators recognized by Visual Basic.

OPERATOR	MEANING
=	is equal to
<	is less than
>	is greater than
<=	is less than or equal to
>=	is greater than or equal to
<>	is not equal to

Here are some valid relational expressions. In each case, when VB evaluates a relational expression, the result is determined to be "True" or "False."

EXPRESSION	EVALUATION
5.4999	True
5 = 4	False
5 < = 4	False
X + 7 − (Y/2) = (X−1) ^ y	may be True or False
"John" + " " + "Smith" = SearchName$	may be True or False
YearsOfService + Age >= 80	may be True or False

The relational expression is actually any expression that VB can evaluate as being True or False, including properties or numbers. If the expression is a True/False-type property (what programmers call a *Boolean* value, after George Boole, the English mathematician who invented it), a relational operator can be omitted. In the following equivalent statements, the message is printed on the form if the Command Button in question is enabled.

```
If command1.Enabled Then Print "Button is enabled"
If command1.Enabled = True Then Print _
  "Button is enabled"
If command1.Enabled  <> False Then Print _
  "Button is enabled"
```

If a numeric value is evaluated as a relational expression, then 0 is considered False and any other value is considered True. Consider this code:

STATEMENT	RESULT
Dim X As Single	declare X
X = −8	X is assigned the value −8
If X Then X = 10	−8 (a nonzero value) is True, so X changes to 10
X = 0	X is assigned the value 0
If X Then X = 10	0 is False; the value of X is not changed

When VB evaluates a relational expression, the printed result is True or False. If the evaluated relational expression is to be used in further computations, a False result is 0 and a True result is −1. For example:

STATEMENT	PRINTED RESULT	COMPUTED RESULT
Print 5 > 4	True	−1
Print 5 < 4	False	0

In the following case,

```
X = X * (X < 0)
```

if X was positive, X becomes 0, because (X < 0) is False, and 0 * X results in 0; but if X was negative, then X becomes positive, because (X < 0) is True, that is, −1, and −1 * a negative value results in a positive value.

Finally, the Not operator may be used to reverse the result of evaluating a relational expression. Therefore, this operator becomes most useful in Visual Basic whenever you want to toggle a True/False property value. For example, the statement

```
command1.Enabled = Not command1.Enabled
```

enables the Command Button, if prior to this statement the Command Button had been disabled; but it disables the Command Button, if prior to this statement the Command Button had been enabled.

If Statements Returning to the original two If statements in the cmd Equal_Click procedure:

```
If mstrOpCode = "+" Then lngAnswer = mlngOperand1 + _ lngOperand2
If mstrOpCode = "-" Then lngAnswer = mlngOperand1 - _ lngOperand2
```

the logic of these statements could be expressed in a variety of ways. The syntax given above is called a *single line If statement*, that is, each entire statement occurs on one line. Since mstrOpCode in this case must contain one of only two possible values, we could achieve the same logical result by the following, and save a wee bit of coding:

```
If mstrOpCode = "+" Then lngAnswer = mlngOperand1 + _
    lngOperand2 Else lngAnswer = mlngOperand1 - lngOperand2
```

In the model

If relational expression Then statement1 Else statement2

statement1 is executed only if the relational expression is True, and statement2 is executed if the relational expression is False.

Instead of the single line If statement, VB also supports the block If statement, which is constructed according to this model:

If relational expression Then

statement1a

statement1b

. . .

statement1n

```
Else
    statement2a
    statement2b
    . . .
    statement2n
End If
```

Statements 1a through 1n constitute a block. A block may contain any number of statements. Using the block If model, the If statements in cmdEqual_Click could have been written this way, with one statement in each block:

```
If mstrOpCode = "+" Then
   lngAnswer = mlngOperand1 + lngOperand2
Else
   lngAnswer = mlngOperand1 - lngOperand2
End If
```

The last few line-by-line explanations follow.

```
lblNum.caption = Str(lngAnswer)
```

The **Str function** is the reverse of the Val function. That is, just as the **Val function** has a string argument and returns the equivalent numeric value, Str has a numeric argument and returns the equivalent string value. In its return value, Str always reserves the first position for the sign of the number—a minus sign if the number is negative, or a space if the number is zero or positive.

```
cmdAdd.Enabled = True
cmdSubtract.Enabled = True
cmdEqual.Enabled = False
```

The three command buttons must be reset for the next computation.

cmdClear This Command Button clears lblNum and readies the other Command Buttons for a new math problem. From the object list, choose cmdClear, and type the Visual Basic statements as they are shown.

```
Private Sub cmdClear_Click()
   cmdAdd.Enabled = True
   cmdSubtract.Enabled = True
   cmdEqual.Enabled = False
   lblNum.caption = ""
End Sub
```

STEP 6. Test and Debug Your Program.

Click the "Start execution" icon or choose Run | Start or press F5. VB will let you know if it finds any syntax errors. When all of your syntax is correct, then the program will run, but you still do not know for sure whether it calculates correctly.

Try several addition and subtraction problems. Work out the correct answers in your head, on paper, or with a calculator, and compare these answers to the answers your program produces. If you discover a discrepancy, go back and examine your program code carefully. You may have miscopied one or more statements, or you may have simply put the correct statements in the wrong order.

STEP 7. Complete the Program Documentation

For this project, the only additional documentation your program needs is some personal identification. Open the project, and open the Code Window for the (declarations) portion of the (general) object. Insert these comment lines:

```
'Project Name:          MYCALC.VBP
'Forms/modules:         frmMYCALC.FRM
'Written by:            <insert your name>
'Original date:         <insert today's date>
['Revision date:        <insert revision date, if any>]
'Adapted from Spear & Spear
```

SUMMARY

This chapter introduced the principal elements of Visual Basic programming. A fundamental concept is the **variable,** a symbolic reference to an address in memory. VB supports these **fundamental data types: Byte, Boolean, Integer, Long, Single, Double, Currency, Date, String, Object,** and **Variant.** By using **Hungarian-notation** prefixes, the **type** and the **scope** (global, form/module level, or local) of a variable can be made clear. Standard abbreviations, similar to Hungarian notation, are also used in naming VB objects.

An **Assignment** is the most common type of VB statement. Variables, constants, or **expressions** can be assigned to variables and to property settings in code.

Structured programming rules help VB programmers write procedures that are intelligible and maintainable. The rules limit the programmer to the use of three **control structures: sequence** (one step after another), **selection** (**If/Then** or **If/Then/Else**), and **iteration.** For project documentation, a **hierarchy table** lists the functional components of a VB project, and **pseudocode** documents the logic flow within a procedure.

PROGRAMMING ASSIGNMENTS

Movie Theater Tickets

This application calculates the cost of movie theater tickets for one customer (who could be purchasing tickets for one or more people).

Place Command Buttons and Labels on a form as shown in Figure 3.09. The left column of Command Buttons obviously indicates the ticket category. The middle column shows how many tickets are being purchased in each category, while the right column shows the cost of the tickets in each category. The totals line indicates the total number of tickets being purchased and the total cost of those tickets.

Set the Command Button Captions as indicated, and set the Names as cmdSenior, cmdAdult, cmdStudent, cmdChild, cmdTwi-Light, and cmdClear.

For all of the Labels, set the Alignment property to 2-Center and the BorderStyle property to 1-Fixed Single. Set the captions of the middle column to 0, and the captions of the right column to $0.00.

Change the size of the font to 18 for the Home and Visitors Command Buttons and Labels. Change the size of the font to 12 for all of the other Command Buttons.

Set the BorderStyle property of the Labels to 1-Fixed Single and the Alignment property to 2-Center.

The names of all controls should be changed to reflect the type and purpose of each: cmdHome, cmdVisitors, lblHome, lblVisitors, cmdTouchdown, cmd1Extra, cmd2Extra, cmdFieldGoal, cmdSafety, and cmdGameOver.

Declare these form-level constants:

```
TOUCHDOWN = 6
ONEEXTRAPOINT = 1
TWOEXTRAPOINTS = 2
FIELDGOAL = 3
SAFETY = 2
```

Also declare a form-level variable, mintScore, as a temporary storage area to hold the value of the score to be added. And declare another form-level variable, mintNumTouchdowns, to keep track of the number of touchdowns scored in the game.

At runtime, when the user clicks a scoring category, assign the appropriate constant to mintScore. Then, when the user clicks the team (Home or Visitor), add mintScore to that team's total, and assign 0 to mintScore.

When the user clicks GameOver, use If/Then statements to display the appropriate message box statement concerning the winner, display another message box statement about the number of touchdowns, and then end the program.

CHAPTER FOUR

CONTROL ARRAYS AND FOR/NEXT LOOPS

Application: Colorful Backdrop

LEARNING OBJECTIVES

Upon completion of Chapter Four, the student will be able to:

- Use Visual Basic's on-line Help System comfortably.
- Create and use control arrays.
- Build simple looping constructs with the For/Next statement.
- Manipulate colors mathematically.

Keywords

ASCII codes
Chr function
Context-sensitive Help (F1)
Control array
For/Next loop
Index property
Jumps
KeyAscii value
KeyPress event
KeyPreview property
Me object reference
QBColor function
RGB color scheme

VISUAL BASIC HELP

As you work in Visual Basic, you will have hundreds of opportunities to call upon the services of VB's Help System. In this section, we will give you a guided tour of the main Help facilities available to you, using some of the new material in the Colorful Backdrop Application as the subject matter for our tour.

Visual Basic's Help System follows the pattern of the Help facilities in all Microsoft Windows-related products. If you already know how to use Help in another Windows application, then you already know how to use VB Help. Conversely, when you learn how to navigate in Visual Basic Help, then that knowledge is immediately transferable to other Windows-based Help systems.

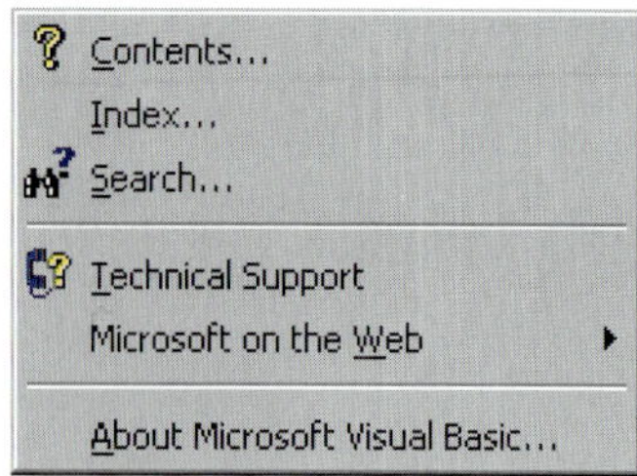

FIGURE 4.01
Help pull-down menu

VB Menu Bar—Help Pull-Down Menu

On the Visual Basic Menu Bar, the Help pull-down menu (Figure 4.01) contains six choices:

- **Contents, Index,** and **Search**—These three selections lead to the same dialog box, with four tabs at the top: **Contents, Index, Search,** and **Favorites.**

  Contents tab: When you are looking for general information or do not know which VB **keyword** to look up, then the best approach may be to start with the Contents tab. From here, click the + sign to the left of MSDN Library Visual Studio 6.0, the + sign again to the left of Visual Basic Documentation, and then click the Visual Basic Start Page, Getting Started with Visual Basic 6.0, Using Visual Basic, or Reference.

  Index tab: This dialog box asks you to type in a keyword or a subject. VB Help then displays all Help topics concerning the keyword you typed in.

  Search tab: This dialog box accepts one or more words from the user; then it locates all help screens that contain those words. Unlike Index, which searches only the Help Topics, the Search feature searches through the entire Help documentation.

  Favorites tab: Click the Add button (at the bottom) to add the current Help topic to your list of favorite help topics. Click a previously listed help topic to return to one of the favorites you added earlier.

- **Obtaining Technical Support**—This menu tells you how to get answers to your questions or VB problems in the event that you cannot get the answers you need directly from the Help system. Note that some tech support services from Microsoft are cheap or free, while other options are much more expensive.
- **Microsoft on the Web**—This service provides online access to additional technical articles on advanced applications development topics.
- **About Microsoft Visual Basic**—As in almost all Windows programs, this selection provides information concerning the software authors, version number, release date, copyright, licensee, and system resources.

Start your Help System tour by clicking on Help | Search. VB's Help screen is divided into two windows: the window on the left lists help topics, while the window on the right displays the actual help screen of the currently selected topic. We will look for information concerning colors, a topic relevant to the Colorful Backdrop Application. Select the Index tab in the topics window on the left, and type "colors" in the text box. From the list of topics under colors, select "defining color values." Click the Display button at the bottom of the screen. (See Figure 4.02.)

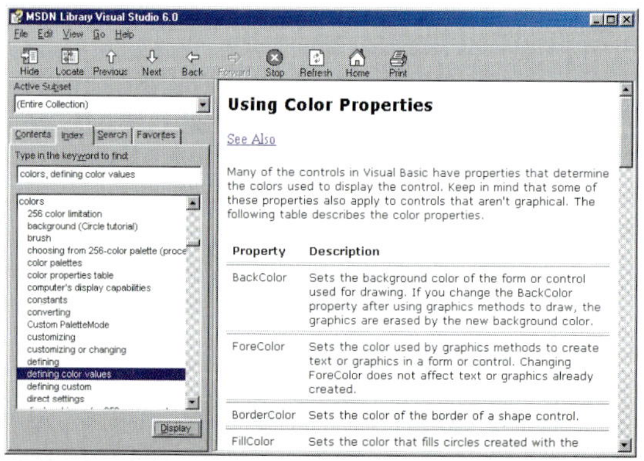

FIGURE 4.02 *Searching for help on colors, defining color values*

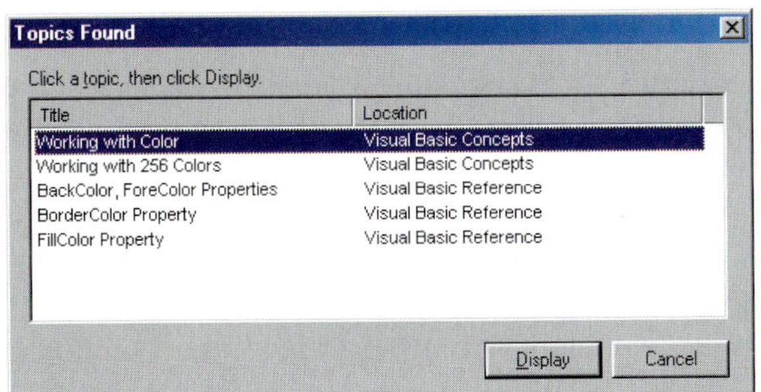

FIGURE 4.03 *See Also pop-up window*

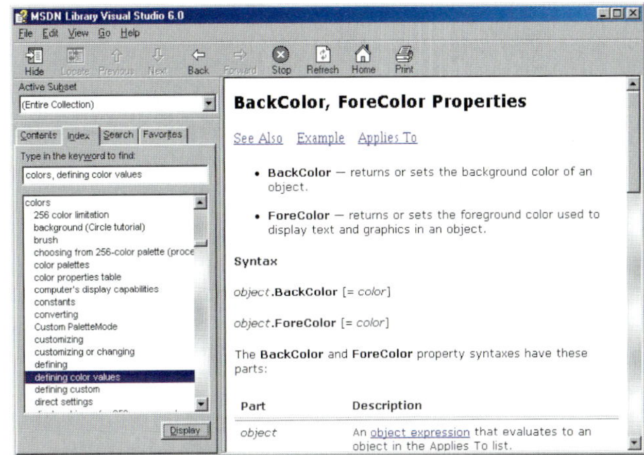

FIGURE 4.04 *BackColor, ForeColor properties help screen*

VB's Help screens often contain information that merely piques your curiosity about related information. In other words, you get some help from Help, but that just leads you to ask for more. For example, the present help screen, "Using Color Properties" has the words "See Also" at the top. Click on See Also, and a pop-up list of related topics appears (Figure 4.03). If you click on one of these, say, "BackColor, ForeColor Properties," VB Help **jumps** to a whole new help screen dealing with that topic. From the BackColor, ForeColor Properties Help screen (Figure 4.04), click on "Applies To", and then click on "Form Object, Forms Collection" from the list of objects to which the BackColor property applies (Figure 4.05). At the top of the Form Help screen, you can click on Properties or Events or Methods related to that object. This system of jumps can be continued indefinitely.

Help Screen's Menu Bar

At the top of every Help screen is a Menu Bar, which includes the entries *File*, *Edit*, *View*, *Go*, and *Help*. The menu selections you will need are these:

File Menu

- **Print**—Prints the current Help topic on paper.
- **Exit**—Leaves the Help system.

Edit Menu

- **Copy**—You can select any or all of the text with the mouse or keyboard. When you click on Edit | Copy, the selected text is copied to the Windows Clipboard, after which you could Paste it in any appropriate Windows application (Notepad or Word, for example, or inside your Visual Basic program).

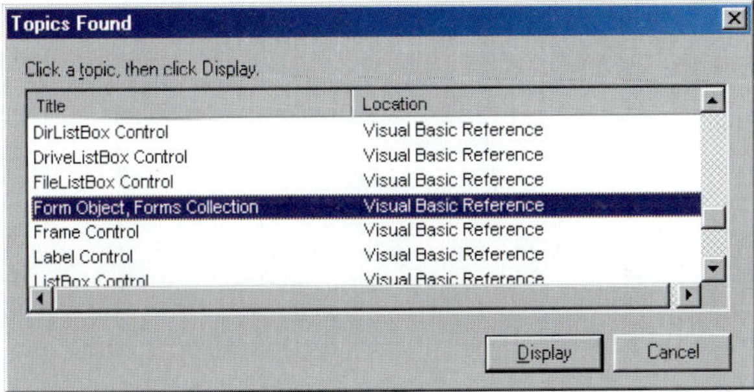

FIGURE 4.05 *Another See Also pop-up window*

Help Screen's Button Bar

Beneath each Help screen's Menu Bar is a Button Bar containing these selections: *Hide, Locate, Previous, Next, Back, Forward, Stop, Refresh, Home,* and *Print.* These buttons accomplish the following:

- **Hide**—Hides the help topics window. When this icon is clicked, it is replaced by the Show icon, which can restore the help topics window.
- **Locate**—Causes the help topics window to display the location in the library where the current help topic came from.
- **Previous**—Displays the previous topic from the list of topics in the table of contents.
- **Next**—Displays the next topic from the list of topics in the table of contents.
- **Back**—Returns to the last help screen displayed.
- **Forward**—After Back has been clicked, Forward becomes available.
- **Stop**—If a help topic is being downloaded from the Web, this button stops the file transfer.
- **Refresh**—Reloads the current help screen.
- **Home**—Displays the MSDN Library home page.
- **Print**—Prints the current Help topic.

Reference Lists

One of the most useful parts of the Help system is the series of reference lists, available at Help | Contents tab, then MSDN Library Visual Studio 6.0 | Visual Basic Documentation | Reference. Subsections of the Reference section contain alphabetical listings of jumps to all programming language topics, including *Objects, Properties, Functions, Methods, Events, Statements, Keywords, Constants, Operators, Intrinsic Controls, ActiveX Controls, Wizards and Add-Ins,* and *Trappable Errors* (Figure 4.06). For example, if you want to find out something about the TabIndex

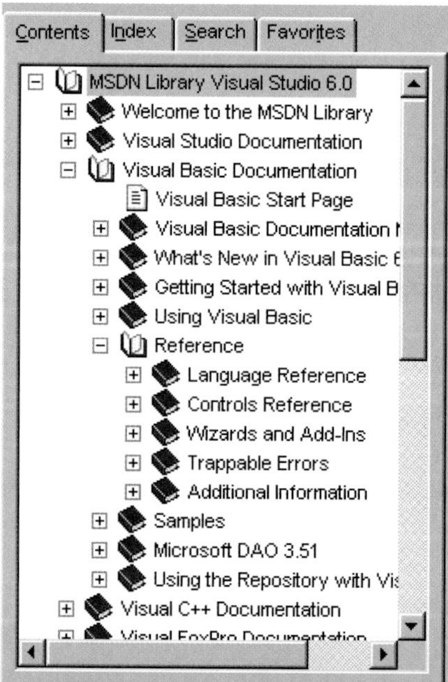

FIGURE 4.06 *MSDN Library table of contents*

property of the Command Button control, you could get to the TabIndex Property Help screen in any of these ways:

- From the Reference entry under the Help | Contents tab, select Language Reference, then select Properties, select the letter T, and select TabIndex.
- Select Help | Index; select the Index tab; type the first few letters of "TabIndex" in the textbox, until TabIndex Property appears in the lower list; click on TabIndex property.
- Perhaps you cannot remember the name "TabIndex," but you know you are looking for a property of the Command Button control. In this case, from the Reference entry under the Help | Contents tab, select Controls Reference, then Intrinsic Controls, and then Command Button Control; at the top of the Command Button Control Help screen, select Properties; in the Properties list, select TabIndex.

Context-Sensitive Help

If you press the F1 function key at any time while you are in Visual Basic, VB Help will display the Help screen that is most appropriate for whatever you are doing, that is, the context in which you are working. Here are several samples of **context-sensitive help:**

- Click on the Shape Control icon in the Toolbox.

- Before placing the control on your form, press the F1 key. The Shape Control Help screen appears (see Figure 4.07).
- You may be typing in a MsgBox statement in a Code Window and forget the correct syntax. After you have typed the word msgbox and a space, a pop-up window automatically displays the correct syntax. If you need to look up additional details concerning this keyword, just place the cursor anywhere within the word MsgBox and press F1; the MsgBox Function Help screen appears (see Figure 4.08).

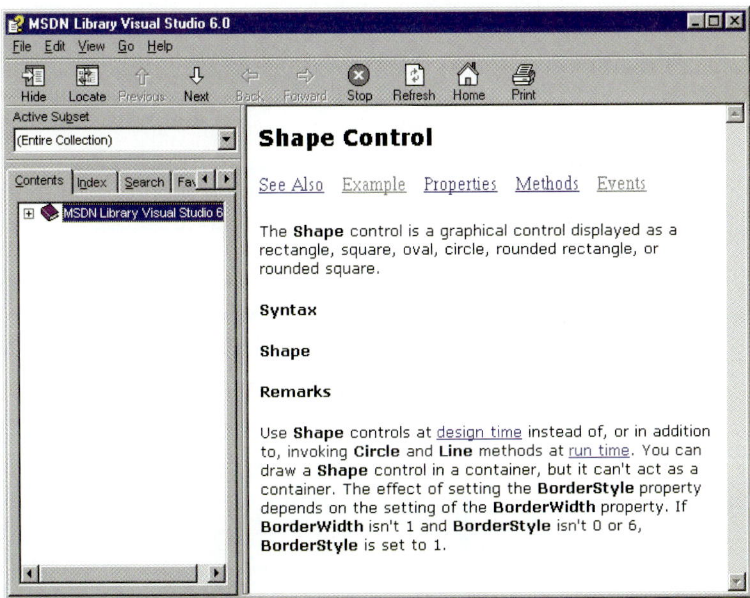

FIGURE 4.07 *Shape Control Help Screen*

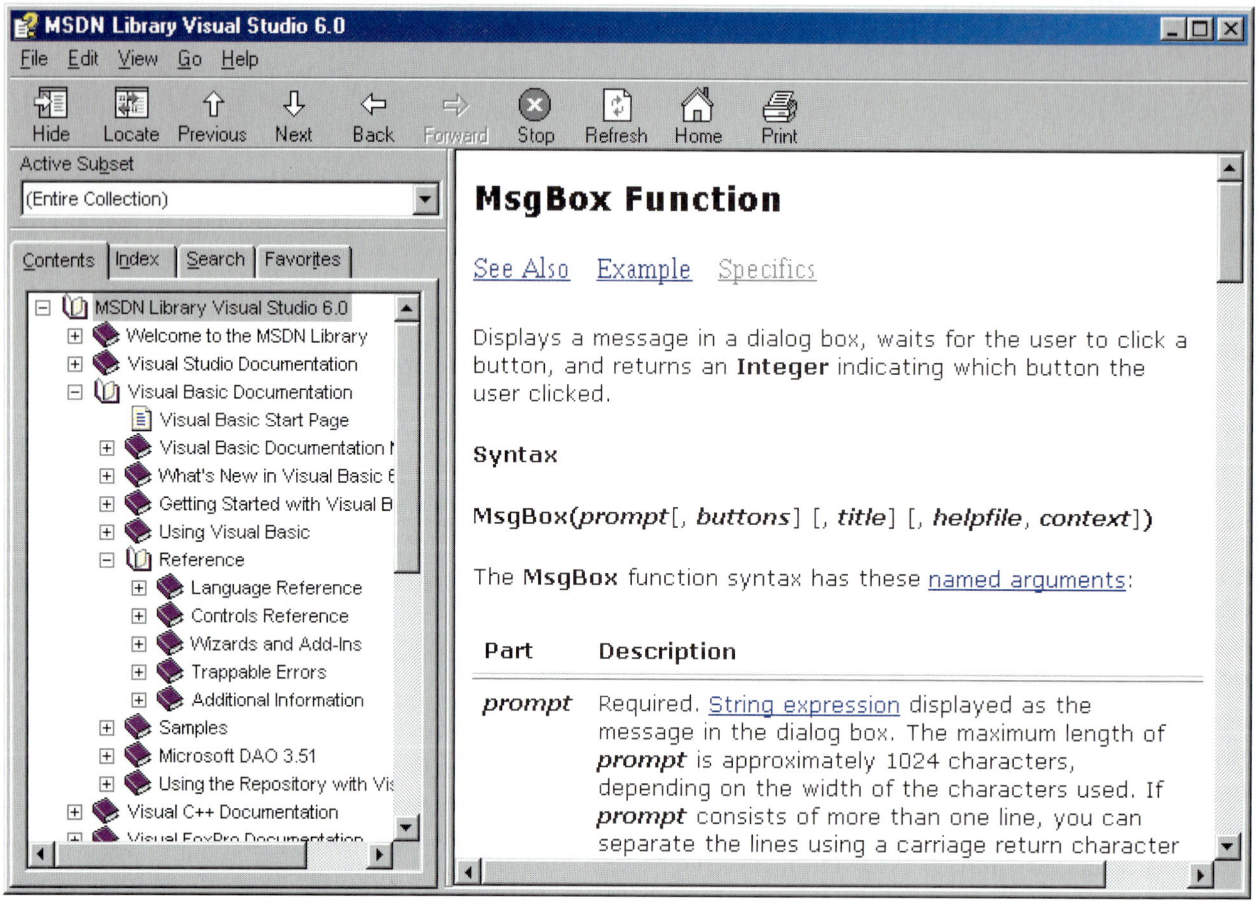

MSDN Library Visual Studio 6.0

File Edit View Go Help

Hide Locate Previous Next Back Forward Stop Refresh Home Print

Active Subset

(Entire Collection)

Contents | Index | Search | Favorites

- MSDN Library Visual Studio 6.0
  - Welcome to the MSDN Library
  - Visual Studio Documentation
  - Visual Basic Documentation
    - Visual Basic Start Page
    - Visual Basic Documentation M
    - What's New in Visual Basic 6
    - Getting Started with Visual B
    - Using Visual Basic
    - Reference
      - Language Reference
      - Controls Reference
      - Wizards and Add-Ins
      - Trappable Errors
      - Additional Information
    - Samples
    - Microsoft DAO 3.51
    - Using the Repository with Vis
  - Visual C++ Documentation
  - Visual FoxPro Documentation

MsgBox Function

See Also Example Specifics

Displays a message in a dialog box, waits for the user to click a button, and returns an **Integer** indicating which button the user clicked.

Syntax

MsgBox(*prompt*[, *buttons*] [, *title*] [, *helpfile*, *context*])

The **MsgBox** function syntax has these named arguments:

Part	Description
prompt	Required. String expression displayed as the message in the dialog box. The maximum length of *prompt* is approximately 1024 characters, depending on the width of the characters used. If *prompt* consists of more than one line, you can separate the lines using a carriage return character

FIGURE 4.08 *MsgBox Function help screen*

- If you encounter an error message and do not understand what it means, press the F1 key for an explanation. The first time you encounter "Variable not defined," for example, you may want an explanation (see Figure 4.09).

Help System Working Examples

Often when you get an error message or when you try to use a new VB statement or function with which you are unfamiliar, it helps to see a live working example

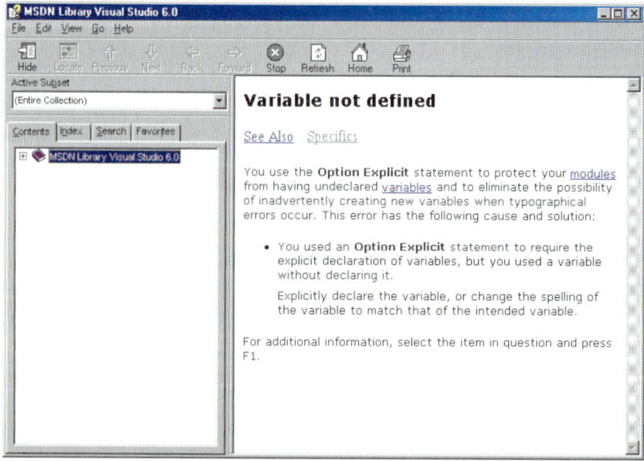

FIGURE 4.09 *Variable not defined help screen*

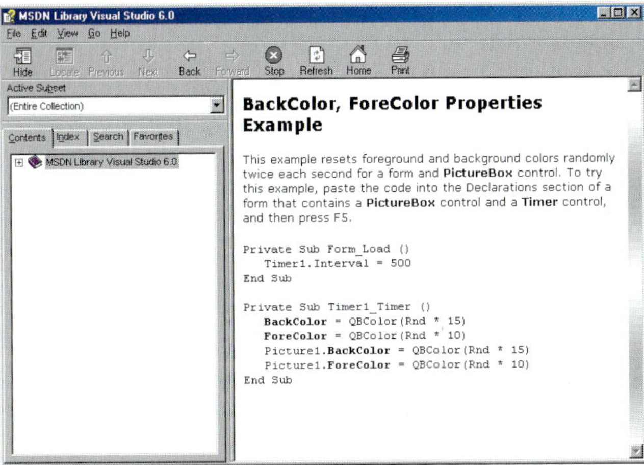
MSDN Library Visual Studio 6.0

BackColor, ForeColor Properties Example

This example resets foreground and background colors randomly twice each second for a form and PictureBox control. To try this example, paste the code into the Declarations section of a form that contains a PictureBox control and a Timer control, and then press F5.

```
Private Sub Form_Load ()
   Timer1.Interval = 500
End Sub

Private Sub Timer1_Timer ()
   BackColor = QBColor(Rnd * 15)
   ForeColor = QBColor(Rnd * 10)
   Picture1.BackColor = QBColor(Rnd * 15)
   Picture1.ForeColor = QBColor(Rnd * 10)
End Sub
```

FIGURE 4.10 *An Example help screen*

in the context of a program. For this reason, many of the Help screens for the VB programming language include a jump to an example of the statement or function in code as in Figure 4.10. In many cases, you can copy the entire example and paste it into a VB application to see how it works. Oftentimes you can paste the example code into your own program, with or without modification, to accomplish your purpose.

To try out this feature, start a new VB project, display the Help screen for the Click Event, and click on Example. Then, in the Example Window, highlight the statement beginning Picture1.Move, and click on Edit | Copy, which copies the highlighted text to the Clipboard. Return to your new project. Place a PictureBox Control in the lower-left corner of the form. Open the Code Window for the declarations section of the general object. Paste the Clipboard contents into that window. (VB will accept this code as the Picture1_Click procedure.) Then run the program and click the PictureBox Control, which will move diagonally across the screen.

INTRODUCING THE COLORFUL BACKDROP APPLICATION

This short project demonstrates two important features of Visual Basic—control arrays and For/Next loops. The application also shows that you can create a rather dramatic visual effect with very little work.

As is now becoming customary, start by running the application, called COLOR.EXE (Figure 4.11). The form contains 16 Command Buttons, numbered 0 through 15. When you click on a Command Button, the background of the form changes to one of 16 colors, and the Label near the lower right corner displays a hexadecimal color code (more about this later). Click as many buttons as you like, then exit the program through the control box or by pressing Alt-F4.

Run the program one more time, this time pressing a numeric key on the keyboard. You can activate any of the first 10 colors (numbered 0 through 9) by pressing the appropriate key.

STEP 1. Understand the Problem.

The selection of 16 as the number of Command Buttons in this application is not arbitrary or accidental. Rather, Visual Basic sports a function called **QBColor,** whose argument is a number from 0 to 15. QBColor returns a number (usually

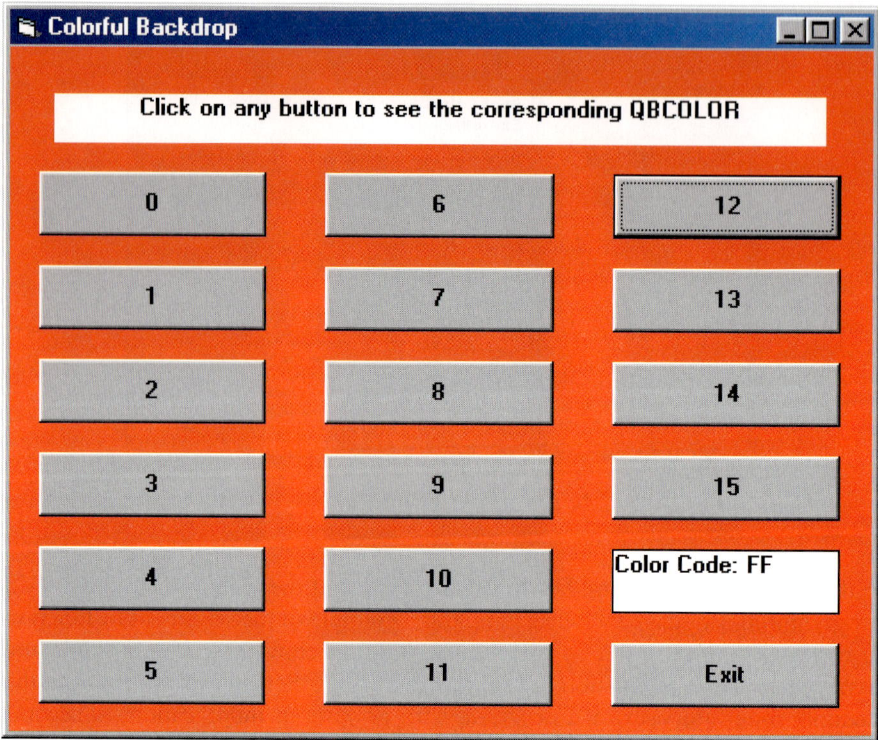

FIGURE 4.11 *Running Color.exe*

expressed as a hexadecimal value) that represents a particular color in Microsoft Windows.

Computer monitors use the **RGB color scheme**, in which any color can be described by the amount of red, green, and blue pigment that the color contains. The hexadecimal representation of a color is in the form BBGGRR, where BB, GG, and RR are hexadecimal digits from 00 to FF and specify the amount of blue, green, and red, respectively, in that color. For example, pure blue is &HFF0000& (the &H at the beginning just means that this value is given in its hexadecimal form; the & at the end means that this number is a long integer). Black, of course, is &H0, since black is defined as the absence of color. And white is given by &HFFFFFF&, that is, 100 percent of all colors. Run the COLOR.EXE program again, and examine the hexadecimal color codes at the bottom of the form. These are the hexadecimal numbers that correspond to the color being displayed.

Although the Colorful Backdrop application uses the QBColor function, offering 16 colors, Visual Basic also supports the far more robust RGB function, offering 256^3 colors. In this function, the intensity of each primary color is given by a decimal value from 0 to 255 (or a hexadecimal value from &H0 to &HFF). For example, to set the form's BackColor property in code, you could use the following:

```
Dim intRed As Integer
Dim intGreen As Integer
Dim intBlue As Integer
intRed = 128 ' or intRed = &H80
intGreen = 0
intBlue = 255 ' or intBlue = &HFF
Me.BackColor = RGB(intRed, intGreen, intBlue)
'Me is always an object reference to the current form
```

STEP 2. Design Your Solution.

Sketch your form on a piece of paper, and decide how you will arrange the 16 Command Buttons. Then number them from 0 to 15. Add the two Labels.

To implement this form design in Visual Basic, you could (but we won't)

- from the Toolbox, put 16 Command Buttons on a form,
- from the Properties Window, change the Caption and Name properties of each Command Button, and
- from the Code Window, write code for the click event procedure for each Command Button.

This would be similar to the technique we used in the Simple Calculator application. However, that would defeat the purpose of this application. Instead, we want to develop this project quickly and with a minimum of redundant effort. For this purpose, we will introduce the notion of a control array.

Control Arrays

A **control array** consists of two or more of the same type of control, which share certain properties and procedures. Most importantly, they all share the same name. The programmer may want them to share other properties as well, such as size and color, but some properties very likely will be different, such as location on the screen and caption. For example, in the present case, 16 Command Buttons will be placed on the form, and all of them will be called cmdColor. cmdColor is a control array of 16 Command Buttons. Each individual control within an array of controls is known as an element of the control array. In order to distinguish a specific element of the control array from any other element, an index is used; that is, the elements are numbered. The first element of any control array has an index of 0, the next has an index of 1, then 2, and so on. When referring to a specific element of a control array, the index appears in parentheses following the array name. So the 16 elements of the cmdColor control array will be numbered (indexed) from 0 to 15. The first element is cmdColor(0), the next is cmdColor(1), and so on through cmdColor(15).

You already know that property values can be set in code as well as at design time. For example, we have been changing the Enabled property of Command Buttons and the Caption property of Labels in both the Hello World and the Simple Calculator applications. Therefore, it would be possible to write a procedure to set the Caption property of all 16 Command Buttons in this application. After establishing the control array of 16 Command Buttons, the brute force version of such a procedure might look like this:

```
cmdColor(0).Caption = 0
cmdColor(1).Caption = 1
cmdColor(2).Caption = 2
cmdColor(3).Caption = 3
cmdColor(4).Caption = 4
cmdColor(5).Caption = 5
cmdColor(6).Caption = 6
cmdColor(7).Caption = 7
cmdColor(8).Caption = 8
cmdColor(9).Caption = 9
cmdColor(10).Caption = 10
cmdColor(11).Caption = 11
cmdColor(12).Caption = 12
cmdColor(13).Caption = 13
cmdColor(14).Caption = 14
cmdColor(15).Caption = 15
```

After typing this in, you might breathe a sigh of relief that the application has only 16 Command Buttons, not 160; and you might also say to yourself, "There must be an easier way to do this."

Guess what. There is.

Looping

A loop in a computer program is a section of code that is designed to be performed more than once. The repeated code may consist of only one statement or it may be long and complicated. You may want to print "Hello, World" five times, or you may want to process 100,000 payroll records. Both of these are examples of loops. Looping or iteration is the third logical construct permitted in structured programming (the other two, sequence and selection, were discussed in Chapter Three).

Looping is absolutely fundamental to computer programming. In fact, without it many computer programs would have no reason to exist. For example, you might not use a computer at all to calculate the payroll for only one employee, nor would you want to write or run a computer program individually for each of 100,000 employees. What makes the computer useful is the fact that the payroll program contains a loop, and the entire process of calculating and paying one employee is repeated for as many times as there are employees.

Because looping is so fundamental, computer programming languages typically include specific syntax to support several versions of loops. A common technique, applicable to the present case, is called an internally controlled loop. The loop is executed a program-specified number of times, based on the value of a loop control variable, whose value is incremented each time the loop is executed. The statement that performs this function in Visual Basic is the **For/Next loop.**

For/Next Loops

Consider this snippet of code, which prints "Hello, World" five times:

```
Dim lcv As Integer
'lcv is the loop control _variable
Print "Start loop"
For lcv = 1 To 5 Step 1
    Print "Hello, World"; lcv
Next lcv
Print "Stop loop"
Print lcv
```

The statement

```
For lcv = 1 To 5 Step 1
```

establishes lcv as the loop control variable for this particular For/Next loop. It then assigns 1 as the initial value of the lcv, that is, the value of lcv as the loop is executed for the first time. The limit value is assigned as 5; that is, when the value of lcv exceeds 5, the limit value, the loop will stop being executed, and the program will continue executing with the first statement following "Next lcv." "Step 1" indicates that the step value (or increment) will be +1: Each time the "Next lcv" statement is executed, the value of lcv will be increased by this step value. (When the Step value = 1, it need not be specified, and in practice it is most often omitted.) The body of the For/Next loop, that is, the statements that are executed iteratively, come between the For statement and the Next statement.

If the previous snippet were executed, the output would be

```
Start Loop
Hello, World 1
Hello, World 2
Hello, World 3
Hello, World 4
Hello, World 5
Stop Loop
6
```

We will encounter numerous applications for For/Next loops, including applications in which the initial, limit, and/or step values are not known ahead of time. All of these can be variables, and all can be of any numeric type. The step value may be positive or negative. For example:

```
Dim i As Integer, s As Single, lg As Long, d _
    As Double
...
For i = s To lg Step d
...
```

Let's say you needed to add up all of the even numbers between 100 and 1000 inclusive. (We can't imagine why you would need to, but let's pretend you did.) The following Form_Click event procedure uses a For/Next loop to accomplish this task and then prints the result on the form. To use this example, start a new project, put this code in the Form_Click event procedure, then run the project and click the form.

```
Private Sub Form_Click()
    Dim i As Integer
    Dim lngSum As Long
    For i = 100 to 1000 Step 2
        lngSum = lngSum + i
    Next i
    Print lngSum
End Sub
```

Here is one more example of the versatility of a For/Next loop. In this case, we want to print out (on paper) every third number from 50 to –50, in descending order (the Printer object directs output to the printer):

```
Private Sub Form_Click()
    Dim vntStart, vntFinish, vntStep, vntLcv
    vntStart = 50
    vntFinish = -50
    vntStep = -3
    For vntLcv = vntStart to vntFinish Step vntStep
        Printer.Print vntLcv,
    Next vntLcv
    Printer.EndDoc
End Sub
```

Getting back to the problem at hand, you can see that we need a loop that is to be executed exactly 16 times. The loop control variable will have integer values from

0 to 15, and each such value will be assigned to the Caption property of the corresponding element of the cmdColor control array. The For/Next loop to effect this result is:

```
Dim i As Integer
For i = 0 To 15
   cmdColor(i).Caption = i
Next i
```

The only remaining design problem concerning the captions of the 16 Command Buttons is how to invoke the code shown here so that the correct captions appear on the Command Buttons as soon as the program starts running. The answer is that a programmable event, called the Form_Load event, occurs while a form is being loaded into memory but before the form is painted on the screen. Assignment of captions to Command Buttons belongs in Sub Form_Load.

Assigning the Background Color and Displaying the Color Code

Elements of a control array share procedures as well as properties. When a trappable event (such as the click event) for an element of a control array occurs, Visual Basic calls the associated event procedure and also passes to that procedure the index of the element that triggered the event. For example, if the user clicks on cmdColor(5), then the common procedure Private Sub cmdColor_Click (Index As Integer) is invoked, and 5 is passed to that event procedure as the Index value.

As mentioned at the outset, the QBColor function (with an argument from 0 to 15) returns a number representing an RGB color recognized by Microsoft Windows. Using the Index passed to Sub cmdColor_Click as the argument of QBColor, the click event procedure changes the form's BackColor property to QBColor's return value, and also displays that value in the Label at the bottom of the form:

```
Me.BackColor = QBColor(Index)
lblColorCode = "Color Code: " & Hex(QBColor(Index))
```

Keyboard Input

One method of obtaining keyboard input during program execution is to program the KeyPress event. Normally, pressing any key on the keyboard fires the **KeyPress event** for whichever object has focus, that is, the currently selected object on the screen. In the present case, we want to program only the KeyPress event for the form. We must also set the form's **KeyPreview property** to True, which means that pressing any key on the keyboard (i.e., any KeyPress) fires the form's KeyPress event procedure first.

VB passes to the KeyPress event procedure the **ASCII code** of the key that was pressed (ASCII codes are listed in Appendix A). In the Colorful Backdrop application, we want to use the keyboard input only if it is a digit—represented by ASCII codes 48 through 57. If the ASCII value of the pressed key (called **KeyAscii** in the KeyPress event procedure) is in the appropriate range, then we first convert the ASCII code to the character it represents (using the **Chr function**), and then convert that character into a numeric value (using the Val function):

```
Index = Val(Chr(KeyAscii))
```

For example, if you press the digit 1 on the keyboard, then KeyAscii is 49, and this is the value that is passed to the KeyPress event procedure. Chr(49) is the character "1," and Val("1") is the number 1, which therefore gets assigned to Index.

We can then repeat the code above, calling on QBColor to set the screen's BackColor property and to fill the Label with the corresponding RGB color.

STEP 3. Develop Your Logic—Hierarchy Table and Pseudocode.

Figure 4.12 displays the hierarchy table for this project, showing the project, the form, and the few procedures which must be programmed. As shown in the pseudocode for this project (Figure 4.13), the control array and For/Next loop make for a simple and efficient logical design.

HIERARCHY TABLE-COLORFUL BACKDROP

```
Project:  Color (Color.vbp)
Form:     frmColor (Color.frm)
          Event procedures:
            Form_Load
            CmdColorClick(Index As Integer)
            CmdExit_Click
            Form_KeyPress(Key Ascii As Integer)
```

FIGURE 4.12 *Hierarchy Table—Colorful Backdrop*

PSEUDOCODE-COLORFUL BACKDROP

```
Event procedure: Sub Form_Load
  FOR/NEXT Loop: FOR I = 0 to 15
    Assign: I as the caption for cmdColor (I)
  NEXT I

Event procedure: Sub cmdColor_Click (Index As Integer)
  Assign: BackColor of Form ← QBColor(Index)
  Assign lblColorCode ← hex value of QBColor(Index)

Event procedure: Sub Form_KeyPress(Key Ascii As Integer)
  IF (the key pressed was a digit)
    True:
      Convert the key pressed to its equivalent Index value
      Assign: BackColor of Form ← QBColor(Index)
      Assign:lblColorCode ← hex value of QBColor(Index)
  ENDIF

Event procedure: cmdExit_Click
  End the program
```

FIGURE 4.13 *Pseudocode—Colorful Backdrop*

STEP 4. Build the Graphical User Interface (GUI).

- Start a new project.
- Name the form frmColor and the form caption Colorful Backdrop.
- Set the form's KeyPreview property to True.
- Change the size and location of the default form as you wish.
- Insert Label1 in the top center of the form, and assign its caption.

- Put the first of the 16 Command Buttons on the form. This first button ultimately will get the caption 0, so position it accordingly and size it to your liking.
- From the Properties Window, change the name of Command1 to cmdColor.
- Click on the form again and select cmdColor. Copy this button to the Clipboard by pressing Ctrl-C or by clicking Edit | Copy. Notice that as soon as you copy cmdColor to the Clipboard, the control is no longer selected—rather, the form is selected.
- Paste the Clipboard contents, that is, cmdColor, onto the form by pressing Ctrl-V or by clicking Edit | Paste. Visual Basic will ask whether you wish to create a control array; answer "Yes." A second cmdColor will appear at the top left of the form. Note that, in the object drop-down list at the top of the Properties Window, the first Command Button you placed on the form is now called cmdColor(0), and the new copy you just created is named cmdColor(1). (See Figure 4.14.)
- After again selecting the form, press Ctrl-V fourteen more times. Each time you press Ctrl-V, another cmdColor is stacked on top of the previous Command Buttons in the top left corner of the form. You will end up with a total of 16 Command Buttons, all called cmdColor(n), where n varies from 0 to 15. To keep track of the number of cmdColor Command Buttons you have created, watch the Properties Window outside your form. Each time you press Ctrl-V, the new copy of cmdColor is positioned at the top left corner of the form (right on top of other copies previously created) and is the currently selected object; hence, that object's name appears at the top of the Properties Window. Stop making copies when the Properties Window tells you that you have created cmdColor(15).
- Put one more Command Button, captioned "Exit" and named cmdExit, at the bottom right of the form.
- Put another Label above the Exit button. Set its Caption property to "Color Code:" and its name to lblColorCode.

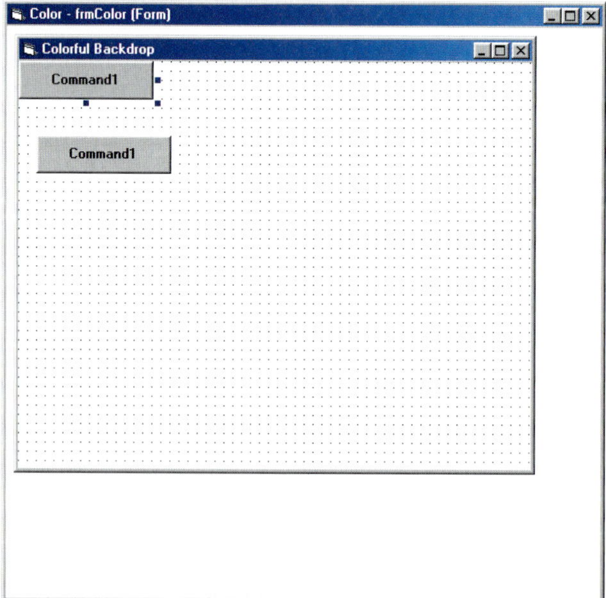

FIGURE 4.14 *Building the cmdColor control array*

- Save the form as MYCOLOR.FRM.
- Save the project as MYCOLOR.VBP.

STEP 5. Write the VB Code.

Only four short procedures need to be written for this application. Double-click on the form to open the Form_Load event procedure, and type in this code:

```
Private Sub Form_Load()
    Dim i As Integer
    For i = 0 To 15
        cmdColor(i).Caption = i
    Next i
End Sub
```

This code was explained earlier.

Double-click any of the Command Buttons (or choose cmdColor() from the Code Window's object drop-down list) to open the code window for Sub cmdColor_Click (Index As Integer). Type in this procedure:

```
Private Sub cmdColor_Click(Index As Integer)
    Me.BackColor = QBColor(Index)
    lblColorCode = "Color Code: " & Hex(QBColor _
        (Index))
End Sub
```

The word **Me** in VB code always refers to the form to which the code is attached. Although you could use the name of the form, it is a good idea to get used to referring to the current form in code as Me. In that way, you will be able later to copy an especially useful code segment between forms or between projects, without having to modify the code so as to accommodate different form names.

QBColor(Index) returns a number that Microsoft Windows recognizes as an RGB color scheme. Actually, the hexadecimal representation of this number shows the amount of Blue, then Green, and then Red in that color. This value is assigned as the background color of Me. The hexadecimal representation of this number (returned by the Hex function) is also displayed in lblColorCode.

In the Code Window, choose Form from the object drop-down list, and then choose KeyPress from the Proc drop-down list. Here is the KeyPress event procedure.

```
Private Sub Form_KeyPress (KeyAscii As Integer)
    Dim intIndex As Integer
    If KeyAscii > 47 And KeyAscii < 58 Then
        intIndex = Val(Chr(KeyAscii))
        Me.BackColor = QBColor(intIndex)
        lblColorCode = "Color Code: " & Hex(QBColor _
            (intIndex))
    End If
End Sub
```

Finally, in Sub cmdExit_Click(), insert the statement "End."

STEP 6. Test and Debug Your Program.

Any mistakes should be fairly easy to find and fix, since this application is so short. (We will get into some handy test and debugging techniques in Chapter Five.)

STEP 7. Complete the Program Documentation.

Open the Code Window for the (declarations) portion of the (general) object. Insert these comment lines:

```
'Project Name:          MYCOLOR.VBP
'Executable file: MYCOLOR.EXE
'Forms/modules:         MYCOLOR.FRM
'Written by:            <insert your name>
'Original date:         <insert today's date>
['Revision date:        <insert revision date, if any>]
'Adapted from Spear & Spear
```

SUMMARY

Visual Basic's online, **context-sensitive Help System** provides a reasonably complete reference tool to assist the VB programmer, especially for questions of syntax.

Control arrays are widely used in GUI design, both to ensure that key properties of objects in the array are the same and to reduce duplicative coding of procedures. The **Index property** identifies a specific control within a control array. **For/Next loops** are widely used for manipulating the elements of a control array. A For/Next loop is VB's internally controlled loop—a loop executed a specified number of times, based on the incrementing value of a loop control variable.

A color in Visual Basic is represented by an RGB value, a hexadecimal long integer indicating the relative intensity of red, green, and blue that make up that color. Programmers can specify a color directly by assigning an RGB value or by using either the **RGB function** (for about 16 million colors) or the **QBColor function** (for 16 colors).

In the **KeyPress event** procedure, VB passes **KeyAscii,** the ASCII code of the key that was pressed. If **KeyPreview** was set to True, the form's KeyPress event procedure will always be fired when any keyboard key is pressed.

PROGRAMMING ASSIGNMENTS

Improved Simple Calculator

Rewrite the Simple Calculator application with these improvements, adapted from the Colorful Backdrop application.

- Use a control array of 10 Command Buttons in lieu of cmd0, cmd1, cmd2, . . . , cmd9.
- Add the ability to perform multiplication.
- Use a control array of three Command Buttons for the three operations—addition, subtraction, and multiplication. In the click event procedure, use a "nested If" selection structure to assign mstrOpCode as "+," "–," or "*," like this:

```
If Index = 0 Then
    mstrOpCode = "+"
Else If Index = 1 Then
    mstrOpCode = "-"
Else mstrOpCode = "*"
End If
```

- To trap keyboard input of each operand, set the Form's KeyPreview property to True and program the Form's KeyPress event procedure.

Olympic Scoring

We have all seen the various systems for subjective judging in Olympic competitions. After each competitor's performance, the judges give their marks, often on a scale of 1 to 10. The competitor's score is the average of the scores awarded by all the judges. (In many sports, the highest and lowest scores are discarded, an element of sophistication that we will omit in this application.) Create a Visual Basic application to facilitate the scoring of Olympic competitions, as in Figures 4.15 and 4.16.

GUI Design:

- Place a top row of five labels containing zeros. This is a control array named lblScore. Set the Alignment property to "2-Centered" and the BorderStyle property to "1-Fixed Single."

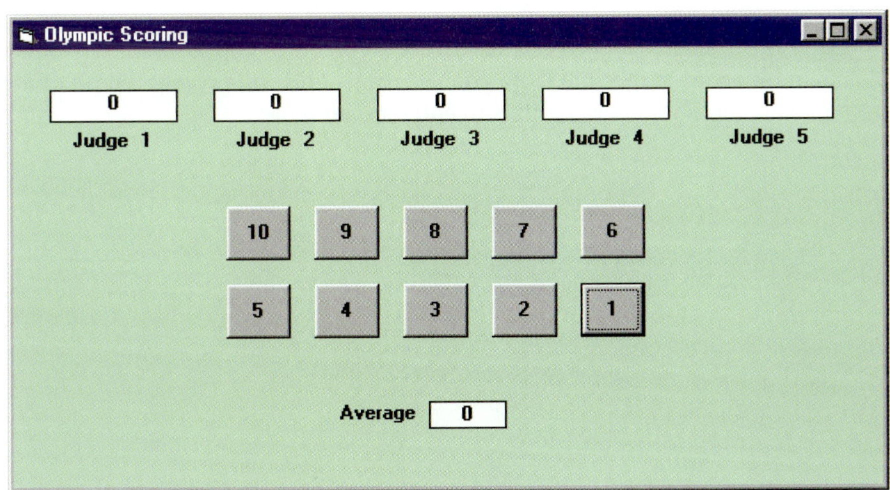

FIGURE 4.15 *Olympic Scoring—Opening Screen*

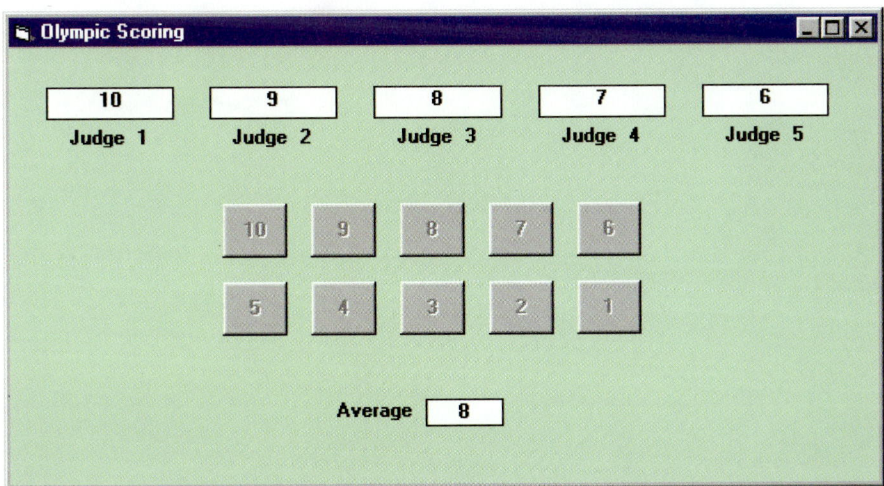

FIGURE 4.16 *Olympic Scoring—After Scoring by All 5 Judges*

- Underneath this row of labels, place another row of five labels. This is a control array named lblJudge. Set the Alignment property to "2-Centered."
- Put 10 small Command Buttons on the form. This is a control array named cmdScore.
- At the bottom, one label contains the word "Average," and another label named lblAverage (centered, with a border) contains 0.
- In the form's Load event procedure, use For/Next loops to:
  - Change the captions of the lblJudge array to "Judge 1," "Judge 2," "Judge 3," "Judge 4," and "Judge 5."
  - Change the captions of the cmdScore array to 10, 9, 8, 7, 6, 5, 4, 3, 2, and 1.

In the cmdScore_Click event procedure, assign the clicked button's value to the next judge's score. In other words, the first click is the score for Judge 1 and replaces the caption in lblScore(0). The next click provides the score for Judge 2, and so on.

When the score for Judge 5 is recorded, the program should automatically calculate the average score and display it in the caption for lblAverage. The score should be accurate to one decimal place.

After the average has been calculated, use a For/Next loop to disable all of the Command Buttons in the cmdScore control array—this will prevent the program from blowing up if the user attempts to enter a sixth score.

CHAPTER FIVE

DEBUGGING, MULTIPLE FORMS, GRAPHICAL CONTROLS

Application: Shapes

LEARNING OBJECTIVES

Upon completion of Chapter Five, you will be able to:

- Use Visual Basic's Debug facility effectively.
- Distinguish among syntax, runtime, and logic errors.
- Use shortcut keys to navigate in the integrated development environment.
- Design a project using multiple forms.
- Understand and apply the twips measurement scale.
- Use the Shape control and the Timer control.
- Position a form in the middle of the screen.

Keywords

Add Watch command
BackStyle property
BorderColor property
BorderWidth property
Breakpoint
Change event
Debug facility
Edit Watch command
Err object
FillColor property
FillStyle property
Focus
Height property
Hide method
Interval property
Left property
Load statement
Logic error
Logical inch
Pixel (measurement scale)
Point (measurement scale)
Quick Watch command
Raise method
Rnd function
Runtime error
ScaleMode property
Screen object
Shape control (prefix: shp)
Shape property
Show method
Start Up form
Step Into command
Step Over command
Step To Cursor command
Syntax error

?Ed/-1 li for pmu

TabIndex property
TextBox control (prefix: txt)
Timer control (prefix: tmr)
Timer event
Toggle Breakpoint (F9)
Top property
Twips measurement scale
Unload statement
View Code (F7)
View Object Browser (F
Watch
Width property

INTRODUCING SHAPES

The sample application for Chapter Five is called SHAPES.EXE. Try running this program.

The initial form (called the **Start Up Form**) appears in the upper left corner of the screen. Four command buttons, captioned "Rectangle," "Square," "Oval," and "Circle," are initially disabled. You are prompted to type in your first name in a TextBox. As soon as you type the first letter, the four command buttons become enabled. When you click on one of the command buttons, a second form appears in the middle of the screen, displaying your name, your chosen design (shape), and a number indicating the sequence of your design selections (see Figure 5.01). Also, the shape on this second form is displayed in a randomly selected color. When you click the OK button on the second form, that form is hidden and you return to the first form.

STEP 1. Understand the Problem.

After you have run the Shapes program several times, this project seems simple enough: The only apparent new components are the use of a second form, the **TextBox control,** and the **Shape control.** You will need to learn how to show and hide a second form on the screen while the program is running, and you will need to learn how to manipulate the properties of the Shape control—specifically, its color and shape. Based on your recent experience with the Colorful Backdrop project as well as the revised Simple Calculator project, you might also correctly surmise that the four command buttons on the Start Up Form that identify shapes (rectangle, square, oval, and circle) constitute a control array. Your program will need to sense when the user types a letter in the TextBox, because that is the trigger for enabling the array of command buttons. The color of each shape is selected with the help of QBColor. Finally, a variable is needed to keep track of the design sequence number.

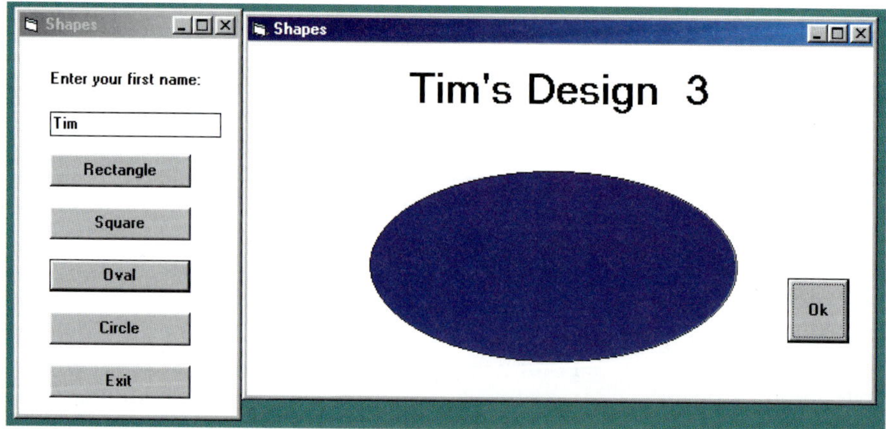

FIGURE 5.01 *Shapes.exe executing*

STEP 2. Design a Solution.

Sketch both of the forms. We will name the Start Up Form frmShapes1 and the second form frmShapes2.

Incorporating a Second Form in a Project

When a Visual Basic program starts executing, the Start Up Form is loaded into memory, then the Form_Load event procedure (if one exists) is executed, and finally the form is displayed on the screen. These three steps occur as discrete, sequential processes, although it may appear to you that they all occur together. Two statements and two methods are related to these processes:

- **Load statement**—loads a form into memory but does not display it on the screen. The syntax is:

    Load *formname*

- **Unload statement**—removes a form from memory. If only one form in the project is loaded, then the unload statement terminates execution of the program. Syntax:

    Unload *formname*

- **Show method**—displays a form on the screen. If the form has not yet been loaded into memory, the Show method first loads the form, triggers the Form_Load event, and then displays the form. Syntax:

    formname.Show

- **Hide method**—removes a form from the screen but leaves the form in memory. Here is the syntax:

    formname.Hide

In the Shapes Project, we used a Form_Load event procedure to locate frmShapes2 in the exact center of the screen. You can see from this project how the Show and Hide methods work.

Run the Shapes Project again. Type in your name, and click on one of the shape names. The Show method loads frmShapes2 into memory, fires the Form_Load event procedure, which locates frmShapes2 in the middle of the screen, and then displays frmShapes2. Now, move frmShapes2 to the upper right corner of the screen (by clicking and dragging the title bar), and then click the OK button, which Hides the form. Next, click another one of the shape command buttons on frmShapes1. As you can see, frmShapes2 appears in the upper right corner of the screen, right where it was when it was hidden. Because frmShapes2 was already in memory when the second shape button was clicked, the Show method neither loads the form again nor does it trigger the Form_Load event.

Twips—and Left, Top, Width, and Height Properties

The size and location of a form on the screen is measured in **twips.** The word twip is derived from its meaning: one twip is a twentieth of a printer's point. You may be familiar with printer's **points,** because font sizes are typically stated in that measurement scale, which is calculated as 72 points per inch when printed on paper. (When we use point sizes for fonts on the screen, whether in Visual Basic or in a word processor, the actual size of an object on the screen is greatly affected by the screen resolution and by capabilities and settings in the screen driver. And so the notion that there are 72 points per inch is an approximation at best. We say, rather, that there are 72 points to a **logical inch.**) Since a twip is 1/20 of a point, there are 1440 twips per logical inch.

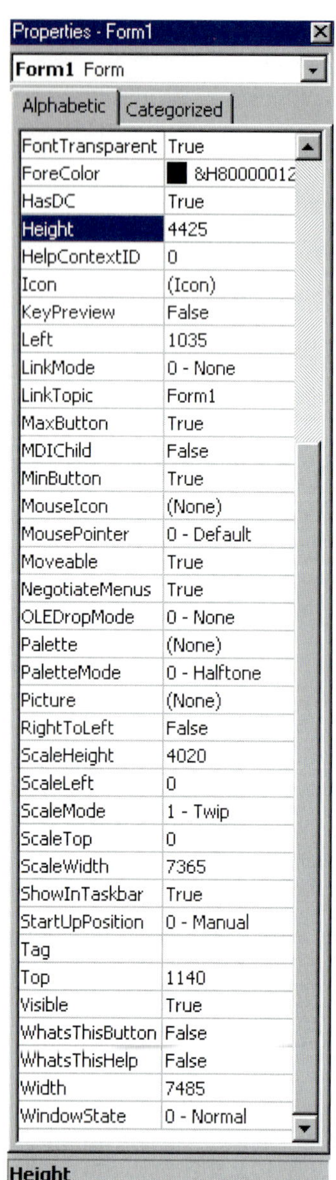

FIGURE 5.03 *Properties window for the form*

Start a new VB project, and look at the numbers in the boxes at the right side of the Toolbar (Figure 5.02). On our computer, the first set of numbers is "1035, 1140," which indicates that the top left-hand corner of the form is 1035 twips from the left edge of the screen and 1140 twips from the top edge of the screen. The second set of numbers, "7485 × 4425," indicates that the form is 7485 twips wide and 4425 twips high. The same values can be viewed in the form's **Left property** (1035 twips), **Top property** (1140), **Width property** (7485), and **Height property** (4425) (Figure 5.03).

Now place a control on the form—any control, it really doesn't matter which one. (Perhaps you should experiment with a new one.) Notice that the location (left, top) and the size (width × height) numbers on the Toolbar have changed. They now reflect the Left, Top, Width, and Height properties of the control you just placed on the form. The measurement scale is still in twips. Left is measured from the inside of the left border of the form, while Top is measured from the underside of the form's title bar.

Put a few more controls on your form. As you click on each object (form or control), the location and size numbers on the Toolbar change. These numbers always reflect the position and dimensions of the currently selected object.

In some cases you may decide that you would rather use a different scale than twips inside your form (Figure 5.04). While the measurement scale for the location and size of the form itself cannot be changed, the scale for all of the controls placed on the form can be selected by the programmer. Select the form's **ScaleMode property,** and change it to whatever you like. In this example, we placed a Shape control and a Command Button on the form, and then set the form's ScaleMode property to pixels (a **pixel** is the smallest unit of monitor resolution). After changing the ScaleMode, select each of the objects on the screen, and note that the location and size properties reflect the new measurement scale, but click on the form, and its location and size are still expressed in twips.

By the way, now that you know how to use the Help System, you can get Help quickly for the ScaleMode property: just open the Properties window for the form, click on ScaleMode, and press the F1 key. Notice that you can resize the Help window, and the screen display automatically adjusts the lines of text inside to fit your window size (Figure 5.05).

The Shape Control

In the Shapes project, frmShapes2 includes a Shape control, which appears as a rectangle, square, oval, or circle.

Obviously, when the user clicks on one of the shape-named command buttons on frmShapes1, we are manipulating some of the properties of the Shape control on frmShapes2, namely FillColor, FillStyle, and Shape:

- **FillColor**—the color that fills the shape. The default color is black.
- **FillStyle**—the pattern or style in which the FillColor appears. The default, unfortunately, is "transparent," so if you do not change the FillStyle, the FillColor does not appear at all. The other choices are "solid" and various combinations of horizontal, vertical, and diagonal lines.

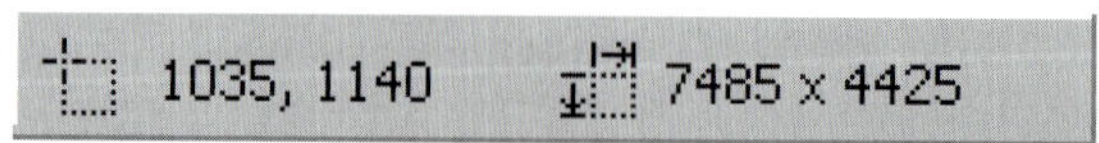

FIGURE 5.02 *Top, Left, Height, and Width property values*

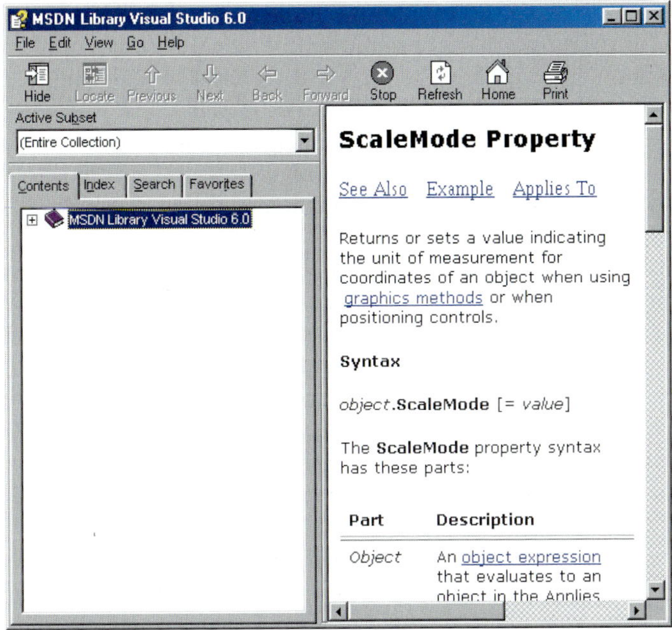

FIGURE 5.05 *ScaleMode property help screen, in a reduced-size window*

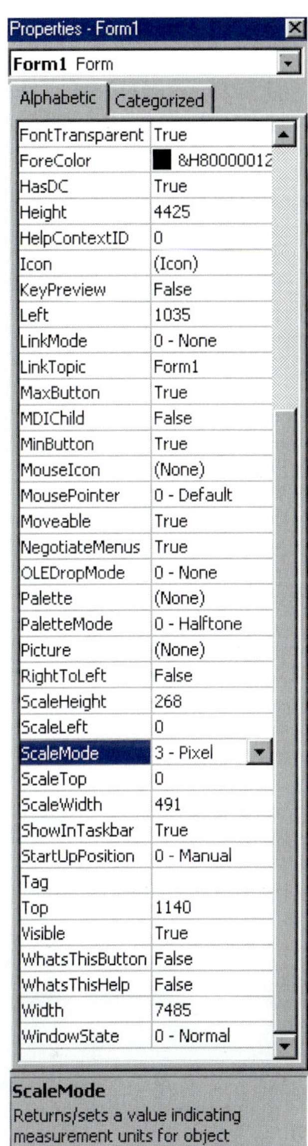

FIGURE 5.04
Setting the ScaleMode property

- **Shape**—a choice of rectangle, square, oval, circle, rounded rectangle, or rounded square.

The TextBox Control and the Notion of "Focus"

The Shapes Project also includes a TextBox control on frmShapes1. This control (in the Toolbox) is one of the principal vehicles for allowing the user to enter information into a VB program during execution.

When you run the Shapes program, you should notice three things about the TextBox:

1. The cursor is blinking inside the TextBox when the program starts. We say that the TextBox "has **focus.**"
2. The array of command buttons is enabled as soon as you type anything into the TextBox. At this time, the blinking cursor is still inside the TextBox.
3. After you click on one of the shape command buttons and then click on OK, the blinking cursor is no longer inside the TextBox; that is, the TextBox no longer has focus. Rather, the command button you had clicked on has a dark border and its caption has a dotted line around it; that is, the Command button has focus.

Whichever control on a form has the lowest value in its **TabIndex property** receives focus when a form is loaded and initially displayed. If the control is not a type that can receive focus, or if the control is not enabled or not visible, then the next control in TabIndex order receives focus. While a form remains active, pressing the tab key on the keyboard advances the focus to the next control, again in TabIndex order.

To see how the focus moves from control to control, run the Shapes Project again. Before typing any letter, press the tab key. Note that the focus moves to the

Exit button. Try typing a letter. Note that nothing happens, because the only control on the form that can receive a typed letter is the TextBox, and it only receives the letter when the TextBox has focus. Press the tab key again, and focus returns to the TextBox. Now type a letter, which goes into the TextBox, and which also triggers the Change event. We wrote a Change event procedure, which enables the four previously disabled command buttons. Now press the tab key repeatedly, and watch the focus move to each of the command buttons and finally back to the TextBox.

The Label on frmShapes1 that says "Enter your first name" actually has a TabIndex property value of 0, but a label cannot receive focus. Therefore, when frmShapes1 first appears, focus goes to the TextBox, whose TabIndex is 1. The four shape-name command boxes have TabIndex properties of 2, 3, 4, and 5. But before these buttons are enabled, they cannot receive focus. The TabIndex property of the Exit button is 6. When the tab key is pressed while the control with the highest TabIndex property has focus, focus returns to the control whose TabIndex is the lowest value. And so the focus continues to move through all of the controls whenever the tab key is pressed.

Clicking on a control that has the ability to receive focus also moves focus to that control.

Pressing the enter key triggers the Click event for whichever control has focus. Hence you could run the Shapes Project without a mouse:

- From the Start Menu, run the Shapes project.
- Type in your name.
- Press the tab key until your desired design has the focus.
- Press the enter key to display frmShapes2.
- Note that the OK button has focus.
- Press the enter key again to hide frmShapes2 and return to frmShapes1.
- Press the tab key until the Exit button has focus.
- Press the enter key to terminate the program.

Scope and Visibility of Form-level versus Procedure-level Variables

The Shapes Project demonstrates the notion that a form-level variable exists for the whole life of the form, while a procedure-level variable exists only while that procedure is being executed. Further, VB is able to keep a procedure-level variable distinct from a form-level variable by the same name.

A form-level integer variable i represents the design sequence number. This variable is incremented each time the user clicks on a shape-named command button on frmShapes1; the value of i is then inserted in the Label on frmShapes2. Notice that the first design sequence number (the number that appears the first time you choose a shape) is 1.

However, before you were able to choose this shape, the array of command buttons had to be enabled. Typing something in the TextBox triggers the **Change event** (which fires every time the contents of a TextBox changes). A procedure-level integer variable i is used as a loop control variable in Sub txt_Change(). This variable i controls the execution of a For/Next loop, which enables the array of four shape-named command buttons. When a loop that begins "For i = 0 To 3" finishes executing, i has a value of 4. But when the procedure finishes executing, this procedure-level variable i ceases to exist. The form-level variable i is not affected by the procedure-level variable i. (We will see this demonstrated later in this chapter when we discuss the VB Debug facility.)

This use of variables named i at both the procedure level and the form level could obviously lead to some confusion and is not recommended as a programming practice. It was used here only to demonstrate that Visual Basic is able to keep the two variables apart.

Step 3. Develop Your Logic.

The Hierarchy Table and pseudocode for the Shapes Project are presented in Figures 5.06 and 5.07, respectively.

```
HIERARCHY TABLE-SHAPES

Project: Shapes (Shapes.vbp)
Form:       frmShapes1 (Shapes1.frm)
            Form variable:
               i - keeps track of the sequential shape design number

            Event procedures:
               cmdExit_Click()
               cmdShape_Click(index As Integer)
               Form_Load()
               Txtname_Change()
Form:       frmShapes2 (Shapes2.frm)
            Event procedures:
               Form_Load
               cmdOk_Click
```

FIGURE 5.06 *Hierarchy Table—Shapes*

```
PSEUDOCODE-SHAPES

FrmShapes1
Event procedure: Sub cmdExit_Click
   End the program

Event procedure: Sub cmdShape_Click(index As Integer)
   Increment i
   Assign the label caption on frmShapes2 ¨ txtName & “'s Design “ & Str$(i)
   Assign the shape of the Shape control on frmShapes2 ← Index
   Assign the FillColor of the shape control on frmShpes2 ← QBColor of a randomly generated integer
   Show frmShapes2

Event procedure: SubForm_Load
   Position the form at the top left of the screen

Event procedure: txtName_Change
   Enable the four cmdShape Command Buttons

FrmShapes2
Event procedure: Sub Form_Load
   Position the form in the exact middle of the screen

Event procedure: Sub cmdOk_Click
   Hide frmShapes2
```

FIGURE 5.07 *Pseudocode—Shapes*

Step 4. Build Your GUI.

The Project Explorer Window

The Project Explorer Window (Figure 5.08) lists all of the files that make up the Visual Basic project you are working on. When a project has only one form in it, then the Project Explorer Window isn't really needed, because you can switch to the form or the code directly from the View Menu. When the project has multiple forms, then you may need to use the Project Explorer Window to select the correct form, after which you switch to the Form Window or the Code Window for the selected form. The Project Explorer Window allows you to select a form and then click on View Form or View Code. The Project Explorer Window is often partially visible while you are designing a VB project; most programmers leave it "docked" in the upper right corner of the screen, although you could move it elsewhere. As you have already discovered, when you click on any part of a window, it becomes selected and moves to the foreground. However, if you cannot see any part of the Project Explorer Window, either because it is covered by other windows on the screen or because it was previously closed, then you can open it again or bring it to the foreground by selecting "View | Project Explorer" or by pressing Ctrl-R or by clicking the View Project icon.

frmShapes1

After creating a new directory on your disk for Chap5, start a new Visual Basic Project. Then set these properties:

Name	frmShapes1
Caption	Shapes
Height	approximately 4700 twips
Width	approximately 2700 twips

Put a Label across the form near the top.

Set these properties:

Caption	Enter your first name
TabIndex	0

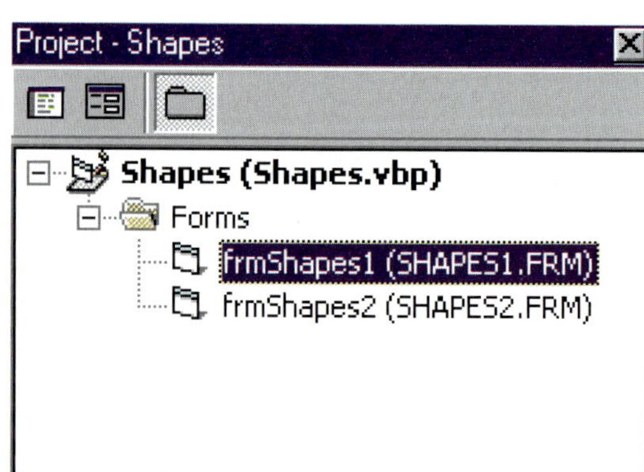

FIGURE 5.08 *Project Explorer window*

Put a TextBox under Label1.

Set these properties:

Name	txtName
TabIndex	1
Text	(blank)

Put a command button under txtName. Set these properties:

Name	cmdShape
Caption	Rectangle
Enabled	False
TabIndex	2

Select cmdShape on the form, and copy it to the Clipboard. Paste cmdShape onto the form. In response to VB's question, yes, you do want to create a control array. Paste cmdShape onto the form two more times. The top copy of cmdShape is now cmdShape(3); drag it into position for the Circle command button. Drag the next copy, cmdShape(2), into position for the Oval command button. Finally, drag cmdShape(1) into position for the Square command button.

Check that the four command buttons have the correct properties:

Name	cmdShape(0)	cmdShape(1)	cmdShape(2)	cmdShape(3)
Caption	Rectangle	Square	Oval	Circle
Enabled	False	False	False	False
TabIndex	2	3	4	5

Put one more command button underneath the other four, and set these properties:

Name	cmdExit
Caption	Exit
Enabled	True
TabIndex	6

Save the project using the Save icon from the Toolbar, the fourth icon from the left.

When prompted by Visual Basic, create a New Folder; then save the form on your disk as SHAPES1.FRM, and save the project as MYSHAPES.VBP.

frmShapes2

From the Toolbar, click on the leftmost icon to start a new form.

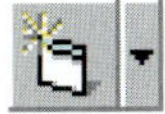

Set these properties:

Name	frmShapes2
Caption	Shapes
ScaleMode	5 – inch

Put a large Label across the top of the form. Set the following properties. Measurements are in inches, because ScaleMode was set to inches. All measurements are approximations:

Name	lbl
Alignment	2-Center
FontSize	24
Height	.5
Left	.1
Top	.1
Width	5

Place a large Shape control under the label. Set these properties:

Name	shp
FillStyle	0 - Solid
Height	1.5
Left	1
Top	1
Width	3

Place a square command button in the lower right quadrant of the form, and set these properties:

Name	cmdOk
Caption	OK

Save this form on your disk as SHAPES2.FRM.

Identifying the Start Up Form

VB assumes that the first form you create for a project is the Start Up Form, but that may not always be the case. You may decide to create a new form for a project, or add a form from another project, and make that the Start Up Form. To designate the Start Up Form, from the VB Menu Bar, select Project | Project Properties, click the General tab, and select Start Up Object. Then click the drop down list and choose the form you wish to designate (Figure 5.09)

STEP 5. Write the VB Code.

There are no constants in the project. As we discussed earlier, this project only has two variables, and both of them are integers named i. The declaration

```
Dim i As Integer
```

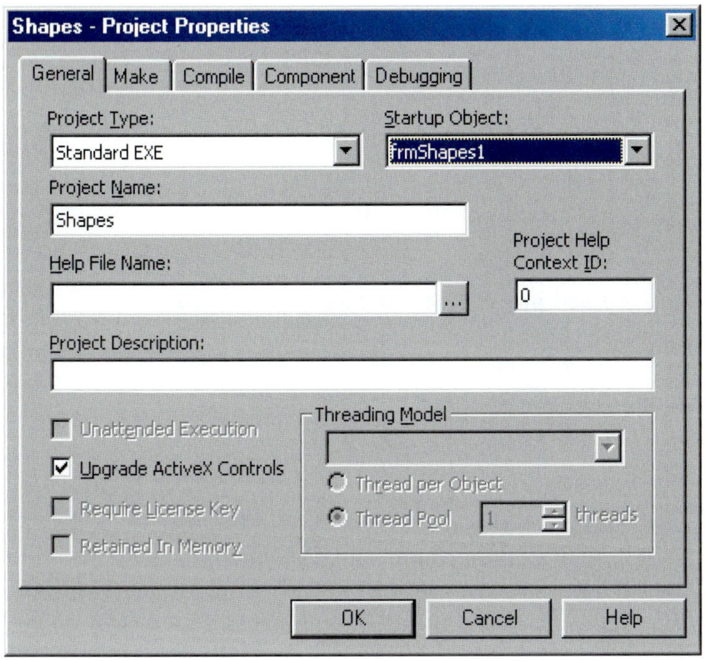

FIGURE 5.09 *Designating the Start Up Form*

should be typed in both the (declarations) portion of the (general) object of frmShapes1, and in the Sub txt_Change() procedure for frmShapes1. VB will not confuse the form-level variable i with the local variable i in Sub Form_Load.

Referring to the Hierarchy Table and pseudocode, you can see that the following procedures need to be written for the Shapes Project.

- under frmShapes1:
  - cmdExit_Click
  - cmdShape_Click
  - Form_Load
  - txtName_Change
- under frmShapes2:
  - cmdOk
  - Form_Load

Private Sub cmdExit_Click

This just ends the program with the single statement

```
End
```

Private Sub Form_Load (for frmShapes1)

Position the form in the top left corner of the screen. This code demonstrates that this positioning could be done at run time—of course, it would have been possible to set the top and left properties at design time. Use this code:

```
Me.Top = 0
Me.Left = 0
```

Private Sub txtName_Change

After declaring the procedure-level variable, a For/Next loop enables the four shape-named command buttons in the cmdShape control array:

```
Dim i As Integer
For i = 0 To 3
   cmdShape(i).Enabled = True
Next i
```

Private Sub cmdShape_Click (Index As Integer)

The form-level integer variable i keeps track of the number of times any button in the cmdShape control array is clicked. Therefore, the cmdShape_Click procedure increments i:

```
i = i + 1
```

We now need to assign the caption of frmShapes2's Label. It consists of the user's name (which the user typed into the TextBox), the literal " 's Design", plus the new value of i (converted to a string). When a procedure references a control on another form, the name of that form must be stated, followed by an exclamation point.

```
frmShapes2!lbl = txtName & "'s Design " & Str(i)
```

We need to assign the Shape property of the Shape control on frmShapes2. The Shape property has possible values of 0, 1, 2, and 3, corresponding (not coincidentally) to the Index values of the cmdShape array:

```
frmShapes2!shp.Shape = index
```

Rnd function

To obtain a randomly selected color each time a shape is selected, we will use Visual Basic's random number generator function, **Rnd.** This function, central to computer simulations and computer video games, will be discussed at greater length in Chapter 8, which deals with mathematical applications and functions. For now, we will only look at this one simple use of Rnd, a function which always returns a fraction <1. To get a randomly selected color with the QBColor function, we need only to generate a randomly selected number from 0 to 15, as follows:

```
frmShapes2!shp.FillColor = QBColor(Int(Rnd * 16))
```

The fraction returned by Rnd is multiplied by 16, giving a real number between 0.000000 and 15.999999. The Int (Integer) function converts this real number into an integer in the 0 to 15 range. The resultant integer is a valid argument for QBColor.

frmShapes2 is now ready to be displayed:

```
frmShapes2.Show
```

In sum, here is the whole procedure:

```
Private Sub cmdShape_Click (Index As Integer)
   i = i + 1
   frmShapes2!lbl = txtName & "'s Design " & Str(i)
```

```
    frmShapes2!shp.Shape = Index
    frmShapes2!shp.FillColor = QBColor(Int(Rnd * 16))
    frmShapes2.Show
End Sub
```

Private Sub Form_Load (for frmShapes2)—Locating the Form on the Screen

Notice that when you run the Shapes program, frmShapes2 appears smack dab in the middle of your screen. And it doesn't matter what computer you run it on; it always appears in the same place. But you may have experienced that this is not always true for the programs you wrote earlier. Depending on the configuration of your computer system at home, at work, and at school, you may have written Visual Basic programs that look great on the machine you used to develop them; but later when you run the program on a different computer, the form appears in a different place on the screen, perhaps even partially off the screen.

The problem is that the location of a form at run time is determined by the form's Top and Left properties, which are measured from the top and left sides of the screen; and the measurement scale is determined by the video card that drives the screen. For example, create a 6-inch-wide form whose left border is 6 inches from the left side of a 17-inch (diagonal) monitor; the right border will be right on the right edge of the screen (on a 17-inch monitor with normal aspect, the viewing area is just over a foot wide). But if you run this program on a computer with a 14-inch (diagonal) monitor, a good chunk of the form will be off the screen to the right.

The way to avoid this problem is to position your form on the screen based on the screen measurements themselves. You can use the width and height of the **Screen Object** for this purpose: The left edge of the form should be placed at (screen width – form width)/2; while the top edge of the form should be located at (screen height – form height)/2. So to position any form in the center of the screen, copy this Form_Load procedure:

```
Private Sub Form_Load()
    Me.Left = (Screen.Width - Me.Width) / 2
    Me.Top = (Screen.Height - Me.Height) / 2
End Sub
```

You could also position a form on the screen relative to the position or size of other forms in the same application. In the Shapes Project, for example, you might want to position frmShapes2 just to the right of frmShapes1. Because frmShapes1 appears at the far left side of the screen, the following statement would place frmShapes2 50 twips (a small fraction of an inch) to the right of frmShapes1:

```
Me.Left = frmShapes1.Width + 50
```

Private Sub cmdOk_Click ()

We use the Hide method to remove frmShapes2 from view but not from memory (out of sight but not out of mind).

```
Me.Hide
```

STEP 6. Test and Debug Your Program.

Have you made any mistakes in building Visual Basic projects so far? If not, you are a rare person indeed! Most of us, even highly experienced programmers, go through a number of false starts and illegal detours in building every program we write. Visual Basic has some internal features that can help.

Computer programs can contain three types of bugs (errors): syntax errors, runtime errors, and logic errors. In this section, we will address each type of programming error and suggest remedies.

In the early years of experimental computers, an electromechanical computer at Harvard University operated with a series of relay switches. On one occasion when the machine malfunctioned, detailed analysis traced the problem to a faulty relay switch at the bottom of the machine. Using a pair of tweezers, a technician removed a cockroach, which had been impaled between the pincers of the relay switch, preventing electrical contact. The log entry was made, "We removed a bug from the computer today!" From then on, any type of hardware or software error in a computer has been known as a bug, and the process of isolating and removing same has been known as debugging.

Syntax Errors

A **syntax error** is a violation of the rules of the programming language. The programmer might use a variable name that is the same as a VB reserved word or that has not been declared, use an expression or constant or literal where only a variable is permissible, make an error in spelling or punctuation, and so on. Syntax errors are the easiest type of errors to discover and correct. This is because VB recognizes them immediately, notifies the programmer, and often provides a helpful error message that explains what caused the problem.

A syntax error may occur in an individual VB statement, or it may occur in the context of the whole program.

If a syntax error occurs in a single statement, VB has a built-in syntax-checking feature that notifies you immediately that the line of code you just typed will not pass muster. This feature may be turned on or off (see Tools | Options | Editor tab | Auto Syntax Check). The syntax-checker built into the VB code editor can simplify your life by letting you know immediately that a line of code cannot be interpreted correctly by Visual Basic.

A syntax error may also occur in the context of a whole program, even though the individual statement may be correct. This is the case with the "Variable not defined" error message. When you type in a line of code and press the enter key, VB checks the line of code you just typed; it does not check the entire program to see if the statement syntax is acceptable in light of all the code in the program. A syntax error caused by the presence or absence of other code in the program will not be discovered until you attempt to run the program. At that time, you will know that you have a syntax error (rather than a runtime or logic error), because the Start icon will still be highlighted on the Toolbar, while the Break and End icons will still be disabled.

Start Break End

You may or may not have enough knowledge of the language to interpret a syntax error message properly; but if you do not understand why the syntax error occurred, you can always press F1 to get VB's immediate explanation, and you can use the Help System further to look up an example of the correct syntax.

Runtime Errors

A **runtime error** occurs when a syntactically correct VB statement asks VB to perform a task it is incapable of performing while the program is running. For example, in Project Two's Simple Calculator Project, a user could enter the number 111222333444 in anticipation of performing an addition operation. When the user clicks the "+" button, an "Overflow" runtime error occurs, because the number being converted from lblNum to mlOperand1 is too large to fit into a variable of type Long. (Try it to see what we mean.)

A runtime error can occur either in a program running within the Visual Basic design environment or in a program running independently as an executable file. The comments in this section pertain to runtime errors encountered while running a program from within the VB design environment.

When the runtime error occurs, Visual Basic suspends execution of the program, changes from [run] mode to [break] mode, and displays an error message.

If you do not understand the error message, press the F1 key (context-sensitive help) for an explanation. For example, start up a new project, put a command button on the form, and in the Command1_Click procedure insert this code:

```
Dim i
Print i/0
```

Run this program and click your command button. You will get an Overflow error (due in this case by an attempt to divide to zero). If you do not understand what Overflow means, press the F1 key (Figure 5.10).

Some runtime errors are so disastrous that they not only crash your program but also crash Visual Basic or even Windows itself. If you run a program that locks up the computer, causes a General Protection Fault in Visual Basic, or crashes Windows, and if you have not saved your project before this calamitous event, then you will lose all of your work since the last time you saved your project. To protect yourself against precisely this disaster, Visual Basic includes an option that saves your project before you run it, if there have been any changes made to the project since the last time you saved it. This option might very well save you a lot of grief the first time a runtime error crashes the system, but it does cost a few seconds to save before each attempted run. To activate this feature, from the VB Menu Bar choose Tools | Options | Environment tab | Save Changes (Figure 5.11).

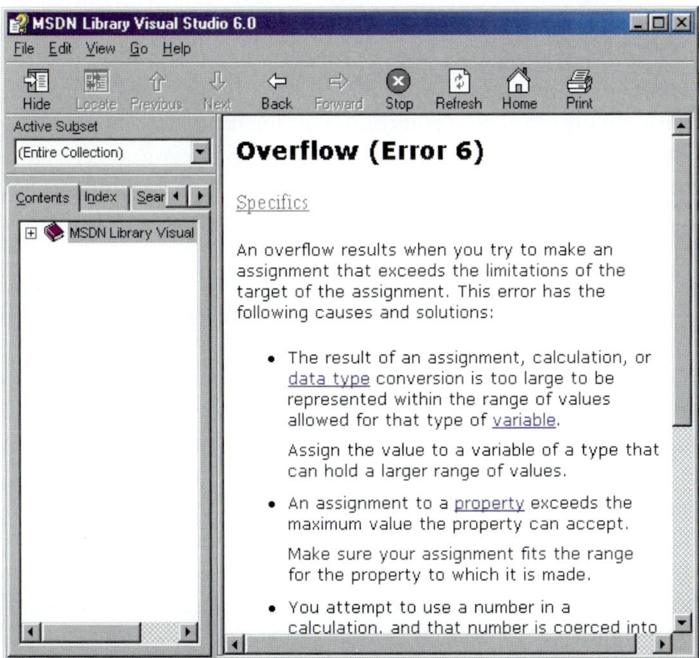

FIGURE 5.10 *Overflow help screen*

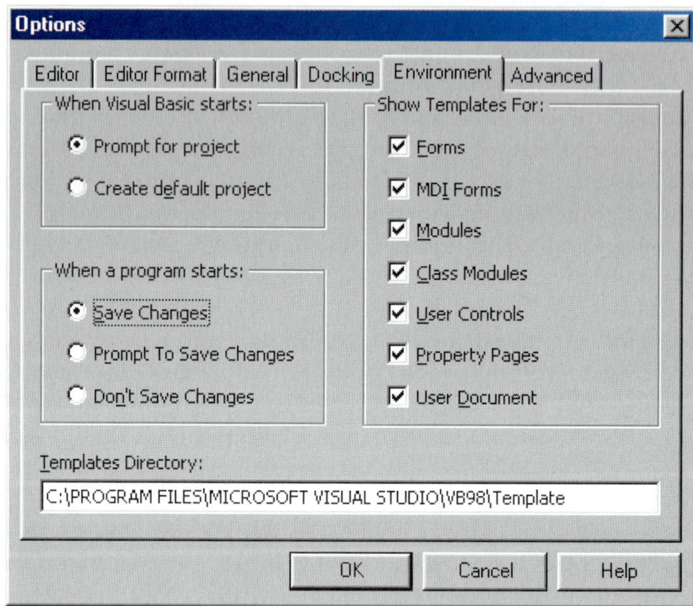

FIGURE 5.11 *Instructing VB to Save Changes before executing a program*

Logic Errors

Your program may be syntactically correct and cause no runtime errors, yet still produce incorrect results. A payroll program, for example, may include the statement

```
NetPay = GrossPay + Deductions
```

which raises nary an objection from Visual Basic but causes your company to go bankrupt.

Logic errors are by far the most difficult type of errors to discover and to ferret out of computer programs. This is partly due to the fact that it took you so much effort just to get the program to run without blowing up, that when it does run with apparent success you think you must be done. Also, the computer discovers syntax errors and runtime errors and gives you at least a hint as to their cause. Logic errors, by contrast, can only be discovered by painstaking human effort; and even then, neither their existence nor their solutions may be obvious.

When the program seems to be producing correct results, you can improve the chances that this is indeed the case by deskchecking your logic and by manually calculating sample data sets.

To deskcheck your logic, you become the computer. Write down an example of the data that your program is supposed to process, and then follow your program's logic step by step, as if you were carrying out your program's instructions. You may discover that certain steps do not make any sense.

To check the program logic using sample data sets, first construct various data samples, including typical data as well as data at the extremes of anticipated real data. For example, in a weekly payroll program, include hourly employees who worked 0, 1, 30, 40, 50, and 80 hours in the week. Then calculate the correct results both by hand and by your computer program. Finally, compare the manual with the computer-generated results. Any discrepancies represent manual calculation errors or logic errors in your program.

Debug Facility

VB provides a complete **Debug facility** to help you find and fix both runtime and logic errors. Debug lets you interrupt processing (to enter [break] mode) whenever and wherever you wish. While in [break] mode, Debug lets you view and change the values of variables and the properties of objects. From [break] mode, you can allow your program to continue to execute one statement or one procedure at a time.

To break into a program while it is running, click the Break icon, press the Ctrl-Break keys, or select Run | Break. Once in [break] mode, all other Debug facilities are available.

You can cause a program to go into [break] mode by designating a **breakpoint** at any executable VB statement, that is, any statement other than a declaration. In [design] or [break] mode, put the cursor on a line of code, and then select Debug | Toggle Breakpoint or click the **Toggle Breakpoint** icon or press the F9 function key. [Note: If you do not see the Toggle Breakpoint icon on a toolbar, then the Debug Toolbar is probably not visible. Right mouse-click any toolbar or the menu bar, and select Debug to make the Debug Toolbar visible.]

Subsequently, when this line of code is about to be executed, program execution will be suspended (Figure 5.12). (If this line of code was already a breakpoint, then this selection will clear this breakpoint. To get rid of all existing breakpoints, select Debug | Clear All Breakpoints.) Breakpoint lines appear in a different color than other lines of code in the program. For example, we set a breakpoint in the Shapes Project, with the results shown in Figure 5.12.

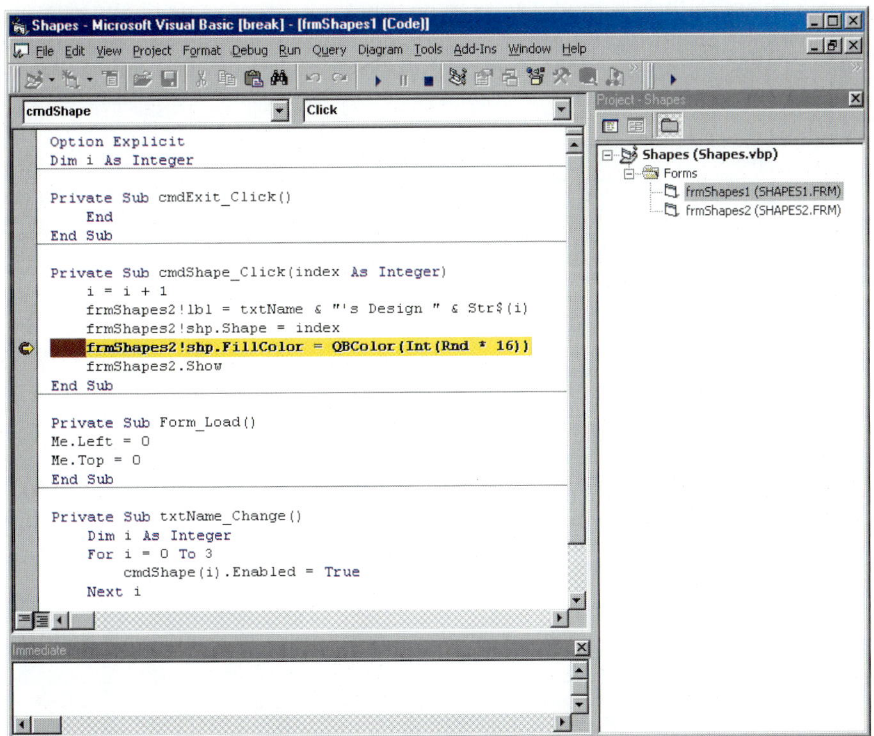

FIGURE 5.12 *Program in Break mode, having encountered a breakpoint*

Occasionally, you may desire to force a runtime error to occur in a program. Insert the statement

```
Err.Raise errornumber
```

in the program. Err is a Visual Basic object, whose Raise method forces an error when this statement is executed, and pressing the F1 key will display an explanation as to what error errornumber refers to (Figure 5.13).

In many cases, the suspected source of a program bug is the value of a particular variable or expression. You can monitor this variable or expression in two ways:

1. Since the Immediate Window is a VB object with a Print method, you can include the statement

```
Debug.Print expression
```

anywhere in your code. When this statement is executed, the value of expression is displayed in the Immediate Window. Figure 5.14 is an example in the cmdShape_Click procedure.

2. Add a **Watch** Expression (Figures 5.15 and 5.16) (or Edit an existing Watch Expression). This feature allows you to designate an expression whose value will appear in a Watches window whenever [break] mode is entered. You can also force a breakpoint with this feature by designating Break When Expression Is True or Break When Expression Has Changed. For example, you could select the expression frmShapes2!shp.Shape in the cmdShape_Click procedure, then select Debug | Add Watch. The selected expression will appear in the **Add Watch** Dialog Box. Click on the option to Break when Expression has Changed, and then click OK.

While you are in [break] mode, you can display the current value of any variable, expression, or property. Just select the item you wish to view in a Code Window

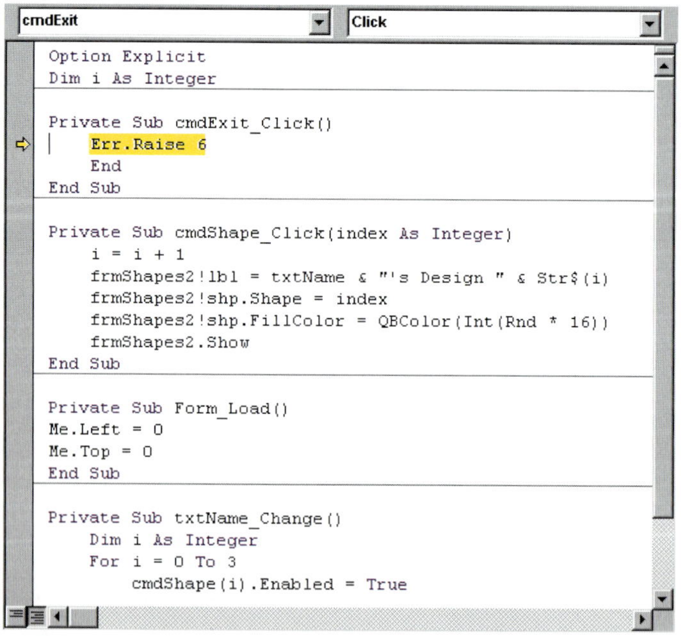

```
cmdExit                                   Click

Option Explicit
Dim i As Integer

Private Sub cmdExit_Click()
    Err.Raise 6
    End
End Sub

Private Sub cmdShape_Click(index As Integer)
    i = i + 1
    frmShapes2!lbl = txtName & "'s Design " & Str$(i)
    frmShapes2!shp.Shape = index
    frmShapes2!shp.FillColor = QBColor(Int(Rnd * 16))
    frmShapes2.Show
End Sub

Private Sub Form_Load()
Me.Left = 0
Me.Top = 0
End Sub

Private Sub txtName_Change()
    Dim i As Integer
    For i = 0 To 3
        cmdShape(i).Enabled = True
```

FIGURE 5.13 *Intentionally forcing error number 6*

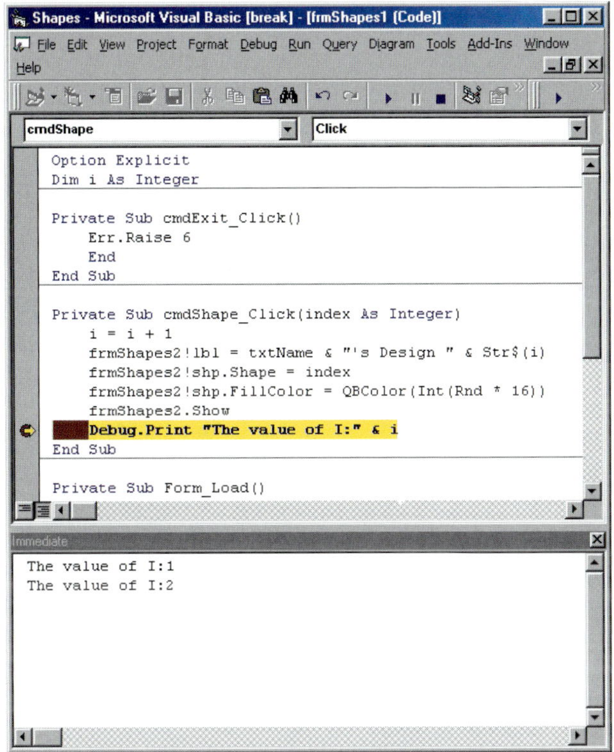

FIGURE 5.14 *Invoking the Debug object's Print method*

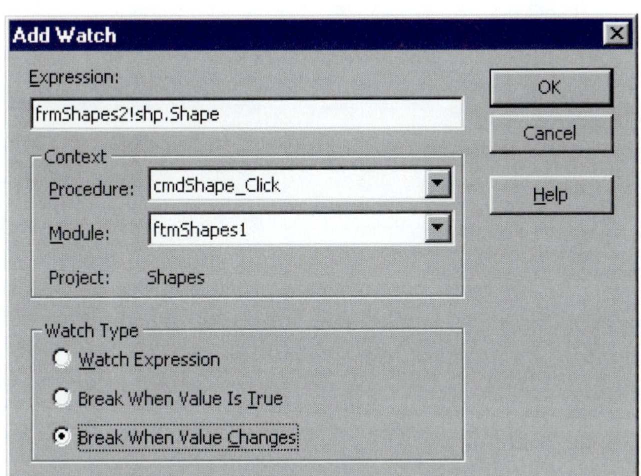

FIGURE 5.15 *Add Watch dialog box*

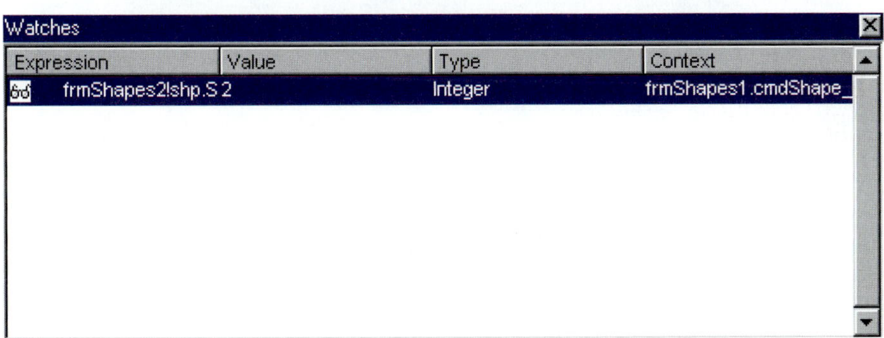

FIGURE 5.16 *The Watch window in break mode*

and then click on Debug | Quick Watch or click the Quick Watch icon or press the Shift-F9 keys.

Of course, the expression you select for Quick Watch must be in existence at the time the program was suspended. In the following examples, the variable index was selected for Quick Watch in Sub cmdShape_Click. In the first instance (Figure 5.17), the Rectangle command button was clicked, frmShapes2 displayed a blue rectangle, and then the program was suspended by clicking the break mode icon

Index was selected in the Code Window, and then the **Quick Watch** icon was clicked.

You can see the result: The variable index was "Not in context" at the time of program suspension. That is, Sub cmdShape_Click had finished processing, and so index went out of existence. In the second instance (Figure 5.18), a breakpoint was set on the first statement inside Sub cmdShape_Click. Again, index was selected for Quick Watch. This time, the value of index was displayed.

A property or variable can also be changed while in break mode, and a method can be executed as well. In Figure 5.19, the Shapes Project began executing, and then was suspended by clicking the break icon before doing anything else. In the

FIGURE 5.17 *Quick Watch—expression Index out of context*

FIGURE 5.18 *Quick Watch—expression Index in context*

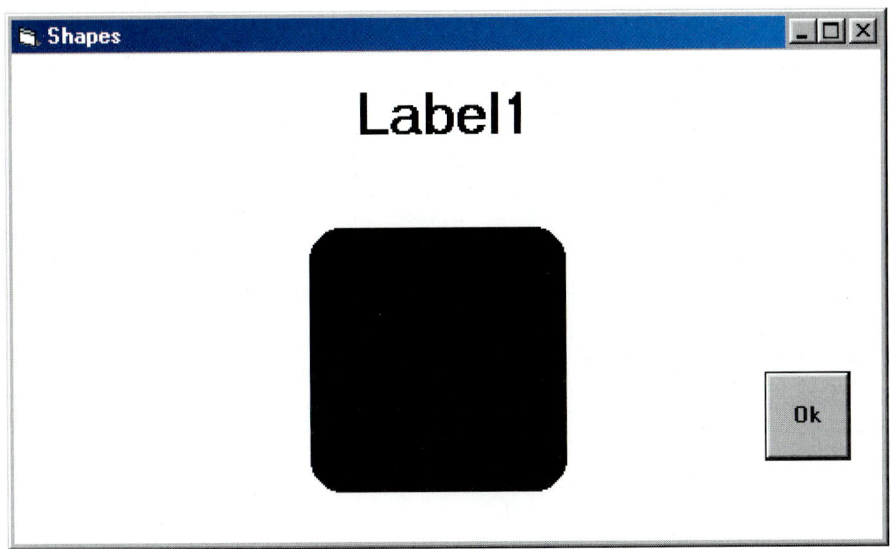

FIGURE 5.19 *Shape property assigned during break time*

Immediate Window, the Shape property of the shp control was set to 5 (a rounded square), and then the Show method was used to show frmShapes2.

From break mode, a suspended program can be continued or restarted, or you can choose to execute program statements one statement or one procedure at a time.

- To continue processing, choose Run | Continue, or click the Continue icon, or press the F5 key.

- To restart the project from the beginning, choose Run | Restart or press the Shift-F5 keys.
- To execute just the very next statement, choose Debug | Step Into, or click the Step Into icon, or press the F8 key.

- To execute the next statement, but to execute an entire procedure in the event that the next statement calls a procedure, choose Debug | Step Over, or click the Step Over icon, or press the Shift-F8 keys.

- To resume execution of the statements in a procedure up to the position of the cursor, choose Debug | Step To Cursor.
- To display the next statement to be executed, choose Debug | Show Next Statement.
- To change which statement within the current procedure will be executed next, choose Debug | Set Next Statement.

Summary of Menu Selections, Toolbar Icons, and Shortcut Keys

We have mentioned most of these menu selections and several of these icons and shortcut keys before, others here for the first time. You may want to begin using them regularly, as they help you navigate quickly through your forms, properties, and code.

While some of these are related to initial program development, many of them are especially helpful while you are testing and debugging your program. This is not an exhaustive list, but rather a list of those items that the authors find most useful.

ICON	SHORTCUT	MENU BAR EQUIVALENT	EXPLANATION
	Ctrl-N	File | New Project	starts a new project
	Ctrl-O	File | Open Project	opens an existing project
		File | Save Project	saves the current project
	Ctrl-S	File | Save Form	saves the current form
		File | Save Form As	saves the current form under a new name
	Ctrl-P	File | Print	prints form images text, or code
	Ctrl-X or Shift-Delete	Edit | Cut	copies the currently selected text or object to the Clipboard and deletes that text or object from its current location
	Ctrl-C or Ctrl-Insert	Edit | Copy	copies the currently selected text or object to the Clipboard
	Ctrl-V or Shift-Insert	Edit | Paste	pastes the Clipboard contents into the currently selected object or text location
	Delete	Edit | Delete	deletes the currently selected text or object
	Ctrl-F	Edit | Find	finds the next occurrence of text in your code
	Ctrl-H	Edit | Replace	finds and replaces text in your code
	F7	View | Code	displays the Code Window for the currently selected form
	Shift-F7	View | Form	displays the Form Window for the currently selected form
	F2	View | Object Browser	displays project components; for a selected form, displays all properties, methods, and procedures; for a selected procedure, switches to the Code Window
	Ctrl-G	View | Immediate Window	displays the Debug Window
	Ctrl-R	View | Project Explorer	displays the Project Explorer Window
	F4	View | Properties	displays the Properties Window for the currently selected object

continued

ICON	SHORTCUT	MENU BAR EQUIVALENT	EXPLANATION
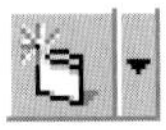		Project | Add Form	adds a new form to your project
		Format | Lock Controls	freezes/unfreezes all controls on a form in their current location (to prevent accidental repositioning)
	F8	Debug | Step Into	executes one statement
	Shift-F8	Debug | Step Over	executes one statement; but if that statement is a procedure call, it executes the entire procedure
	Ctrl-F8	Debug | Run to Cursor	executes from the current statement up to the cursor position
		Debug | Add Watch	adds a watch expression
	Ctrl-W	Debug | Edit Watch	displays all watch expressions for editing
	Shift-F9	Debug | Quick Watch	displays the value of the currently selected expression
	F9	Debug | Toggle Breakpoint	inserts or removes a breakpoint at the current code line
	Ctrl-Shift-F9	Debug | Clear All Breakpoints	removes all breakpoints
	Ctrl-F9	Debug | Set Next Statement	specifies the next statement to be executed
		Debug | Show Next Statement	identifies the next statement to be executed
	F5	Run | Start or Run | Continue	runs the current program, or continues running after a program was suspended
	Ctrl-Break	Run | Break	suspends a running program
		Run | End	ends the current program
	Shift-F5	Run | Restart	restarts the current program after it was suspended
	Ctrl-E	Tools | Menu Editor	Opens the Menu Editor
		Tools | Options	provides Environment, Project, Editor, and Advanced option tabs
	F1		context-sensitive help

STEP 7. Complete the Program Documentation.

Insert the program identification and descriptive remarks in the (declarations) portion of the (general) object of the Start Up Form, frmShapes1:

```
'Project Name:          MYSHAPES.VBP
'Forms/modules:         frmSHAPES1.FRM
                        frmSHAPES2.FRM
'Written by:            <insert your name>
'Original date:         <insert today's date>
['Revision date:        <insert revision date,   if any>]
'Adapted from Spear & Spear
'Purpose:               This program demonstrates
'                       a multiform project, TextBox
'                       control, and Shape control
```

A VARIATION ON SHAPES

We could make the Shapes program operate on its own, without the necessity of the user clicking on the command buttons. Try running this variation, named AUTOSHAPES.EXE. As you can see, as soon as you begin typing your name into the text box, the program takes over and begins displaying frmShapes2, rotating through the four shapes. You can also watch the focus move from one command button to the next on frmShapes1.

This effect is accomplished through a **Timer control** placed on frmShapes1. You will find that a Timer control is useful for creating all kinds of visual effects.

Timer Control

In the Toolbox, the Timer control's icon looks like a clock:

When enabled, a Timer control fires its **Timer event** at an interval (measured in milliseconds) set by the programmer. For example, if you want the message "Hello, World" to be printed to a form once every second, then

- put a Timer control on the form—it doesn't matter where you put it, because the Timer control is invisible at run time;
- set its Interval property to 1000 (milliseconds); and
- in Sub Timer1_Timer, insert the statement

```
Print "Hello, World"
```

In the sample program TIMER.EXE (Figure 5.20), we included a module-level variable (mintSeconds) to keep track of the number of times the timer event has fired. We set the Timer control's **Interval property** to 1000. Since the Interval is 1000, this variable equals the number of seconds the program has been running for the first five seconds of execution. When this module-level variable reaches a value of 5, the Timer control is disabled. (The Timer1_Timer event procedure will not fire if the Enabled property is False or if the Interval property is 0.) Here is the key procedure:

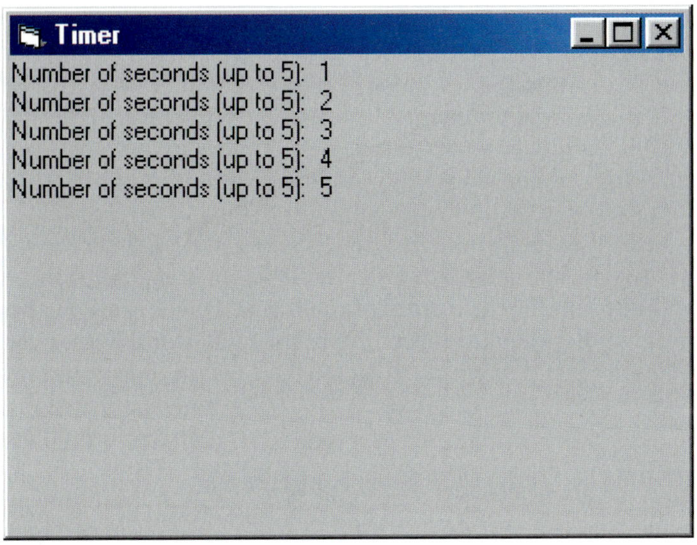

Timer

Number of seconds (up to 5): 1
Number of seconds (up to 5): 2
Number of seconds (up to 5): 3
Number of seconds (up to 5): 4
Number of seconds (up to 5): 5

FIGURE 5.20 *Timer.exe, executing*

```
Private Sub Timer1_Timer
    mintSeconds = mintSeconds + 1
    Print "Number of seconds (up to 5): "; mintSeconds
    If mintSeconds = 5 Then Timer1.Enabled = False
End Sub
```

To accomplish the desired effect in the AutoShapes program, we placed a Timer control on frmShapes1, initially disabled, and set its Interval property to 1000 milliseconds (that is, 1 second). We also inserted a module-level Integer variable called mintShapeCounter. When the Timer event fires, it increments mintShapeCounter, then sets mintShapeCounter back to 0 when it reaches 4. Then the Timer event procedure calls cmdShape_Click(mintShapeCounter), which executes that procedure just as if the user had clicked one of the cmdShape command buttons directly.

Try this code yourself, modifying the Shapes project you created while studying this chapter. Follow these three easy steps:

1. Place a Timer control anywhere on frmShapes1.
2. In the General object of frmShapes1, declare:

```
Dim mintShapeCounter As Integer
```

3. Then insert this code for the Timer event:

```
Private Sub Timer1_Timer()
    mintShapeCounter = mintShapeCounter + 1
    If mintShapeCounter = 4 Then mintShapeCounter = 0
    Call cmdShape(mintShapeCounter)
End Sub
```

SUMMARY

Visual Basic's **Debug facility** is most useful in testing your program and in isolating and fixing program bugs. Debug lets you **step** through your program one step at a time, **watch** (monitor) key variables or expressions during execution, and assign new values to variables during break time.

Programs can contain three kinds of errors: A **syntax error** is a violation of the grammar rules of the programming language. A **runtime error** occurs when the syntactically correct program directs the computer to do something it cannot possibly do. A **logic error** violates no computer rules; it just produces the wrong results.

All of Visual Basic's objects are measured in a scale called **twips.** From the Visual Basic design environment, a programmer can add multiple forms to a project and can put colorful **Shape controls** on forms. By accessing the **Screen object,** the programmer can position a form in the middle of the screen at runtime. With the **Timer** control, events can be timed to occur automatically.

PROGRAMMING ASSIGNMENTS

Busy Box

a. Design a Really Nice "Busy Box" Form—something with colors and shapes that would excite a small child. Include on this form a control array of eight shapes, each in a different combination of BackColor, **BorderColor, BorderWidth,** FillColor, FillStyle, and Shape. Set the **BackStyle** to Opaque. Use the Help system to look up and experiment with any of the properties that you do not understand. Hint: If BackColor is yellow while FillColor is red and FillStyle is horizontal lines, then the inside area of the shape will appear as horizontal red lines over a yellow background.

b. Whenever the form is clicked (program the Form_Click event procedure), change all of the following properties for every one of the eight shape controls: Top, Left, Height, Width, BackColor, BorderColor, BorderWidth, FillColor, FillStyle, and Shape. This is accomplished simply with a For/Next loop and a series of assignment statements, incrementing or resetting or randomly selecting each property value. For example, the Shape Property can have six legitimate values, ranging from 0 to 5. The following code will randomly select a shape for a Shape control named shp, and it will move this control across the form from left to right until it almost leaves the form, when it starts over on the left:

```
shp(i).Shape = Int(Rnd * 6)
shp(i).Left = shp(i).Left + 500
If shp(i).Left > Me.Width Then shp(i).Left = 0
```

c. When you are satisfied with the look and operation of this rather static busy box, automate it by putting a Timer control on the form, and set the Interval to 500 ms. In the Timer event, call the Form_Click event.

d. Add your "Hello, World" form (from Chapter Two) to this project. Make the "Hello, World" form the Start Up Form. Add a command button on the "Hello, World" form, which will Show the "Busy Box" form. Add a command button on the "Busy Box" form to hide it.

e. Also randomly select the background color for the BusyBox form each time the Timer event fires.

Layout

Use Line controls to draw the complete layout of the main floor of your house or apartment. Include walls, windows, and doors. Put a Command Button in the living room with the caption "Living Room—click for details." Add an exit button to end the program.

Draw an additional form for the living room. Use Shape controls and Line controls to display the details and the furniture in this room. Use the color properties of the form and the Shape controls to display the actual color scheme. Include a Command Button with the caption "Return"; when this button is clicked, hide this form.

At run time, the user initially sees only the overall layout. When the user clicks the Living Room Command Button, that room's detail design form should be displayed.

Use your imagination to spice up the visual effects. If it looks really cool, email it to us—maybe we can win a prize!

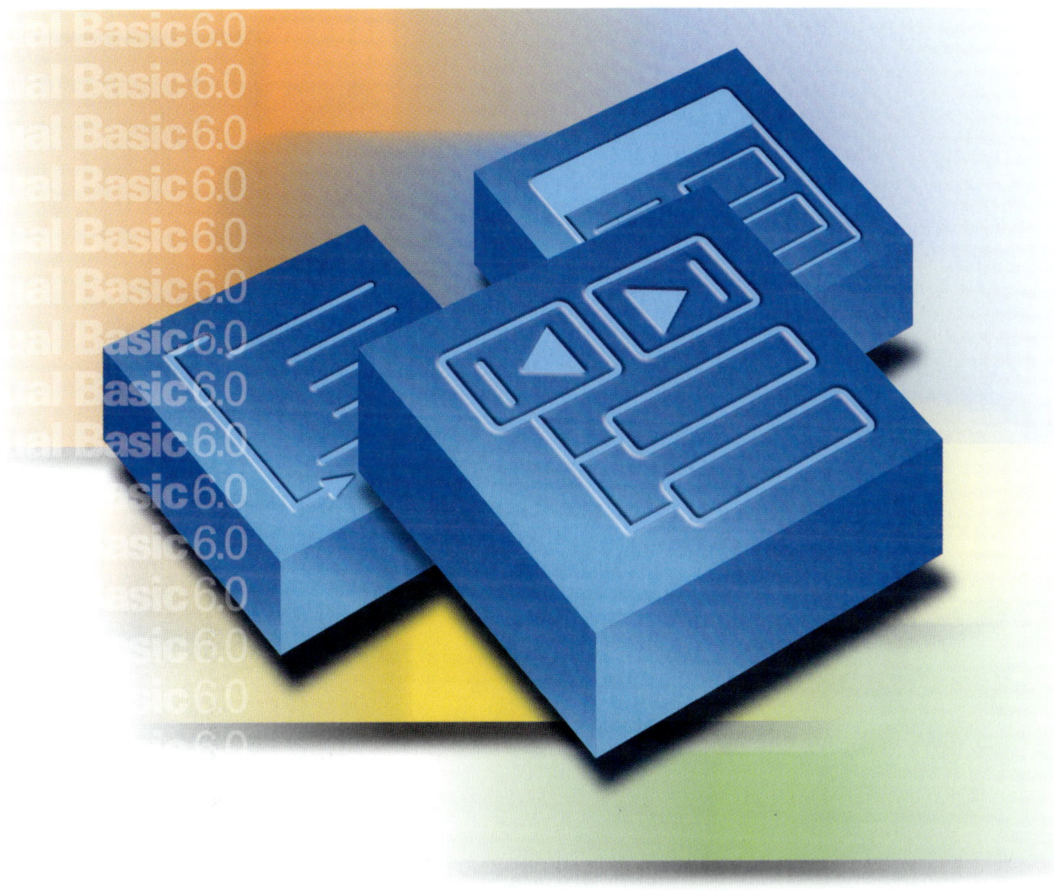

PART THREE

PROGRAMMING THE FRONT-END: THE GRAPHICAL USER INTERFACE

CHAPTER SIX

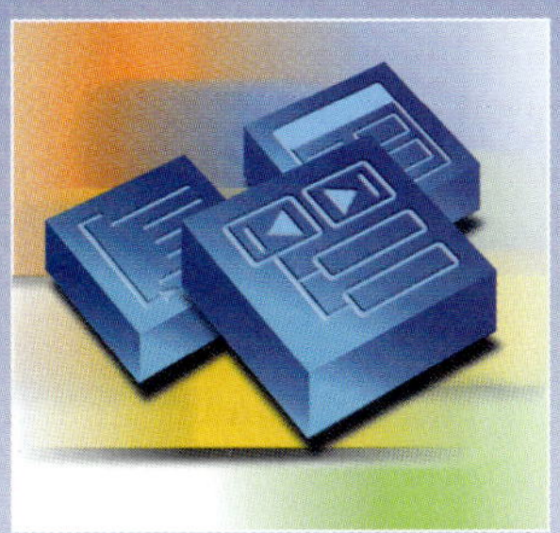

DO LOOPS, FUNCTIONS, ARRAYS OF VARIABLES

Application: Finance (Version 1)

LEARNING OBJECTIVES

Upon completion of Chapter Six, the student will be able to

- Implement Do loops.
- Use the Frame control.
- Use Option Buttons.
- Learn about symbolic constants and the Object Browser.
- Use the Format function.
- Declare and manipulate variable arrays.
- Define and use Boolean variables.
- Build financial functions into an application.

Keywords

DDB function	InputBox function	SLN function
Do/Loop statement	Mod operator	SYD function
Format function	MultiLine property	Until conditional
Frame control (prefix: fra)	Option Button control (prefix: opt)	While conditional
FV function	Pmt function	

INTRODUCING THE FINANCE PROJECT

The Finance Project entails a bit of complexity, and therefore it will be introduced to you in stages through Chapters Six, Seven, and Nine. Building this program in stages will let you begin to assemble all of the Visual Basic skills that you have learned so far.

Visually, the first version of the Finance Project has just two new controls (Frames and Option Buttons) and a new TextBox property (MultiLine). Most of the new material in this chapter relates to the VB code: variable arrays, another looping construct (the Do Loop), the Mod operator (for modulo arithmetic), a dialog box for soliciting user input (the InputBox function), the notion of Boolean values and variables, and the use of several of VB's built-in financial functions.

Run FINANCE1.EXE (Figures 6.01 through 6.05) and experiment with it. The financial concepts underlying loan payments, future value, and depreciation may not be fresh in your memory, so we will review them for you here. Obviously, you do not need to be a finance major to learn Visual Basic programming; but since we are using a financial motif for this project, it will help in writing this project if you do understand those concepts.

The first command button, Loan Payment, calculates the amount of a fixed monthly payment on a loan. The user is prompted to provide the amount of the loan, the interest rate, and the number of monthly payments. With these data, VB's Pmt function calculates the amount of each month's payment. The user inputs and the payment amount are displayed in the TextBox.

The second command button, Future Value, calculates the future value of a fixed monthly investment, such as a payroll deduction savings plan. The user is

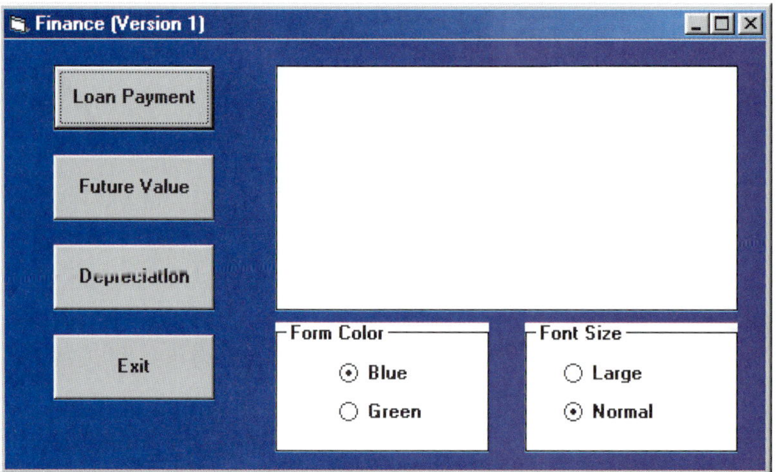

FIGURE 6.01 *Finance.exe—opening screen*

FIGURE 6.02 *InputBox dialog box*

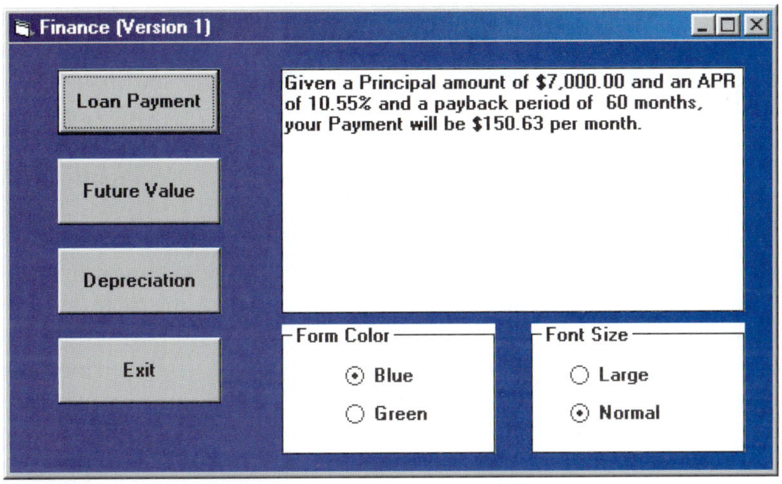

Finance (Version 1)

Loan Payment

Future Value

Depreciation

Exit

Given a Principal amount of $7,000.00 and an APR of 10.55% and a payback period of 60 months, your Payment will be $150.63 per month.

Form Color: Blue (selected), Green

Font Size: Large, Normal (selected)

FIGURE 6.03 *Results from Loan Payment calculation*

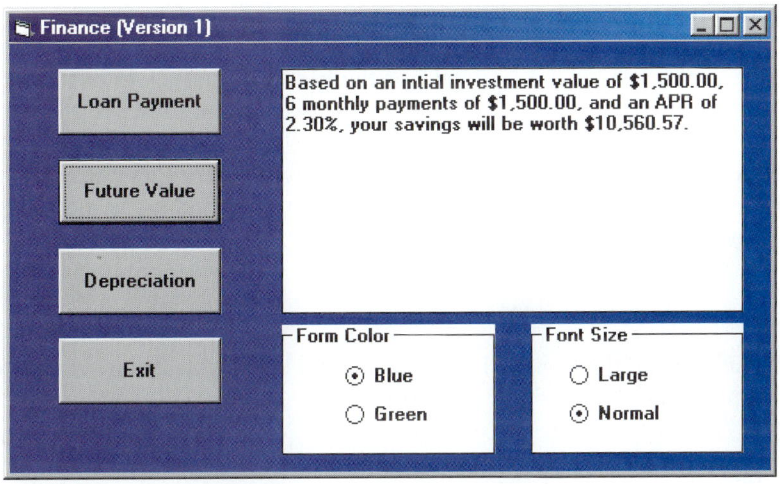

Finance (Version 1)

Loan Payment

Future Value

Depreciation

Exit

Based on an intial investment value of $1,500.00, 6 monthly payments of $1,500.00, and an APR of 2.30%, your savings will be worth $10,560.57.

Form Color: Blue (selected), Green

Font Size: Large, Normal (selected)

FIGURE 6.04 *Results from Future Value calculation*

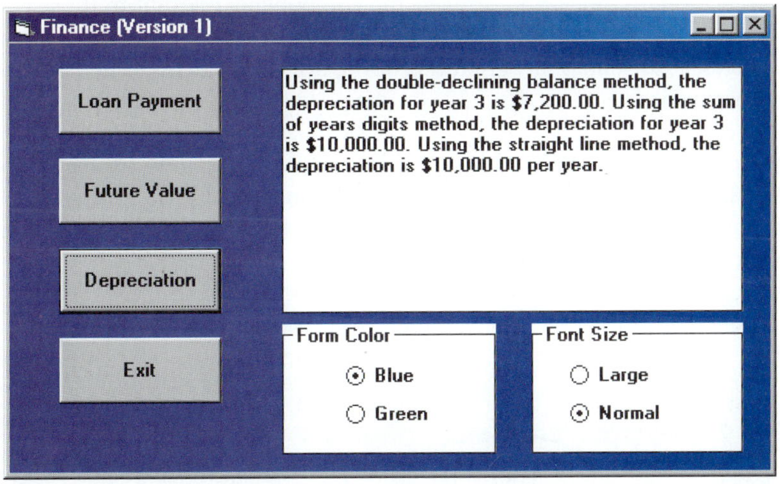

Finance (Version 1)

Loan Payment

Future Value

Depreciation

Exit

Using the double-declining balance method, the depreciation for year 3 is $7,200.00. Using the sum of years digits method, the depreciation for year 3 is $10,000.00. Using the straight line method, the depreciation is $10,000.00 per year.

Form Color: Blue (selected), Green

Font Size: Large, Normal (selected)

FIGURE 6.05 *Results from Depreciation calculation*

prompted to provide the amount of each monthly investment, the interest rate that the investment will earn, the number of months investments will be made, the current value of the investment (the initial investment or starting point), and a determination as to whether investments are made at the beginning or at the end of each investment period. With all of these user inputs as arguments, VB's FV function calculates the future value of the investment. The user inputs and the future value are displayed in the TextBox.

The third command button, Depreciation, calculates depreciation according to the three most common depreciation schedules: the double-declining balance method, the sum of years' digits method, and the straight line method. The user is prompted to provide the initial cost of the depreciable asset, its salvage value at the end of its useful life, the months of useful life, and the year for which depreciation is to be calculated. Using these inputs, VB's DDB function calculates the depreciation for the requested year according to the double-declining balance method; and VB's SYD function calculates the depreciation for the same year according to the sum of years' digits method. Straight line depreciation, which, as its name implies, is the same for each year, is calculated by VB's SLN function. The user inputs and the results from all three function calls are displayed in the TextBox.

The Finance form includes two Frames, titled Form Color and Font Size. The default selections for the Option Buttons inside these Frames are Blue (for the Form Color frame) and Normal (for the Font Size frame). While Finance is running, the user may toggle back and forth between Blue and Green Form Colors, and between Large and Normal Font Sizes.

When the user selects the Exit command button, the program displays in the TextBox the number of times each financial function was chosen, and concludes with an ending message.

STEP 1. Understand the Problem.

After you have run the Finance1 program several times, you should be able to see that the program performs four principal tasks:

1. Calculates a loan payment amount and displays the relevant components in that calculation;
2. Calculates the future value of an investment and displays the relevant components in that calculation;
3. Calculates depreciation of an asset for a given year according to three different depreciation methods, and displays the components relevant to those calculations; and
4. Displays, at the end of program execution, how many times each financial task was performed.

The first three tasks are complete unto themselves. That is, each time the task is performed, no impact on a subsequent performance of that task occurs. The fourth task, however, requires knowledge of previous tasks, namely, how many times each of those tasks was performed.

The project also includes two ancillary functions: The user may select a form background color of either blue or green, and the user may decide to display the TextBox in the default font size or in a larger font size.

STEP 2. Design a Solution.

Try drawing the graphical user interface for this application directly on the screen, without first drawing it by hand on a sheet of paper. Place four command buttons positioned vertically down the left-hand side, a large TextBox in the upper right center, and two rectangles representing frames along the bottom center-right. Place the option buttons inside the frames. Use the suggested captions for all of the objects.

Many Visual Basic programmers become quite adept at drawing GUIs directly on the screen rather than using paper first, and you too may find that this approach suits you. Even if you make mistakes in your early on-screen "sketches," the graphics-drawing software is so quick and user-friendly that you won't mind drawing the same form several times over in order to get it right, whether to satisfy yourself or someone else (instructor or customer).

Array of Simple Variables

To keep track of the number of times each financial function is performed, we will use an array of integers called "maintCountClicks" (the prefix maint will be explained as we go along). When the loan, future value, or depreciation command button is clicked, the corresponding element of the integer array will be incremented. When the Exit button is clicked, the program will display the number of times each financial function was clicked.

At the form level, the dimension (Dim) statement is used to declare an array of variables, just as Dim is used to declare any variable. The maximum element number in the array is placed in parentheses after the array name. The prefix "a" indicates that this is an array. The "a" follows the "m," indicating a form-level variable. For example,

```
Dim mastrFamilyName(10) As String
```

declares a module level array of strings called mastrFamilyName. As is customary in Visual Basic, the first element is numbered 0. Therefore, this declaration actually reserves storage space for an array of 11 strings: mastrFamilyName(0), mastrFamilyName(1), mastrFamilyName(2), . . . , mastrFamilyName(10).

You will recall that, when referring to a particular element of an array of controls, the number in parentheses following the common control name is called an index; for an array of variables in VB, the term subscript is generally employed rather than index, but they mean exactly the same thing. Back in the Colorful Backdrop project, if the user clicked on the command button captioned "2," then the index value 2 was passed to the click event procedure, and cmdColor(Index) referred to cmdColor(2). Similarly, if the subscript value is 2, then mastrFamilyName(2) refers to element number 2 within the mastrFamilyName array.

An array may be created from any variable type. As with simple variables, the data type may be indicated by an As VarType clause (the preferred method) or by a type declaration character (a less accepted method), or the data type may be omitted (not a recommended practice at all). For example,

```
Dim x(5) As Integer
Dim x%(5)
Dim x(5)
```

all declare an array named x whose maximum subscript = 5. The first two Dim statements declare an Integer array, while the third declares an array of type Variant.

In this text, we will continue to follow Microsoft's naming convention, so that the above declaration, if x represented some kind of counter, would be

```
Dim maintX(5) As Integer 'module level array of integers
```

When declaring an array of variables, the range of subscripts may be stated explicitly. For example,

```
Dim maintAmericanYear(1776 To 2000) As Integer
Dim mastrDayOfWeek(1 To 7) As String
```

When the (lower To upper) option is used in an array declaration, the range of subscripts may include negative numbers. A module-level array of long integers intended to hold the population of Rome for each year from its founding in 753 BC until the fall of the Byzantine Roman Empire in 1453 AD could be declared like this:

```
Dim malngRomanYear(-753 To 1453) As Long
```

The Dim statement may also be used to declare an array at the procedure level:

```
Dim aintNumberOfStudents(1 To 4) As Integer
'1=frsh,2=soph,3=jr,4=sr
```

At the procedure level, the size of an array may be dynamic, that is, dependent on the value of a variable, in which case the ReDim statement is used to declare it:

```
Private Sub ProcedureLevel
    Dim i as Integer
    i = 5
    ReDim asngLastSample(i) As Single
```

As indicated above, in version 1 of the Finance application we will use a module-level array of integers to keep track of the number of times each command button has been clicked. In the General object, the declaration is

```
Dim maintCountClicks(0 To 2) As Integer
```

Frames and Option Buttons

Each group of two **Option Buttons** is placed within a Frame. The action associated with each Option Button is implemented with a single Visual Basic statement, assigning a new value to a property.

A **Frame Control** serves primarily as a container for other controls. In this case, each Frame contains two Option Buttons. Only one Option Button within a given group of Option Buttons may be True (selected) at any one time. Hence, if the programmer wants the user to be able to make two selections concurrently—such as form color and font size—then each group of Option Buttons must exist in its own container. Of the Visual Basic objects introduced to you so far, both a form and a frame can serve as a container. Therefore, it would be possible to have only one Frame with two Option Buttons inside it, and then two more Option Buttons placed directly on the form itself. Each pair of Option Buttons would be in a separate container. But this design would not look right. The preferred design technique when the user is being given essentially parallel kinds of choices is to place all of them in parallel structures; hence we have used two Frames.

At run time, the user can click an unselected Option Button, which makes that Option Button's Value property True (–1) and also triggers that Option Button's click event. Alternatively, when the focus is on an Option Button, the user can use the arrow keys to select a different option, again triggering the newly selected Option Button's click event.

STEP 3. Develop an Algorithm.

Hierarchy Table

The Hierarchy Table for the Finance Project (Figure 6.06) is straightforward, and the pseudocode is in Figure 6.07. The only form-level variable is the integer array maintCountClicks(0 to 2). Under the form are nine event procedures: Form_Load, the four command buttons, and the four Option Buttons.

```
HIERARCHY TABLE-FINANCE (VERSION 1)

Project:    Finance1 (Finance1.vbp)
Form:       frmFinance (frmFinance1.frm)
            Form variable:
              Dim maintCountClicks(0 To 2) As Integer—integer array to track the number of
                  times each financial function is selected
            Event procedures:
              cmdExit_Click
              Form_Load
              cmdLoan_Click
              cmdFuture Value_Click
              cmdDepreciation_Click
              optBlue_Click and optGreen_Click
              optLarge_Click and optNormal_Click
```

FIGURE 6.06 *Hierarchy Table—Finance (Version 1)*

```
PSEUDOCODE-FINANCE (VERSION 1)

Event procedure: Sub Form_Load
   Position the form in the exact middle of the screen
   Set the form's BackColor to blue

Event procedure: Sub optblue_Click and Sub optGreen_Click
   Set the form's BackColor to blue or green, respectively

Event procedure: Sub optLarge_Click and Sub optNormal_Click
   Add 2 to (or subtract 2 from) txtResult's Font.Size

Event procedure: cmdLoan_Click
   Increment maintCountClicks(0)
   Using InputBoxes, get from the user the following information about a loan: principal,
         annual percentage rate (APR), and duration of loan. [Note: adjust the decimal place
         on APR, in case the user enters ten percent as 10 rather than as .1]
   Use the Pmt function to calculate the monthly payment, like this:
         curPayment = Pmt(sngAPR/12, intTotPmts, -curPrincipal, 0,0)
         [Note that the principal is entered as a negative value]
   Display the loan details and monthly payment in txtResult

Event procedure: cmdFuture Value_Click
   Increment maintCountClicks(1)
   Using InputBoxes, get from the user the following information about an annuity type
         investment: amount of monthly investment, annual percentage rate, duration of
         investment, beginning value of the investment, and an indication of whether the
         monthly payment is made at the beginning or end of the month. [Note: adjust the
         decimal place on APR, if the user enters ten percent as 10 rather than as .1]
   Use the FV function to calculate the future value of the investment, like this:
      curFutureValue = FV(sngAPR/12, intTotPmts, -curPayment, -curPresentValue, blnPayType)
      [Note that the monthly payment and the present value are entered as negative values]
   Display the details concerning this investment and its future value in txtResult
```

(continued on page 132)

FIGURE 6.07 *Pseudocode—Finance (Version 1)*

FIGURE 6.07 *(continued)* *Pseudocode—Finance (Version 1)*

```
Event procedure: cmdDepreciation_Click
   Increment maintCountClicks(2)
   Using InputBoxes, get from the user the following information about a depreciable asset:
         initial cost of the asset, salvage value, number of months of useful life, and the
         year for which the depreciation calculation is requested. [Note: useful life must be
         at least 12 months.]
   Use the DDB, SYD, and SLN functions to calculate depreciation according to the double-
         declining balance method, the sum of years digits method, and the straight line
         method, like this:
      curDepreciation = DDB(curInitialCost, curSalvage Value, intLifeTime,
            IntYearForDepreciation)
      curDepreciation = SYD(curInitialCost, curSalvage Value, intLifeTime,
            IntYearForDepreciation)
      CurDepreciation = SLN(curInitialCost, curSalvage Value, intLifeTime)
   Display the details concerning this asset and its depreciation for the requested year
         according to all three methods in txtResult

Event procedure: Sub cmdExit_Click
   Display in txtResult the number of times each financial function was selected.
   Display a farewell message in a message box (so that the user has a chance to read
         txtResult).
   End the program.
```

Event Procedures

The program logic for the Finance Project is more complicated than its Hierarchy Table suggests, but you can understand it by following the discussion below carefully. We have packed a heavy dose of computer program logic and Visual Basic language syntax into these few paragraphs.

The click event procedures associated with the four Option Buttons are trivial, so we can dispense with them quickly. In each case, a property value is being changed. To program Option Buttons correctly, you need only to know these basic characteristics:

1. The implied property of an Option Button is its Value, which must be True or False.
2. Only one Option Button within a group can be True at any one time. When a new Option Button within a group is selected (either by the programmer at design time or by the user during execution), the Value property of all other Option Buttons within that group becomes False.
3. During execution, the click event fires only when an Option Button whose Value property was False is clicked. Multiple click events do not occur if the user repeatedly clicks an Option Button that is already True.

Command Button Click Event Procedures Pseudocode

The Loan, FutureValue, and Depreciation click event procedures demonstrate a number of new logical constructs and Visual Basic features. The pseudocode for these procedures is in Figure 6.07. The new syntax includes the following:

- User input is solicited with the InputBox function.
- User input is tested with a Do . . . Loop Until construct.
- The Mod operator is used in conjunction with a Boolean value.

- The MsgBox function is introduced (similar to the MsgBox statement you have used before).
- Numeric values are converted to strings and concatenated onto strResult.

InputBox Function

The **InputBox function** construct is one of the many ways in which user input can be provided to a Visual Basic program during execution. The usual form of this function is

```
variable = InputBox (stringexpression)
```

where *stringexpression* is the prompt that asks for the user input, and *variable* is the name of the variable that gets its value from whatever the user types in response to the prompt. At run time, the InputBox function causes a modal Dialog Box to be displayed. (A modal form is one that requires a response before the user can do anything else.) This Dialog Box contains the *stringexpression* prompt, a TextBox for user input (which has focus, that is, the blinking cursor), and OK (the default) and Cancel Command Buttons. The user is expected to input a value and then press the enter key or click OK. At that point, the value entered by the user is assigned to *variable*, and the Input Dialog Box disappears. Incidentally, the value returned by InputBox is a Variant, so *variable* can be any of VB's fundamental data types. Figure 6.08 demonstrates the result of this statement at the beginning of Sub Depreciation in the Finance Project:

```
curInitialCost = InputBox _
("What's the initial cost of the asset?")
```

Do Loop Construct

In Chapter Four we introduced the notion of looping and demonstrated one form of looping, namely, Visual Basic's internally controlled loop, the For/Next loop. In this chapter we will examine the use of externally controlled loops, implemented through the **Do loop construct** in Visual Basic.

Essentially, the distinction between internally and externally controlled loops is that the number of iterations performed with an internally controlled loop is determined by a loop control variable, whose initial, step, and limit values are all part of the looping construct itself. An externally controlled loop does not have a loop control variable with initial, step, and limit values built into the looping construct. Rather, it has only the statements that bracket the block of statements to be repeated (that is, mark the beginning and end of the loop) as well as a test (a condition) that provides for an exit from the loop.

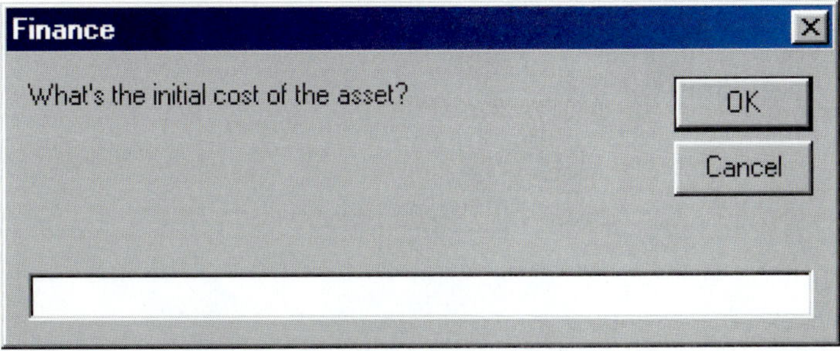

FIGURE 6.08 *Dialog box resulting from InputBox function call*

The syntax of VB's Do loop is as follows:

Do [While | Until relational expression]
    statement 1
    statement 2
    statement n
Loop [While | Until relational expression]

The **While** or the **Until** condition can appear either at the beginning of the loop (as part of the Do statement) or at the end of the loop (as part of the Loop statement). The difference is that, when the test appears at the end of the loop, the statements inside the loop will always be performed at least once, since the test of whether or not to repeat the loop is encountered only after the first time the body of the loop is executed. When the test appears at the top of the loop, the body of the loop may not be performed at all.

Here are some typical Do loops:

```
Dim strAnswer As String
Do
   'block of statements which play a video game
   strAnswer = InputBox("Do you want to " & _
      "play again?(Y/N)")
Loop Until strAnswer = "N"
```

```
Dim strAnswer As String
Do
   'block of statements which play a video game
   strAnswer = InputBox("Do you want to " & _
      "play again?(Y/N)")
Loop While strAnswer = "Y"
```

```
Dim intNumber As Integer, intTest As Integer
intTest = 10
Do Until intNumber = intTest Or intTest = 0
   intTest = intTest - 1
   intNumber = InputBox("Pick a number between" &_
      " 1 and 10")
   If intNumber = intTest Then Print "You Win!"
   If intNumber < intTest Then Print "Too low."
   If intNumber > intTest Then Print "Too high."
Loop
```

In the Finance Project, Do loops are used to ensure that user input falls within specified parameters. For example, this code from the Depreciation procedure ensures that intMonthLife has a value of at least 12 (YRMOS has been declared as a constant with a value of 12).

```
intMonthLife = InputBox _
   ("What's the asset's useful life in months?")
Do While intMonthLife < YRMOS
   'Ensure period is >= 1 year
   MsgBox "Asset life must be a year or more."
   intMonthLife = InputBox _
      ("What's the asset's useful life in months?")
Loop
```

In the first statement, the user is asked to input the asset's useful life in months, and this value is assigned to intMonthLife. The Do While statement tests to see whether intMonthLife is less than 12; if it is, the statements within the Do loop are executed, otherwise those statements are skipped. The program continues to loop inside this Do loop until the user enters a number >= 12 in response to the InputBox prompt.

Mod Operator

Immediately after the above code, the asset life in months (intMonthLife) is converted into the asset life in years. The integer variable intLifeTime is divided by YRMOS (a constant declared = 12 earlier in the procedure). However, if the months do not convert evenly to years, the fractional value will be truncated, and intLifeTime needs to be incremented. For instance, if the asset life is 30 months, then dividing intMonthLife by YRMOS gives a result of 2. In this case, intLifeTime needs to be incremented to 3.

The **Mod operator** (also called the remainder function) gives only the remainder of an integer division operation: 7 Mod 3 is 1; if x Mod 2 = 0, then x is an even number. In the present case, if intMonthLife Mod 12 is anything other than 0, then intLifeTime (the asset life in years) is one less than it needs to be for purposes of calculating depreciation. The following code uses both the Mod operator and the notion of a Boolean expression, discussed in the next section.

```
' Convert months to years:
intLifeTime = intMonthLife / YRMOS
'If intMonthLife not evenly divisible by 12
'then add 1 to intLifeTime:
If intMonthLife Mod YRMOS Then
   intLifeTime = intLifeTime + 1 '
End If
```

Boolean expressions and variables

The expression intMonthLife Mod YRMOS in the code above is used as a Boolean expression, that is, a numeric expression treated by Visual Basic as True or False. When evaluating the truth or falsehood of an expression, a value of 0 is treated as false, and any other value is treated as true. Thus in this instance, if intMonthLife is an even multiple of 12, then intMonthLife Mod 12 will be 0, the whole expression will be considered false, and intLifeTime will not be incremented. However, if intMonthLife is not an even multiple of 12, then the expression intMonthLife Mod 12 will evaluate to an integer in the range of 1 to 11, which, when treated as a Boolean, will be considered true (since any nonzero value is true), and intLifeTime will be incremented.

Visual Basic also offers a Boolean data type. A variable declared as a Boolean can be assigned the constant values True or False (True = –1 and False = 0). Consider this example (Sub cmdLove_Click() in project LOVE.VBP):

```
Private Sub cmdLove_Click()
   Const JOES_LOVE = True
   Const FRANKS_LOVE = False
   Dim blnLove As Boolean, strLover As String
   strLover = "Joe": blnLove = JOES_LOVE
   If blnLove Then
      Print strLover & " loves me"
   Else Print strLover & " loves me not"
   End If
   strLover = "Frank": blnLove = FRANKS_LOVE
```

```
    If blnLove Then
        Print strLover & " loves me"
    Else Print strLover & " loves me not"
    End If
End Sub
```

blnLove is a Boolean variable (actually I think mothers warn us about that). When JOES_LOVE is assigned to blnLove, then blnLove is True (because JOES_LOVE is constantly True); but when FRANKS_LOVE is assigned to blnLove, then blnLove is False (because the constant FRANKS_LOVE is False). Look at the two If statements to see how True Love plays out (Figure 6.09).

MsgBox Function

In the Finance Application, the pseudocode for the FutureValue procedure includes a call to the MsgBox function. You have seen the MsgBox statement ever since Chapter Two, but this is your first exposure to the MsgBox function. The new wrinkle here is that the function returns a value indicating which of several possible command buttons the user has clicked.

Now that you are accustomed to using VB's Help System, let's use it to gain an understanding of this function. Start a new project, open the code window for Sub Form_Click, and type in this procedure:

```
Private Sub Form_Click()
    Dim intChoice As Integer
    intChoice = MsgBox("Please click Yes or No," _ vbYesNo)
    If intChoice = vbYes Then Debug.Print "Yes was selected"
    If intChoice = vbNo Then Debug.Print "No was selected"
End Sub
```

Run the program and click the form. Note the message that appears in the Immediate window. (The Print method is defined for the Debug object, sending output to the Immediate window at run time.)

Place the cursor on MsgBox in the above code, and press the F1 key to call up context-sensitive help for this function. With the "MsgBox Function" Help Screen that appears automatically, you should be able to decipher the code you just typed in.

VB's Library of Symbolic Constants

Declarations for many symbolic constants are built into Visual Basic. You may have discovered some of these on your own—from sample programs or from the Help System. In the above code snippet, we introduce you formally to the VB library of symbolic constants. In this example, we have used vbYesNo, vbYes, and vbNo. In the MsgBox function call, vbYesNo (that is, 4) indicates that the message box should

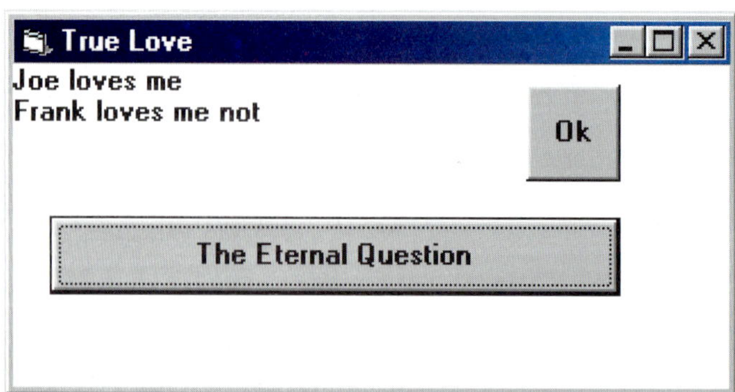

FIGURE 6.09 *How true love plays out*

contain two buttons marked Yes and No. vbYes and vbNo are defined respectively as 6 and 7, that is, the possible return values from the MsgBox function call.

For one more variation, modify the above code to incorporate a third button, Cancel, and add the question mark icon to the message box.

```
Private Sub Form_Click()
    Dim intChoice As Integer
    intChoice = MsgBox("Please click Yes, No, " & _
        "or Cancel", vbYesNoCancel + vbQuestion)
    If intChoice = vbYes Then Debug.Print "Yes was selected"
    If intChoice = vbNo Then Debug.Print "No was selected"
    If intChoice = vbCancel Then Debug.Print "Cancel was selected"
End Sub
```

Please note in this code how the programmer can use constants effectively to elucidate the code. The above code is far more intelligible than the following version, which omits the constants:

```
Private Sub Form_Click()
    Dim intChoice As Integer
    intChoice = MsgBox("Please click Yes, No, " & _ "or Cancel", 35)
    If intChoice = 6 Then Debug.Print "Yes was selected"
    If intChoice = 7 Then Debug.Print "No was selected"
    If intChoice = 2 Then Debug.Print "Cancel was selected"
End Sub
```

What, pray tell, does 35 mean in the MsgBox function call; and what do 6, 7, and 2 signify in the If statements? For ease of program maintenance, do yourself a huge favor: Use symbolic constants liberally to enhance the intelligibility of your code.

Object Browser

How do you know what constants are defined? Unfortunately, that is not always easy or intuitive. As you learn a new piece of Visual Basic, you may discover the constants in the help files. You can also look through the libraries listed in the Object Browser. To do this, press the F2 function key or click the Object Browser icon.

Select a library from the drop-down list at the top of the Object Browser Dialog Box. Many sets of constants are listed under Visual Basic objects and procedures. Click on ColorConstants, for example. Then choose vbRed, and the definition (255, or hexadecimal FF) appears at the bottom of the Dialog Box (Figure 6.10).

Another less scientific method of discovering a symbolic constant is just to make one up and try it. Many of the built-in constants start with the abbreviation vb. So if, for example, you want to use a color, you could try vbWhite (which is defined and therefore works) or vbBrown (which is not defined and therefore generates a "Variable not defined" syntax error).

Format Function

All of the financial functions in the Finance application use or return currency values. Naturally, we would prefer output in a currency format ($1,204.50) rather than a general numeric format (1204.5). We would also like 10 percent interest to look like "10%" rather than ".1." The Format function provides this type of formatting. You are invited to read the Help Screen for the details—it goes on for

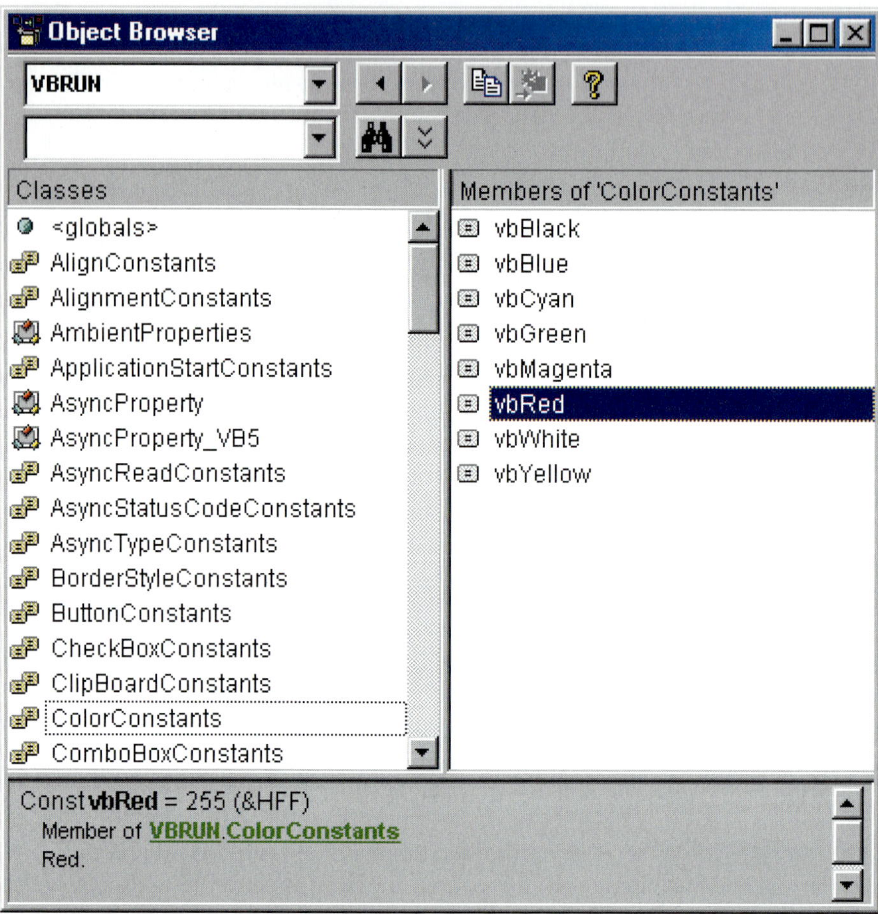

FIGURE 6.10 *Selection and definition of vbRed*

about 10 pages. But here is the short version for our immediate need. The general model for the **Format function** is

```
Result = Format(expression, "fmt")
```

where *expression* means the data to be formatted, and *fmt* is a predefined or custom-developed print format. Lucky for us, Percent and Currency are both predefined Visual Basic formats. Try these examples in the Form_Click event of a new project.

```
Private Sub Form_Click()
    Print "Here is percentage:"; Format(.135, _ "Percent")
    Print "and here is currency,"; Format(13.5, _ "Currency")
End Sub
```

Run the project and click the form to see the Format function in operation (Figure 6.11).

DDB, SYD, and SLN Depreciation Functions

These three functions calculate depreciation according to three common depreciation methods: double-declining balance (generated by Visual Basic's **DDB function**), sum of years' digits (**SYD function**), and straight line (**SLN function**). All three share the first three arguments: initial cost, salvage value, and useful life (usually expressed in years). The DDB and SYD functions also share a fourth ar-

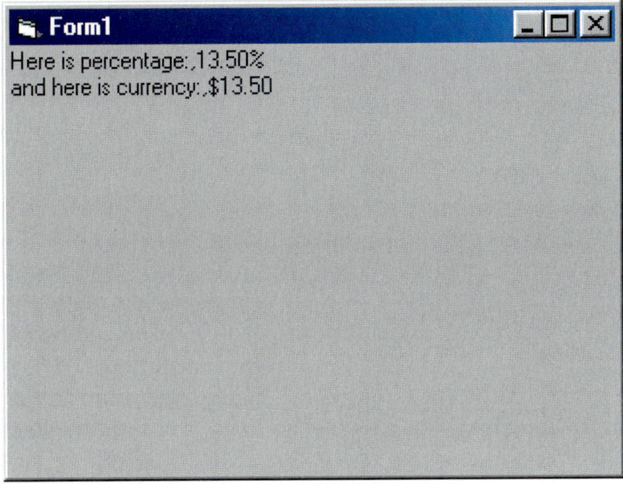

FIGURE 6.11 *Using the Format function*

gument, the period (that is, year) for which depreciation is to be calculated. (The SLN function does not require this fourth argument, since the depreciation amount is the same for every period.) To see how these functions work, put this code in the Form_Click event of a new project, and run it:

```
Private Sub Form_Click()
    Dim curDepr As Currency, i As Integer
    Debug.Print
    For i = 1 To 4
        Debug.Print "Depreciation for Year "; i
        curDepr = DDB(10000, 2500, 4, i)
        Debug.Print "DDB method:"; Format(curDepr, _  "Currency")
        curDepr = SYD(10000, 2500, 4, i)
        Debug.Print "SYD method:"; Format(curDepr, _  "Currency")
        curDepr = SLN(10000, 2500, 4)
        Debug.Print "SLN method:"; Format(curDepr, _  "Currency")
    Next i
End Sub
```

This code prints in the Debug window the amount of depreciation according to each depreciation method for an asset that costs $10,000 originally, has a useful life of 4 years, and has a salvage value of $2,500. See Figure 6.12.

```
Immediate

Depreciation for Year  1
DDB method:$5,000.00
SYD method:$3,000.00
SLN method:$1,875.00
Depreciation for Year  2
DDB method:$2,500.00
SYD method:$2,250.00
SLN method:$1,875.00
Depreciation for Year  3
DDB method:$0.00
SYD method:$1,500.00
SLN method:$1,875.00
Depreciation for Year  4
DDB method:$0.00
SYD method:$750.00
SLN method:$1,875.00
```

FIGURE 6.12 *Depreciation calculations (Immediate window)*

FV and PV Functions; Pmt, NPer, and Rate Functions

The Future Value and Present Value functions both calculate value (future or present, respectively) for an annuity based on constant, periodic payments and a constant interest rate. The models are

```
FV(rate, nper, pmt, pv, due)
PV(rate, nper, pmt, fv, due)
```

where *rate* is the interest rate per period, *nper* is the number of periods, *pmt* is the amount of the periodic payment, *pv/fv* is the present value or future value, and *due* indicates whether payments are made at the end (0) or beginning (1) of each period. Money paid out must be entered as a negative value.

In the present application, we used the **FV function** to calculate the future value of an investment, based on a certain number of monthly payments at a fixed interest rate.

The Pmt, NPer, and Rate functions are also related to annuity calculations. Essentially, when any four of the five key terms (payment amount, number of periods, rate, present value, and future value) are known, the fifth term can be determined by the function that returns the missing ingredient.

The **Pmt function** was used to determine the amount of a monthly payment in the Loan procedure. When performing this calculation, the present value is actually the amount of the loan (this is the total value of the annuity today), and the future value is zero, after the loan payments have all been made. From the standpoint of the lending institution, the present value (principal) is a negative cash flow, that is, an amount paid out from the annuity, while all of the annuity payments are cash inflows. Hence the syntax of the function call is

```
curPayment = Pmt(sngAPR / 12, intTotPmts, -curPrincipal, _ 0, 0)
```

STEP 4. Build Your GUI.

Start a new form, change its name to frmFinance1; change its caption property to "Finance"; and change its BackColor property to blue. Follow these steps carefully to place the controls for this project correctly on the form (refer again to Figure 6.01).

1. Place four command buttons along the left side of the form. Change the captions of the four command buttons as shown, and change their names to cmdLoan, cmdFutureValue, cmdDepreciation, and cmdExit.
2. Draw the TextBox on the form and name it txtFinance. Delete its caption (text property). Set its **MultiLine property** to "True," which will allow text appearing in the TextBox to wrap around onto multiple lines.
3. Draw the first Frame control on the form. Size and position it as shown. Change its caption to "Form Color."

4. This next step must be done carefully. Click once on the Option Button icon (in the Toolbox). Then draw the Option Button *inside the Frame*. In a similar fashion, draw a second Option Button inside the Frame. Change the names of the two option buttons to optBlue and optGreen, and change their captions to Blue and Green.

Do not double-click on the Option Button icon in the Toolbox, because that will place the Option Button on the form rather than inside the Frame, even if you subsequently move the Option Button within the Frame borders. After you have the Option Buttons inside the Frame, you can tell if they are really inside it by selecting the Frame and then moving the Frame. If the Option Buttons are contained within the Frame as they should be, then when the Frame moves, the Option Buttons will move with it.

5. Select the Frame on the Form, and copy it to the Clipboard. Then paste the Clipboard to the Form. This time you do not wish to create a control array, so answer that question "No." Move the new Frame into its proper position, and change its caption to Font Size. Change the names of the two option buttons to optLarge and optNormal, and change their captions to Large and Normal.

Following is a summary listing of all of the property settings for frmFinance1, except for the default settings and the size and location properties.

OBJECT	PROPERTY	SETTING
Form	Name	FrmFinance1
	Caption	"Finance (Version 1)"
Frame	Name	FraFont
	Caption	"Font Size"
OptionButton (inside fraFont)	Name	OptNormal
	Caption	"Normal"
	Value	True
OptionButton (inside fraFont)	Name	OptLarge
	Caption	"Large"
Frame	Name	FraColor
	Caption	"Form Color"
OptionButton (inside fraColor)	Name	OptBlue
	Caption	"Blue"
	Value	True
OptionButton (inside fraColor)	Name	OptGreen
	Caption	"Green"
CommandButton	Name	CmdLoan
	Caption	"Loan Payment"
CommandButton	Name	CmdFutureValue
	Caption	"Future Value"
CommandButton	Name	CmdDepreciation
	Caption	"Depreciation"
CommandButton	Name	CmdExit
	Caption	"Exit"
TextBox	Name	TxtResult
	MultiLine	True
	Text	"" (empty)

STEP 5. Write the VB Code.

Before you examine the code for the Finance Project, try writing it yourself based on the pseudocode. Then compare your coding to that shown below. Pay particular attention to the indentation, which helps to make program code more readable.

As indicated in previous chapters, the Option Explicit declaration should appear automatically in every form you create. If it does not, then from the Menu Bar select Tools | Options | Editor tab, and check the box for "Require Variable Declaration."

```
Option Explicit
Dim maintCountClicks(0 To 2) As Integer

Private Sub cmdDepreciation_Click()
    Dim strResult As String
    maintCountClicks(2) = maintCountClicks(2) + 1

    'DDB, SYD, and SLN Functions Example

    'Using the double-declining balance method, the sum of years' digits method,
    'and the straight line method, this example returns the depreciation
    '(curDepreciation) of an asset for a specified period, given the initial
    'cost (curInitialCost), the salvage value at the end of the asset's useful
    'life (curSalvageValue), the total life of the asset in years (intLifeTime),
    'and the year for which the depreciation is calculated (intYearForDepreciation).

    Const YRMOS = 12 ' Number of months in a year.
    Dim curInitialCost As Currency
    Dim curSalvageValue As Currency
    Dim intMonthLife As Integer
    Dim intLifeTime As Integer
    Dim intYearForDepreciation As Integer
    Dim curDepreciation As Currency

curInitialCost = InputBox("What's the initial cost of the asset?")
curSalvageValue = InputBox("Enter the asset's value at end of its life.")
intMonthLife = InputBox("What's the asset's useful life in months?")
Do While intMonthLife < YRMOS ' Ensure period is >= 1 year.
    MsgBox "Asset life must be a year or more.", , "Finance"
    intMonthLife = InputBox("What's the asset's useful life in months?")
Loop
    intLifeTime = intMonthLife / YRMOS ' Convert months to years.
    'Note both the Mod operator and the notion of a Boolean value:
    If intMonthLife Mod YRMOS Then 'If intMonthLife not evenly divisible by 12
    intLifeTime = intLifeTime + 1 ' Round up to nearest year.
End If
    intYearForDepreciation = InputBox("Enter year for depreciation calculation.")
    Do While intYearForDepreciation < 1 Or intYearForDepreciation > intLifeTime
        MsgBox "You must enter at least 1 but not more than " & intLifeTime, , "Finance"
        intYearForDepreciation = InputBox("Enter year for depreciation calculation.")
Loop
    curDepreciation = DDB(curInitialCost, curSalvageValue, intLifeTime,
        intYearForDepreciation)
    strResult = "Using the double-declining balance method, the depreciation for year " & intYearForDepreciation & " is " &
Format(curDepreciation, "Currency") & "."
    curDepreciation = SYD(curInitialCost, curSalvageValue, intLifeTime, intYearForDepreciation)
    strResult = strResult & " Using the sum of years digits method, the depreciation for year " & intYearForDepreciation & " is " &
Format(curDepreciation, "Currency") & "."
    curDepreciation = SLN(curInitialCost, curSalvageValue, intLifeTime)
    strResult = strResult & " Using the straight line method, the depreciation is " & Format(curDepreciation, "Currency") & " per year."
    txtResult = strResult
End Sub

Private Sub cmdExit_Click()
    Dim strResult As String
```

```
    strResult = "Number of times each function was called: "
    strResult = strResult & vbCrLf
    strResult = strResult & " Loan: " & maintCountClicks(0)
    strResult = strResult & " Future Value: " & maintCountClicks(1)
    strResult = strResult & " Depreciation: " & maintCountClicks(2)
    txtResult = strResult
    MsgBox "That's all folks", , "Finance"
    End
End Sub

Private Sub cmdFutureValue_Click()
    Dim strResult As String
    maintCountClicks(1) = maintCountClicks(1) + 1

    'FV Function Example

    'This example returns the future value (curFutureValue) of an
    'investment given the percentage rate that accrues per monthly
    'period (sngAPR / 12), the total number of payments (intTotPmts),
    'the amount invested each month (curPayment), the current
    'value of the investment (curPresentValue), and a Boolean value
    'that indicates whether the curPayment is made at the
    'beginning or end of the period (blnPayType). Note that
    'because curPayment represents cash paid out, it's a negative number.
    Const ENDPERIOD = False, BEGINPERIOD = True ' When payments are made.
    Dim curPayment As Currency 'amount invested each month
    Dim sngAPR As Single  'annual percentage rate
    Dim intTotPmts As Integer 'duration of the investment (months)
    Dim blnPayType As Integer 'used as a Boolean value
    Dim curPresentValue As Currency  'Present Value -- initial investment
    Dim curFutureValue As Currency  'Future Value of the investment

    curPayment = InputBox("How much do you plan to save each month?")
    sngAPR = InputBox("Enter the interest rate (annual percentage rate)?")
    If sngAPR > 1 Then sngAPR = sngAPR / 100 ' Ensure proper form.
    intTotPmts = InputBox("For how many months do you expect to save?")
    If MsgBox("Do you make payments at the end of month?", vbYesNo) = vbNo Then
    blnPayType = BEGINPERIOD
Else
    blnPayType = ENDPERIOD
End If
    curPresentValue = InputBox("How much is in this savings account now?")
    curFutureValue = FV(sngAPR / 12, intTotPmts, -curPayment, -curPresentValue, blnPayType)
    strResult = "Based on an initial investment value of " & Format(curPresentValue, "Currency")
    strResult = strResult & ", " & Str$(intTotPmts) & " monthly payments of " & Format(curPayment, "Currency")
    strResult = strResult & ", and an APR of " & Format(sngAPR, "Percent")
    strResult = strResult & ", your savings will be worth " & Format(curFutureValue, "Currency") & "."
    txtResult = strResult
End Sub

Private Sub cmdLoan_Click()
    Dim strResult As String
    maintCountClicks(0) = maintCountClicks(0) + 1
```

```
    'This routine returns the monthly payment amount for a loan,
    'given the principal amount borrowed, the annual interest rate (APR),
    'and the number of payments.

    Dim curPrincipal As Currency
    Dim sngAPR As Single
    Dim intTotPmts As Integer
    Dim curPayment As Currency

    curPrincipal = InputBox("How much do you want to borrow?")
    sngAPR = InputBox("What is the annual percentage rate of your loan?")
    If sngAPR > 1 Then sngAPR = sngAPR / 100 ' Ensure proper form.
    intTotPmts = InputBox("How many monthly payments will you make?")
    curPayment = Pmt(sngAPR / 12, intTotPmts, -curPrincipal, 0, 0)
    strResult = "Given a Principal amount of " & Format(curPrincipal, "Currency")
    strResult = strResult & " and an APR of " & Format(sngAPR, "Percent")
    strResult = strResult & " and a payback period of " & Str$(intTotPmts) & " months, "
    strResult = strResult & " your Payment will be " & Format(curPayment, "Currency")
    strResult = strResult & " per month."
    txtResult = strResult
End Sub

Private Sub Form_Load()
    Me.Top = (Screen.Height - Me.Height) / 2
    Me.Left = (Screen.Width - Me.Width) / 2
    Me.BackColor = vbBlue
End Sub

Private Sub optBlue_Click()
    Me.BackColor = vbBlue
End Sub

Private Sub optGreen_Click()
    Me.BackColor = vbGreen
End Sub

Private Sub optLarge_Click()
txtResult.FontSize = txtResult.FontSize + 2
End Sub

Private Sub optNormal_Click()
txtResult.FontSize = txtResult.FontSize - 2
End Sub
```

STEP 6. Test and Debug.

Now that you know how to use the Debug facility, you can go to town with various tests, breakpoints, watch expressions, step-intos, step-overs, and so on. Have fun.

STEP 7. Complete the Program Documentation.

Add appropriate comments to the program code.

SUMMARY

An **array of simple variables** contains a number of repetitions of a fundamental data type, identified by one variable name. A specific element in the variable array is identified by a subscript, also sometimes called an index or element number.

A **Boolean** variable has a value of True (-1) or False (0). Boolean variables may be used as switches in a program. Any numeric expression can also be treated as a Boolean, in which case a value of 0 is treated as False and any nonzero value is treated as True.

The **InputBox function** provides a convenient method to solicit user input during program execution. Visual Basic affords a number of financial functions for accomplishing standard financial management and accounting-type tasks.

A **Do/Loop** is an externally controlled loop, unlike the For/Next, which is an internally controlled loop. Both are examples of iteration control structures. A Do loop construct is most useful when an action(s) needs to be repeated an unknown number of times, or until some condition exists.

The **Frame control** is a container for other controls. The **Option Button** control, also called the Radio Button control, allows the user to select from among mutually exclusive choices. Several Frame controls may be used in conjunction with several sets of Option Button controls on a single form. Only one Option Button control within a container may be True at any one time.

PROGRAMMING ASSIGNMENTS

Lotto

Draw a form with a control array of six textboxes, a control array of six labels (with borders), a frame with three option buttons, three command buttons, and another textbox (txtResult) (see Figure 6.13).

- The command buttons read "Play" (initially disabled), "Clear", and "Exit".
- The frame is captioned "Amount of Wager." The three option buttons inside the frame are designated \$1, \$5, and \$10, with \$1 as the initial selection.
- Set the Index and the TabIndex properties of the TextBox control array so that focus is on the leftmost TextBox when the program starts, and pressing the tab key moves the user through the remaining TextBoxes from left to right.
- At runtime, the user enters a two-digit number (00 through 99) in each TextBox. The program permits the user to enter only digits (hint: program the KeyPress event for the TextBox control array). The program also limits the number of digits in each TextBox to two, and it automatically sets focus to the following TextBox after the user has entered the second digit in any of the first five TextBoxes (Hint: program the Change event to achieve this functionality, along with the SetFocus method). The Play button is only enabled when two-digit numbers have been entered in all six TextBoxes, regardless of the order in which the user has entered the numbers (Hint: use a Boolean variable and a For/Next loop, also inside the Change event). Duplicate entries are permitted.
- The Play button causes the generation of six randomly selected numbers between 0 and 99, which appear in the Labels. Again, duplicate randomly generated numbers are permitted. The user can play as often as he wants without having to enter new numbers in the TextBoxes.
- Each time the Play button is clicked, the program displays the results in txtResult:
  \$0 for no matches

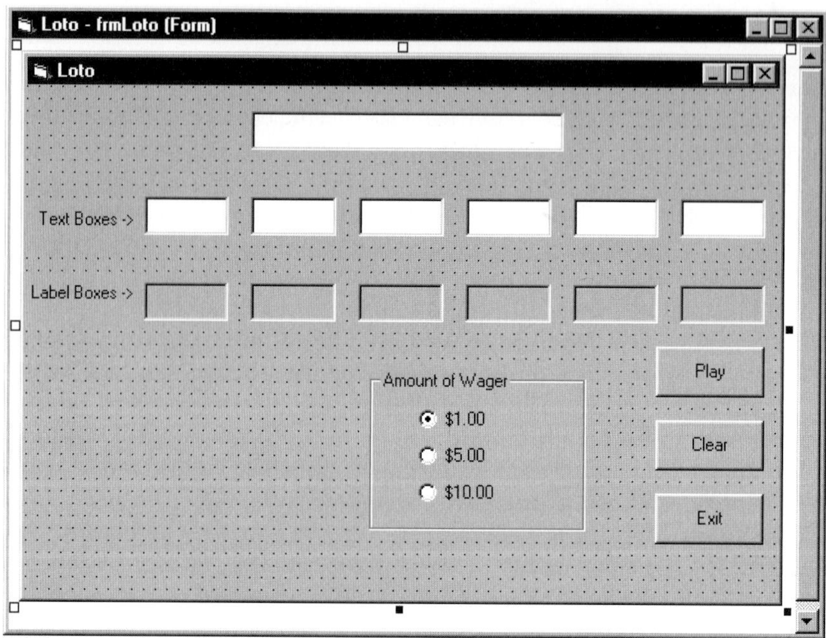

FIGURE 6.13 *Lotto form*

$1 for one number match, multiplied by the amount wagered.
$5 for two number matches, multiplied by the amount wagered.
$10 for three number matches, multiplied by the amount wagered.
$100 for four number matches, multiplied by the amount wagered.
$1,000 for five number matches, multiplied by the amount wagered.
$10,000 for six or more number matches, multiplied by the amount wagered.

- The Clear button clears the six user-selected numbers in the TextBoxes, the six randomly-selected labels, and txtResult. It also disables the Play button.
- When the Exit button is clicked, the program displays the user's net results in a message box, that is, total winnings less total amount wagered; and then the program ends.

Now add two more command buttons to the form, captioned Help and About:

- The Help selection results in instructions for playing LOTTO (use a MsgBox statement).
- The About selection brings up an About form, which displays standard information about this program: application name, author, copyright, and so on. (The layout of the About form is up to you.)

Revised Finance1

Modify the Finance1 Project to include the three functions named Choose, InStr, and IRR instead of Pmt, FV, and the depreciation functions.

CHAPTER SEVEN

GENERAL PROCEDURES, CASE STRUCTURE, ERROR TRAPS

Application: Finance (Version 2)

LEARNING OBJECTIVES

Upon completion of Chapter Seven, the student will be able to:

- Use general procedures attached to a form.
- Pass parameters to a called procedure.
- Distinguish between static and dynamic variables.
- Define and use the Case construct.
- Understand the principles of reusable code.
- Code error traps in a Visual Basic procedure.

Keywords

Actual parameter	Exit Sub statement	Select Case statement
ByVal parameter	Formal parameter	Static declaration
Call statement	On Error Goto statement	
Case structure	Resume statement	
End Select statement		

INTRODUCING THE FINANCE PROJECT (VERSION 2)

From the user's viewpoint, this version of the Finance Project looks exactly like version 1. However, the coding is significantly more sophisticated, more professional, more like the kind of application you are likely to encounter or create yourself when you are being paid to do so. As in the last chapter, the new material in this chapter relates to the VB code: general procedures, parameter passing, static variables, reusable code, and a multiple selection structure (the **Select Case statement**).

This chapter also discusses error traps, an important topic in all commercial programming. Error traps allow the programmer to "trap" anticipated runtime errors, so as to permit the user to recover from the error or provide for an orderly termination of the program, rather than allowing the runtime error to cause the program to "blow up" during execution.

STEP 1. Understand the Problem.

The objectives of this project are (1) to rewrite Finance1 so that the core elements of the code—the three financial functions of loan payments, future value, and depreciation calculations—may be easily reused in another project, and (2) to insulate the program from abnormal termination ("blowing up") due to erroneous user input.

STEP 2. Design a Solution.

Reusable Code

Successful programmers copy and borrow code from their own previous projects and from other programmers and external sources. An amazing amount of code is available for free in the marketplace of software ideas, from bulletin boards to newsletters and magazines. Smart programmers write new code with the constant idea in the back of their minds that this new code may someday be applicable to another project not now envisioned, and that, therefore, the new code should be written in such a way that it is easily transportable to a different application.

Suspend your disbelief, and buy for the moment our premise that the three financial tasks in this Finance Project (Loan Payment, Future Value, and Depreciation) have applicability to other future projects. In that case, wouldn't it make sense to design these tasks in such a way that the code could be reused in another project? We will try to do just that.

One method of making a task independent of its current project application (and therefore reusable later) is to code it in a procedure that is not tied to a control. Such a procedure can still be part of a form, but it will be attached to the form's general object rather than to a specific control on the form. We will use this principle for coding the Loan Payment, Future Value, and Depreciation tasks in the Finance Project. These general procedures will be named Loan, FutureValue, and Depreciation. When the command button captioned "Loan Payment" is clicked, the click event procedure will call the general procedure Loan; when the command button captioned "Future Value" is clicked, the click event procedure will call the general procedure FutureValue; and when the command button captioned "Depreciation" is clicked, the click event procedure will call the general procedure Depreciation. Ideally, a reusable general procedure should not directly reference any controls by name, since the procedure may later be reused on a VB form that does not include the same control names.

The notion of a control array was introduced in the Colorful Backdrop application in Chapter Four. A control array of four command buttons has been usefully employed in this project. The index of the array element will be used to identify which of four tasks is to be performed. If one of the first three command buttons is clicked, the corresponding general procedure will be called. If the fourth (that is, Exit) button is clicked, the actions to be taken are rather unique to this project, and so they are coded within the click event procedure for the command button array.

Static Versus Dynamic Variables

In order to create computer programs that are easy to understand and to maintain, programmers strive mightily to push variable declarations down to the lowest possible level. Form-level variables are to be preferred over global variables, and procedure-level variables are to be preferred over form-level variables. By following this principle consistently, good programmers avoid writing code that accidentally modifies variables declared at a higher level. This is especially significant with respect to the reusable code discussed earlier. Take the case, for example, in which you want to use a procedure in Project B that you originally wrote for Project A. Inside this procedure, you refer to variable X, which was a form-level variable in Project A. Project B, however, has no form-level variable X or, much worse, Project B does have a form-level variable X but it means something totally different in Project B than it did in Project A. In either case, when you try to use this procedure in Project B, variable X becomes a significant problem.

Hence, we would prefer to declare variables at the local (procedure) level wherever possible. However, if the value of a variable is changed within a procedure, and that value is needed the next time the procedure is called, then a local variable declared with the Dim statement (or a local array declared with the ReDim statement) will not suffice. This is because all such variables are dynamic, that is, they come into existence when the procedure is executed, and they cease to exist when execution of that procedure is completed.

Here is a simple example. Put a command button in the middle of a form. Every time the user clicks the command button, you want to print on the form the number of clicks so far. Try this code:

```
Private Sub cmdIncrement1_Click()
    Dim i As Integer
    i = i + 1
    Print i,
End Sub
```

The result after five clicks is shown in Figure 7.01. The problem is simply that the variable i, which you want to be a counter for the number of times the procedure is executed, is recreated every time the click event procedure starts executing. A bad solution to this problem is to make i a form-level variable, that is, put the "Dim i As Integer" statement in the (declarations) portion of the general object of

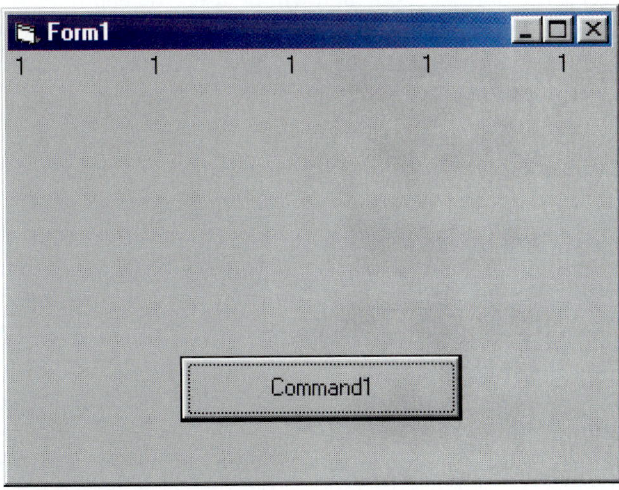

FIGURE 7.01 *Dynamic i*

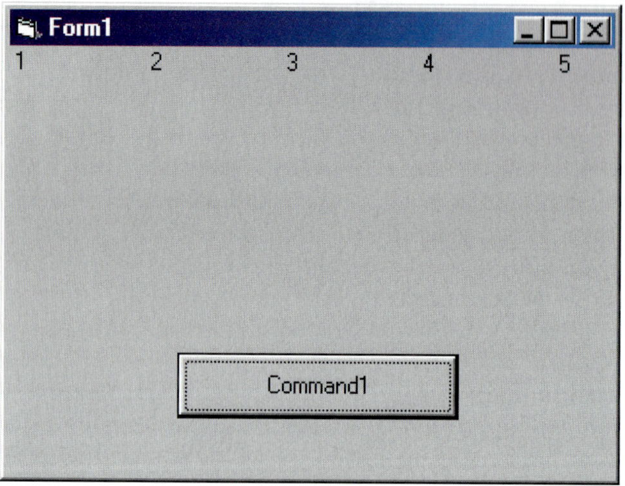

FIGURE 7.02 *Static i*

the form. This solves the problem of the persistence of i between procedure calls, but in a large and complicated project, this practice leads to bugs: You may have multiple procedures in the project developed over time, all of which inadvertently reference (and change) the same counter.

A far better solution to the problem of persistence is to make i a static variable, that is, a variable that, having once been declared, remains in existence until the program stops running. Try this code in lieu of the above:

```
Sub cmdIncrement1_Click()
    Static i As Integer
    i = i + 1
    Print i,
End Sub
```

Now you will get the desired result (Figure 7.02). If you want to declare a fixed-size array at the procedure level, you must use **Static** (for a static array), or Dim or ReDim (for a dynamic array).

In conclusion, the Finance2 application calls for the declaration of a static, procedure-level array of integers, which will be used to keep track of the number of times each command button is clicked. The declaration will look like this:

```
Static staintCountClicks(0 To 3) As Integer
```

The prefix *staint* means a *st*atic *a*rray of *int*egers.

STEP 3. Develop an Algorithm.

Hierarchy Table and Pseudocode

The Hierarchy Table for Finance Version 2 is shown in Figure 7.03. Note that cmdFinance_Click has replaced the four individual command button click event procedures, and that this one procedure calls the three general procedures: Loan, FutureValue, and Depreciation.

Sub cmdFinance_Click introduces several new programming concepts. These include 1) a multiple selection structure, termed the case structure; 2) a variable array in parallel with a control array; 3) calls to separately written general procedures; and 4) parameter passing.

HIERARCHY TABLE-FINANCE (VERSION 2)

```
Project:    Finance2 (Finance2.vbp)
Form:       frmFinance2 (frmFinance2.frm)

            General procedures:
                Sub Loan(rstrMsg As String)
                Sub FutureValue(rstrMsg As String)
                Sub Depreciation(rstrMsg As String)

            Event procedures:
                cmdFinance_Click(Index As Integer)
                Form_Load
                optBlue_Click and optGreen_Click
                optLarge_Click and optNormal_Click)
```

FIGURE 7.03 *Hierarchy Table–Finance (Version 2)*

Case Structure

Many modern programming languages have implemented the case structure through syntax that both clarifies the program's intent and also greatly simplifies the programming effort needed to handle a question that has several possible answers. Remember that the If/Then and the If/Then/Else selection structures discussed in Project 2 both require a relational expression that has a single Yes/No answer. If a question has multiple possible answers, then each answer must be tested separately using the If/Then or If/Then/Else logic.

For example, consider a program that bills utility customers for electricity usage at one of four different rates, depending on the customer category of Commercial, Residential, Government, or Special (customer category codes of C, R, G, and S). Assume that the corresponding usage rates are 9¢, 7¢, 6¢, and 4¢ per kilowatt hour. If the input data always conform to the expected category codes of C, R, G, and S, then four If/Then selection structures will handle the task of assigning the correct rate. The Visual Basic code could be either one of these:

a) Four single-line If statements:

```
If strCategoryCode = "C" Then sngUsageRate = .09
If strCategoryCode = "R" Then sngUsageRate = .07
If strCategoryCode = "G" Then sngUsageRate = .06
If strCategoryCode = "S" Then sngUsageRate = .04
```

b) Four block If statements:

```
If strCategoryCode = "C" Then
   sngUsageRate = .09
End If
If strCategoryCode = "R" Then
   sngUsageRate = .07
End If
If strCategoryCode = "G" Then
   sngUsageRate = .06
End If
If strCategoryCode = "S" Then
   sngUsageRate = .04
End If
```

However, if the input data might have erroneous data, then a set of nested If/Then/Else selection structures are called for resulting in this monstrosity:

```
If strCategoryCode = "C" Then
   sngUsageRate = .09
Else If strCategoryCode = "R" Then
   sngUsageRate = .07
   Else If strCategoryCode = "G" Then
      sngUsageRate = .06
      Else If strCategoryCode = "S" Then
         sngUsageRate = .04
         Else MsgBox "Error. Commercial is assumed"
            sngUsageRate = .09
         End If
      End If
   End If
End If
```

The case structure makes for much more intelligible code. Here is Visual Basic's version of the **Case structure,** followed by notes concerning the syntax:

```
Select Case strCategoryCode
Case "C": sngUsageRate = .09
Case "R": sngUsageRate = .07
Case "G": sngUsageRate = .06
Case "S": sngUsageRate = .04
Case Else
   MsgBox "Error. Commercial is assumed."
   sngUsageRate = .09
End Select
```

The first statement:

Select Case *testexpression*

serves as the header for this selection structure and also identifies a numeric or string variable (the *testexpression*) whose current value will be tested against the individual Cases in the lines that follow.

Each case then follows this syntax:

Case *expressionlist*
    statement(s)

where *expressionlist* provides one or more possible values of *testexpression. Expressionlist* may be a single numeric or string value, as in the electric utility's strCategoryCode example above, or it may be a range of values, such as:

```
Case 3 To 9      'for a numeric testexpression, or
Case Is > 10     'for a numeric testexpression, or
Case "A" To "D" 'for a string testexpression
```

Expressionlist could be a variable:

```
Case strAddress
Case Is < curGrossPay
```

Expressionlist could also include multiple expressions, separated by commas:

```
Case "Sam", "Bob", "Bill"
   Print "Named after his uncle"
```

Please note that we usually follow the well-established practice of putting only one Visual Basic statement on each line, even though VB permits multiple statements on the same line, separated by colons. However, the conventional practice in a case structure, if *statement* is short and singular, is to write

Case *expressionlist: statement*

rather than

Case *expressionlist*
    statement

If *expressionlist* is followed by multiple statements, then put each on a separate line. All of the statements following a Case statement remain part of that case, up to the next Case statement or the **End Select statement.**

After all of the anticipated values of *testexpression* have been listed in the appropriate Case statements, any other value of *testexpression* can be treated with the Case Else statement:

Case Else
    statement(s)

You are not required to include a Case Else statement, but usually it is a good idea. If you do not include Case Else, and *testexpression* has a value unmatched by any Case *expressionlist,* then no case is executed, and execution continues with the first statement following End Select.

If *testexpression* matches values in more than one Case *expressionlist,* only the statement(s) in the first matching Case is/are executed.

The Case structure is terminated by the End Select statement, which is required.

Parallel Arrays of Variables and Controls

This idea was discussed earlier in theory; now we want to put it into practice. First, a static integer array is declared:

```
Static staintCountClicks(0 To 3) As Integer
```

Note that this array has four elements, corresponding to the four elements of the cmdFinance control array. When it comes to using the data in the integer array, we will only really be interested in the contents of staintCountClicks(0) (which will tell us how many times the Loan Payment button, cmdFinance(0), was clicked), staintCountClicks(1) (which will tell us how many times Future Value, cmdFinance(1), was clicked), and staintCountClicks(2) (which will tell us how many times Depreciation, cmdFinance(2), was clicked). So you might wonder why the integer array needs to have four elements rather than just three. The reason is that, when the Exit button, whose name is cmdFinance(3), is clicked, the cmdFinance_Click() procedure will try to increment staintCountClicks(3); and if at that point staintCountClicks(3) does not exist, the program will blow up with a

"Subscript out of range" error. (Of course, we could have avoided this problem in alternative ways. For instance, if staintCountClicks( ) had only three elements, we could have written

```
If index <> 3 then
   staintCountClicks(Index) = staintCountClicks _ (Index) + 1
End If
```

but that would wreck the poetic symmetry of our parallel arrays.)

Figure 7.04 shows that the staintCountClicks( ) array is referenced twice in the procedure logic. The first reference is incrementing staintCountClicks(Index). The second reference is part of a For/Next loop that is executed when Index = 3, that is, when the Exit button is clicked. This For/Next loop cycles through both the control array and the parallel integer array from 0 to 2, and it concatenates onto strResult the caption of the command button along with the number of times that button was clicked. (strResult is used throughout the cmdFinance_Click( ) procedure as the temporary holder for the text that will be assigned to txtResult at the end of the procedure.)

Procedure Calls

The cmdFinance_Click event procedure includes calls to three general procedures, namely Loan, FutureValue, and Depreciation. When a procedure call is encountered during execution of a program, Visual Basic

1. suspends execution of the statements in the calling procedure;
2. begins executing the statements in the called procedure;
3. when the called procedure finishes its execution, returns control to the next statement following the procedure call in the calling procedure.

For example, consider this code:

```
Sub CallingProc()
   Print "Start"
   Call CalledProc
   Print "Done"
End Sub

Sub CalledProc()
   Print "Middle"
End Sub
```

When CallingProc is executed, the following gets printed on the form:

```
Start
Middle
Done
```

Any procedure in Visual Basic can call any other procedure. The Finance program demonstrates a click event procedure calling a general procedure, but actually a click event procedure could call another click event procedure, or a general procedure could call a click event procedure or another general procedure.

```
PSEUDOCODE-Finance (Version 2)

Event procedure: Sub Form_Load
   Position the form in the exact middle of the screen
   Set the form's BackColor to yellow

Event procedure: Sub optYellow_Click and Sub optRed_Click
   Set the form's BackColor to yellow or red, respectively

Event procedure: Sub optLarge_Click and Sub optNormal_Click
   Add 2 to (or subtract 2 from) txtResult's Font.Size

Event procedure: Sub cmdFinance_Click(Index As Integer)
   Static staintCountClicks(0 To 3) As Integer—keeps track of the number of times each
      financial function is selected. [Note: element 3 prevents the program from blowing
      up when the Exit button is selected.]
   Increment staintCountClicks(Index)
   Call the appropriate general procedure, depending on which financial function was selected.
      [Note: use a Case structure for this.] Pass a local string variable in the procedure call:
   CASE (Index):
      0: Call Loan (strResult)
      1: Call FutureValue (strResult)
      2: Call Depreciation (strResult)
      3: Display in txtResult the number of times each financial function was selected.
         Display a farewell message in a message box.
         End the program.
   ENDCASE

General procedure: Sub Loan(rstrMsg As String)
   Copy this procedure from cmdLoan_Click in frmFinance1. Substitute rstrMsg for txtResult.

General procedure: Sub FutureValue(rstrMsg As String)
   Copy this procedure from cmdFutureValue_Click in frmFinance1. Substitute rstrMsg
      for txtResult.

General procedure: Sub Depreciation(rstrMsg As String)
   Copy this procedure from cmdDepreciation_Click in frmFinance1. Substitute rstrMsg
      for txtResult. Include an error trap.
```

FIGURE 7.04 *Pseudocode—Finance (Version 2)*

The word *Call* in a procedure call is optional. We generally include the word *Call* because it seems clearer, and clarity in programming is of the utmost importance. However, you should know that these two statements are equivalent, if MyProc is a procedure in an application:

```
Call MyProc
MyProc
```

Scope of General Procedures

The default scope of a general procedure is Public, which means that this procedure can be called by a procedure in another form or module of the application. A Private procedure, by way of contrast, can be called only by another procedure in its own form. Since this particular application has only one form, it doesn't really make any difference whether the scope is public or private. However, remembering that one of our objectives is to write reusable code, it makes some sense to write a general procedure as public, which is why Public is the default. (You will see the default when we actually create the procedure below.)

Parameter Passing

Quite often a called procedure needs to use or modify data values that exist in the calling procedure. Of course, a programmer could satisfy this requirement by declaring global variables (available to both the calling and the called procedure), but that approach is fraught with the risks described earlier. Global variables should be used sparingly if at all, and limited to cases where a variable is needed extensively throughout an application. More typically, a local (procedure-level) variable or constant or even a literal data value in a calling procedure is needed only by the called procedure. In this case, the data value in the calling procedure needs to be passed to the called procedure.

Here is an example. Suppose you have a procedure that prints any number of employment applications. The actual number to be printed must be passed to this procedure as part of the procedure call.

The value passed from the calling to the called procedure is known as a parameter. The list of parameters is placed in parentheses after the name of the procedure in the Call statement (or without parentheses, if the word Call is omitted); the corresponding list of parameters then appears in the heading of the called procedure. For example, in the case cited above, a calling procedure (Sub Example_Click) could call a public procedure called PrintEmploymentApplication and ask for 5 copies of the form:

```
Private Sub Example_Click()
    Call PrintEmploymentApplication (5)
End Sub

Public Sub PrintEmploymentApplication _
    (intNumToPrint As Integer)
    Dim i As Integer
    For i = 1 To intNumToPrint
        'put here all of the statements which print
        'one copy of the employment application, and
        'then page eject
    Next i
End Sub
```

A parameter listed in the heading of a called procedure is known as a **formal parameter.** Think of the formal parameter as a substitute or design-time stand-in for the actual data values that will be passed to the procedure when the program is run. Within the called procedure, a formal parameter's value can be used or changed just the same as a variable.

Parameters appearing in the procedure call are known as **actual parameters.** A variable, a constant, a literal, or an expression may serve as an actual parameter. However, the number and type of data values in the actual parameter list must match exactly the number and type of formal parameters.

Example:

```
Call ProcX("George", 5, intNum)

Private Sub ProcX(strSample As String, intFirstNum As Integer, intSecondNum As Integer)
```

Actual parameter (in Call statement)	Formal parameter (in Sub heading)
"George"	StrSampl As String
5	IntFirstNum As Integer
IntNum	IntSecondNum As Integer

If the actual and formal parameters (arguments) do not agree in number or type, one of the following error messages will be generated, either when the program is compiled, or at runtime when the offending Call statement is executed:

Error Message	Explanation	Example
Argument not optional	The Call statement includes too few actual parameters	Call ProcX(5) Sub ProcX(y As Integer, z As Integer)
Wrong number of arguments or invalid property assignment	The Call statement includes too many actual parameters	Call ProcX(5,7) Sub ProcX("Frank") Sub ProcX(y As Integer)
Type mismatch	The data type of an actual parameter is incompatible with the data type of a formal parameter.	Call ProcX("Frank") Sub ProcX(Y As Integer)

Parameters can be passed from the calling to the called procedure in two ways: by reference and by value. When data is passed by reference, the calling procedure does not pass the actual data value to the called procedure; rather, it passes the address in the computer's memory (i.e., its reference) where that variable is stored. The called procedure uses the address to manipulate directly (access and/or change) the variable's value. In this way, a procedure can modify the value of a variable that is passed to it.

However, only a variable can be passed by reference, because, of course, only a variable can vary. The value of a constant, by definition, cannot change; the same is true of a literal. When an expression appears in a parameter list, Visual Basic resolves the expression into a single value, and then passes that value the same as if it were a literal. All of these data categories (constant, literal, and expression) must be passed by value rather than by reference.

Although, by default, VB passes variables by reference, you can force a variable to be passed by value either by preceding the actual parameter with the keyword **ByVal** or by placing that parameter inside parentheses (which makes it look like an expression). As a general rule, you should force variables to be passed by value (using the very clear keyword ByVal), except when you specifically want the called procedure to modify the variable's value.

The naming convention for the formal parameter list provides that a parameter that is expected to be passed by reference should carry an "r" prefix, while a parameter expected to be passed by value should have a "v" prefix. For example, the PrintEmploymentApplication procedure might actually have two parameters—one an indicator of the number of copies to print, and the other a Boolean (set within the procedure itself) indicating whether or not the print operation was successful. In this case, the heading might be:

```
Public Sub PrintEmploymentApplication _
(ByVal vintNumToPrint As Integer, rblnPrintOk As Boolean)
```

vintNumToPrint is seen to be a number (Integer) passed by value, while rblnPrintOk is seen to be a Boolean passed by reference.

The project PROCCALL.VBP demonstrates many of these concepts. Sub Command1_Click declares an integer variable and an integer constant, x and Y.

This click event procedure prints the initial values of x and Y, and then calls the procedure Sub Sample three times, again printing the values of x and Y after each call. The actual parameters include these variations: a simple variable, x; a constant, Y; a literal, 7; an expression, x + 4; and a variable passed by value, (x). The general procedure Sub Sample receives two integers from the calling procedure, Sub Command1_Click. Sub Sample prints the actual parameter values it receives, doubles them, and prints them again. Examine its output (Figure 7.05) and its code carefully to see how it works:

```
Private Sub Command1_Click
    Const Y = 2
    Dim x%
    x = 3
    Print "in main," x, Y
    Call Sample(x, Y)
    Print "after 1st call," x, Y
    Call Sample(x + 4, 7)
    Print "after 2nd call," x, Y
    Call Sample((x), Y)
    Print "after 3rd call," x, Y
End Sub
Public Sub Sample (i As Integer, j As Integer)
    Print
    Print "begin sample," i, j
    i = i * 2
    j = j * 2
    Print "end sample," i, j
End Sub
```

Initially, the variable x is given the value 3, and Y is defined as a constant with the value 2. As you can see, the values of the actual parameters before and after each call to Sub Sample are as follows:

- The first call to Sub Sample passes x as a simple variable and Y as a constant. x is passed by reference, while Y is passed by value because it is a constant.

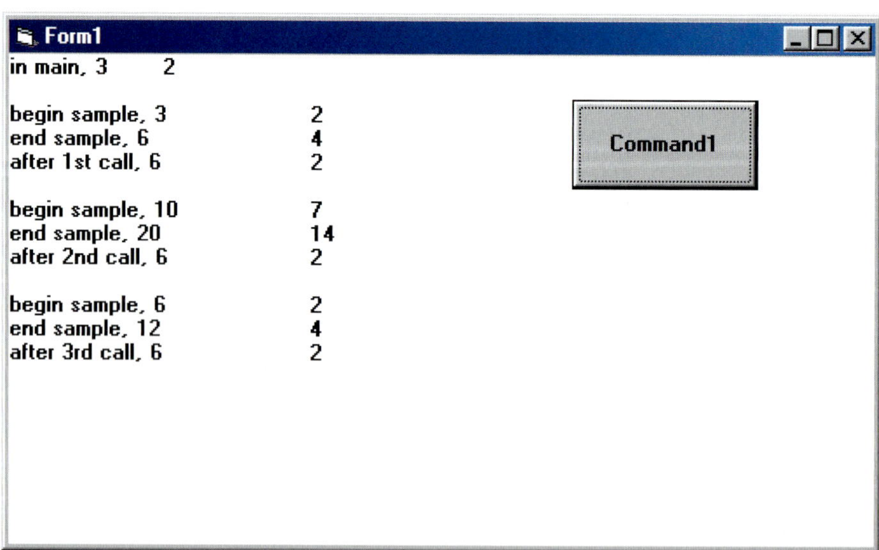

FIGURE 7.05 *Result from running Proccall.exe*

- After the call, x returns from the called procedure doubled.
- While the value of Y was doubled within the called procedure, its value has not changed after control returns to the calling procedure, since by definition a constant cannot change.
- The second call passes an expression, x + 4, and a literal, 7. These are both passed by value, so that doubling these values within the called procedure has no effect in the calling procedure.
- The third call passes the variable x by value (by enclosing it within parentheses, making it look to VB as an expression). Y is again passed by value, because it is a constant. Neither parameter is altered by the doubling that occurs in Sub Sample.

Getting back to the Finance2 Project, you may have noticed that one variable is passed as a parameter to Sub cmdFinance_Click. Specifically, when any of the command buttons in the cmdFinance control array is clicked, VB fires Sub cmdFinance_Click and passes Index as a parameter to the click event procedure. The value of Index indicates which of the four command buttons was clicked. To see how this works, look at the project INDEX.VBP. The form contains a control array of five Option Buttons. When you click on a button, the value of Index is printed on the form (Figure 7.06). Remember that the members of a control array are numbered starting at 0:

```
Private Sub Option1_Click (Index As Integer)
    Print Index;
End Sub
```

Also in Finance2, within the Sub cmdFinance_Click procedure, procedure calls are made to the general procedures Loan, FutureValue, and Depreciation. And in each case, a string variable called strResult is passed to the general procedure. Each of the three general procedures declares "rstrMsg As String" as its formal parameter. After rstrMsg is initialized, values are concatenated onto it throughout the general procedure. Since strResult was passed by reference, changes to rstrMsg in the general procedure are actually changes to the local variable strResult in the cmdFinance_Click procedure. When the general procedure finishes

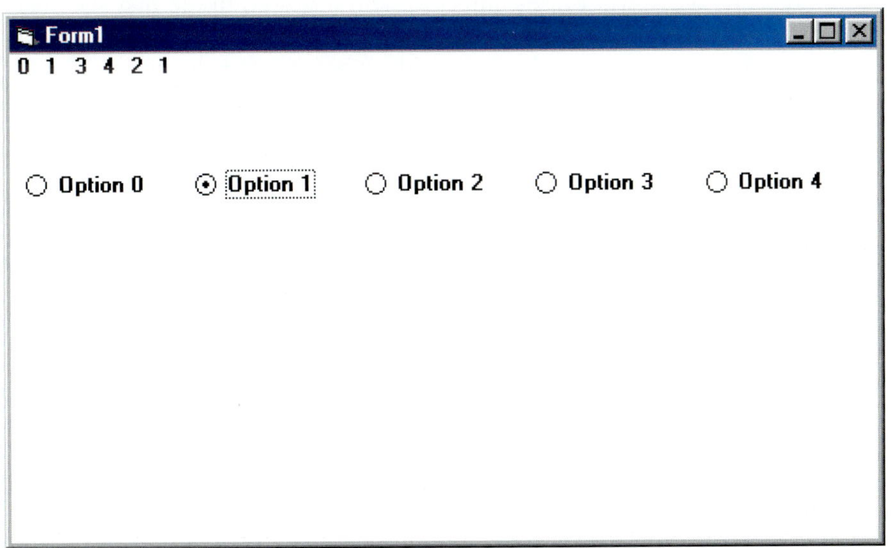

FIGURE 7.06 *Result from running Index.exe*

running and control returns to cmdFinance_Click, the next statement executed in cmdFinance_Click assigns the value of strResult to the TextBox on the form.

Error Traps

Run Chapter Six's Finance1 application again, and try the following:

- Select Loan Payment.
- Oops! You did not mean to select Loan Payment; you wanted to select Depreciation instead, but you accidentally clicked the wrong command button. Maybe you can get out of this by just selecting Cancel in response to the InputBox.
- Select Cancel.
- Your program blows up with a "Type Mismatch" error.

What actually happens here is that, if the user selects the cancel button, the InputBox function returns an empty string (""), which cannot be assigned to a numeric variable. Any runtime error is immediately fatal, and so the program aborts with an error message from the operating system.

To avoid this type of error, you can insert an error trap. An error trap consists of code in your program that traps a runtime error and permits you to deal with the error inside your program rather than letting the operating system deal with it. In most cases, the operating system's method of dealing with an error is rather crude: It cancels your program and issues an error message to the user.

Why do we say that this is crude? Imagine asking your word processing software to read a file from your floppy disk, only you forgot to put the disk in. The word processor traps this error, issues the message "Disk not ready," and lets you try again or cancel the operation. The word processor itself does not come crashing down, which would be downright rude if it were to occur. Programmers put error traps in programs in order to avoid having their user treated so rudely by the operating system.

In Visual Basic, an error trap is set within a procedure by the statement

```
On Error Goto <line label>
```

where *line label* identifies a location within the current procedure. After the **On Error Goto statement** is executed, any runtime error that occurs while that procedure remains active will cause control to be transferred to the first statement following *line label.* The error-handling code can fix the error and resume execution at the same line that caused the error, the next line after the line that caused the error, or another line label location within the current procedure. Alternatively, the error handler could simply exit the current procedure or, if an unanticipated type of error is encountered, allow the program to crash.

Typically, programmers put the error handler at the end of a procedure. Of course, if the procedure executes normally (without causing any error), then we do not want the error-handling code to be executed. Therefore, an **Exit Sub statement** immediately precedes the error handler.

ERRORS.VBP (Figure 7.07) provides examples of some typical error trap variations. The basic program asks the user to supply a dividend and a divisor for a division problem. The quotient is then calculated and displayed.

The first command button just performs the user input and division operation without any error traps.

```
Private Sub Command1_Click ()
    'Division without error trap
    Dim sngDivisor As Single
```

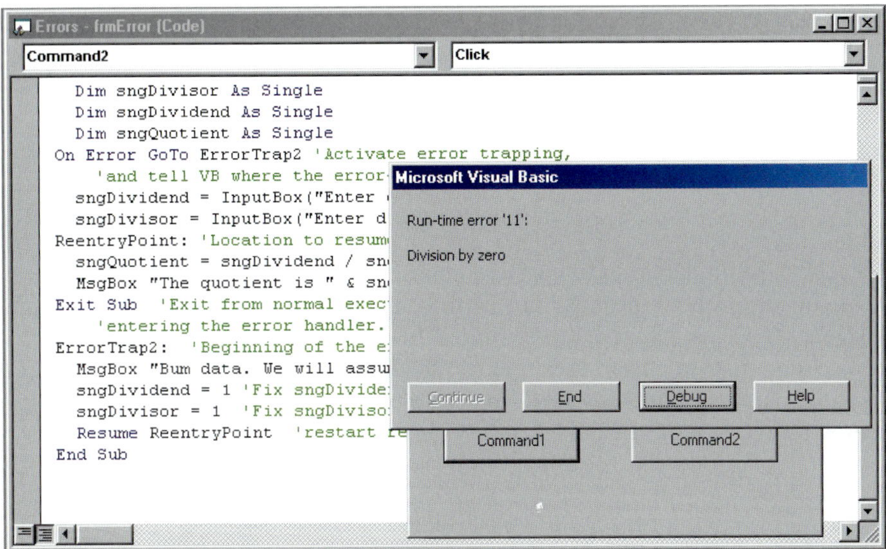

FIGURE 7.07 *Result from running Errors.exe*

```
    Dim sngDividend As Single
    Dim sngQuotient As Single
    sngDividend = InputBox("Enter dividend")
    sngDivisor = InputBox("Enter divisor")
    sngQuotient = sngDividend / sngDivisor
    MsgBox "The quotient is " & sngQuotient
End Sub
```

A user could cause two kinds of errors in this routine. One is the Type mismatch error discussed above, which could occur when assigning the return value from either InputBox function call. The other is a Division by zero error, which would occur if the user enters 0 as the divisor.

One solution to a runtime error is to fix the error and then resume execution of the procedure. In the present case, we do not know which statement caused the error—one of the two assignments that called the InputBox function, or the division operation itself. So the safe approach to fixing this error is to assign legitimate values to sngDividend and sngDivisor in the error handler, and then resume execution of the procedure at the point where the division takes place. In the following code, all of the statements related to the error trap are annotated.

```
Private Sub Command2_Click ()
    'Fix the error
    Dim sngDivisor As Single
    Dim sngDividend As Single
    Dim sngQuotient As Single
On Error GoTo ErrorTrap2 'Activate error trapping,
        'and tell VB where the error-handler is.

    sngDividend = InputBox("Enter dividend")
    sngDivisor = InputBox("Enter divisor")
ReentryPoint: 'Location to resume after an error
    sngQuotient = sngDividend / sngDivisor
    MsgBox "The quotient is " & sngQuotient
Exit Sub 'Exit from normal execution without
        'entering the error handler.
```

```
ErrorTrap2: 'Beginning of the error handler
   MsgBox "Bum data. We will assume the" & _
   "dividend and divisor are both 1"
   sngDividend = 1 'Fix sngDividend
   sngDivisor = 1 'Fix sngDivisor
   Resume ReentryPoint 'restart regular execution
End Sub
```

Of course, when the programmer fixes the error on behalf of the user, the choices made by the programmer may not be the ones really desired by the user. In this instance, the user may not have wanted to divide 1 by 1. So perhaps a better choice would be to let the user reenter the data. However, if the error occurred after the data was entered, such as the Division by zero error, then the error handler will have to assume valid values for sngDividend and sngDivisor.

```
Private Sub Command3_Click ()
   'Give the user another chance
   Dim sngDivisor As Single
   Dim sngDividend As Single
   Dim sngQuotient As Single
On Error GoTo ErrorTrap3 'Activate error handling

   sngDividend = InputBox("Enter dividend")
   sngDivisor = InputBox("Enter divisor")
   sngQuotient = sngDividend / sngDivisor
   MsgBox "The quotient is " & sngQuotient
Exit Sub
ErrorTrap3:
   MsgBox "Bum data. Try again"
   sngDividend = 1
   sngDivisor = 1
   'if the error was in the first InputBox
   'assignment, then the user gets another chance. If the error was a division by zero, then
   'the quotient of 1/1 will be calculated.
   Resume 'resumes at the line which caused the
   'error
End Sub
```

Another program choice is to cancel the current operation. The following code notifies the user that some data input is unacceptable, and then cancels the procedure by exiting. Note that, at runtime, an error handler must always result in either a **Resume statement** or an Exit Sub statement.

```
Private Sub Command4_Click ()
   'Cancel the operation
   Dim sngDivisor As Single
   Dim sngDividend As Single
   Dim sngQuotient As Single
On Error GoTo ErrorTrap4

   sngDividend = InputBox("Enter dividend")
   sngDivisor = InputBox("Enter divisor")
   sngQuotient = sngDividend / sngDivisor
   MsgBox "The quotient is " & sngQuotient
Exit Sub
```

```
ErrorTrap4:
    MsgBox "Bum data. Operation canceled"
Exit Sub
End Sub
```

Also note that every line label must be within its procedure. If two line labels were named ErrorTrap, then the second such line label would generate a Duplicate label compile-time error. Also, line label must occur within the current procedure. If we tried to construct a single error handler, and the statement

```
On Error Goto ErrorTrap
```

were placed in each procedure, with the actual ErrorTrap code placed in only one procedure, then the compiler error message "Label not defined in this procedure" would be issued in the first procedure that did not include the ErrorTrap label.

The most sophisticated error handlers examine the cause of the error, and take appropriate action based on that information. The following code resumes the operation after an appropriate error message if the cause of the error is a Type mismatch, which happens to be error code 13. (The code of the current error is returned by the Err function. A listing of all trappable runtime errors in Visual Basic appears in the VB Help files: On the Contents tab, select MSDN Library Visual Studio 6.0 | Visual Basic Documentation | Reference | Trappable Errors.) If the cause of the error is Division by zero, which is error code 11, then the procedure is exited after an appropriate message to the user. If any other, unanticipated error interrupts execution, then the error code (returned by Err) and the corresponding error message (returned by Err.Description) are printed in the Debug Window before exiting the procedure.

```
Private Sub Command5_Click ()
    'Action depends on the error code
    Dim sngDivisor As Single
    Dim sngDividend As Single
    Dim sngQuotient As Single
On Error GoTo ErrorTrap5

    sngDividend = InputBox("Enter dividend")
    sngDivisor = InputBox("Enter divisor")
    sngQuotient = sngDividend / sngDivisor
    MsgBox "The quotient is " & sngQuotient
Exit Sub
ErrorTrap5:
    If Err = 13 Then
        MsgBox "Bum data. Try again"
        Resume
    ElseIf Err = 11 Then
        MsgBox "Division by zero. " & _
        " Operation cancelled"
        Exit Sub
    End If
    Debug.Print Err, Err.Description
Exit Sub
End Sub
```

To see how an unanticipated error is handled by this procedure, generate an intentional error other than a Type mismatch or Division by zero anywhere within the executable code. Insert, for example, the statement

```
Err.Raise 6
```

before the first Exit Sub in the procedure. When the procedure is executed, the error message

```
6 Overflow
```

will appear, as if you had assigned a numeric value too large to fit into a given variable.

In sum, this brief treatise introduces an important topic in serious, commercial programming. Businesses need a great deal of data; obtaining accurate data is the most compelling problem in commercial data processing, without question. Error trapping is one of the many techniques used by professional programmers to validate user input and to ensure that their programs execute without unwanted runtime interruptions.

To demonstrate the notion of error traps, we inserted error trapping code into the Depreciation procedure, and we will use it again as appropriate throughout the remaining chapters of this book.

STEP 4. Build Your GUI.

Open Finance1.vbp. Rename frmFinance1 as frmFinance2. Then save frmFinance2 as frmFinance2.frm, and save the project as Finance2.vbp. Follow these steps to modify the command buttons for this project.

Rename the four command buttons so that they become a control array named cmdFinance. Do this by renaming cmdLoan as cmdFinance, and then setting its Index property to 0. Rename cmdFutureValue as cmdFinance, and note that VB assigns an Index property of 1. Similarly, rename both cmdDepreciation and cmdExit as cmdFinance, and note that their Index properties become 2 and 3, respectively.

Following is a summary listing of all of the property settings for frmFinance2, except for the default settings and the size and location properties.

OBJECT	PROPERTY	SETTING
Form	Name	FrmFinance2
	Caption	"Finance (Version 2)"
Frame	Name	FraFont
	Caption	"Font Size"
OptionButton (inside fraFont)	Name	OptNormal
	Caption	"Normal"
	Value	True
OptionButton (inside fraFont)	Name	OptLarge
	Caption	"Large"
Frame	Name	FraColor
	Caption	"Form Color"
OptionButton (inside fraColor)	Name	OptBlue
	Caption	"Blue"
	Value	True
OptionButton (inside fraColor)	Name	OptGreen
	Caption	"Green"

continued

OBJECT	PROPERTY	SETTING
CommandButton	Name	CmdFinance
	Caption	"Loan Payment"
	Index	0
CommandButton	Name	CmdFinance
	Caption	"Future Value"
	Index	1
CommandButton	Name	CmdFinance
	Caption	"Depreciation"
	Index	2
CommandButton	Name	CmdFinance
	Caption	"Exit"
	Index	3
TextBox	Name	TxtResult
	MultiLine	True
	Text	"" (empty)

STEP 5. Write the VB Code.

cmdFinance Click Event Procedure

As explained earlier in this chapter, the cmdFinance click event procedure declares the static local integer array staintCountClicks in place of the module-level array maintCountClicks in Finance1. Since the Index indicates which of the four command buttons was clicked, one statement increments the appropriate element of this array: staintCountClicks(Index) = staintCountClicks(Index) + 1. A case construct is used to call the appropriate general procedure (Loan, FutureValue, or Depreciation), depending on the value of Index.

When the user clicks the Exit button (Index=3), a string is constructed to tell the user how many times each financial function had been called. Note that this message is somewhat easier to construct because of the parallel array (the control array and the integer array): With a For/Next loop, the caption of the command button is paired with the corresponding counter from staintCountClicks. One other tiny improvement was incorporated in Finance2 for this display: a carriage return/line feed (vbCrLf) was added after each line.

```
Private Sub cmdFinance_Click(Index As Integer)
   Static staintCountClicks(0 To 3) As Integer
   Dim strResult As String
   staintCountClicks(Index) = staintCountClicks(Index) + 1
   Select Case Index
   Case 0: Call Loan(strResult)
   Case 1: Call FutureValue(strResult)
   Case 2: Call Depreciation(strResult)
   Case 3 'exit button
      Dim i As Integer
   strResult = "How many times each financial function "_
   & "was selected:" & vbCrLf
   For i = 0 To 2
      strResult = strResult & " " & cmdFinance(i).Caption & _
         Str(staintCountClicks(i)) & vbCrLf
   Next i
   txtResult = strResult
   MsgBox "That's all folks", , "Finance"
   End
```

```
    End Select
    txtResult = strResult
End Sub
```

Depreciation General Procedure

All three general procedures are similar. To write a general procedure:

- From the Menu Bar, select Insert | Procedure.
- In the Insert Procedure Dialog Box (Figure 7.08), the default selection of Sub is correct, and the Name textbox has the focus. Type the name of the procedure, such as "Depreciation"; include neither the formal parameter list nor the parentheses.
- As discussed above, the default scope of a general procedure, Public, is usually to be preferred.
- Local variables in this procedure should be dynamic—re-created upon each call to the procedure. Therefore, declaring such variables as Static would be a mistake so do not check that box.
- Choose OK or press the enter key.
- VB presents the Code Window for the new procedure. Insert the formal parameters between the parentheses in the heading line, such as "rstrMsg As String" in Sub Depreciation.
- Type the body of the procedure in the same way as you would for an event procedure.

However, in the present case, the code for the three general procedures already exists, with only minor modifications required: You can copy most of this code from the command button click event procedures left over from frmFinance1. To do this, in the code window find the General object, then look for cmdDepreciation_Click in the procedure list. The cmdDepreciation_Click procedure appears now as a general procedure, because it no longer has a command button object with which to associate itself (recall that we changed the name of cmdDeprecia-

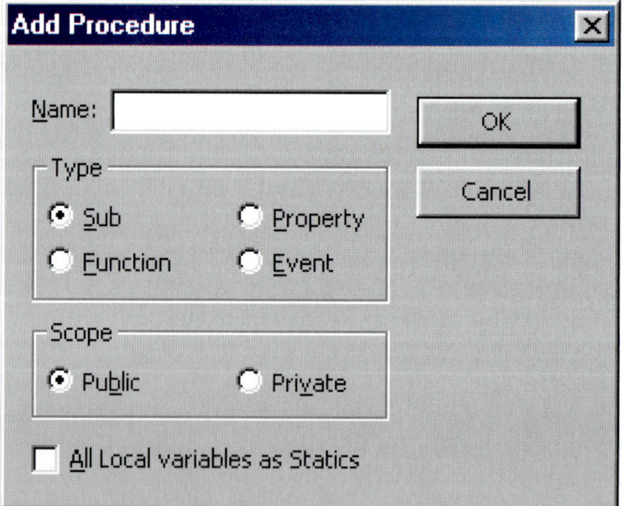

FIGURE 7.08 *Insert Procedure dialog box*

tion to cmdFinance). Select and cut all of the code in cmdDepreciation_Click (exclusive of the Sub and End Sub statements), and paste this code into Public Sub Depreciation. Now use the Edit | Replace feature to change every occurrence of strResult to rstrMsg (but only within this procedure), and delete the last line before End Sub (assigning the message to the textbox). You now have a general procedure containing reusable code: it performs a useful, generalized function (calculating the depreciation of an asset); its functionality is totally encapsulated within the procedure, so that it can be used without the programmer ever bothering to look inside it; its variables are all local, except for one variable passed as a parameter; and it references no external variable or object.

The final step in the transformation of cmdDepreciation_Click into the general procedure Depreciation is to add an error-handling routine. The suggested code displays the message, "Function cancelled—invalid data", which may not be truthful in every case, since the user may have simply clicked the Cancel button. In any case, if the user makes some other kind of error, like typing alphabetic data in response to a request for a number, at least the error handler prevents the program from blowing up.

```
Public Sub Depreciation(rstrMsg As String)
    'DDB, SYD, and SLN Functions Example

    'Using the double-declining balance method, the sum of years' digits method,
    'and the straight line method, this example returns the depreciation (curDepreciation)
    'of an asset for a specified period, given the initial cost (curInitialCost),
    'the salvage value at the end of the asset's useful life (curSalvageValue),
    'the total life of the asset in years (intLifeTime), and the year for which
    'the depreciation is calculated (intYearForDepreciation).

    Const YRMOS = 12 ' Number of months in a year.
    Dim curInitialCost As Currency
    Dim curSalvageValue As Currency
    Dim intMonthLife As Integer
    Dim intLifeTime As Integer
    Dim intYearForDepreciation As Integer
    Dim curDepreciation As Currency
On Error GoTo ErrorTrap
    curInitialCost = InputBox("What's the initial cost of the asset?")
    curSalvageValue = InputBox("Enter the asset's value at end of its life.")
    intMonthLife = InputBox("What's the asset's useful life in months?")
    Do While intMonthLife < YRMOS ' Ensure period is >= 1 year.
        MsgBox "Asset life must be a year or more.", , "Finance"
        intMonthLife = InputBox("What's the asset's useful life in months?")

    Loop
    intLifeTime = intMonthLife / YRMOS ' Convert months to years.
    'Note both the Mod operator and the notion of a Boolean value:
    If intMonthLife Mod YRMOS Then 'If intMonthLife not evenly divisible by 12
        intLifeTime = intLifeTime + 1 ' Round up to nearest year.
    End If
    intYearForDepreciation = InputBox("Enter year for depreciation calculation.")
    Do While intYearForDepreciation < 1 Or intYearForDepreciation > intLifeTime
        MsgBox "You must enter at least 1 but not more than " & intLifeTime, , "Finance"
        intYearForDepreciation = InputBox("Enter year for depreciation calculation.")
    Loop
```

```
    curDepreciation = DDB(curInitialCost, curSalvageValue, intLifeTime, intYearForDepreciation)
    rstrMsg = "Using the double-declining balance method, the depreciation for year " &
        intYearForDepreciation & " is " &
Format(curDepreciation, "Currency") & "."
    curDepreciation = SYD(curInitialCost, curSalvageValue, intLifeTime, intYearForDepreciation)
    rstrMsg = rstrMsg & " Using the sum of years digits method, the depreciation for year " &
        intYearForDepreciation & " is " &
Format(curDepreciation, "Currency") & "."
    curDepreciation = SLN(curInitialCost, curSalvageValue, intLifeTime)
    rstrMsg = rstrMsg & " Using the straight line method, the depreciation is " & Format(curDepreciation, "Currency") & " per year."
    Exit Sub
ErrorTrap:
    MsgBox "Function cancelled -- invalid data", vbCritical
End Sub
```

Create, copy, and modify the other two general procedures (FutureValue and Loan) based on the original code in cmdFutureValue_Click and cmdLoan_Click in a similar fashion. Afterwards, you can delete the original four click event procedures for cmdLoan, cmdFutureValue, cmdDepreciation, and cmdExit.

STEP 6. Test and Debug.

Add error traps to the Loan and FutureValue general procedures, as needed to insulate the program from user errors.

STEP 7. Complete the Program Documentation.

Add appropriate comments to the program code.

Summary of Naming Conventions for Variables

Initial prefix indicates scope:

g	global (public)
m	module or form level
st	static, procedure level
r	formal parameter, passed by reference
v	formal parameter, passed by value
[none]	dynamic, procedure level

Next, an "a" indicates a variable array, if applicable.

Data type is indicated by the next abbreviation:

bln	boolean
byt	byte
col	collection object
cur	currency
dtm	date/time
dbl	double, that is, a double-precision floating-point number
err	error

int	integer
lng	long integer
obj	object
sng	single, that is, a single-precision floating-point number
str	string
udt	user-defined type
vnt	variant
vb	symbolic constant built into Visual Basic

SUMMARY

The **Case structure** is a selection control structure, used when only one of several possible logic paths is to be followed, depending on the value of a particular variable or expression.

In order to facilitate code reusability, **static** or dynamic procedure-level variables may be declared, and **general procedures** (rather than event procedures) can contain most of the executable code. General procedures, usually **Public,** are attached to the general object of a form rather than to a visual object (form or control). Needed parameters are passed to the general procedure from an event procedure, which calls the general procedure. The procedure call includes the list of **actual parameters** that are passed to the **called procedure,** whose header includes the list of **formal parameters.** The formal and actual parameter lists must agree as to the number and type of parameters.

Error traps are used in commercial programs in order to prevent such programs from blowing up (terminating abnormally, or abending, or aborting). The **On Error Goto statement** sets an error trap within a procedure. Within the error trap code, the **Err** function is tested to see if the error was anticipated. After the error is fixed, **Resume** returns control to the normal logic flow.

PROGRAMMING ASSIGNMENTS

QBColors Revisited

(Challenging assignment, but a lot of fun!)

Create a form containing a series of control arrays (see Figure 7.09):

6 Command buttons, named cmd, placed on top of 6 shapes, named shp

8 Option buttons, named opt

5 Text boxes, named txt

7 Labels, named lbl

Arrange the controls on this form so that it is visually attractive.

When any control is clicked, call a general procedure called proc, and pass to that procedure the name and the index of the control that was clicked. Exception: when cmd is clicked, pass the name shp instead of cmd.

In the general procedure proc:

Declare a static local integer variable called stint.

Set the BackColor property of the object that was clicked to the color returned by QBColor(stint).

Decrement stint.

If stint becomes a negative number, reset it to 15.

Hints: Maximize the form. In procedure proc, declare a formal parameter vobj As Object.

Revised Finance2

Modify the Finance2 Project to include the three functions named Choose, InStr, and IRR instead of Pmt, FV, and the depreciation functions.

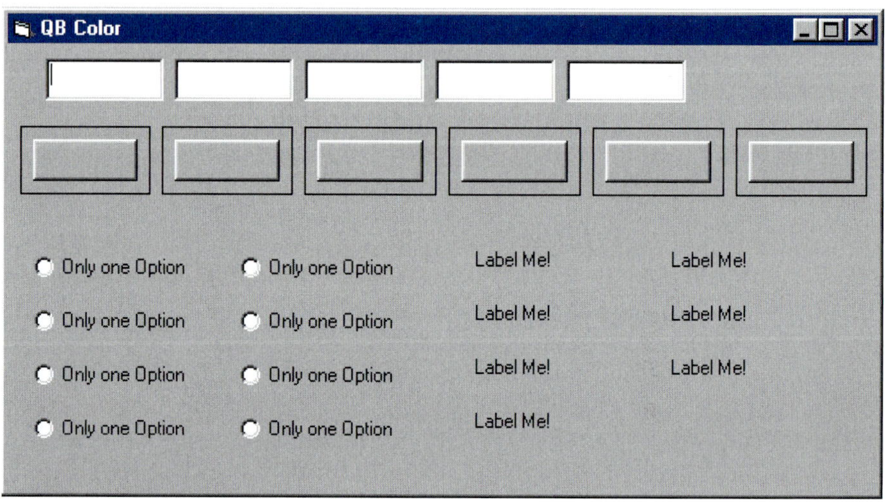

FIGURE 7.09 *QBColors*

CHAPTER EIGHT

MATH, SIMULATIONS, FUNCTION PROCEDURES

Application: Math Magic

LEARNING OBJECTIVES

Upon completion of Chapter Eight, the student will be able to:

- Reuse previously written code.
- Understand the notion of a simulation.
- Generate random numbers and use them in a simulation application.
- Write function procedures.
- Use the built-in mathematical functions.
- Derive other (non-intrinsic) trigonometric functions.

Keywords

Asc function	Exit Function statement	Sgn function
Atn function	Exp function	Sqr function
Choose function	Function statement	Tan function
Computer simulation	Log function	WindowState property
Derived math functions	Intrinsic math functions	
End Function statement	Randomize statement	

INTRODUCING MATH MAGIC

This project represents a minor digression from the main business-oriented theme of this text. We are convinced that computer programming is in its essence a practical application of mathematical-type logic, and that therefore students who are drawn to computer programming might also be drawn to mathematical problem-solving. We trust that you will be as exhilarated by these topics as we are in writing about them. But if you are not, you may safely proceed to the next business problem in Chapter Nine.

This chapter elaborates on the notion of random numbers, first described in Chapter Five. Random numbers form the basis for all computer simulations and applications of probability theory and, in a sense, the notions of inference and artificial intelligence. We encourage you to read on!

An application of software reuse, the Math Magic Project is an adaptation of the Finance Project (Version 2), using the same form design and event procedures to implement three mathematical tasks rather than three financial tasks. If you have already built the Finance2 Project, then you can modify it to create the Math Magic form and controls about as fast as you can read about it. Only the general procedures which implement the three specific mathematical tasks will need to be written from scratch. We have also introduced a couple of new functions within the option button click event procedures. And finally, the Math Magic program employs **function procedures**—a new type of general procedure.

STEP 1. Understand the Problem.

As usual, begin by running the completed project, MAGIC.EXE (see Figure 8.01). The three mathematical tasks, Primes, Fibonacci, and Guess A Number, replace the three financial tasks, Loan Payment, Future Value, and Depreciation.

The first command button, captioned "Primes", provides a list of all of the prime numbers from 2 up to a user-selected maximum (limited to 500) (Figure 8.02). A prime number is an integer > 1, whose only factors are itself and 1, that is, a number which is evenly divisible only by itself and 1. The first three primes are 2, 3, and 5. The number 6 is not a prime because it can be factored into 2 * 3. When the user selects "Primes", a Dialog Box asks the user to input a number up to 500. The program then displays all of the prime numbers from 2 up to the user-selected maximum. The limit of 500 was chosen both so that the prime

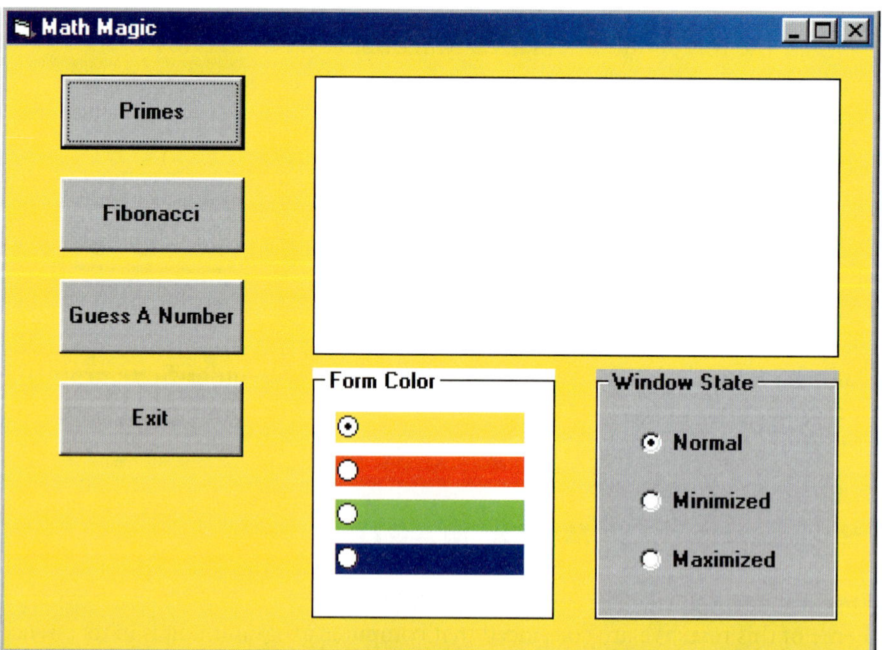

FIGURE 8.01 *Magic.exe, opening screen*

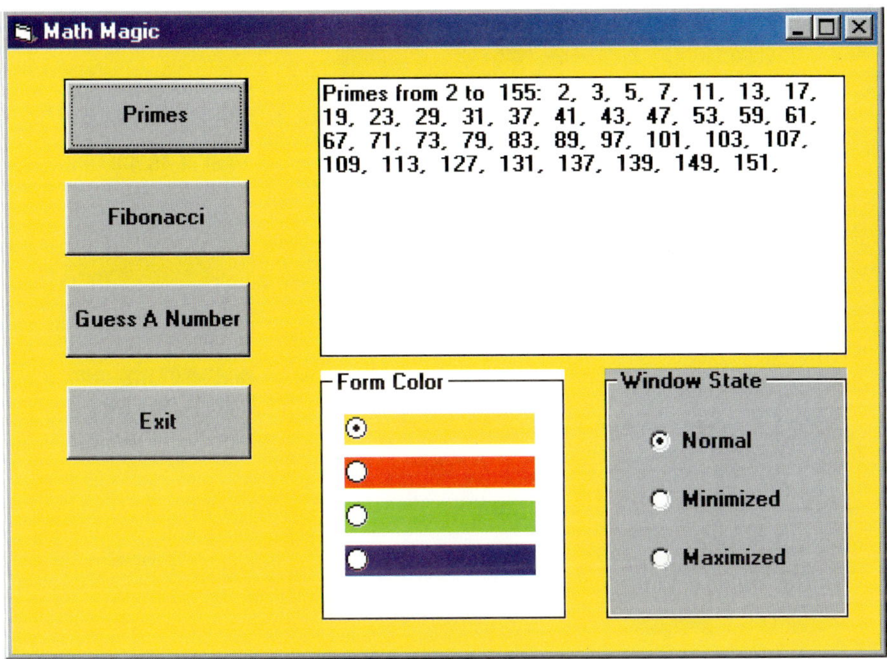

FIGURE 8.02 *Magic, after selecting Primes*

numbers would fit in the TextBox on the form and so that the program would complete the calculations in a reasonable amount of time.

The second command button is titled "Fibonacci". Leonardo Fibonacci was a medieval Italian mathematician who invented the sequence of numbers named after him. It works like this: Imagine that you started with one pair of newborn rabbits, one male and one female. Say it takes rabbits one month to reach the age of fertility, and that the gestation period for a litter of rabbits is also one month. Assume further that, after becoming fertile, the female has a new litter every month, and each litter consists of exactly one pair of new rabbits, one male and one female. Finally, assume that each new pair of rabbits behaves in exactly the same way as the first pair, and that none of the rabbits ever dies. The question is, how many pairs of rabbits would you have after *n* months? Here are the first 10 months:

MONTH	ADULT PAIRS	NEWBORN PAIRS	TOTAL PAIRS
1	0	1	1
2	1	0	1
3	1	1	2
4	2	1	3
5	3	2	5
6	5	3	8
7	8	5	13
8	13	8	21
9	21	13	34
10	34	21	55

Each number in the Fibonacci sequence is calculated as the sum of the previous two numbers in that sequence. Notice that each list (adult pairs, newborn pairs, and total pairs) contains exactly the same sequence. The sequence for total pairs begins in month 1, for adult pairs in month 2, and for newborn pairs in month 3.

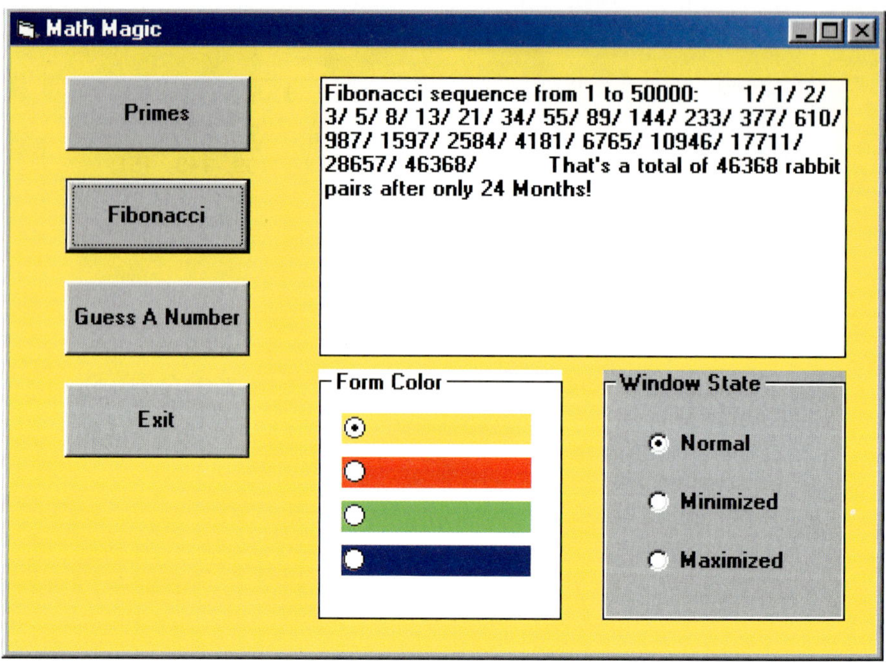

FIGURE 8.03 *Magic, after selecting Fibonacci*

One could postulate a Fibonacci-like sequence with any two initial values: given 5 and 6 as the first two numbers, the first 10 numbers in the sequence would be 5, 6, 11, 17, 28, 45, 73, 118, 191, 309.

The Fibonacci sequence has proven useful in many theoretical and practical applications in nature—not just for calculating the potential overpopulation of rabbits in medieval Europe. For instance, the Fibonacci sequence reflects the increasing radii of the concentric circles on seashells. And lots of other neat stuff. In any case, the Math Magic program displays the Fibonacci sequence for rabbits up to a user-selected maximum of 1 billion rabbit pairs and also shows the user how many months it takes to get there. The maximum of 1 billion was chosen in order to avoid a numeric overflow problem with Long Integers. See Figure 8.03 for a sample Fibonacci sequence.

"Guess A Number" is the caption of the third command button. The computer randomly picks a number from 1 to 100 and then asks the user to guess what it is. After each guess, Math Magic states whether your guess is high, low, or correct. You should be able to guess the correct number in at most seven guesses, using a binary search technique: always guess the middle number in the range of numbers which are still possible. For example, your first guess should always be 50. If 50 is too high, your next guess is 25; but if 50 is too low, your next guess is 75. If your second guess is 25 and is too low, then your third guess is 37—midway in the range of potential right answers, that is, halfway between 26 and 49. Since 2^7 is 128, dividing the number of potential answers in half seven times will invariably isolate the correct answer, since you started with fewer than 128 possibilities. See Figure 8.04.

The frames in Math Magic are a little different from the frames in Finance1 and Finance2. Both sets of option buttons (in the Window State frame and in the Color frame) are control arrays, and the index value of the control array directly determines the action in the click event procedure. The color frame has four colors and provides an interesting example of the **Choose function.**

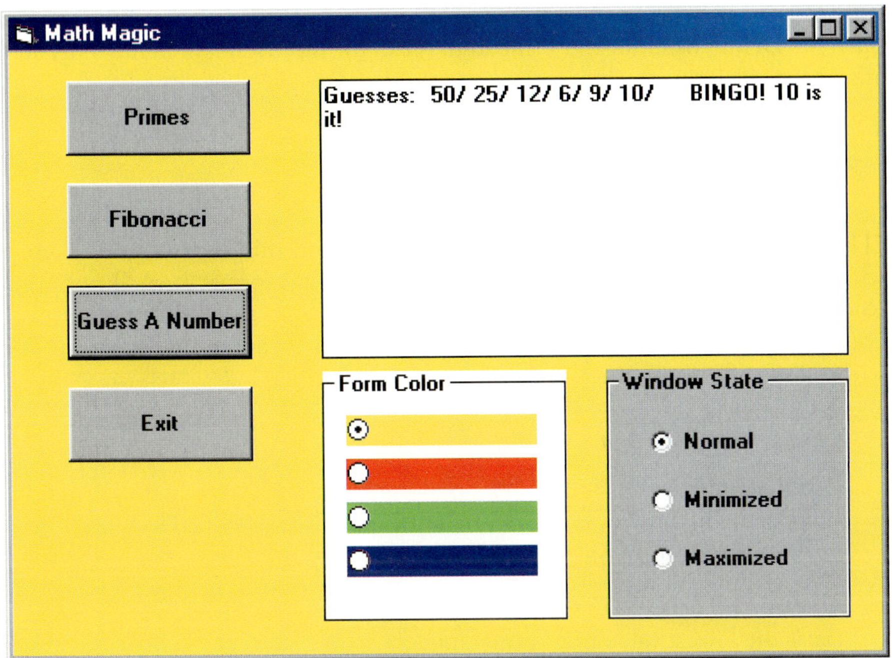

FIGURE 8.04 *Magic, after selecting Guess A Number*

STEP 2. Design a Solution.

The design of this project is a ready-made adaptation of the Finance2 Project from the last chapter. You can use the same form with new captions for the three financial tasks, substituting the three mathematical tasks in this project. Three new general procedures—"Primes", "Fibonacci", and "Guess" will substitute for "Depreciation", "FutureValue", and "Loan". The click event procedures for the option buttons are also new.

The new programming concepts in this chapter include the random number generator, computer simulations, intrinsic and derived mathematical functions, and function procedures.

Rnd Function and Randomize Statement

The random number generator is needed in the "Guess A Number" component of the Math Magic program, wherein your program is supposed to randomly select an integer in the range of 1 to 100. Random numbers are an important part of computer programming, and so they merit a somewhat detailed discussion.

Imagine playing a new video game, in which your token sits in the middle of the screen, and the bad guy can attack you from the top, bottom, left, or right. The first time you play the game, the first attack comes from the right; but as you turn to meet it, another attack comes from the left, catching you by surprise, and you die. The next time you play, the first attack is from the right, then from the left, then the bottom, then the right again. The third time the attacks come in the same order, and you are beginning to get bored. Every time you play the video game, the bad guys do exactly the same thing in exactly the same order.

If we could not generate random numbers, that is exactly the sorry state our video games would be in.

Visual Basic has a random number generator function called *Rnd*, which returns a fractional value *n* where 0 < = n < 1. (The data type of this fractional value is Single.) To test this function, run any VB program, then click into Break mode, open the Debug window, and Print Rnd. A call for three random numbers generated these results:

?rnd,rnd,rnd

.533424 .5795186 .2895625

(The "?" is a shortcut for typing "Print". If you typed this line inside a VB code window, rather than the Debug window, VB would reformat it as "Print Rnd, Rnd, Rnd".)

The Rnd function is usually used to generate a randomly selected integer within a specific range of integers, by using this formula:

variable = Int(Rnd * *range*) + *low*

where *variable* receives the result

range is the number of integer possibilities, and is determined by

(the high value – the low value + 1)

the function *Int* returns an integer from any numeric argument

low is the lowest value within the range

For example, in the Guess procedure in the Math Magic Project, to obtain a randomly selected integer from 1 to 100, we will use the statement

```
n = Rnd * 100 + 1
```

(Note that we omitted the *Int* function, since *n* will be declared as an Integer anyway, so the resulting random number will be forced into an Integer format even without the Int conversion function.)

Another example: a random number from 5 to 7 would be generated by

```
Int(Rnd * (7 - 5 + 1) + 5)
```

Rnd is sometimes called a pseudo-random number generator. This is because the set of random numbers generated within a given program follows a particular sequence, in which the first number is based on a *seed* value. Each call to the Rnd function returns the next random number in the given sequence.

In some computer applications, the programmer needs the same sequence of random numbers to be generated every time a program runs. For instance, a botanist conducting a series of experiments may need to randomly select certain plants from a group of plants, but the botanist may want to retain the sequence of randomly generated numbers so that further experimental treatments could be given to the same plants or so that the experiment itself could be replicated later.

In other cases—even most cases—the programmer wants to generate a different set of random numbers every time the program runs. This is certainly true of video games.

By default, VB generates the same sequence of random numbers every time a computer program runs. If you want to generate a new set of random numbers each time the program runs, you must insert the **Randomize statement,** which re-seeds the random number generator. After this statement is executed, subsequent calls to the Rnd function follow the new, randomly selected, sequence.

To see how this works, examine this code from RANDOM.VBP:

```
Private Sub Command1_Click()
    Dim i
    For i = 1 To 5
        Print Int(Rnd * 100);
    Next i
    Randomize
    Print
    For i = 1 To 5
        Print Int(Rnd * 100);
    Next i
End Sub
```

The first five calls to Rnd occur before the **Randomize statement,** so the same five random numbers are generated every time the program runs. The second five calls to the Rnd function follow the Randomize statement, so a different sequence of random numbers is generated each time the program runs. Here are the results of running RANDOM.EXE three times:

```
70 53 57 28 30
56 9 21 38 17
70 53 57 28 30
73 73 82 95 26
70 53 57 28 30
99 6 49 93 36
```

Computer Simulation

A random number generator is key to many aspects of computer modeling, simulations, expert systems, and other artificial intelligence applications. Here is a tiny demonstration of the use of random numbers to help construct a computer simulation.

Assume a bank wants to simulate the servicing of a queue of customers waiting for a bank teller. The bank wants to know, for example, how long can the queue be expected to get, how much time will on average a customer have to wait in the queue, and how much time will the bank teller be idle, awaiting the arrival of a customer. The two critical factors in determining the number of people in the queue are 1) how often do customers arrive at the bank and join the queue and 2) how long does it take the teller to service one customer. Quite possibly, a customer joins the queue every four minutes on average, and quite possibly the teller services a customer in three minutes on average. But these averages cannot be used to imply that the queue never has more than one person in it, and that the teller is idle for one minute after each customer, which are clearly unrealistic implications. Rather, the computer program must simulate the random behavior of real customers, such as this:

- 10 percent of the time, a customer comes in right behind the previous customer—essentially simultaneously.
- 20 percent of the time, an interval of 1 minute between customers exists.
- 20 percent of the time, an interval of 2 minutes exists.
- 40 percent of the time, an interval of 4 minutes exists.
- 10 percent of the time, an interval of 6 minutes exists.

To determine when the next customer will arrive at the bank (the Interval), the program must generate a random number from 1 to 100, and then divide the possibilities into the above-mentioned percentages with a Select Case statement, as follows:

```
Public Sub GetCustomerInterval (rintInterval As Integer)
    Dim intRandomPercent As Integer
    Randomize
    intRandomPercent = Rnd * 100 + 1
    Select Case intRandomPercent
        Case 1 To 10: rintInterval = 0
        Case 11 To 30: rintInterval = 1
        Case 31 To 50: rintInterval = 2
        Case 51 To 90: rintInterval = 4
        Case 91 To 100: rintInterval = 6
    End Select
End Sub
```

And the bank's customers require services that take anywhere from 2 to 20 minutes, such as this:

- cash a check, 20 percent of the customers, 2 minutes
- make a deposit or withdrawal, 60 percent of the customers, 3 minutes
- open a new account, 5 percent of the customers, 20 minutes
- miscellaneous services, 15 percent of the customers, 5 minutes

A similar procedure can assign the customer service time randomly, yet maintain these overall probabilities:

```
Public Sub GetCustomerServiceTime _(rintServiceTime As Integer)
    Dim intRandomPercent As Integer
    Randomize
    intRandomPercent = Rnd * 100 + 1
    Select Case intRandomPercent
        Case 1 To 20: rintServiceTime = 2
        Case 21 To 80: rintServiceTime = 3
        Case 81 To 85: rintServiceTime = 20
        Case 86 To 100: rintServiceTime = 5
    End Select
End Sub
```

The sample programs for this text include the Dice Project, a simulation of a dice-throwing game, written as a favor for a mathematics professor for use in a course on probability. This program demonstrates many of the typical characteristics of computer simulations: heavy dependence on the random number generator, graphical display of the results, and some level of interactivity with the user. We won't discuss the program further here, but if you have an interest in writing computer simulations, an examination of the Dice program may be a good place to start.

Other Mathematical Functions

The Math Magic application uses only a few of the mathematical functions built into Visual Basic. If you implement the Math Magic program yourself, you could easily substitute a procedure to use any of these:

Function	Argument	Return Value
Asc	an ASCII character	the number representing that character in ASCII
Atn	Size of an angle, in radians	arctangent of the angle
Cos	Size of an angle, in radians	cosine of the angle
Exp	A natural log value	the number whose natural log = the argument
Log	A number	the natural log (e) of the argument
Sgn	Any numeric expression	–1, 0, or +1, depending on the sign of the argument—negative, 0, or positive
Sin	Size of an angle, in radians	sine of the angle
Sqr	A positive number	the square root of the argument
Tan	Size of an angle, in radians	the tangent of the angle

VB's Help screens contain examples of all of the mathematical functions. Here, for example, is a routine which displays the sine of an angle. Since the Sin function requires an argument in radians, the example first converts the user's input from degrees to radians:

```
Private Sub Form_Click()
    Dim Degrees, Msg, Pi, Radians ' Declare variables.
    Pi = 4 * Atn(1)        ' Calculate Pi.
    Degrees = InputBox("Enter an angle in degrees.")
    Radians = Degrees * (Pi / 180) ' Convert to radians.
    Msg = "The sine of a " & Degrees
    Msg = Msg & " degree angle is "
    Msg = Msg & Sin(Radians) & "."
    MsgBox Msg        ' Display results.
End Sub
```

The list of functions above is hardly exhaustive. All of the common mathematical functions are either included as part of the Visual Basic language or can be readily derived from the built-in functions. For instance, if you need the secant of an angle, just use the inverse of the cosine:

```
Secant = 1/Cos(x)
```

In VB Help, look up the topic "Derived Math Functions" for the complete list, reproduced below:

Function	Derived equivalents
Secant	Sec(X) = 1 / Cos(X)
Cosecant	Cosec(X) = 1 / Sin(X)
Cotangent	Cotan(X) = 1 / Tan(X)
Inverse Sine	Arcsin(X) = Atn(X / Sqr(–X * X + 1))
Inverse Cosine	Arccos(X) = Atn(–X / Sqr(–X * X + 1)) + 2 * Atn(1)
Inverse Secant	Arcsec(X) = Atn(X / Sqr(X * X – 1)) + Sgn((X) – 1) * (2 * Atn(1))
Inverse Cosecant	Arccosec(X) = Atn(X / Sqr(X * X – 1)) + (Sgn(X) – 1) * (2 * Atn(1))
Inverse Cotangent	Arccotan(X) = Atn(X) + 2 * Atn(1)
Hyperbolic Sine	HSin(X) = (Exp(X) – Exp(–X)) / 2
Hyperbolic Cosine	HCos(X) = (Exp(X) + Exp(–X)) / 2
Hyperbolic Tangent	HTan(X) = (Exp(X) – Exp(–X)) / (Exp(X) + Exp(–X))
Hyperbolic Secant	HSec(X) = 2 / (Exp(X) + Exp(–X))
Hyperbolic Cosecant	HCosec(X) = 2 / (Exp(X) – Exp(–X))

continued

Function	Derived equivalents
Hyperbolic Cotangent	HCotan(X) = (Exp(X) + Exp(–X)) / (Exp(X) – Exp(–X))
Inverse Hyperbolic Sine	HArcsin(X) = Log(X + Sqr(X * X + 1))
Inverse Hyperbolic Cosine	HArccos(X) = Log(X + Sqr(X * X – 1))
Inverse Hyperbolic Tangent	HArctan(X) = Log((1 + X) / (1 – X)) / 2
Inverse Hyperbolic Secant	HArcsec(X) = Log((Sqr(–X * X + 1) + 1) / X)
Inverse Hyperbolic Cosecant	HArccosec(X) = Log((Sgn(X) * Sqr(X * X + 1) + 1) / X)
Inverse Hyperbolic Cotangent	HArccotan(X) = Log((X + 1) / (X – 1)) / 2
Logarithm to base N	LogN(X) = Log(X) / Log(N)

But enough about random numbers and derived functions and trigonometry. Let's go on to function procedures.

Function Procedures

A function procedure is akin to a general procedure, with the following differences:

- It is used in an expression rather than being the object of a Call statement.
- It always returns a single value. Both a general procedure and a function procedure may modify variables passed to them by reference, but only a function procedure is syntactically designed to return a value to the calling statement.
- A function procedure's return value is assigned to the name of the function in the body of the function.
- Function procedures, unless declared Private, are Public by default.
- A function procedure header begins with the word Function, while a general procedure header begins with the word Sub. Function procedures end with the words **End Function**, general procedures end with the words EndSub.
- To see the difference in practice, consider the following example. The purpose of both of the following procedures is to double the value of Y—the first case is written as a familiar general procedure, while the second is written as a function procedure:

```
Subsample
   Dim Y As Integer
   Dim X As Integer
   Y = 5
   Call SubDoubleMe(Y)
   Print Y
   Y = 5
   X = FuncDoubleMe(Y)
   Print X
   Print FuncDoubleMe(Y)
End Sub

Private Sub SubDoubleMe(rn As Integer)
   rn = rn * 2
End Sub

Function FuncDoubleMe (ByVal vn As Integer) As Integer
   FuncDoubleMe = vn * 2
End Function
```

The procedure SubDoubleMe doubles the value of Y, which is passed to it by reference. The function FuncDoubleMe returns an integer value (note the As Integer at the end of the function header). It does not matter that vn is passed to the function by value, since vn is not changed within the procedure. The value of vn doubled is assigned to the name of the function, which therefore becomes the return value.

In the Math Magic Application, we used a function procedure to determine whether one particular integer is or is not a prime number. As the prior example shows, we could have accomplished the same task with a general procedure. However, function procedures provide a handy additional coding choice and can be used effectively to simplify coding or improve readability.

STEP 3. DEVELOP AN ALGORITHM.

Hierarchy Table and Pseudocode

The Hierarchy Table for Math Magic (Figure 8.05) looks almost exactly like the Hierarchy Table for Finance2.

```
HIERARCHY TABLE-Math Magic

Project:   Magic (Magic.vbp)
Form:      frmMagic (frmMagic.frm)

           General procedures:
              Sub Primes(rstrMsg As String)
              Sub Fibonacci(rstrMsg As String)
              Sub Guess(rstrMsg As String)
              Function IsPrime(m As Integer) As Boolean

           Event procedures:
              cmdMath_Click(Index As Integer)
              Form_Load
              optColor_Click(Index As Integer)
              optWindowState_Click(Index As Integer)
```

FIGURE 8.05 *Hierarchy Table—Math Magic*

Window State Option Buttons With one statement, the click event procedure for the control array of three option buttons in the Window State frame sets the WindowState property of the form:

```
frmMagic.WindowState = Index
```

This works because the index values of the three option buttons (0, 1, and 2) match the three WindowState property values (0=vbNormal, 1=vbMinimized, and 2=vbMaximized).

Form Color Option Buttons Also with one statement, the click event procedure for the control array of four option buttons in the Form Color frame sets the BackColor property of the form. However, in this case the index values of the option buttons (1, 2, 3, 4) do not match the desired colors (vbYellow, vbRed, vbGreen, and vbBlue). Therefore, we introduce the Choose function in order to correlate the index values of the option buttons with the four colors:

```
Me.BackColor = Choose(Index, vbYellow, vbRed, _ vbGreen, vbBlue)
```

The first argument of the Choose function, Index, must be a positive integer from 1 to the number of choices following that argument. In this case, there are four color choices, so Index must have a value between 1 and 4. Note that the first option button has an index value of 1, not 0. The easiest way to create this set of option buttons is to create one of them, set its index to 0, then copy it four times (creating option buttons with index values 1, 2, 3, and 4), and then go back and delete the option button whose index value is 0.

General Procedures

Refer to the pseudocode for the general procedures Primes, Fibonacci, and Guess (Figure 8.06) to help you understand the following discussion.

PSEUDOCODE-Math Magic

```
Event procedure: Sub Form_Load
  Position the form in the exact middle of the screen
  Set the forms BackColor to yellow

Event procedure: Sub optColor_Click (Index As Integer)
  Set the form's BackColor to yellow, red, green, or blue, depending on the value of
    Index. [Use the Choose function.]

Event procedure: Sub optWindowState(Index As Integer)
  Assign: WindowState ← Index

Event procedure: Sub cmdMath_Click(Index As Integer)
  Static staintCountClicks(0 To 3) As Integer—keeps track of the number of times each
    math function is selected. [Note: element 3 prevents the program from blowing up
    when the Exit button is selected.]
  Increment staintCountClicks(Index)
  Call the appropriate general procedure, depending on which math function was
    selected:
  CASE (Index):
    0:Call Primes (strResult)
    1:Call Fibonacci (strResult)
    2:Call Guess (strResult)
    3:Display in txtResult the number of times each math function was selected.
      Display a farewell message in a message box.
      End the program
  ENDCASE

General procedure: Sub Prime(rstrMsg As String)
  Define a prime number in a message box
  Get user input for a positive number intMaxPrime up to 500
  rstrMsg ← "Primes from 2 to & intMaxPrime & ": 2,"
  FOR/NEXT Loop: FOR (I = 3 To intMaxPrime) Step 2 [Note: examine odd integers only]
    IF (IsPrime(I))
      True: Assign: rstrMsg ← rstrMsg & I & ","
    ENDIF
  NEXT I

General procedure: Function IsPrime(m As Integer) As Boolean
  Assign: intTest ← 3
  Assign: IsPrime ← True
  DO/WHILE Loop: DO WHILE IsPrime AND intTest <=Sqr(m) [Note: stop testing m after
    IsPrime is False or after passing the square root of m.)
    IF(m Mod intTest = 0)
      True: Assign: IsPrime ← False
    ENDIF
    Add 2 to intTest
  ENDDO
```

Primes

continued

FIGURE 8.06 *Pseudocode for Math Magic (continued)*

Fibonacci

```
General procedure: Sub Fibonacci(rstrMsg As String)
   Define the Fibonacci sequence in a message box
   Get user input for a positive number n up to 1 billion
   Use four long integers to develop the sequence: n, n1, n2, and n3
   Assign: n2 ← 1
   Assign: rstrMsg ← "Fibonacci sequence from 1 to" & Str(n) &": "
   DO/WHILE Loop: DO WHILE n2 <= n
      Assign: n3 ← n1 + n2 [Note: compute the sum]
      Assign: n1 ← n2           [Note: reassign n1, and then n2]
      Assign n2 ← n3
      Assign: rstrMsg ← rstrMsg & Str(n1) & "/"
      intMonths = intMonths + 1
   ENDDO
      Assign: rstrMsg ← rstrMsg & "   That's a total of" _
         & Str(n1) & "rabbit pairs after only" &_
         Str(intMonths) & "Months!"
```

Guess

```
General procedure: Sub Guess(rstrMsg As String)
   Randomize
   Pick a random number n in the range of 1 to 100
   Assign: rstrMsg ← "Guesses:"
   DO/UNTIL Loop: DO UNTIL intTest=n
      intTest ← InputBox ("Guess a number")
      Keep track of the user's guesses by concatenating each guess onto rstrMsg
      Let the user know whether each guess is low or high
   ENDDO
   Add congratulations to rstrMsg
```

Public Sub Primes()

After the user selects intMaxPrime (the maximum number to be tested as a potential prime number), rstrMsg is initialized to start the list of primes with the number 2. This allows us to avoid testing all other even numbers, since 2 is the lowest prime number, and all other even numbers are not prime by definition, since they are all divisible by 2. Thus we can construct a For/Next Loop which tests all of the odd numbers *i* from 3 up to intMaxPrime. If any number *i* between 3 and intMaxPrime turns out to be prime, then that number is concatenated onto rstrMsg.

The function procedure IsPrime examines each *i* and returns a Boolean true if *i* is a prime number and a Boolean false if *i* is not a prime number. Therefore, the statement

```
If IsPrime(i) Then rstrMsg = rstrMsg & Str(i) & ", "
```

concatenates *i* (but only if it is a prime number) onto rstrMsg.

Within the function procedure IsPrime, to find out if the integer *m* passed to the function procedure is a prime number, we start by assuming that *m* is a prime number, that is, the function IsPrime is True. We then use a Do loop (rather than a For/Next loop) to test each potential factor of *m*. This is because we want to exit the loop as soon as we know that *m* is not prime.

The potential factors of *m* are the odd numbers from 3 up to the square root of *m*. (Remember that even numbers > 2 had been eliminated earlier from the list of potential prime numbers; hence no even number needs to be tested as a potential factor of *m*.)

The reason we only have to go up to the square root of *m* is that division by any divisor > Sqr*(m)* will result in a quotient < Sqr*(m)*, and therefore we would already have tested this quotient as a divisor. For example, forgetting about prime numbers for a moment, if we just want to list the pairs of factors of 120, we obtain this list:

```
2 * 60
3 * 40
4 * 30
5 * 24
6 * 20
8 * 15
10 * 12
12 * 10
15 * 8
20 * 6
24 * 5
30 * 4
40 * 3
60 * 2
```

The square root of 120 is 10.95445. Note that after the first factor gets larger than the square root, each pair repeats a previous pair in reverse order.

Within the Do loop, we divide each of the odd numbers from 3 up to the square root of *m* (given by the **Sqr function**) into *m;* if any of these divisions has a remainder of 0, then *m* is not a prime number. Our divisor in this operation (and the loop control variable) is called *intTest*. Note that intTest is initialized to 3 prior to the Do loop, and it is incremented by 2 inside the Do loop.

To determine if *m* is evenly divisible by intTest, we employ the Mod operator, also sometimes known as the *remainder function* or the *modulo arithmetic operator*, which was introduced in the Finance1 Project. Mod calculates the integer remainder from integer division. For instance, 18 divided by 7 is 2 remainder 4; therefore 18 Mod 7 equals 4. Therefore, if the result of *m* Mod intTest is 0, then *m* is evenly divisible by intTest and *m* is not prime. In this case, IsPrime is set to False, and the function procedure is exited.

If IsPrime is still true when the Do loop terminates, then no factor of *m* was found, which means that *m* is a prime number.

Public Sub Fibonacci()

The four Integers needed to compute the Fibonacci sequence *(n, n1, n2,* and *n3)* are all declared as Long Integers, because regular integers can hold values only up to 32767, and we want to accommodate a Fibonacci sequence as high as 1 billion.

No additional new syntax appears in this procedure.

The logic of the Fibonacci procedure is also relatively straightforward: *n* is the user-selected maximum number in the Fibonacci sequence, while rstrMsg serves as the string which holds the sequence of numbers as it is being built. *n1* and *n2* are the current last pair of numbers at the end of the sequence; these are summed to produce *n3*, after which *n1* is assigned the value of n2 and then n2 is assigned the value of *n3*. *n1* is then concatenated to the end of the sequence, and the month counter is incremented. This process continues as long as *n2* <= *n*.

Public Sub Guess()

The Guess procedure features one of the most interesting and versatile capabilities of computers, namely, their ability to generate and use random numbers. Random number generators are at the core of computer simulations, many kinds of models based on statistical probabilities, and all computer video games.

The algorithm to implement the Guess procedure is short and straightforward. After selecting a random number in the 1 to 100 range, a Do loop prompts the user to guess the number, and the Do loop continues executing until the user guesses the correct number. Each guess is concatenated onto rstrMsg (keeping a record of the sequence of user-guesses), and a message is issued with each incorrect guess, indicating that that guess was either too low or too high.

STEP 4. Build Your GUI.

The graphical user interface for Math Magic is copied mostly from the Finance project. To accomplish this, follow these steps:

- Start a new project.
- Select File | Remove File, which deletes Form1 from this new project.
- Select File | Add File, and select FINANCE2.FRM as the file to be added.
- Change the form name to frmMagic, and the form caption to "Math Magic".

Select Project | Project1 Properties, and select the General tab. Change the Project Name to "Magic", and designate frmMagic as the Startup form.

Change the captions of the first three Command Buttons to "Primes", "Fibonacci", and "Guess A Number".

Delete the Font Size frame and insert the Window State frame in its place. Put a control array of three option buttons inside the Window State frame, with the captions "Normal", "Minimized", and "Maximized".

- Delete the option buttons inside the Form Color frame, and insert a control array of four option buttons instead. Make their index values 1, 2, 3, and 4. Set their BackColor properties to yellow, red, green, and blue.
- Select File | Save frmFinance2.frm As . . . , and save the form under the name frmMagic.frm.

Finally, select File | Save Project As . . . , and save the project under the name Magac.vbp.

STEP 5. Write the VB Code.

Press F2 to open the Object Browser, select frmMagic as the object, and select the Depreciation procedure. Highlight the entire procedure in the Code Window, and then press the Delete key on the keyboard; this will delete this general procedure. Perform the same surgical procedurectomy on the FutureValue and Loan procedures.

Then create the three new procedures for the mathematical tasks in Math Magic: Sub Primes, Sub Fibonacci, and Sub Guess. Also create the IsPrime function procedure.

As in the Finance Project, there are no global or form-level variables or constants. The declarations in Sub cmdMath_Click need not be altered; only the Call statements need to be changed, in order to call Primes, Fibonacci, and Guess, rather than Loan, FutureValue, and Depreciation. The local declarations in each of the four general procedures (three Sub procedures and one Function procedure) are those needed to perform each mathematical task:

```
Public Sub Primes (rstrMsg As String)
    Dim i As Integer ' used as a loop control variable
    Dim intMaxPrime As Integer ' maximum Prime number
```

The function procedure IsPrime will be needed by the Sub Primes procedure.

```
Public Function IsPrime(m As Integer) As Boolean
    Dim intTest As Integer
```

Fibonacci's declarations require a bit more explanation:

```
Public Sub Fibonacci (rstrMsg As String)
    Dim n As Long, n1 As Long, n2 As Long, n3 As Long
    Dim intMonths As Integer
```

Four integers must be manipulated to develop the Fibonacci sequence. We used n as the user-selected maximum value in the sequence. At any point in the development of the sequence, the new value to be appended to the sequence is given by

n3 = n1 + n2

where n3 is the new number, and n1 and n2 are the two previous numbers in the sequence. intMonths is used to keep track of the number of numbers in the Fibonacci sequence.

The fourth general procedure is Guess, with declarations as follows:

```
Public Sub Guess (rstrMsg As String)
    Dim n As Integer 'the random number to be guessed
    Dim intTest As Integer 'the user's current guess
```

As with the earlier projects, try first to write the code by following the pseudocode. Then compare your completed code with our version below. By now, you are hopefully coming to realize that there can be any number of correct solutions to a programming problem. In addition to creating a program that works correctly, you should also strive for clarity, consistency, and reusability. To the extent that you achieve all of these objectives, you are well on the way to becoming a successful and accomplished computer programmer.

FrmMagic—filename frmMAGIC.FRM—Code

```
Option Explicit
Private Sub Fibonacci(rstrMsg As String)
    Dim n As Long, n1 As Long, n2 As Long, n3 As Long
    Dim intMonths As Integer
    MsgBox "The Fibonacci sequence-Each number is " _
        & "the sum of the previous two numbers"
    Do
        n = InputBox("Enter a number up to 1,000,000,000")
    Loop Until n > 0 And n < 1000000001
    n2 = 1
    rstrMsg = "Fibonacci sequence from 1 to" + Str$(n) + ": "
    Do While n2 <= n
        n3 = n1 + n2
        n1 = n2
        n2 = n3
        rstrMsg = rstrMsg + Str$(n1) & "/"
        intMonths = intMonths + 1
    Loop
    rstrMsg = rstrMsg & "That's a total of" & _
```

```
        Str$(n1) & "rabbit pairs after only" & _
        Str$(intMonths) & " Months!"
End Sub
Private Sub Guess(rstrMsg As String)
    Dim n As Integer
    Dim intTest As Integer
    Randomize
    n = Rnd * 100 + 1
    MsgBox "Math Magic randomly picked a number from 1 to" _
        & " 100. Now you have to guess the number. You" _
        & " get as many tries as it takes!"
    rstrMsg = "Guesses: "
    Do Until intTest = n
        intTest = InputBox("Guess a number")
        rstrMsg = rstrMsg & Str(intTest) & "/"
        If intTest < n Then MsgBox "low"
        If intTest > n Then MsgBox "high"
    Loop
    rstrMsg = rstrMsg & "BINGO!" & Str(intTest) & _ " is it!"
End Sub
Private Sub Primes(rstrMsg As String)
    Dim i As Integer ' used as a loop control variable
    Dim intMaxPrime As Integer ' maximum Prime number
    MsgBox "A Prime number is a positive integer evenly " & _
        "divisible only by itself and 1. Pick the " & _
        "maximum prime to see all primes from 2 to " & _
        "that maximum prime."
    Do
        intMaxPrime = InputBox("Enter a number up to 500")
    Loop Until intMaxPrime > 1 And intMaxPrime < 501
    rstrMsg = "Primes from 2 to " & Str(intMaxPrime) & _
        ": 2, "
    For i = 3 To intMaxPrime Step 2
        If IsPrime(i) Then rstrMsg = rstrMsg & Str(i) & ", "
    Next i
End Sub
Private Sub cmdMath_Click(Index As Integer)
    Static staintCountClicks(0 To 3) As Integer
    Dim strResult As String
    staintCountClicks(Index) = staintCountClicks(Index) + 1
    Select Case Index
    Case 0: Call Primes(strResult)
    Case 1: Call Fibonacci(strResult)
    Case 2: Call Guess(strResult)
    Case 3
        Dim i As Integer
        strResult = "How many times each math function " _
        & "was selected:" & vbCrLf
        For i = 0 To 2
        strResult = strResult & " " & cmdMath(i).Caption _
                & Str(staintCountClicks(i)) & vbCrLf
        Next i
        txtResult = strResult
        MsgBox "That's all folks", , "Finance"
        End
```

```
    End Select
    txtResult = strResult
End Sub
Private Sub Form_Load()
    Me.Top = (Screen.Height - Me.Height) / 2
    Me.Left = (Screen.Width - Me.Width) / 2
    Me.BackColor = vbYellow
End Sub
Private Sub optColor_Click(Index As Integer)
    Me.BackColor = Choose(Index, vbYellow, vbRed, _
vbGreen, vbBlue)
End Sub
Private Sub optWindowState_Click(Index As Integer)
    frmMagic.WindowState = Index
End Sub
Public Function IsPrime(m As Integer) As Boolean
    Dim intTest As Integer
    IsPrime = True
    intTest = 3
    Do While IsPrime And intTest <= Sqr(m)
        If m Mod intTest = 0 Then IsPrime = False
        intTest = intTest + 2
    Loop
End Function
```

STEP 6. Test and Debug.

Make sure it works! Add error traps!

STEP 7. Complete the Program Documentation.

Add appropriate comments to the program code.

SUMMARY

Rnd generates a **random real number** between 0 and <1. This random number can be manipulated to create random values in any range. The **Randomize** statement reseeds the Rnd function, so that each subsequent computer run results in a unique series of random numbers. Random numbers are at the core of **computer simulations.**

Function procedures, unlike Sub procedures, return a value to the calling routine. The Function header identifies the functionname, parameter list, and data type of the function's return value. In the body of the function, the **return value** is assigned to the functionname. **Exit Function** permits early exit from the body of a function, and **End Function** marks the end of the function definition. A typical function call is an assignment statement in which the return value from the function is assigned to a variable.

Software reuse is again emphasized, since the whole project is an adaptation of the Finance2 Project. Visual Basic includes a full complement of **mathematics functions,** either as **intrinsic** or as **derived functions.** The **Choose** function returns one value from an enumerated list of choices.

PROGRAMMING ASSIGNMENTS

1. New Math

Rewrite the Math Magic program with three new mathematical functions in lieu of the current Primes, Fibonacci, and Guess A Number routines presented in the text. Choose two mathematical functions which are built into Visual Basic, such as Sin (Sine) and Cos (Cosine), and one derived function, such as Hyperbolic Sine. (Hint: Look up *Math Functions* in Help | Search.) Make sure that your program explains the functions you are using. Program these functions within general procedures, as was done in the original Math Project. Include error trapping in all three general procedures. Include also at least one new function procedure.

2. Randomly Selected Student Groups

Your psychology instructor would like to have a computer program which divides students in a class into randomly selected groups. The input data consists of the number of student groups and the number of students in each group. The program first calculates the total number of students in the class. Assume that students are assigned a unique Student ID number, an integer in the range from 1 to the number of students. Thus the output should be a listing of the randomly selected Student ID numbers in each student group. Sample output for 3 student groups of 10 students per group appears in Figure 8.07.

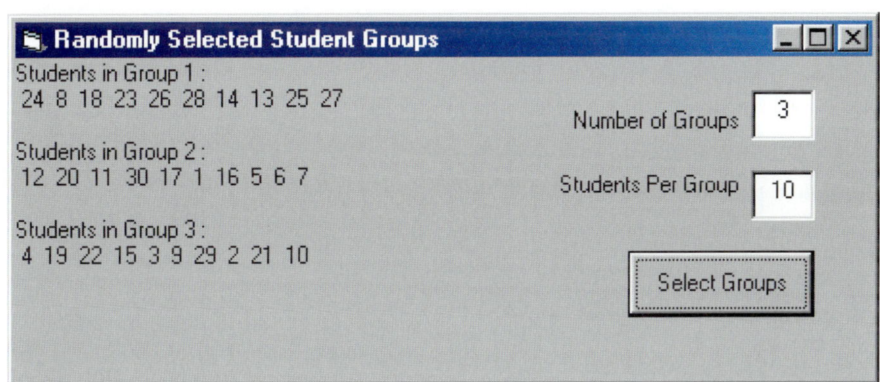

FIGURE 8.07 *Output from Random Selection*

CHAPTER NINE

MENUS AND MDI FORMS

Application: Finance (Version 3)

LEARNING OBJECTIVES

Upon completion of Chapter Nine, you will be able to:

- Implement an application using a Multiple Document Interface (MDI) Form.
- Arrange child forms (cascade, tile horizontal, tile vertical, arrange icons).
- Use the Menu Editor to incorporate a menu into an application.
- Use the Picture control and the Image control.
- Place a Toolbar underneath the Menu on an MDI form.
- Design a splash screen to start up an application.

Keywords

Align property
Arrange Icons arrangement
Arrange method
Cascade arrangement
Checked property
Child form
Icon property
Image control (prefix: img)
LoadPicture function
Make EXE command
MDIChild property
MDI Form object (prefix: mdi)
Menu control
Menu Editor
MousePointer property
Multiple Document Interface (MDI) application
Picture Box control (prefix: pic)
Picture property
Splash screen
Stretch property
Tile Horizontal arrangement
Tile Vertical arrangement
WindowList property
WindowState property

INTRODUCING FINANCE (VERSION 3)

Run FINANCE3.EXE, the third version of our Finance Application. Like several earlier projects, Finance3 includes multiple forms, but in this case the several forms are displayed under the control of a single master form, called a Multiple Document Interface Form (MDI Form). After an initial splash screen (Figure 9.01), the MDI Form (Figure 9.02) contains both a menu and a toolbar, allowing the user to activate each of the other forms: Loan Payment (Figure 9.03), Future Value (Figure 9.04), Depreciation (Figure 9.05). (The "About" selection is a repeat of the splash screen.) The functional tasks performed by this application are the now-familiar ones of calculating the monthly payment for a loan, the future value of an annuity, and the depreciation deduction for an asset for a given year.

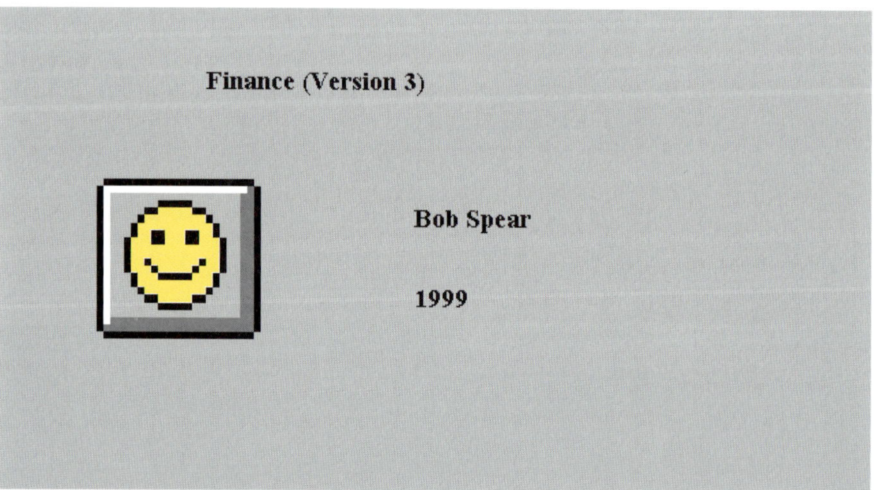

FIGURE 9.01 *Splash screen for Finance Version 3*

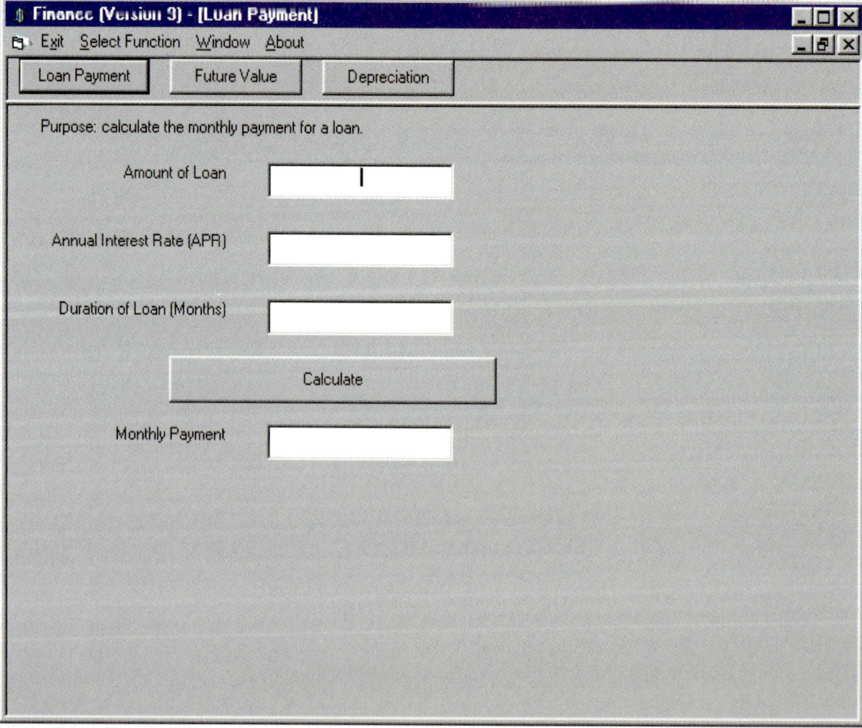

FIGURE 9.02 *Finance3 MDI Form*

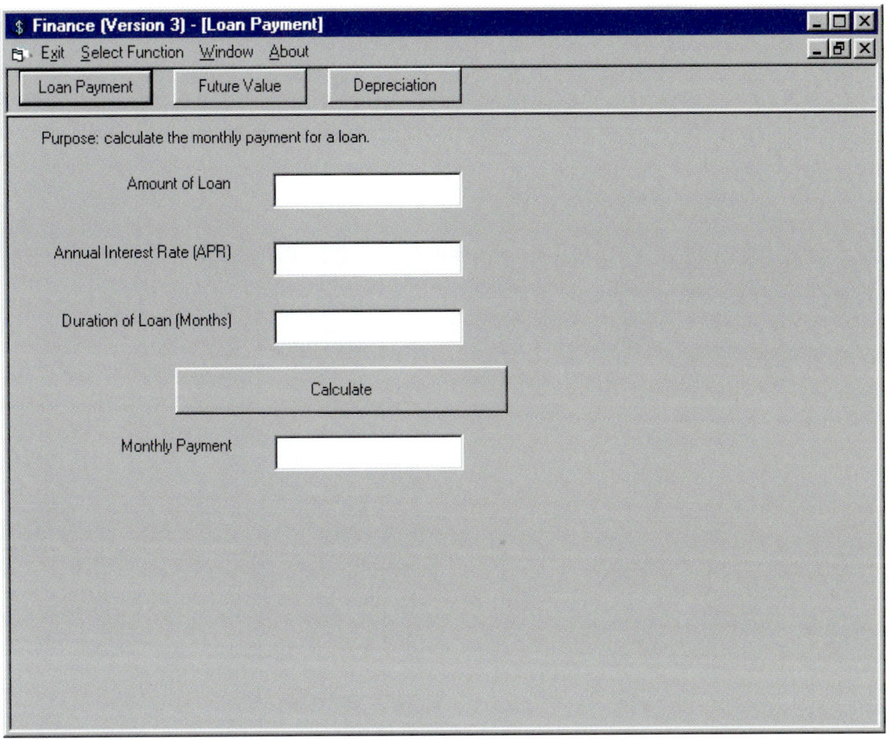

FIGURE 9.03 *Loan Payment child form*

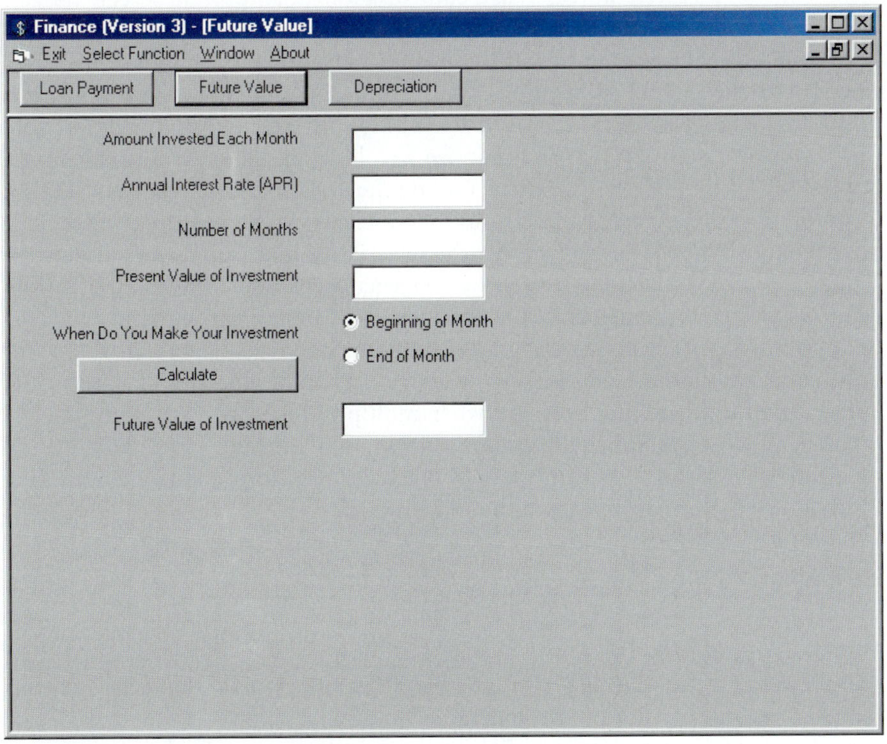

FIGURE 9.04 *Future Value child form*

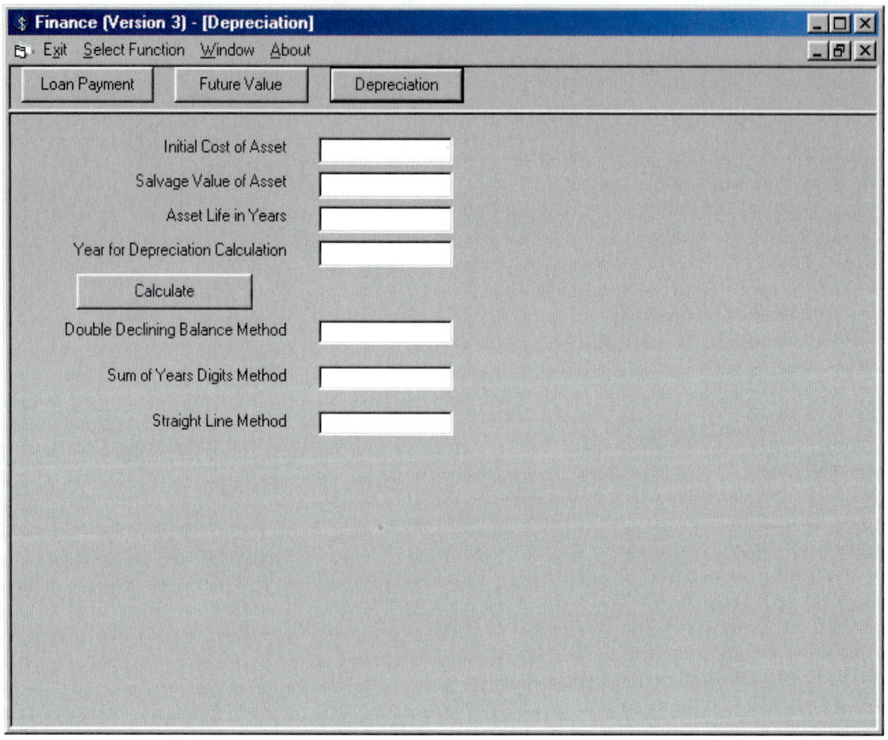

FIGURE 9.05 *Depreciation child form*

STEP 1. Understand the Problem.

The central new GUI feature in this chapter is the use of a Multiple Document Interface Form and several "child" forms that operate under the MDI Form. The menu control, picture control, image control, toolbar, and splash screen are also new features of the Finance3 application.

Run the program several times to discover its principal operational characteristics. Note that a child form always exists within the borders of the parent MDI Form. If you move or resize the MDI Form, any active child form remains within the MDI Form's borders. If you minimize a child form, the child form's icon appears at the bottom of the MDI Form (not on the desktop outside the MDI Form).

Note also the effects of the various menu selections. Before any child form is activated, the Window menu has only the selections **Cascade, Tile,** and **Arrange Icons,** and these selections have no effect whatever. When one or more child windows are open, the names of the open windows appear in the **WindowList** at the bottom of the Window menu. Selecting an open window from the WindowList makes the selected window the active form. Note the effects of **Cascade, Tile Horizontal,** and **Tile Vertical** when multiple child forms are open (but not minimized). Now minimize the open child windows, move the icons around, and then choose Window | **Arrange Icons.** Finally, if you close a child window, then that window no longer appears in the WindowList.

STEP 2. Design a Solution.

Menu Control

Visual Basic's **Menu Control** gives you the ability to create a Menu Bar for your VB application, with all of the functionality of any Windows Menu Bar. The Menu can have any number of main selections, and a drop-down list can be associated with each Menu Bar entry. Entries on a drop-down list can be further subdivided into submenus. Any entry can be checked or unchecked, enabled or disabled, visible or invisible. Selecting any menu entry triggers the click event for that entry or, if that entry's click event procedure was not programmed, displays the next lower submenu for that entry.

VB provides a **Menu Editor,** which makes it easy to design a complete set of Menu Bar entries and drop-down lists. To experiment with this feature, let's build the Menu Control for a hypothetical Windows-based text editor called Personal Edit. The menu bar, Figure 9.06, offers the following choices.

File
- Open . . .
- Close
- ________
- Print
- Printer Setup . . .
- ________
- Exit

Edit
- Cut
- Copy
- Paste

Help
- Contents
- Search . . .
- ________
- About Personal Edit

To start building this Menu Control, start a new project, change Form1's caption to "Personal Edit," and then choose Tools | Menu Editor from VB's Menu Bar, or press the Ctrl-E keys, or click the Menu Editor icon, the sixth icon from the left on the Toolbar. (This is the only control whose icon is on the Toolbar rather than in the Toolbox.) This opens the Menu Editor window (Figure 9.07).

Type in the caption for the first Menu Bar entry, "&File". The ampersand (&) before the letter F indicates that F will be underlined in the menu (File), and that the user will be able to access this menu item from the keyboard by pressing Alt-F rather than by clicking the word *File* with the mouse.

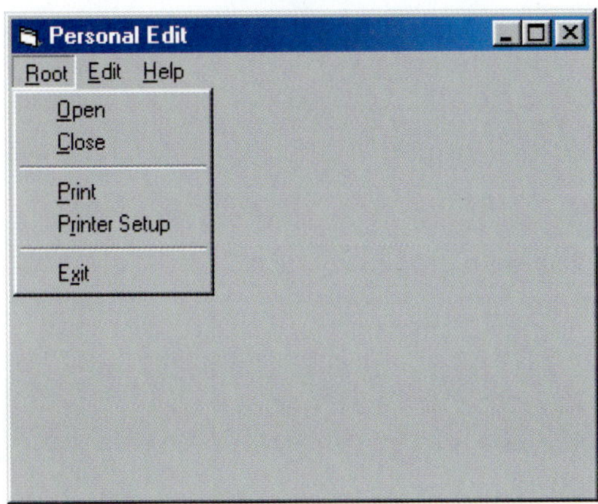

FIGURE 9.06 *Menu bar for Personal Edit*

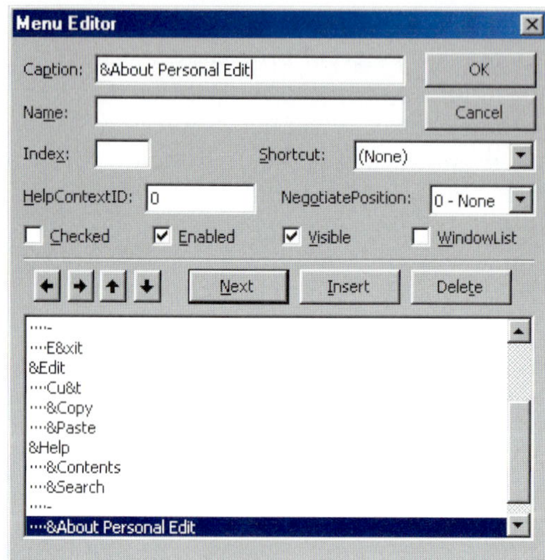

FIGURE 9.07 *Menu Editor window*

Type a name for this menu entry, in this case "mnuFile". Every entry in the menu requires a name, by which you will refer to this menu entry in code. The name must be entered, even if you have no intention of writing a click event procedure for this menu item. Then click on the "Next" command button.

The first item in the drop-down list is Open . . . , then Close, followed by a separator bar; but we are not concerned with them right now and will get back to the Open . . . entry later. The next menu entry we are concerned with is the item in the drop-down list under File named Print. Type the caption "&Print", and give it the name mnuFilePrint. Now click the OK button. As you can see (Figure 9.08), we have created a Menu Bar with the entries File and Print. But we wanted Print to appear as part of the drop-down list under File, not as a Menu Bar selection. Re-enter the Menu Editor, click on &Print, and then click the right arrow on the Menu Editor (pressing the right arrow key on the keyboard will not work). "----" appears before the menu item. Now click OK. The Menu Bar has only one item, File, and if you click that item, the drop-down list will appear, containing Print (Figure 9.09). Press the escape key twice to leave your Menu Bar.

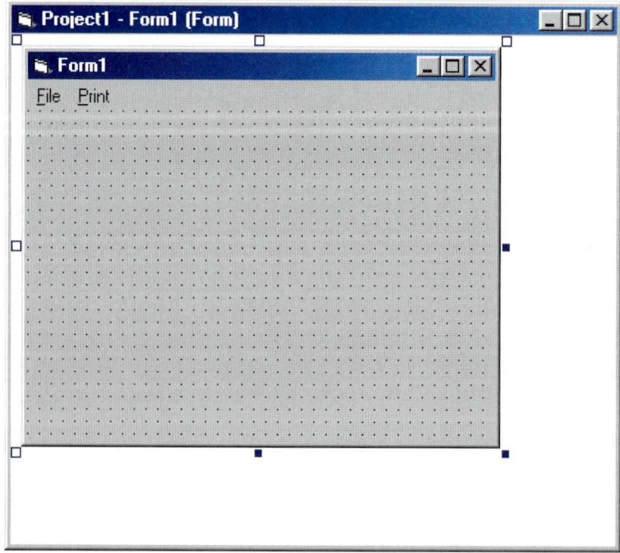

FIGURE 9.08 *An incorrect menu bar*

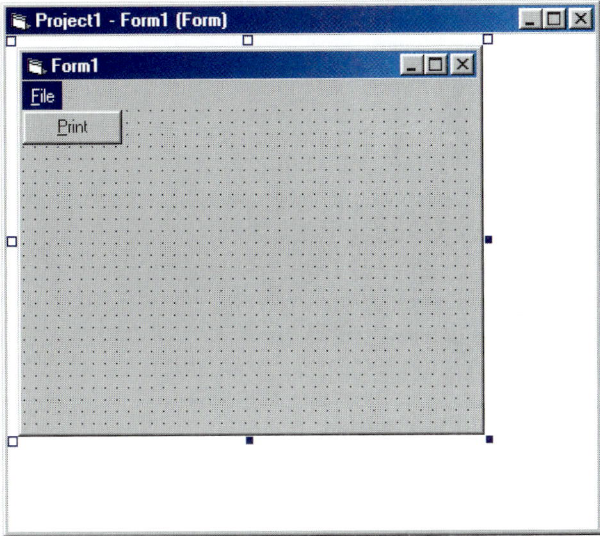

FIGURE 9.09 *The corrected menu bar*

Re-enter the Menu Editor to create the rest of the Personal Edit menu. Click on the &Print entry, and then click on the Insert command button. Note that space for a new entry has been created, and this new entry will be automatically indented one level. Type "&Open . . ." as the caption and "mnuFileOpen" as the name. (The File | Open menu selection in our hypothetical application would lead to a Dialog Box, in which the user would select a file to be opened. Remember that the ellipsis (. . .) is the Windows convention for a menu selection that leads to a Dialog Box. You should also adopt this convention, because then your users will know what to expect.)

Click on the &Print entry again, and then click on the Insert command button again. Insert the menu selection &Close, and name this entry mnuFileClose. Click on the &Print entry again, and then click on the Insert command button for a third time. The separator bar in a menu is created by typing a single hyphen in the caption field. You still need to provide a unique name for this separator bar, such as mnuFileSep1. The Menu Editor now appears as in Figure 9.10.

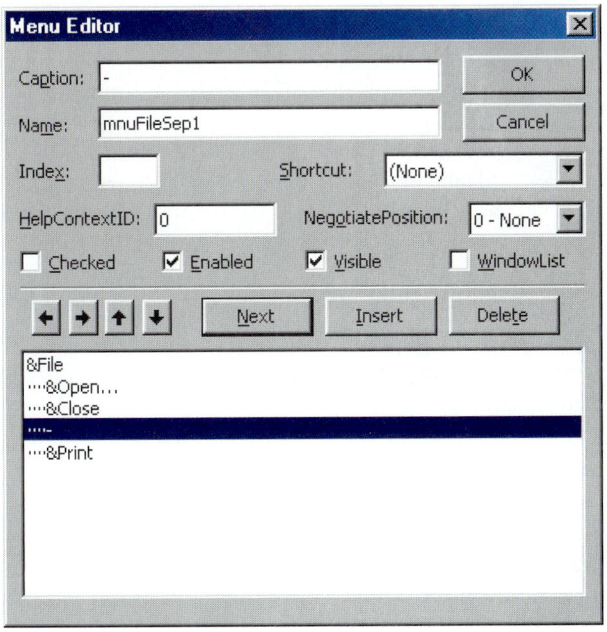

FIGURE 9.10 *Creating a separator bar*

- In the list of menu entries at the bottom of the Menu Editor, click on the last item, &Print. Then click Next.
- Enter the caption "P&rint Setup . . ." and the name "mnuFilePrintSetup."
- Click again on Next. The caption should again be a hyphen and the name "mnuFileSep2."
- Click again on Next. The caption is "E&xit" and the name "mnuFileExit."
- Click on OK.

The File drop-down menu is now complete, though we have not yet written any code behind the menu selections. Let's write a little code so you can see how the Menu Control works.

Click on File | Open in your Form Window. The template for Sub mnuFileOpen_Click appears. The Click event is the only event defined for the Menu Control. Type into this procedure the statement

```
Print "File | Open selected"
```

From the object drop-down list in the Code Window, choose mnuFilePrint, and type this statement into the Sub mnuFilePrint_Click event procedure:

```
Print "File | Print selected"
```

Now run the program. With the mouse, select File | Open, and the "File | Open selected" message should appear on the form; select File | Print, and the "File | Print selected" message should appear. Press Alt-F O, and the "File | Open selected" message should appear on the form; press Alt-F P, and the "File | Print selected" message should appear. Note that you cannot click on a separator bar, although you could refer to mnuFileSep1 in code.

Re-enter the Menu Editor, and complete the construction of the entire Menu Control. Click on the E&xit entry, and then click the Next command button. The next entry should be "&Edit," an entry on the Menu Bar itself. Click the left arrow to remove the indentation, and type "&Edit" as the caption and "mnuEdit" as the name of this entry. Complete the Menu Control for this form with these remaining entries.

LEVEL	CAPTION	NAME
indented	Cu&t	mnuEditCut
indented	&Copy . . .	mnuEditCopy
indented	&Paste	mnuEditPaste
Menu Bar	&Help	mnuHelp
indented	&Contents	mnuHelpContents
indented	&Search	mnuHelpSearch
indented		mnuHelpSep1
indented	&About Personal Edit	mnuHelpAboutPersonalEdit

Run the program to see the entire Menu Control, even though no code exists for most of the menu selections.

Three more Menu Control options are important and should be demonstrated here: Checked, Enabled, and Visible. To see the effect of these options, re-enter the Menu Editor, and select the entry "&Search". Click the Visible check box. Since the default value of the Visible property is True, clicking this box will make this menu selection invisible. Similarly, select the entry "&Contents", and click the Enabled check box. Since the default value of the Enabled property is True, clicking this box will disable this item. Select the entry "&Paste", and click the **Checked property.** Since the default value of the Checked property is False, clicking this box will cause a checkmark to appear next to the item. Click OK to leave the Menu Editor.

Now run the program, and click on the Menu Bar selections. Note that Search does not appear, Contents is disabled, and Paste is checked.

All of these toggle switches can be reversed in code. Put a Command Button on the form, and enter this code:

```
Private Sub Command1_Click()
   mnuHelpSearch.Visible = Not _
      mnuHelpSearch.Visible
   mnuHelpContents.Enabled = Not _
      mnuHelpContents.Enabled
   mnuEditPaste.Checked = Not mnuEditPaste.Checked
End Sub
```

Run the program, and note the effect of clicking Command1.

Finally, a Shortcut key may be assigned in the Menu Editor for any indented menu item. For example, in most Windows-based editing software, Ctrl-X is a shortcut key for Edit | Cut; Ctrl-C is a shortcut for Edit | Copy; and Ctrl-V is a shortcut for Edit | Paste. In each case, the shortcut key fires the click event procedure for the associated menu entry.

MDI Form

A Multiple Document Interface Form (MDI Form) is a window object in a Visual Basic application that serves as a container for other forms. If a VB application has many forms, the programmer may find it useful to ensure that all of these forms appear within the same application window on the screen. An MDI Form provides such an application window.

A VB application can have only one MDI Form. To demonstrate:

- start up a new project;
- choose Project | Add MDI Form;
- click the Project Explorer icon or choose View | Project Explorer, and note that this project now contains two forms, Form1 and MDIForm1;

- choose Project from the Menu Bar again, and note that the Add MDI Form selection has been disabled.

An MDI Form can serve as the container for any number of child forms. A child form is simply any regular (non-MDI) form whose **MDIChild property** is set to True. At run time, a child form always appears within the borders of the parent MDI Form. Within those borders, the child form can be moved, resized, maximized, or minimized. When a child form is maximized, its caption is added to the MDI Form's caption in the MDI Form's Title Bar. Whenever a child form is the active form, if the child form has its own menu, the child's menu replaces any MDI Form menu. When a child form is minimized, an icon representing the child form appears at the bottom of the MDI Form. Experiment with these features (Figure 9.11).

1. Choose View | Project Explorer, select MDIForm1, and then click on View Object. Set the MDI Form's caption property to "mdi sample", and name property to "mdiSample".

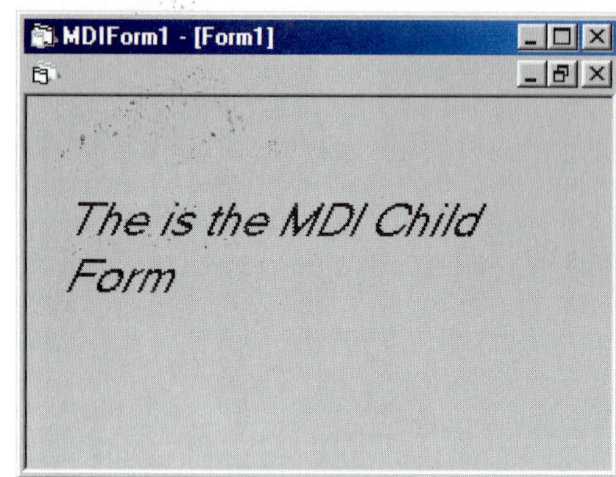

FIGURE 9.11 *An MDI child form is maximized*

2. Put a Menu Control on the MDI form. Just put one entry in the menu; use the caption "mdi sample" and the name "mnuMDISample".
3. Double-click the MDI Form, which opens the Code Window for Sub MDIForm_Load. Put the statement "child2.Show" into this procedure.
4. Choose View | Project, select Form1, and then click on View Form. Change the caption and name properties of this form to "child1".
5. Drag several controls from the Toolbox onto child1.
6. Put a Menu Control on child1 with just two entries, "one-1" and "one-2".
7. Open the Properties Window, and set the MDIChild property to True.
8. Click on the New Form icon (the leftmost icon on the Toolbar), which adds Form2 to the project. Change the name and caption properties of Form2 to "child2".
9. Drag several different controls from the Toolbox onto child2.
10. Put a Menu Control on child2 with just two entries, "two-1" and "two-2".
11. Open the Properties Window, and set the MDIChild property to True.

Now run this application (see Figures 9.12, 9.13, and 9.14). By default, child1 is the Start Up Form. When a child form is loaded, its parent MDI Form is automatically loaded. And the MDIForm_Load event procedure loads child2. Therefore, when the application first appears on the screen, child1, the Start Up Form, is the active form. Note that the menu that appears on the MDI Form is that belonging to child1.

Child2, which appears cascaded behind child1, is also open but is not active (only one form can be the active form at a time). Continue with the following steps.

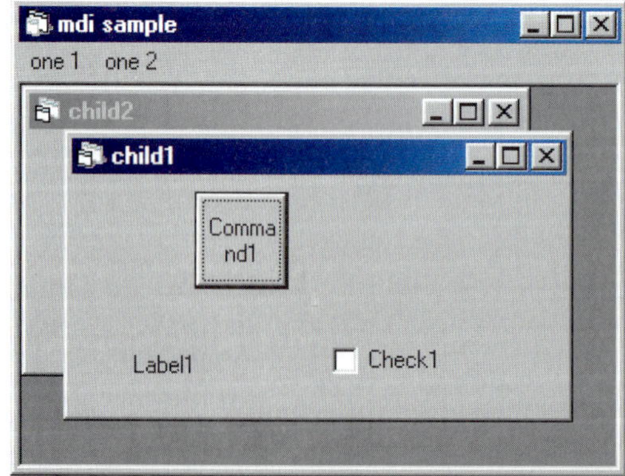

FIGURE 9.12 *Child1 is the active form; child2 is also open*

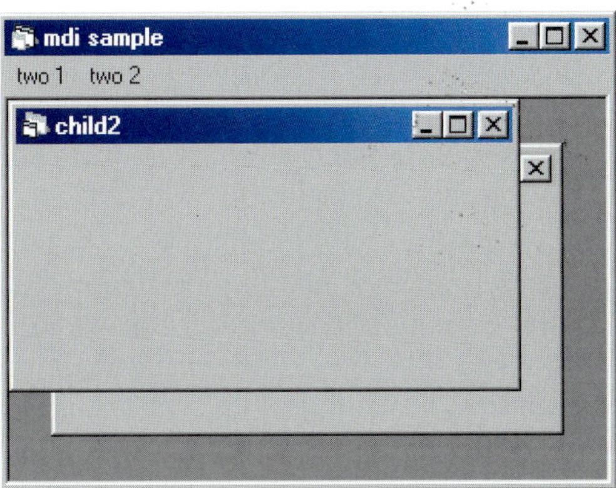

FIGURE 9.13 *Child2 is the active form; child1 (mostly hidden) is also open*

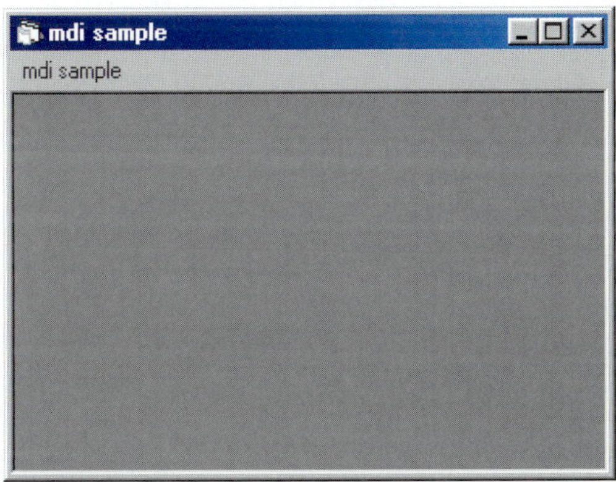

FIGURE 9.14 *No child form is open*

- Click on child2. Note that the menu on the MDI Form switches to the menu belonging to child2.
- Maximize child2. Note that child2 fills the entire MDI client area (the area within the borders and under the MDI Form's Title Bar). Note also that the Title Bar now contains the caption of both the MDI parent form and the child form: "mdi Sample—[child2]" (Figure 9.15).

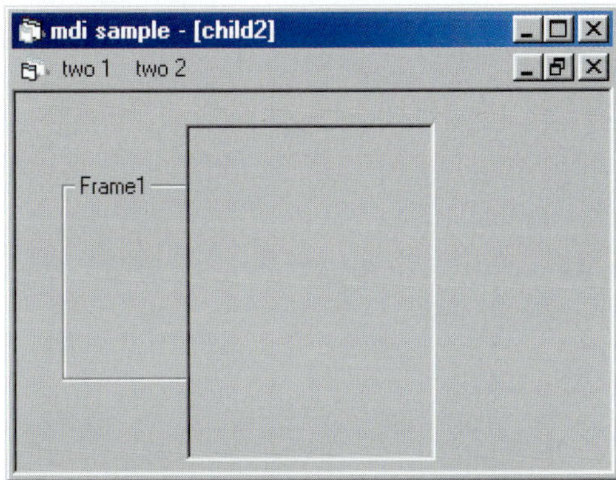

FIGURE 9.15 *MDI sample, with Child2 maximized*

- Minimize child2 by clicking child2's Control Box and choosing Minimize. An icon representing child2 appears at the bottom of the parent MDI form. The menu reverts to that belonging to child1, since child1 is now the active form.
- Maximize child1. Then resize the MDI Form. Note that child1 continues to fill all of the available space within the application window.
- Close child1 either by double-clicking child1's control box (not the MDI Form's control box), or by clicking Child1's control box and choosing Close, or by pressing the Ctrl-F4 keys). (Ctrl-F4 closes the active window within an application; Alt-F4 closes the application.) Note that child2, which had been minimized, is now maximized. VB maintains the current maximized window state for the active child.
- Now close child2. Note that the menu that appears on the MDI Form is that written for the MDI Form itself (Figure 9.16).
- End the application.

In the sample application we have described here, we have no method of showing a child form after it has been closed. Typically, therefore, MDI applications include menu selections to show each of the child forms in the project. In the present experiment, open the Code Window for Sub mnuMDISample_Click, and insert this code:

```
child1.Show
child2.Show
```

Now when you run the program, if you close both child forms and then click MDIForm1's menu selection "mdi Sample", both forms will be loaded and displayed.

For the last MDI Form experiment, we need a menu only on the parent form. So select child1, enter the Menu Editor, and delete all of the items in this menu. Click OK. Then do the same thing for child2, deleting its menu.

Now open the Menu Editor for the MDI Form. Currently, the only entry in this menu is "mdi sample." Add new items, as follows:

LEVEL	CAPTION	NAME
Menu Bar	&Window	mnuWindow
indented	&Cascade	mnuWindowCascade
indented	Tile &Horizontal	mnuWindowTileHorizontal
indented	Tile &Vertical	mnuWindowTileVertical
indented	&Arrange Icons	mnuWindowArrangeIcons

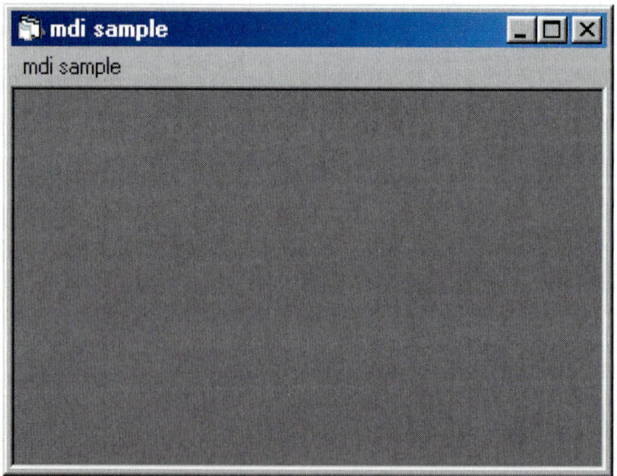

FIGURE 9.16 *MDI sample, with no child form open*

After entering all of these items in the Menu Editor, select the "&Window" entry and click its WindowList property. When a menu item has its WindowList property set to True, Windows will maintain a list of all open child forms in an MDI application and will display this list at the bottom of the drop-down list under that menu item. The currently active child form is also checked. (You have probably seen this feature in other Windows-based programs. In Word, WordPerfect, Excel, Quattro Pro, and many other commercial software products, the list of open child forms appears under the "Window" menu. The WindowList property lets you add this functionality to your own applications.) Only one menu entry in a Menu Control can have a WindowList.

The **Arrange method** applies to an MDI Form. It can be employed to control how the open and active child forms under the MDI Form are displayed within the application window. The available selections are similar to those in the Windows Task List called Cascade, Tile, and Arrange Icons. The syntax of this method is

```
object.Arrange arrangement
```

where *object* is the name of the MDI Form, and *arrangement* is an integer from 0 to 3:

0	Cascade. Open child forms that are not minimized are displayed in an overlapping series, with the currently active form on top.
1	Tile horizontally. Each open child form that is not minimized is displayed across the entire width of the application window. From top to bottom, the available window space is divided among the displayed forms. (However, if any child forms are currently minimized, space is left below the displayed child forms for those icons to appear.)
2	Tile vertically. Each open child form that is not minimized is displayed from the top of the client area (under the MDI Form's Menu Bar) to the bottom of the MDI Form. (However, if any child forms are currently minimized, space is left below the displayed child forms for those icons to appear.) From left to right, the available window space is divided among the displayed forms.
3	Arrange icons. Icons representing open but minimized child forms are displayed across the bottom of the MDI Form.

This demonstration will be more illustrative of these features if we have at least three child forms to work with, and if we use the entire screen. Therefore, add child3 to the project by clicking the New Form icon. Change the name and caption properties of this new form to "child3", and set its MDIChild property to True. Then return to the MDI Form and add the statement

```
Child3.Show
```

to Sub mnuMDISample_Click. Then, open the Properties Window for mdiSamp, and change the WindowState property setting to "2—Maximized".

The click event procedures for the items in the drop-down list under the "Window" selection of the MDI Form's Menu Bar need to be written as follows:

```
Private Sub mnuWindowCascade_Click
    mdiSample.Arrange 0
End Sub
Private Sub mnuWindowTileHorizontal_Click
    mdiSample.Arrange 1
End Sub
```

```
Private Sub mnuWindowTileVertical_Click
    mdiSample.Arrange 2
End Sub
Private Sub mnuWindowArrangeIcons_Click
    mdiSample.Arrange 3
End Sub
```

Now run the project.

- Click on "mdi Sample" to display all three child forms (Figure 9.17).
- Then click on Tile Horizontal, Tile Vertical, and Cascade to see the different effects when none of the child forms are minimized.
- Note the WindowList display under the Window menu. Change the active form (either by clicking the form itself or by selecting it from the WindowList). The active form always has a checkmark in the WindowList.
- Next, minimize one of the child forms (Figures 9.18 and 9.19).
- Again, click on Tile Horizontal, Tile Vertical, and Cascade to see the different effects.
- Restore the MDI Form (by clicking the Restore button in the upper right corner of the screen, or by choosing Restore from the Control Menu). Note that horizontal and vertical scroll bars automatically appear along the bottom and right borders of the MDI Form. This is because the restored size of the MDI Form is not large enough to display the child forms, whose size was established when the MDI Form was maximized.

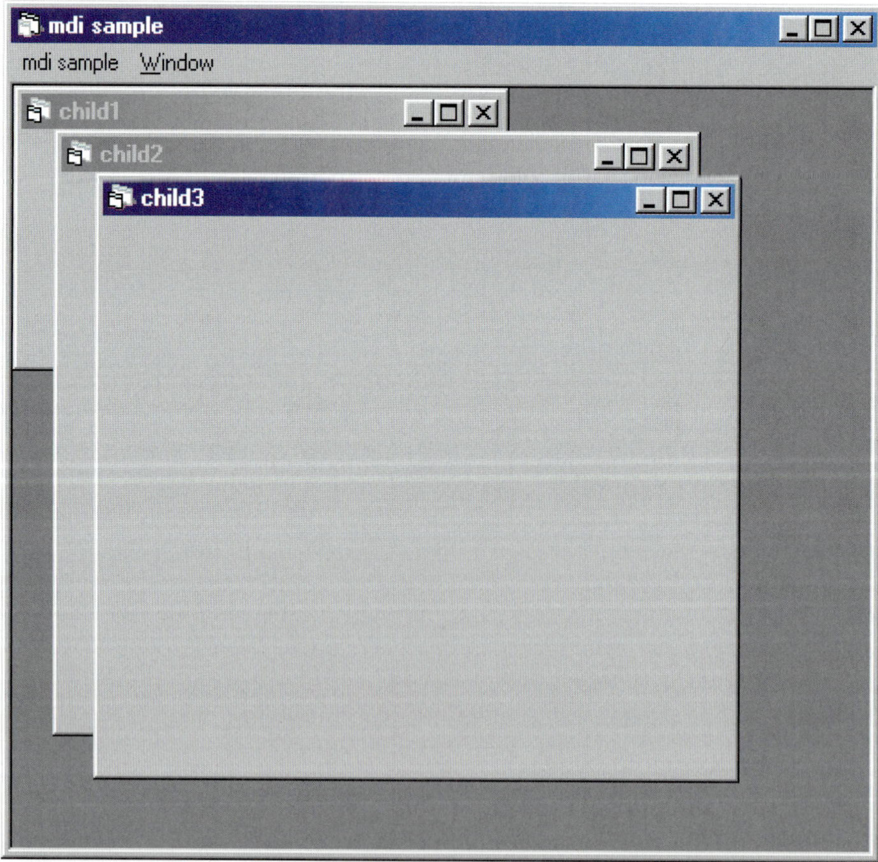

FIGURE 9.17 *Revised MDI sample, showing all 3 child forms*

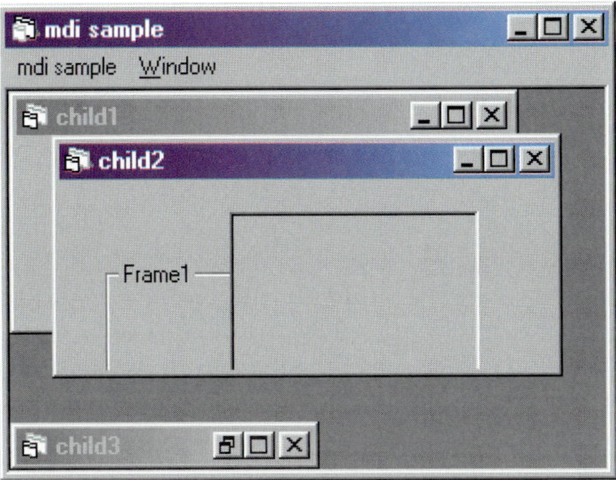

FIGURE 9.18 *Child3 is minimized; child1 and child2 are cascaded*

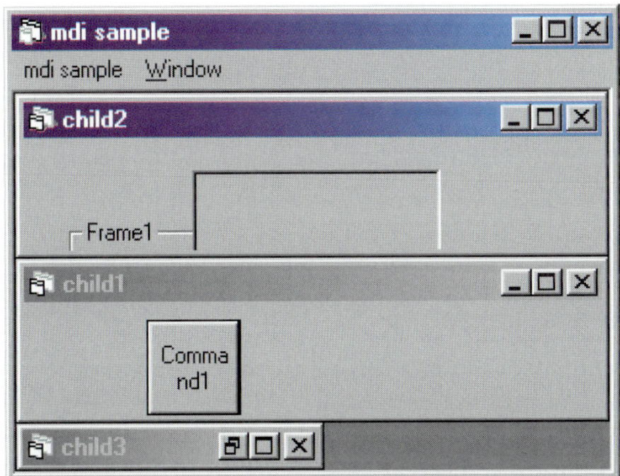

FIGURE 9.19 *Child3 is minimized; child1 and child2 are tiled horizontally*

- Minimize all three child forms. Note where they appear on the screen. Maximize the MDI Form again. Note the position of the three icons. Choose Window | Arrange Icons to order the icons neatly at the bottom of the screen.
- Now restore the MDI Form again. You probably cannot see the icons at all. Choose Window | Arrange Icons to order the icons again at the bottom of the application window.
- End the application.

Image Control

VB offers two controls that can contain pictures, the **Image control** and the Picture control, both introduced in this chapter. The Image control's icon in the Toolbox looks like a painting of a mountain with the sun in the background:

An Image control can be used to display relatively simple graphics files: icons (.ICO files), bitmaps (.BMP files), and Windows metafiles (.WMF files), among others. Two new properties are critical to using the Image control: the Stretch property and the Picture property.

The Stretch property is either True or False. When True, the size of the picture is adjusted to fit the size of the control. When False (the default setting), the size of the control is adjusted to fit the size of the picture. For instance, if you want a small icon to appear as a large image on your form, draw the Image control as large as you want the picture to appear and set the Stretch property to True.

The Picture property identifies the file containing the image that you wish to display. This property can be loaded at design time or at run time.

To load the Picture property at design time, select the property and click the ellipsis in the Properties window settings box. A Dialog Box prompts you to select a file containing the image you want to display. If you want to load an icon into an image control, you could select one of the hundreds of icons shipped with VB 6.0 (you can find them on the VB 6.0 CD in the folder \Common\Graphics\Icons). In that icons folder, in a subfolder called Flags, you could load FlgUSA01.ico into an Image control.

To load the Picture property of an Image control at run time, you must use the LoadPicture function. To load the same USA flag at run time into a control named Image1, the VB statement (assuming your VB 6.0 CD is in Drive D) would be

```
Image1.Picture = LoadPicture _
   ("d:\common\graphics\icons\flags\flgusa01.ico")
```

A Timer control and an Image control can be combined to produce an image that flashes on and off (Figure 9.20). Try this sample on a new project.

1. Set the form's caption to "Image Sample" and the form name to frmImage.
2. Place an Image control on Form1. Set its Stretch property to True, and make it about one inch square in size.
3. For the Image control's Picture property, select the Don't Walk icon, stored in \icons\traffic\trffc18b.ico.
4. Place a Timer control on the form.
5. Set the Timer control's Interval property to 1000 (milliseconds)
6. In Sub Timer1_Timer, toggle the visible property of the Image control:

```
Image1.Visible = Not Image1.Visible
```

7. Run this program. Note that the image flashes on and off every second.

FIGURE 9.20 *Image sample, flashing icons*

By extension, you can easily flash alternating icons on the screen. To modify this sample to this effect, continue as follows.

1. Copy the Image control to the Clipboard, and then paste it onto the form. You do not want to create a control array.
2. Place Image2 in the middle of the form, and change its Picture property to the Walk icon, that is, \icons\traffic\trffc18a.ico.
3. Place Image1 directly on top of Image2.

Run this program. Image1 (still the Don't Walk icon) flashes on and off every second. When Image1 is not visible, the Walk icon (Image2), hidden behind Image1, appears.

Icon Property

The same techniques used to load the Picture property of the Image control at design time or at run time can also be used to load the **Icon property** of a form. Only an icon stored in a file with the extension .ICO can be loaded into a form's Icon property. The selected icon appears at the top left corner of a form, and, at run time, when a form or an application is minimized, the icon used to represent that form or application is taken from the form's Icon property.

To try out this feature, set the Icon property of frmImage to \icons\traffic\trffc09.ico, the image of a traffic light. The traffic light icon appears at the top left of the form.

Splash Screen

The Start Up Form for Finance3, called a "splash screen," stays on the screen for three seconds and then disappears, giving way to the main part of the project. You have probably seen this technique in many Windows applications. The alternating icons (images of the smiley face) reside in two Image controls placed on top of each other; a Timer control toggles the visibility of the Image control on top. The automatic time-out feature on this form is also controlled by the Timer control. The images used in this screen are bitmaps, although a number of different graphic image formats could be used. Visual Basic comes with a collection of icons and other images that can be loaded into an Image control. Alternatively, you could modify an existing image or build your own from scratch, using Windows Paintbrush or some other drawing program.

Picture Box Control and Toolbar

The **Picture Box control,** whose icon is a desert landscape, is similar to the Image control, in that both of these controls have a **Picture property** that can be used to display a graphic. Picture Box and Image controls can hold the following kinds of graphics files, recognized by Visual Basic: bitmaps (.BMP), run-length encoded (.RLE), icons (.ICO), and Windows metafiles (.WMF). But there are important differences as well:

- The Image control has a Stretch property that if set to True, stretches or shrinks the image to fit the borders of the Image control.
- The Image control uses much fewer Windows resources than the Picture Box control, as a result of which the Image control executes much more quickly.
- The Picture Box control has an **Align property,** which is required for a control to appear on an MDI Form. A Picture Box control may be Aligned at the top or the bottom of a regular form or an MDI Form; or, on a regular form, it may be

unaligned. The only other controls with this Align property are the Menu control and the Data control (which we will meet in the next chapter). As a result, a Menu control and a Picture Box control can be placed directly on an MDI Form.

- A Picture Box control, like a Frame control, also serves as a container for other controls. Therefore, via a Picture Box control, you can place other controls on an MDI Form indirectly.

In the Finance3 Application, the MDI Form includes a Picture Box control at the top underneath the Menu control. It is used here as a Toolbar, containing a series of command buttons. Programmers often employ a Picture Box control as a container for a toolbar.

MousePointer Property

Loading and displaying an application with multiple forms might take a few seconds, during which time the user should be encouraged to wait patiently, rather than take some precipitate action while disk accesses are in progress. This encouragement can be accomplished with a splash screen by changing the **MousePointer property** to the familiar hourglass icon at the beginning of the Form_Load procedure and by changing the mouse pointer back to the northwest arrow (the default MousePointer icon) after the main form has been displayed. To see a list of all of the available MousePointer icons, click the drop-down list in the settings box for the MousePointer property of the form.

To see this feature in action, return to your frmImage, and place a second Timer control on the form, with an Interval of 5000. In the Form_Load() procedure, set the form's MousePointer property to 11 (the hourglass). In the Timer event for the second Timer control, disable Timer1 and also set the MousePointer property to 0. Now run the program again. When the form is initially displayed at run time, the mouse pointer will be the hourglass, and the alternating icons will flash on the screen. After five seconds, the flashing will stop and the MousePointer will return to its normal (default) shape.

STEP 3. Develop Your Logic.

There's nothing much new here. The logic for the financial functions on the three child forms is adapted from Finance1, while the click events for the MDI Form's menu items are obvious. The splash screen's logic was demonstrated above.The Hierarchy Table is Figure 9.21. We skipped the pseudocode, since the logic mirrors that in Finance1 (Chapter 6, Figure 6.07).

STEP 4. Build Your GUI.

The listings of property settings for this version of the Finance Application are quite lengthy—a bit much to include in a textbook, and rather pointless, since a picture is worth a thousand words, and with the picture, you can design the GUI yourself.

In the figures below, we have listed all of the forms and have included the object names that we used in building our version of this program.

Here is the list of components (form files) in FINANCE3.VBP:

- mdiFinance—mdiFinance.frm (MDI Form) (Figure 9-21)
- frmLoan—frmLoan.frm (Child Form) (Figure 9-22)
- frmFutureValue—frmFutureValue.frm (Child Form) (Figure 9-23)
- frmDepreciation— frmDepreciation.frm (Child Form) (Figure 9-24)

```
HIERARCHY TABLE-FINANCE (VERSION 3)
Project:  Finance3 (Finance3.vbp)
Form:     frmAbout (frmAbout.frm)
          Event procedures:
             Form_Load
             Timer1_Timer
  MDI Form: mdiFinance (mdiFinance.frm)
          Event procedure:
             MDIForm_Load
          Click event procedures:
             cmdLoan
             cmdFutureValue
             cmdDepreciation
             mnuExit
             mnuAbout
             mnuSelectLoan
             mnuSelectFuturevalue
             mnuSelectDepreciation
             mnuWindowArrangeIcons
             mnuWindowTileHorizontal
             mnuWindowTileVertical
             mnuWindowCascade
  Child Form: frmLoan (frmLoan.frm)
          Event procedure:
             cmdCalculate_Click
  Child Form: frmFutureValue (frmFutureValue.frm)
          Event procedure:
             cmdCalculate_Click
  Child Form: frmDepreciation (frmDepreciation.frm)
          Event procedure:
             cmdCalculate_Click
```

FIGURE 9.21 *Hierarchy Table—Finance (Version 3)*

- frmAbout—frmAbout.frm (Form) (Figure 9-25)
- frmAbout.frx (Pictures used by frmAbout.frm—this file is created automatically by VB when frmAbout.frm is saved.)

STEP 5. Write the VB Code.

You should attempt to write the program yourself before looking at the code below.

mdiFinance-mdiFinance.frm (MDI Form) (Figure 9.22)

```
Option Explicit
Private Sub cmdDepreciation_Click()
   Call mnuSelectDepreciation_Click
End Sub

Private Sub cmdFuture_Click()
   Call mnuSelectFuturevalue_Click
End Sub

Private Sub cmdLoan_Click()
   Call mnuSelectLoanpayment_Click
End Sub
```

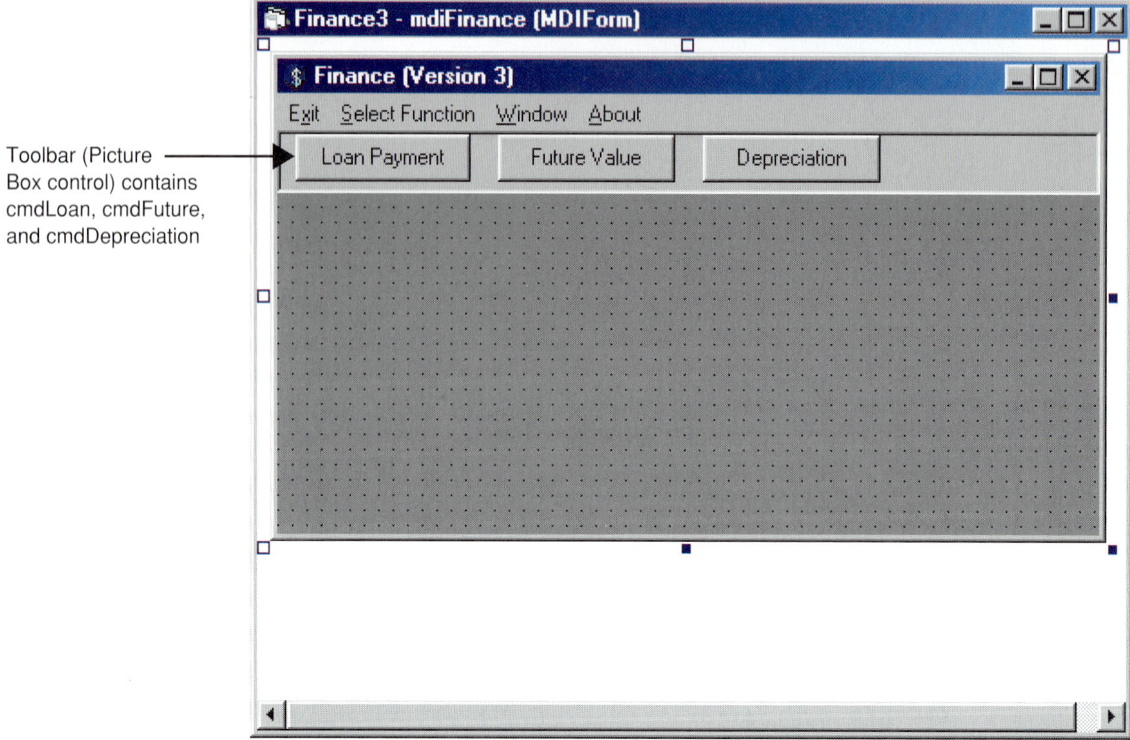

FIGURE 9.22 *Finance3, opening screen*

```
Private Sub MDIForm_Load()
   Me.Height = Screen.Height / 2
   Me.Width = Screen.Width / 2
   Me.Top = Screen.Height / 4
   Me.Left = Screen.Width / 4
End Sub

Private Sub mnuAbout_Click()
   frmAbout!Timer1.Enabled = True
   frmAbout.Show
End Sub

Private Sub mnuExit_Click()
   End
End Sub

Private Sub mnuSelectDepreciation_Click()
   frmDepreciation.Show
End Sub

Private Sub mnuSelectFuturevalue_Click()
   frmFutureValue.Show
End Sub

Private Sub mnuSelectLoanpayment_Click()
   frmLoan.Show
End Sub
```

```
Private Sub mnuWindowArrangeicons_Click()
   Me.Arrange vbArrangeIcons
End Sub

Private Sub mnuWindowCascade_Click()
   Me.Arrange vbCascade
End Sub

Private Sub mnuWindowTilehorizontal_Click()
   Me.Arrange vbTileHorizontal
End Sub

Private Sub mnuWindowTilevertical_Click()
   Me.Arrange vbTileVertical
End Sub
```

frmLoan—frmLoan.frm (Child Form) (Figure 9.23)

```
Option Explicit
Private Sub cmdCalculate_Click()
   'This routine returns the monthly payment amount for a loan,
   'given the principal amount borrowed, the annual interest rate (APR),
   'and the number of payments.

On Error GoTo ErrorTrap
   Dim sngAPR As Single 'annual percentage rate
   sngAPR=txtAPR
   If sngAPR > 1 Then sngAPR = sngAPR / 100 ' Ensure proper form.
   lblMonthlyPayment = Format(Pmt(sngAPR / 12, _
      txtDuration, -txtAmountOfLoan, 0, 0), "currency")
   Exit Sub
```

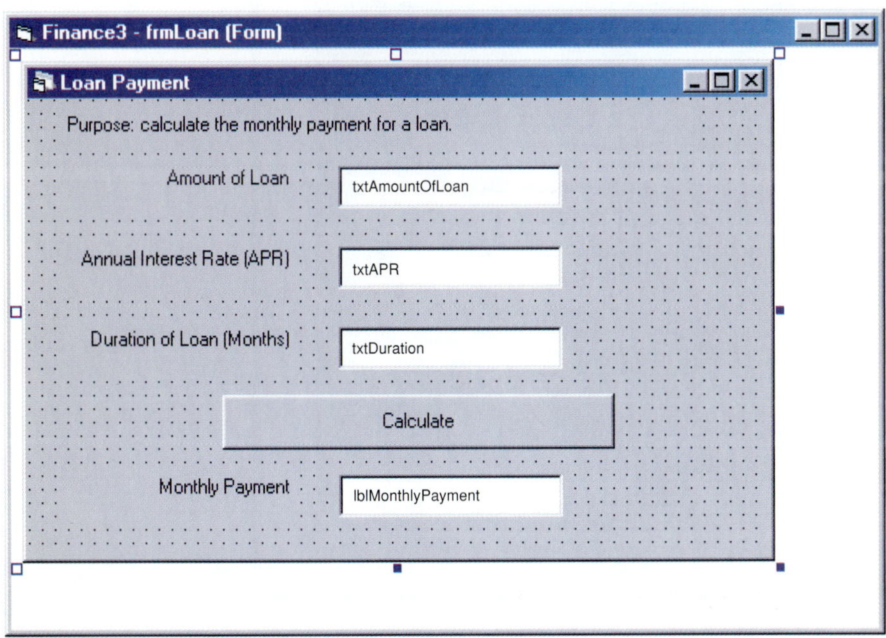

FIGURE 9.23 *Loan Payment child form*

```
ErrorTrap:
    MsgBox "Calculation aborted -- Check your input data"
End Sub
```

frmFutureValue—frmFuture.frm (Child Form) (Figure 9.24)

```
Option Explicit
Private Sub cmdCalculate_Click()
    'This procedure returns the future value of an investment given
    'the percentage rate that accrues per monthly
    'period (sngAPR / 12), the total number of payments (intTotPmts),
    'the amount invested each month (fPayment), the current
    'value of the investment (fPVal), and a Boolean value that indicates
    'whether the fPayment is made at the
    'beginning or end of the period (blnPayType). Note that
    'because fPayment represents cash paid out, it's a negative number.

On Error GoTo ErrorTrap
    Dim sngAPR As Single 'annual interest rate percentage
    sngAPR = txtAPR
    If sngAPR > 1 Then sngAPR = sngAPR / 100
    lblFutureValue = Format(FV(sngAPR / 12, txtDuration, -txtAmountInvested, _
        -txtPresentValue, optBegin.Value), "currency")
    Exit Sub
ErrorTrap:
    MsgBox "Calculation aborted-Check your input data"
End Sub
```

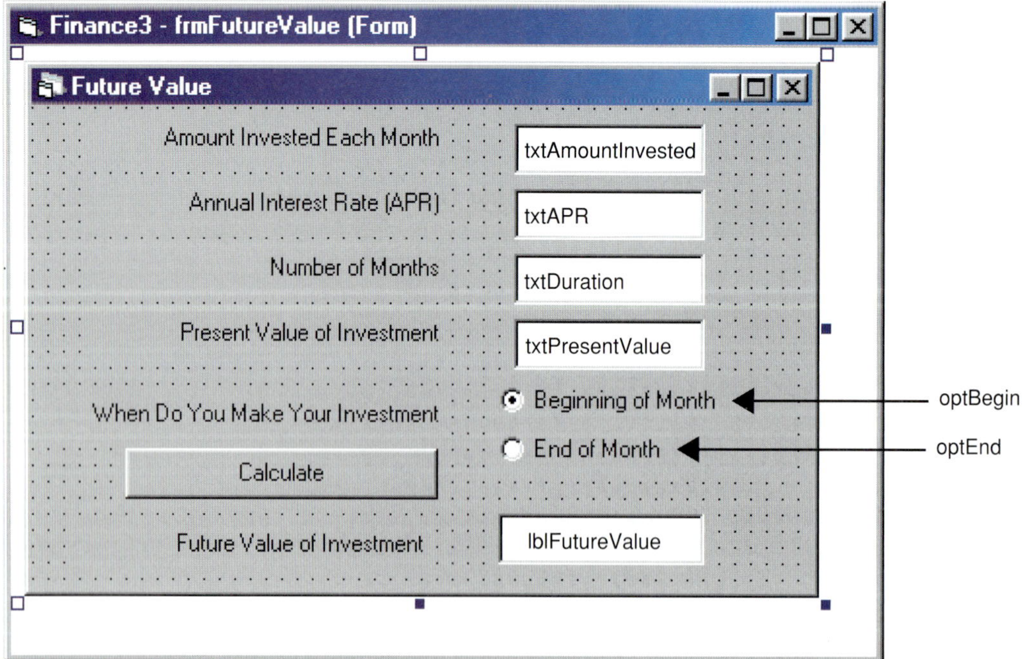

FIGURE 9.24 *Future Value child form*

frmDepreciation— frmDepreciation.frm (Child Form) (Figure 9.25)

```
Option Explicit

Private Sub cmdCalculate_Click()
   'DDB, SYD, and SLN Functions Example

   'Using the double-declining balance method, the sum of years' digits method,
   'and the straight line method, this example returns the depreciation
   'of an asset for a specified period, given the initial cost,
   'the salvage value at the end of the asset's useful life,
   'the total life of the asset in years, and the year for which
   'the depreciation is calculated. The inputs are a control array of textboxes;
   'the outputs are a control array of labels. Note the use of constants to
   'identify each textbox and label.
   Const INITIALCOSTOFASSET = 0
   Const SALVAGEVALUEOFASSET = 1
   Const LIFEINYEARS = 2
   Const YEARFORDEPRECIATIONCALCULATION = 3
   Const DDBMETHOD = 0
   Const SYDMETHOD = 1
   Const SLNMETHOD = 2
   On Error GoTo ErrorTrap
   lblOutput(DDBMETHOD) = Int(DDB(txtInput(INITIALCOSTOFASSET), _
      txtInput(SALVAGEVALUEOFASSET), txtInput(LIFEINYEARS), _
      txtInput(YEARFORDEPRECIATIONCALCULATION)))
   lblOutput(SYDMETHOD) = Int(SYD(txtInput(INITIALCOSTOFASSET), _
      txtInput(SALVAGEVALUEOFASSET), txtInput(LIFEINYEARS), _
      txtInput(YEARFORDEPRECIATIONCALCULATION)))
```

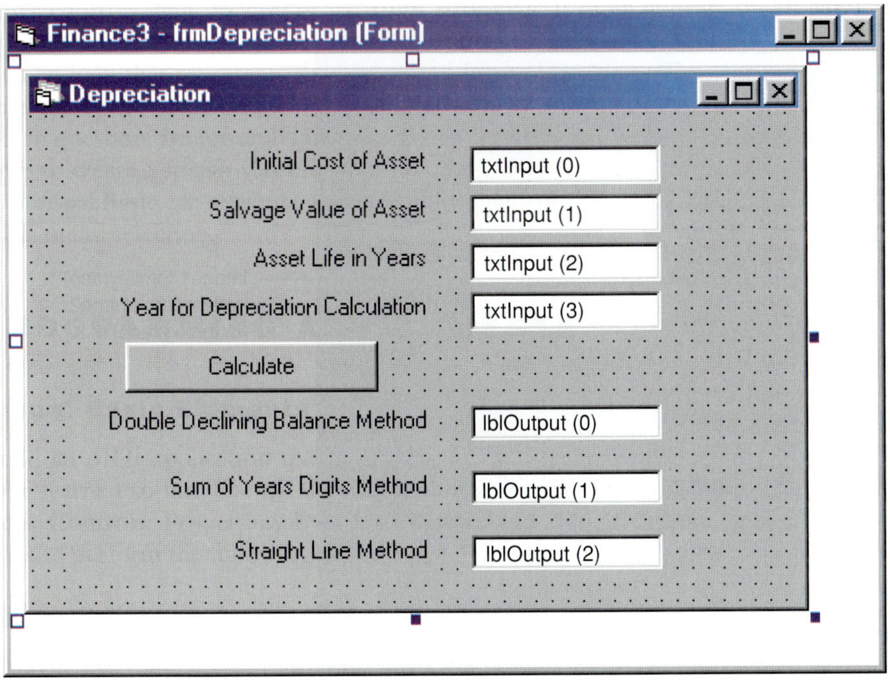

FIGURE 9.25 *Depreciation child form*

addressed by the next child form), Screen, Debug, and Printer. When the user clicks one of these labels, a glossary-type definition of the object should appear in a Text Box.

- **Controls**—Load a child form containing a sample of each of VB's controls. If the control has a Caption property, use it to identify the control and, in parentheses, its standardized abbreviation. Example: "Command Button (cmd)." If the control has no caption property, or if the control is not visible at run time, identify the control and its abbreviation in a Label control. When the user clicks a sample control or its identifying label, a glossary-type definition of the control should appear in a Text Box.
- **Properties, Events, Methods**—Load the same child form for all three of these MDI Form menu selections. The child form should also have a menu containing the three selections Properties, Events, and Methods. Each of these menu selections should have alphabetically sorted submenu selections appearing in a drop-down list, identifying all of the keywords that you have learned in that category. For example, list all of the events to which you have been exposed in this text, such as Click, Double-Click, Load, Change, GotFocus, LostFocus, and Timer. Note that you can fit only about 25 items in a drop-down list (the maximum is a function of your monitor). VB lets you put more items into the drop-down list than will fit on your screen, but you won't be able to see them at run time. Therefore, you may need to subdivide the properties list into several separate sublists, such as "Properties A through M" and "Properties N through Z." At run time, when the user clicks an item in one of the drop-down lists, a glossary-type definition of the item should appear in a Message Box.
- **About**—Be creative! Make a fancy About form. Include your name and the title of your program, as well as shapes, colors, icons, and action controlled by timers.

Math Magic (MDI Version)

Rewrite the Math Magic application from Chapter Eight as an MDI app. Include a menu on the MDI form, as follows:

- Exit
- Math Functions
  - Prime Numbers (show a child form)
  - Fibonacci Sequence (show a child form)
  - Guess a Number (show a child form)
- Window (set the WindowList property)
  - Cascade
  - Tile Horizontal
  - Tile Vertical
  - Arrange Icons
- About (show a child form)

The functionality of the three math function child forms should be copied from Math Magic, but use textboxes for the user input and labels for the output. The About child form should display the author's name and date, along with a flashing icon (the same icon should be loaded into the MDI form's Icon property).

Also include a toolbar underneath the MDI form's menu. The toolbar should contain three command buttons, which activate the three math functions and have the captions Prime Numbers, Fibonacci Sequence, and Guess a Number.

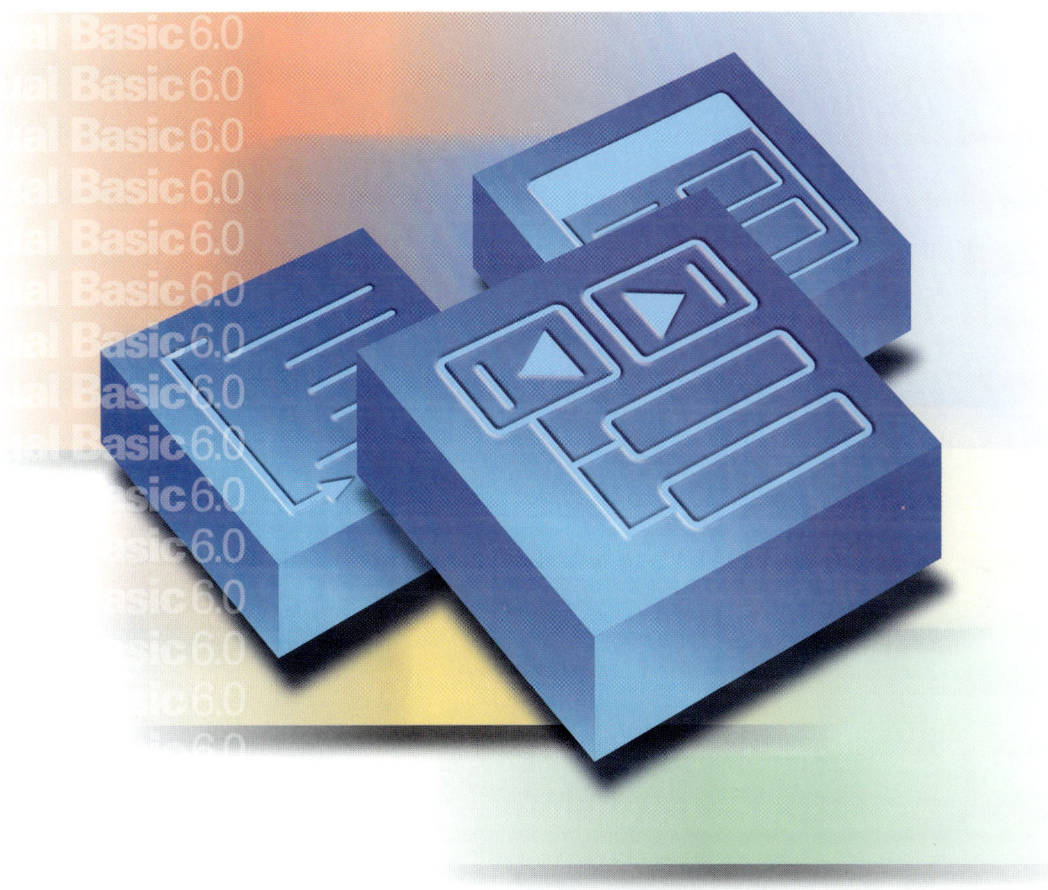

PART FOUR

PROGRAMMING THE BACK-END: DATABASES, ActiveX, AND THE WEB

CHAPTER TEN

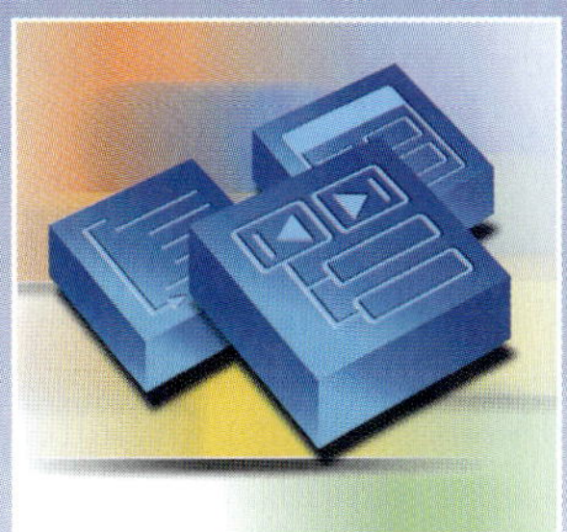

DATABASES AND DATA CONTROL (VIEWABLE)

Application: Class Scheduling (Version 1)

LEARNING OBJECTIVES

Upon completion of Chapter Ten, you will be able to:

- Understand the basics of database management systems and the relational model.
- Access a database and create a Recordset from within a VB program via the Data control.
- Display fields within a table of a database through bound controls.
- Scroll through the records of a Recordset created from a Microsoft Access table using a Data control.
- Find a user-requested record within a Recordset.
- Identify and use the application object and application path (App.Path).
- Use the IIf (Immediate If) function, the last of Visual Basic's selection structures.

Keywords

App object
Data control (prefix: db)
Database object
DatabaseName property
DataField property
DataSource property
Dynaset RecordsetType
FindFirst method
FindLast method
FindNext method
FindPrevious method
IIf function
MoveFirst method
MoveLast method
MoveNext method
MovePrevious method
NoMatch property
Path property
Recordset object
RecordsetType property
RecordSource property
Refresh method
Reposition event
Right function
Snapshot RecordsetType
Table RecordsetType

FILES AND DATABASES

Up to this point, the programs we have written have produced only transient outputs—text and graphics that appear on the screen but cease to exist as soon as the program stops running. Real world business information systems, in contrast, are characterized by permanent or semi-permanent records. Employee records, credit card customer accounts, store or warehouse inventory information, automobile engineering design data, and patient medical history files all persist over long stretches of time. Businesses need computer systems that create, maintain, update, and store records indefinitely. These records exist in what are called data files, stored on a secondary storage device, which means essentially a hard disk, a floppy disk, or a magnetic tape.

Traditional File Structures

In earlier computing times, programmers stored information in sequential files and, later, in random access files. These traditional file structures are still used infrequently, and some instructors still like to cover them early in an introductory text. Other professors believe, as we do, that traditional files have gone the way of the automobile stick shift—it's nice to know if you are an automobile history buff, and still quite useful for driving a sports car, but hardly necessary for getting your driver's license. The purpose of this text is for you to get your Visual Basic driver's license, so to speak. For this reason, we have placed traditional sequential and random access file structures at the end of the book (Chapter Thirteen). In Chapter Ten, we focus on the much more widely used relational database file structure and on the use of Visual Basic's Data control to retrieve information from a database. Chapter Eleven continues with the Data control, focusing on database maintenance. And Chapter Twelve covers the ActiveX Data Object Data Control (ADODC) and related facilities for accessing a database on the World Wide Web.

Databases

A **database,** in its simplest definition, is a collection of data. In this sense, a college's course schedule, student rosters for class, the inventory data for the local grocery store, the weather data for the next national forecast, the engineering drawings for the space shuttle, and all the holdings of the Library of Congress each constitutes a database.

In the parlance of modern computer information systems, a database is defined more precisely as a collection of records organized into a series of one or more tables. For example, a college's "course schedule" database could include one master record for each course the college offers, one record for each section of each course offered in a given semester, and one record for each faculty member who teaches one or more sections of courses. Multiple tables are used in order to reduce the total amount of space needed to store all of the data and to reduce or eliminate data redundancy. To take the college database a step further, these data could be organized into three tables, called the Courses Table, the Sections Table, and the Faculty Table. We will be using this database throughout Chapters Ten, Eleven, and Twelve, and so it behooves us to describe the entire database here.

COLLEGE.MDB

COLLEGE.MDB is a Microsoft Access Database that contains three interrelated Tables.

- Courses—contains the master record for each course in the college catalog.
- Sections—contains one record for each section offered each semester.
- Faculty—contains one record for each faculty member.

As you read the more detailed description of each of these tables below, note the internal structure of the table, but also look for the ways in which the tables can be interrelated.

- Course description information is placed in the Courses Table: Fields include course identifier (such as "CIS 214"), course title, credits, the department that offers the course, and a flag indicating whether or not this is a required course. It would be terribly redundant to duplicate all of this information for every section of the course that is offered. Rather, the course description information is stored only once, where it is available to any program that needs it. Internally, a Table is organized into columns and rows, where the columns represent data fields and the rows represent records. Most often, an individual record can be uniquely identified by some key field or by a combination of fields, which is known as the primary key. In Courses, CourseID is the primary key. Here is the structure and some sample records for Courses.

TABLE NAME:	COURSES
Index Name:	CourseIndex
Primary Key:	Course ID

FIELD NAME	FIELD TYPE	WIDTH
CourseID	Text	8
Title	Text	30
Credits	Integer	System Determined
Department	Text	10
Required*	Boolean	System Determined

*In MS Access, a false Boolean value appears as 0, while a true Boolean appears as –1.

COURSEID	TITLE	CREDITS	DEPARTMENT	REQUIRED
CHM 101	Inorganic Chemistry 1	4	Chemistry	0
CIS 101	Computer Literacy	3	Computer Science	–1
CIS 214	Visual Basic Programming	4	Computer Science	0
EGL 101	Composition	3	English	–1
EGL 232	British Literature	3	English	0
HIS 102	History of the Modern World	3	History	0
MAT 241	Analysis I	4	Math	0
PED 100	Physical Education	1	Health and Phys Ed	–1
PHY 107	Introduction to Astronomy	4	Physics	0
PSY 101	General Psychology	3	Psychology	0
PSY 207	Human Growth and Development	3	Psychology	0

- The Faculty Table contains one record for each member of the faculty. The elements include the faculty ID (the primary key), last name, first name, department, and rank. Here is the structure and several records of this Table:

TABLE NAME:	FACULTY
Index Name:	FacultyIndex
Primary Key:	Faculty ID

FIELD NAME	FIELD TYPE	WIDTH
FacultyID	Text	3
LastName	Text	15
FirstName	Text	10
Department	Text	10
Rank	Text	10

FACULTYID	LASTNAME	FIRSTNAME	DEPARTMENT	RANK
A04	Allbright	Mary	Health and Phys Ed	Assistant Professor
B04	Bradley	Andrew	English	Instructor
B17	Smithson	Gladys	Mathematics	Professor
E01	Elliot	Carl	Computer Science	Associate Professor
J03	Josephson	Daryl	Psychology	Professor
S01	Spear	Timothy	Computer Science	Professor
S09	Spear	Robert	Computer Science	Professor
S12	Sullivan	Nancy	Computer Science	Assistant Professor
T01	Tracey	Anne	English	Associate Professor
T03	Tomlin	Reginald	Chemistry	Instructor
T09	Torrino	Peter	Physics	Assistant Professor
Z14	Zarin	Boris	English	Associate Professor

- Section offerings are entered into the Sections Table. Each record in this table describes one offering of one course. The elements of information include the course reference number (the primary key, and the number used by students to register for a particular section of a course); the course ID; the faculty ID of the faculty member assigned to teach the course; and the meeting days, times, and location. Each course in the Courses Table may be listed 0, 1, or more times in the Sections Table. The structure and a few sample records in this table follow.

TABLE NAME:	SECTIONS
Index Name:	SectionIndex
Primary Key:	RefNum

FIELD NAME	FIELD TYPE	WIDTH
RefNum	Text	4
CourseID	Text	8
FacultyID	Text	3
Days	Text	5
StartTime	Text	4
StopTime	Text	4
Location	Text	8

REFNUM	COURSEID	FACULTYID	DAYS	STARTTIME	STOPTIME	LOCATION
1200	EGL 101	T01	MW	1830	1945	AAFB
1201	EGL 101	B04	S	0900	1200	B213
3421	CIS 101	E01	MWF	0900	0950	L122
3422	CIS 101	S12	MWF	1000	1050	L122
3423	CIS 101	E01	TR	0930	1045	L126
3510	CIS 214	S01	TR	1930	2200	L208A
4000	PED 100	A04	R	1200	1400	N100
4040	MAT 241	B17	MWRF	1300	1350	M3022
4117	EGL 101	Z14	TR	1100	1215	B204
4433	PHY 107	T09	MTRF	1300	1415	B104
6972	EGL 232	B04	TR	0800	0915	M2072
6974	EGL 232	T01	MF	1000	1200	B214

- Relationships among the three tables have been defined as follows: A course in the Courses Table may appear many times in the Sections Table (that is, the college may offer multiple sections of any course); and a faculty member in the Faculty Table may appear many times in the Sections Table (that is, a faculty member may teach many sections)[1]. These relations are defined by placing the primary key of the Courses Table and of the Faculty Table in the Sections Table, and then drawing the relationship (see Figure 10.01).

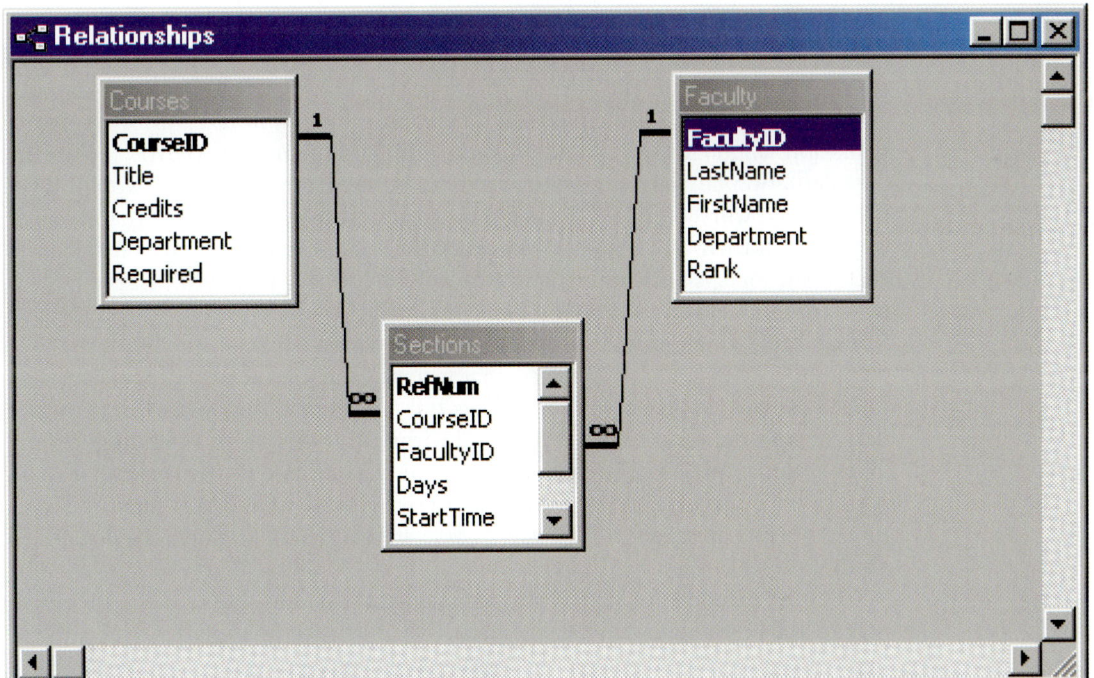

FIGURE 10.01 *Drawing the relationship between courses, sections, and faculty.*

[1]Right up until the faculty member faints from overwork, or the students faint from boredom.

Using this database of three tables, the college's schedule of classes can be produced by extracting appropriate information from each table. Here is a small sample of some possible output:

```
                    Official Schedule of Classes

CIS 101        Computer Literacy          3 Credits

Reference Num      Instructor    Days      Times       Location
     3421          Elliot        MWF     0900-0950       L122
     3422          Sullivan      MWF     1000-1050       L122
     3423          Elliot        TR      0930-1045       L126

CIS 214        Visual Basic               4 Credits

Reference Num      Instructor    Days      Times       Location
     3510          Spear         TR      1930-2200       L208A

EGL 101        Composition                3 Credits

Reference Num      Instructor    Days      Times       Location
     1200          Tracey        MW      1830-1945       AAFB
     1201          Bradley       S       0900-1200       B213
```

Database Management Systems (DBMS)

A database management system (DBMS) is a software package that allows the user to establish and maintain a database, such as the student registrations database described above. The DBMS performs most of the detailed and complex database tasks behind the scenes, intentionally hidden from the user—another good example of the principle of information hiding. The DBMS offers a data definition language (DDL) and a data manipulation language (DML). With the data definition language, the user is able to define from a logical viewpoint what the database will look like. The user names each table in the database, names all of the fields in each table, determines what type and size of data will be stored in each field, and specifies any indices (the unique primary key, by which the table is ordered; as well as any secondary keys, by which the table may also be accessed; or foreign keys, which provide entrée to another table). Through the DDL the user defines the schema of the database, that is to say, the logical view of the data. The DBMS, unbeknown to the user, defines the subschema, the physical view of the data, or how the data are actually stored within the rules of the operating system. The data manipulation language (DML) of the DBMS allows the user to add (also called insert), delete, or edit database records. Many DBMSs support Structured Query Language (SQL), the *de facto* standard DBMS language developed by IBM.

Several models of database management systems have been invented, namely the hierarchical model, the network model, the relational model, and the object-oriented model. By far the most popular of these is the relational DBMS model, developed by E. J. Codd around 1970 and based on a branch of mathematics called relational algebra and relational calculus. In the peculiar argot of relational algebra, a table is known as a relation, data fields (columns) are called attributes, and records (rows) are called tuples. A particular data value (such as "Introduction to Visual Basic" in the course title field) is known in DBMS terminology as an A-V (attribute-value) pair. This A-V pair is associated with a particular object, in this case, the college course that is associated with every A-V pair in that tuple. The association of an A-V pair with an object creates, again in DBMS terminology, what is called an A-V-O triplet. The terminology introduced in this paragraph is important only for reading the literature concerning DBMSs; we will stick to the more mundane terms table, field, data value, and record.

Microsoft Access is a relational database management system. Since Visual Basic is a product of Microsoft Corporation, Visual Basic works very well with Microsoft Access, but VB's Data control (everything covered in this chapter) also works well with most of the other popular microcomputer-based DBMSs. Using a powerful protocol called Open Database Connectivity (ODBC), VB also works quite well with many large-scale, mainframe DBMSs. VB supports SQL, allowing Structured Query Language statements to be embedded in certain VB statements and functions. Finally, databases on the World Wide Web can best be manipulated within VB by using ActiveX Data Objects (ADO) and the ActiveX Data Object Data Control (ADODC), covered in Chapter Twelve.

INTRODUCING THE CLASS SCHEDULING PROJECT (VERSION 1)

Version 1 of the Class Scheduling Project demonstrates the retrieval of data from a Microsoft Access database using Visual Basic's Data control. The database to be accessed has already been created for you and is on the Web under the name COLLEGE.MDB. This first version of the program uses only the Faculty Table within COLLEGE.MDB.

VB's Visual Data Manager allows you to design and create tables within a Microsoft Access Database. The Visual Data Manager and the Data control provide a shortcut to defining, storing, and manipulating a database with minimum programmer effort.

STEP 1. Understand the Problem.

Run FACULTY1.EXE, the first portion of our Class Scheduling Database application. The menu offers the selections Exit and Window (Figure 10.02). The drop-down list under Window has two selections: Browse allows the user to scroll through the list of faculty members in the Faculty Table of our College Database (Figure 10.03); Find allows the user to type in a faculty member's last name, and then search for that name in the Faculty Table (Figure 10.04). This first version of the Class Scheduling application deals only with a single table, namely the Faculty Table. And the user's access to the information in this table is limited to inquiry. That is, the user is not permitted to make any changes to the information stored in the Faculty Table, whose format and contents were determined outside of this VB program.

Experiment a little bit with this program to discover its main features. Note that when you click Window | Browse, a Data control called "Faculty Table" becomes visible. The arrows reposition the Data control within the **Recordset;** that is, they change which record is the current record. The arrows mean, from left to right, Move to the First record in the Recordset, Move to the Previous record, Move to the Next record, and Move to the Last record. When you select Window on the Menu Bar again, Browse has a checkmark in front of it. If you again click Browse, the Data control becomes invisible, and when you subsequently click Window, the checkmark in front of Browse is gone. Label controls containing the values of the fields within the Faculty Table are called bound controls, that is, they are bound to the values of the current record in the Recordset created by the Data control.

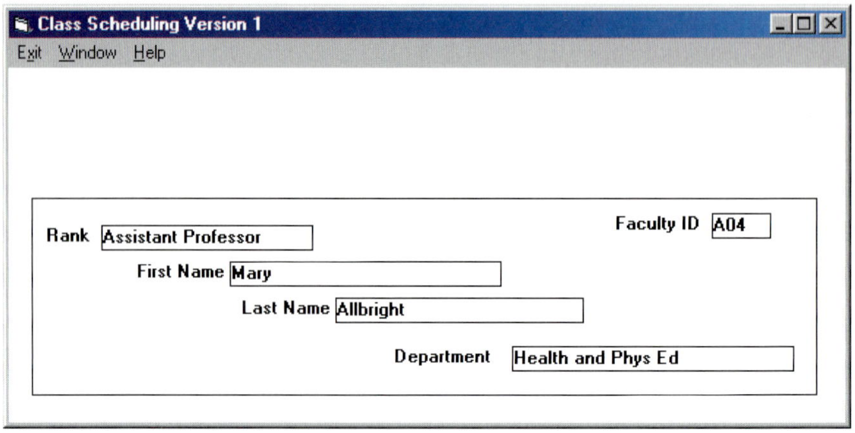

FIGURE 10.02 *Faculty1, opening screen*

The Window | Find menu selection makes the "Find Faculty Member" Frame visible at the top of the screen. The user is prompted to type in the last name of a faculty member in the TextBox, and then click the "Find" Command Button. The program either repositions the current record to the record containing that faculty member's name, or it issues a gentle error message to the user in the event that that name cannot be found in the Faculty Table. Again, note that Find is now checked in the Window drop-down list; and, if Window | Find is again selected, both the Frame and the checkmark disappear.

If you are interested in where we are headed with this application, you can also experiment with running version 2 of the Class Scheduling Application: FACULTY2.EXE (in Chapter Eleven) incorporates database update functionality—the ability to add, delete, and change records in the Faculty Table; and it uses a Common Dialog Box control to locate the College database. And at the end of this chapter, SCHEDULE1.EXE demonstrates the use of three interconnected data controls to access all three tables of the College.mdb database in order to display the Schedule of Classes.

STEP 2. Design a Solution.

Sketch out the form needed for the Class Scheduling version 1 Project.

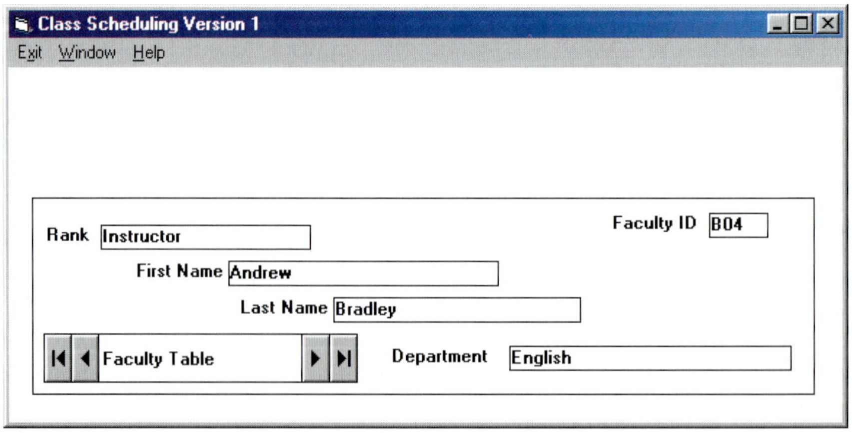

FIGURE 10.03 *Browsing through the Faculty table*

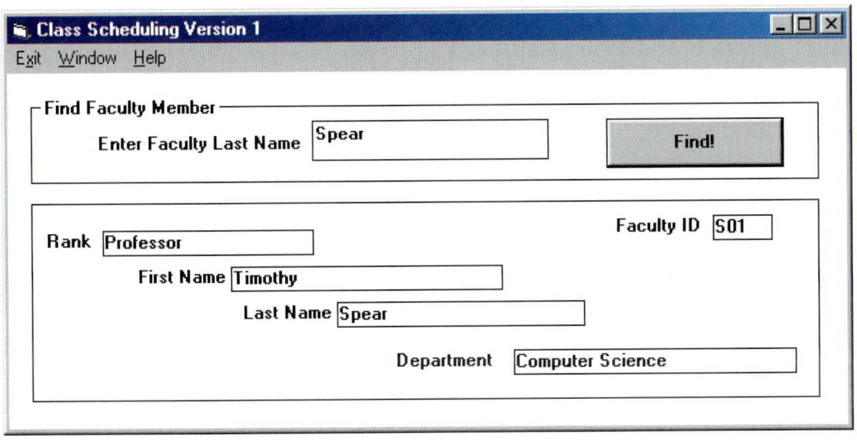

FIGURE 10.04 *Finding a faculty member*

We have asked you to sketch your form designs on paper right from the first chapter. Have you actually done this or have you adopted the practice of designing your forms on the screen?

Actually, many professional Visual Basic programmers do most of their design work right on the computer. As you get more accustomed to Visual Basic programming, you too may find that sketching a form design on paper takes you more time than "sketching" that same design on the screen. There is nothing wrong with designing your forms from within the VB design environment. Just do be careful that you continue to treat your first computerized "sketches" the same as you would the paper variety: These are first drafts, or rough approximations of the finished product. Don't become too enamored of your first draft, and don't start writing code in back of a rough-draft form design. You need to think the design all the way through, consider alternatives, plan all of the other forms in the application, and develop your algorithms before you start writing code. If you start with "Step 5. Write Your VB Code" before completing steps 1 through 4 of the programming process, you will end up wasting an awful lot of time fixing and rewriting. But if you have the self-discipline to develop your application according to a logical, linear methodology, then nothing will be lost by "Designing your solution" right on the screen in Visual Basic.

Before proceeding any further with the design, we will describe the new controls, statements, and functions needed to implement our solution.

Visual Basic's Data Control

The **Data control** is used in a Visual Basic application to display, insert (add), delete, or change (edit) records in a database.

When opened, the Data control creates a **Recordset**—that is, a set of records created from one or more underlying tables in a database. The Data control affords the capability to move from record to record within that Recordset. Labels and TextBoxes bound to that Data control display the data values of individual fields in the current record.

VB's Data control provides access to data stored in databases that were previously created either through VB's Visual Data Manager or through one of the other software packages that the Data control supports (Access, Paradox, dBase, Foxpro, Excel, text files, or ODBC—Open Database Connectivity Protocol). The

Data control itself accesses a database through its **DatabaseName property,** and a specific Table of that Database through its **RecordSource** property, as follows:

- For an Access Database

  To open an Access Database with a Data control, set the DatabaseName property with the path and name of the Access Database (.MDB file). Then set the RecordSource property to the name of a table in the database. These properties can be set at design time or at run time. The conventional prefix for the name of a Data control is db. The code to access a Microsoft Database might look like this.

```
dbTitles.DatabaseName = "C:\VB98\BIBLIO.MDB"
dbTitles.RecordSource = "Titles"
```

- For a dBase, Paradox, or Foxpro Database

  To open a dBase, Paradox, or Foxpro Database with a Data control, set the DatabaseName property with the path to the directory that contains the Database files. Then set the RecordSource property to the name of the file containing a Table (.DBF or .DB file). These properties can be set at design time or at run time. The code to access a dBase file might look like this.

```
dbFaculty.DatabaseName = "C:\DBASE\LIBRARY\"
dbFaculty.RecordSource = "TITLES.DBF"
```

Based on the DatabaseName and RecordSource properties, a Data control opens the database and retrieves the specified set of records, represented within the Data control by the Recordset object at run time. Initially, the Data control points to the first record in the Recordset as the current record. The user can change the current record (move to another record) by clicking the arrows on the right and left sides of the Data control (see Figure 10.05).

By itself, the Data control does not display any information from its Recordset. Rather, you can bind other controls on the same form to the Data control through the use of the other controls' **DataSource** and **DataField properties.** (Other methods, discussed in later chapters, also exist for accessing data values from the current record.) The controls that may serve as bound controls include the Label, TextBox, Image, CheckBox, and Picture controls.

Let's try this out. Start a new project, and put a Data control on the form. Name the Data control dbTitles, and set the caption to "Titles." Select dbTitles' DatabaseName property and click the ellipsis (Figure 10.06). A dialog box

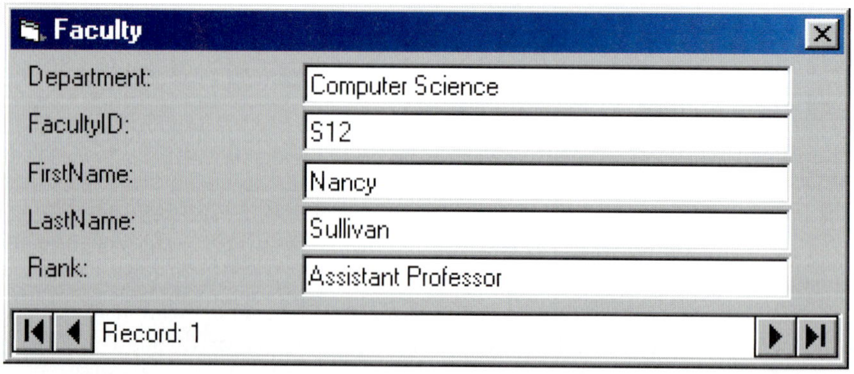

FIGURE 10.05 *Moving from record to record in VB's Data control*

appears, prompting you to identify the database file that you wish to assign to this Data control. In the VB98 directory, you will find the Access database file BIBLIO.MDB. Select this file (Figure 10.07).

Then select the RecordSource property, click its drop-down list to see the list of tables in BIBLIO.MDB, and select the Titles Table (Figure 10.08), as indicated above, so that dbTitles will open the Titles Table of BIBLIO.MDB.

Now to display the book titles in the Titles Table, put a Label control on the form, and name the Label control lblTitle. Then set lblTitle's DataSource property to dbTitles (the DataSource property may only be set at design time). To set this property, click the down-arrow in the Settings Box, and a drop-down list of all of the Data controls on that form will appear (Figure 10.09); select dbTitles. Next, select the DataField property, again click the down-arrow in the Settings Box, and a drop-down list of all of the fields in the Data control's RecordSource property will appear (Figure 10.10); select Title.

If no drop-down list of data fields is available, check to see that the path in the DatabaseName property is correct. When setting the DataSource and DataField properties of a bound control, it is always better to use the drop-down lists provided by VB rather than just typing in the property settings yourself, even if they are short

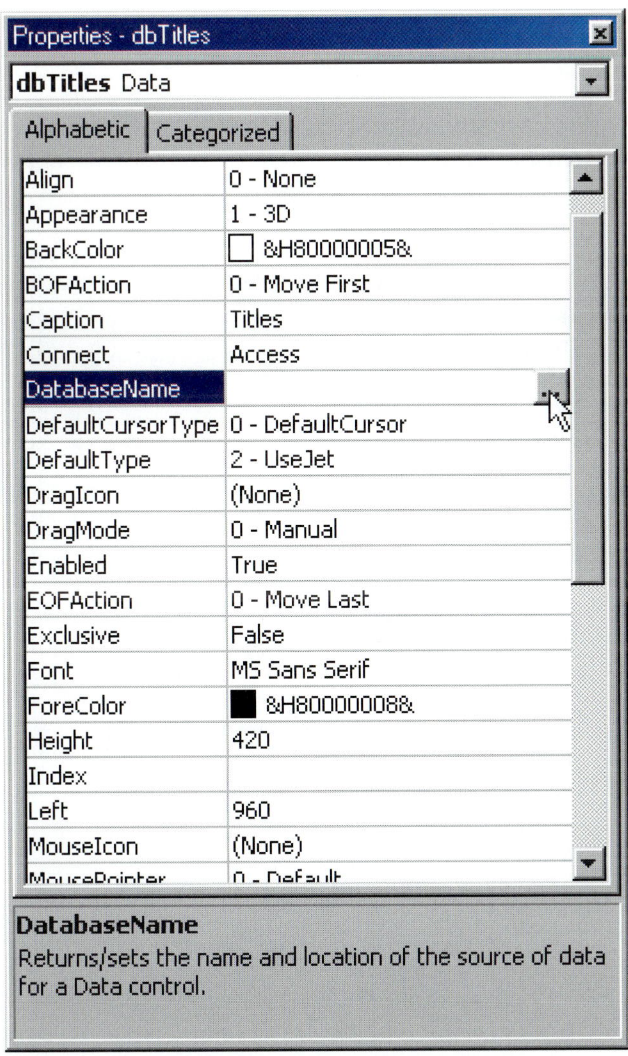

FIGURE 10.06 *Selecting the DatabaseName property*

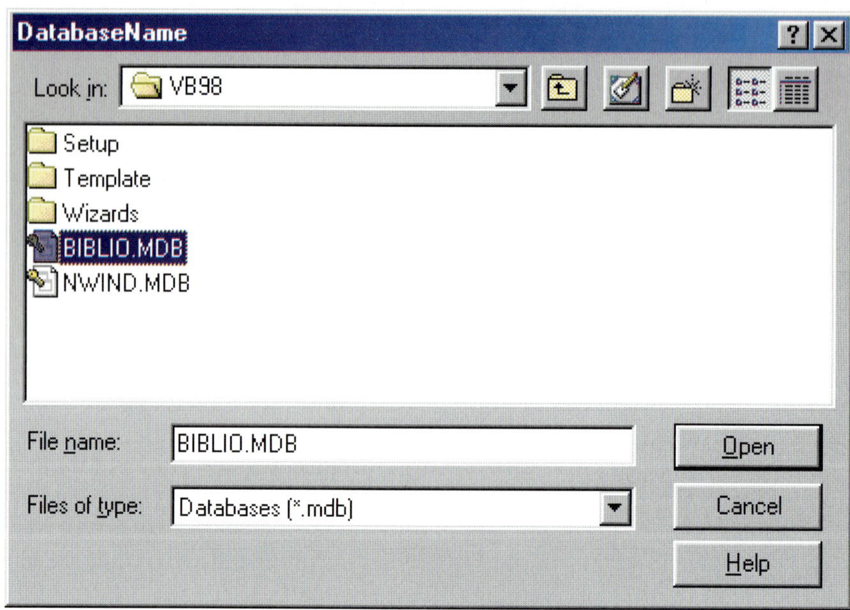

FIGURE 10.07 *The DatabaseName property's dialog box*

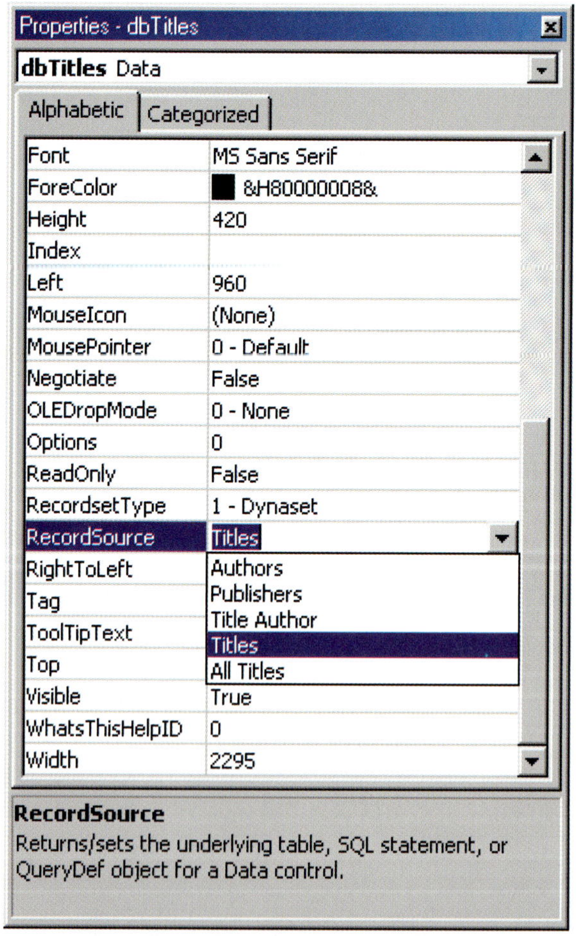

FIGURE 10.08 *The RecordSource property's drop-down list*

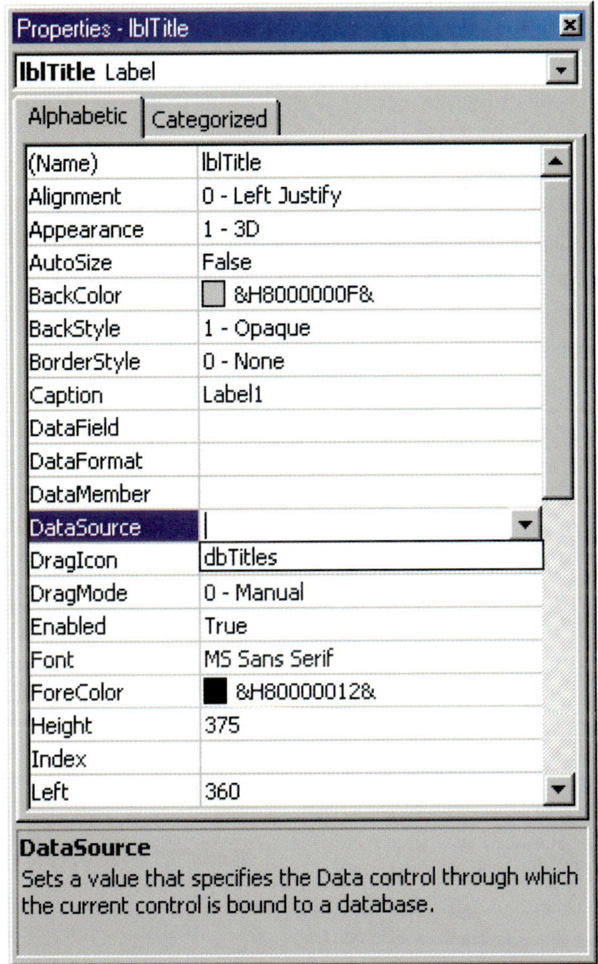

FIGURE 10.09 *The DataSource property's drop-down*

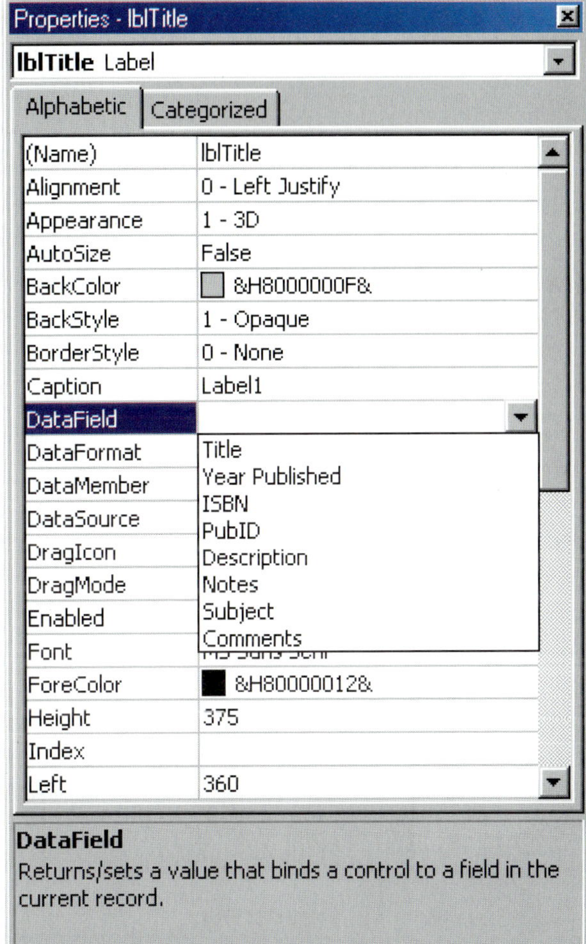

FIGURE 10.10 *The DataField property's drop-down list*

and simple and you are sure you know what they are supposed to be. Using the drop-down lists ensures that you have set the properties in the Data control correctly so that the drop-down lists can be accessed; and using the drop-down lists to set the bound control's properties also ensures that they are spelled correctly.

Run this program (see Figure 10.11). lblTitle displays the Title of the first record in the Recordset. Click on the right arrow (not the far right arrow) to move one record to the right in the Recordset (that is, in the Titles Table). Click the far right arrow to move to the last record in the Recordset. Click the left arrow (not the far left arrow) to move one record to the left, and click the far left arrow to return to the first record in the Recordset.

As you can see, you can display all of the information in a table without writing any code at all. Just create a set of bound controls tied to the Data control and to the fields within a RecordSource. Automatically, the information will be updated in each bound control whenever the current record in the Recordset changes.

Furthermore, you could use a TextBox as a bound control, in which case the user could change the information in the TextBox. The updated information in the TextBox is automatically saved in the database whenever the current record changes. Of course, you may not always want the user to have the ability to make changes to the database.

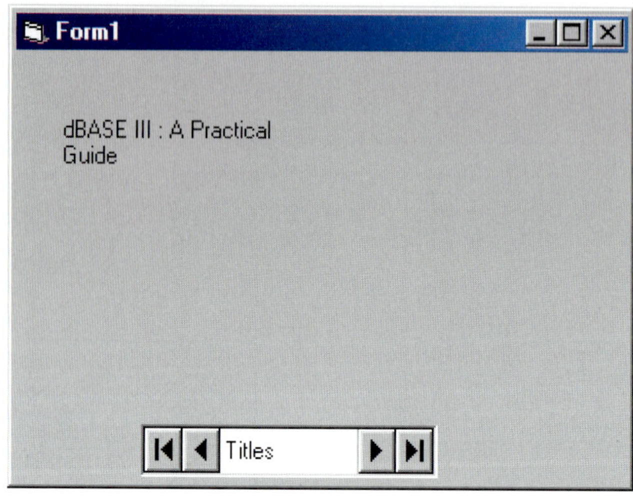

FIGURE 10.11 *Browsing through the titles in Biblio.mdb*

A Data control can create three types of Recordsets, determined by its RecordsetType property.

- **Table-type Recordset**—created from a single Table; may be updatable; records can only be accessed sequentially.
- **Dynaset-type Recordset** (the default RecordsetType property setting)—created from one or more tables or as the result of a Database Query; may be updatable; records can be accessed randomly or sequentially.
- **Snapshot-type Recordset**—created from one or more tables or as the result of a Database Query; not updatable; records can be accessed randomly or sequentially.

If you do not want the user to make any changes to the underlying table, just set the RecordsetType property to Snapshot. A Snapshot-type Recordset also requires fewer system resources, and so it executes more quickly. It is a good choice when no update functionality is required.

You can also move from record to record within your code with the **MoveFirst** method, which makes the first record in the Recordset the current record; **MoveLast,** which moves to the last record; **MoveNext,** which moves one record to the right; and **MovePrevious,** which moves one record to the left. These methods correspond to the four arrows on the Data control.

Try these methods by adding four Command Buttons to your form (Figure 10.12). Caption them First, Previous, Next, and Last, and name them cmdMoveFirst, cmdMovePrevious, cmdMoveNext, and cmdMoveLast. Program each Command Button's click event procedure following this model for cmdMoveFirst.

```
Private cmdMoveFirst_Click()
   dbTitles.Recordset.MoveFirst
End Sub
```

Then run the program and compare the results of clicking the arrows with the results from clicking the Command Buttons (they should be the same).

Finally, you can search for a record matching specific criteria with the **FindFirst, FindLast, FindNext,** and **FindPrevious methods.** The syntax for such a

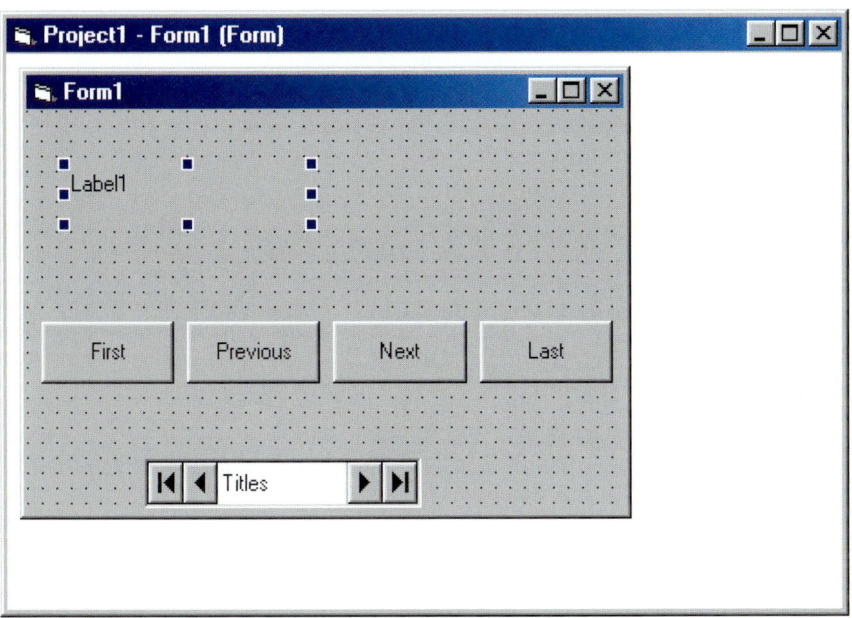

FIGURE 10.12 *Command buttons equivalent to the Data control's arrows*

search is a little bit cumbersome, so examine this code carefully, constructed for another Command Button named cmdFindFirst.

```
Private Sub cmdFindFirst_Click()
    Dim strCriteria As String
    Dim strSearchTitle As String
    strSearchTitle = "Gone with the Wind"
    strCriteria = "Title = '" & strSearchTitle & "'"
    dbTitles.Recordset.FindFirst strCriteria
    If dbTitles.Recordset.NoMatch Then
        Me.BackColor = vbBlue
    Else: Me.BackColor = vbWhite
    End If
End Sub
```

Note that the title to be searched must be enclosed within single quotation marks, because the entire search argument is a string enclosed within double quotation marks. Specifically, the final value of strCriteria in this code is "Title = 'Gone with the Wind'".

If a FindFirst, FindPrevious, FindNext, or FindLast operation fails to find a matching record, then the Recordset's **NoMatch property** is set to True, and the current record remains the record that was current before the Find method was invoked. In the example above, since the Titles Table of BIBLIO.MDB does not contain "Gone with the Wind," the form's BackColor changes to blue when cmdFindFirst is clicked.

STEP 3. Develop Your Logic.

See the Hierarchy Table (Figure 10.13) and the pseudocode (Figure 10.14.)

```
HIERARCHY TABLE-CLASS SCHEDULING VERSION 1

Project:   Faculty1 (Faculty.vbp)
Form:      frmFaculty1 (frmFaculty1.frm)
           Click event procedures:
             cmdFind
             mnuExit
             mnuHelp
             mnuWindowBrowse
             mnuWindowFind
```

FIGURE 10.13 *Hierarchy Table—Class Scheduling Version 1*

```
PSEUDOCODE-CLASS SCHEDULING VERSION 1

Event procedure: Sub cmdFind_Click
   Set an error trap
   Assign: strCriteria ← "LastName= "' & txtSearch & "'"
   Find the first record in the table that matches the requested surname
   If no match is found, issue an error message

Event procedure: mnuExit_Click
   End the program

Event procedure: mnuHelp_Click
   Display a message box with instructions for using this program

Event procedure: mnuWindowBrowse_Click
   Toggle the checked property of mnuWindowBrowse
   Toggle the visibility of dbFaculty

Event procedure: mnuWindowFind_Click
   Toggle the checked property of mnuWindowFind
   Toggle the visibility of fraFind
```

FIGURE 10.14 *Pseudocode—Class Scheduling Version 1*

STEP 4. Build Your GUI.

If you did "sketch" your forms on-line, then the only remaining task is to verify those designs and to name all forms and all controls that might be referenced in code. When you are satisfied with the appearance of all of the controls on the form, click the Lock Controls icon on the Form Editor toolbar (if visible) or select Format | Lock Controls to prevent any accidental movement of controls from one place to another on the form.

Use the following table to name and assign properties for all of the objects in frmFaculty1:

OBJECT	PROPERTY	SETTING
Form	Name	FrmFaculty1
	Caption	"Class Scheduling (Version 1)"
	BackColor	White

continued

OBJECT	PROPERTY	SETTING
Menu control (root)	Name	MnuExit
	Caption	"E&xit"
Menu control (root)	Name	MnuWindow
	Caption	"&Window"
Menu control (indented)	Name	MnuWindowBrowse
	Caption	"&Browse"
Menu control (indented)	Name	MnuWindowFind
	Caption	"&Find"
Menu control (root)	Name	MnuHelp
	Caption	"&Help"
Frame	Name	FraFind
	Caption	"Find Faculty Member"
	Visible	False
	BackColor	White
Label (inside fraFind)	Name	Label1
	Caption	"Enter Faculty Last Name"
Textbox (inside fraFind)	Name	TxtSearch
	Caption	<none>
Command Button (inside fraFind)	Name	CmdFind
	Caption	"Find"
Frame	Name	FraBrowse
	Caption	<none>
	BackColor	White
Data control (inside fraBrowse)	Name	DbFaculty
	Caption	"Faculty Table"
	DatabaseName	"C:\VBStudentDemos\Chap10\College.mdb"
	RecordSource	Faculty
Label (inside fraBrowse)	Name	Label2
	Caption	"Faculty ID"
Label (inside fraBrowse)	Name	LblFacultyID
	BackColor	White
	BorderStyle	1-Fixed Single
	DataSource	DbFaculty
	DataField	FacultyID
Label (inside fraBrowse)	Name	Label3
	Caption	"Rank"
Label (inside fraBrowse)	Name	LblRank
	BackColor	White
	BorderStyle	1-Fixed Single
	DataSource	DbFaculty
	DataField	Rank
Label (inside fraBrowse)	Name	Label4
	Caption	"First Name"
Label (inside fraBrowse)	Name	LblFirstName
	BackColor	White
	BorderStyle	1-Fixed Single
	DataSource	DbFaculty
	DataField	FirstName
Label (inside fraBrowse)	Name	Label5
	Caption	"Last Name"
Label (inside fraBrowse)	Name	LblLastName
	BackColor	White
	BorderStyle	1-Fixed Single
	DataSource	DbFaculty
	DataField	LastName

continued

OBJECT	PROPERTY	SETTING
Label (inside fraBrowse)	Name	Label6
	Caption	"Department"
Label (inside fraBrowse)	Name	LblDepartment
	BackColor	White
	BorderStyle	1-Fixed Single
	DataSource	DbFaculty
	DataField	Department

Note the location of the Microsoft Access database file in the folder C:\VBStudentDemos\Chap10\. You may need to modify this reference in your own code, depending on where the Student data was loaded.

Finally, from the Project menu, select Project1 Properties, and type in the name Faculty1 in the Project Name textbox. Save the form as frmFaculty1.frm and the project as Faculty1.vbp. These files should be in the same folder as your copy of the College.mdb database.

STEP 5. Write the VB Code.

This project, FACULTY1.VBP, includes only frmFaculty1, and very little code:

```
Option Explicit

Private Sub cmdFind_Click()
    Dim strCriteria As String
    On Error GoTo ErrorTrap
    txtSearch.SetFocus
    strCriteria = "LastName = '" & txtSearch & "'"
    dbFaculty.Recordset.FindFirst strCriteria
    If dbFaculty.Recordset.NoMatch Then
        MsgBox "That name was not found " & _
        "in the Faculty Table"
    End If
    Exit Sub
ErrorTrap:
    MsgBox "Type the name of a Faculty " & _
        "member; then click the Find button"
    Exit Sub
End Sub

Private Sub Form_Load()
    'Note to instructors: The following line is needed
    'so that the Data control finds the Database
    '(COLLEGE.MDB) no matter where the student places the
    'directory containing this program.
    dbFaculty.DatabaseName = IIf(Right(App.Path, 1) = "\", _
    App.Path & "college.mdb", App.Path & "\college.mdb")
End Sub

Private Sub mnuExit_Click()
    End
End Sub

Private Sub mnuHelp_Click()
    MsgBox "Under Window, choose Browse to " _
```

```
        & "scroll through all of the records, " _
        & "Find to search for a Faculty member"
End Sub

Private Sub mnuWindowBrowse_Click()
    dbFaculty.Visible = Not dbFaculty.Visible
    mnuWindowBrowse.Checked = Not mnuWindowBrowse.Checked
End Sub

Private Sub mnuWindowFind_Click()
    mnuWindowFind.Checked = Not mnuWindowFind.Checked
    fraFind.Visible = Not fraFind.Visible
End Sub
```

STEP 6. Test and Debug Your Program.

Put in some error traps to prevent the user from blowing up the program. Afterward, your debugging should include attempts to blow up your program on purpose, exercising your error traps. If you are able to cause a runtime error, then you need more error traps.

STEP 7. Complete the Program Documentation.

DISPLAYING THE SCHEDULE OF CLASSES

STEP 1. Understand the Problem.

Most commonly, Visual Basic provides a GUI as a front-end to a database, and in many if not most applications, only data retrieval (rather than data update) is required. Oftentimes, you will want to develop a simple VB program to display data contained in one table or derived from one predefined query. This is easily accomplished, as demonstrated above. [Note: when you click the down-arrow in the Data control's **RecordSource property,** you get a list of not only all of the tables in the database to which the Data control is attached, but also all QueryDefs (predefined queries) associated with that database. At runtime, the Data control actually creates a Recordset by executing a query, either retrieving all records from a table or retrieving the records resulting from the QueryDef.]

However, you will also encounter many applications in which you must retrieve data from multiple tables, but a predefined query matching your requirements does not exist within the database. In such a case, you can use a series of interrelated Data controls. Basically, you will assign one Data control to each required table of the database. Then, in code, you will reposition the current record of each Data control so as to keep all of the recordsets in synch.

SCHEDULE1.EXE (Figure 10.15) demonstrates this technique. The project contains three Data controls (dbSection, dbCourse, and dbFaculty), although only one of them (dbSection) is visible. Generally in a program of this kind, the visible Data control actually controls the movement of records in all of the Data controls. When the user moves to a new current record (a new section of a course), the program locates the corresponding records in the dbCourse Recordset (to display course information) and in the dbFaculty Recordset (to display the name of the instructor for that section).

This project also includes program code to assign the DatabaseName property of the Data controls at runtime. In Form_Load, the program accesses the name of the current folder (the folder where Schedule1.exe resides) and concatenates onto

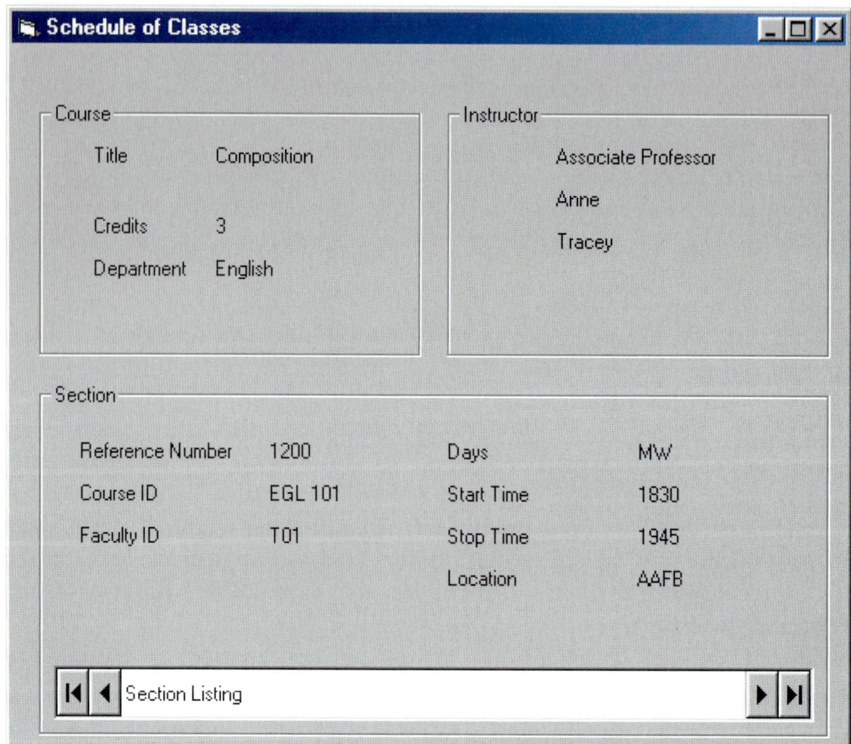

FIGURE 10.15 *Schedule1, displaying related records from three tables*

the folder name the name of the database (College.mdb). This complete folder and filename is then assigned to the DatabaseName property of the Data controls, and the Recordsets are re-created through the Refresh method.

Table Join Operations and Embedded SQL

Rather than programming a secondary Data control to look up the corresponding record in an associated table, professional programmers actually use the built-in query capabilities of the DBMS to accomplish this task effortlessly. A query builds an Answer Table based on user-specified criteria, and the results can combine information from a series of Tables. When more than one Table is employed to generate the results of the query, the operation is referred to as a Table Join. In the case of the Display of the Schedule of Classes, for example, the Table Join operation would result in an Answer Table with the same number of records as the Sections Table; but, in addition to all of the information in the Sections Table, the record for each section would also contain the course description information extracted from the Courses Table and the faculty-identifying information extracted from the Faculty Table.

Typically, DBMS software offers users a friendly graphical or menu-driven interface for asking even complex queries: "Show me all airline passengers whose destination was Jacksonville/Ft. Lauderdale/Orlando during March 1997 and who used the Student Discount 'Spring Break' coupons." A DBMS must also allow programmers to generate such queries in code, and the language most often supported for this purpose is the IBM-created *de facto* standard programming language for DBMS called Structured Query Language (SQL).

Visual Basic supports SQL. You could use an SQL statement as the RecordSource property in order to define the Recordset to be created by a Data control. The statement for the present application would be "Select * from Sections, Courses, Faculty where Sections.CourseID = Courses.CourseID and Sections.

FacultyID = Faculty.FacultyID". Only one Data control would be needed, rather than three.

We realize that we are giving this topic short shrift here, but we do not want this textbook to digress into an introductory text in SQL. Suffice it to say that, if you become proficient in the Structured Query Language, practically everything you learn in that language can be directly incorporated in your Visual Basic programs. Some of the tasks and solutions presented in this and the next two chapters would be easier to implement by embedding SQL statements into your Visual Basic programs. Having said that, we will now restrict ourselves to solutions written entirely in native VB.

STEP 2. Design a Solution./ STEP 4. Build Your GUI.

The form for this project (Figure 10.16) has three frames, one for each table. Within each frame, a Data control is assigned to a table of the College database, and label controls are bound to selected fields within that table:

- In fraSection, the RecordSource for the dbSection Data control is the Section table. Labels are bound to every field of the Section table (RefNum, CourseID, FacultyID, Days, StartTime, StopTime, and Location).
- In fraCourse, the RecordSource for dbCourse is the Courses table, and dbCourse's Visible property is set to false. This is done because the user is not supposed to scroll through the Courses table in this application; rather, the

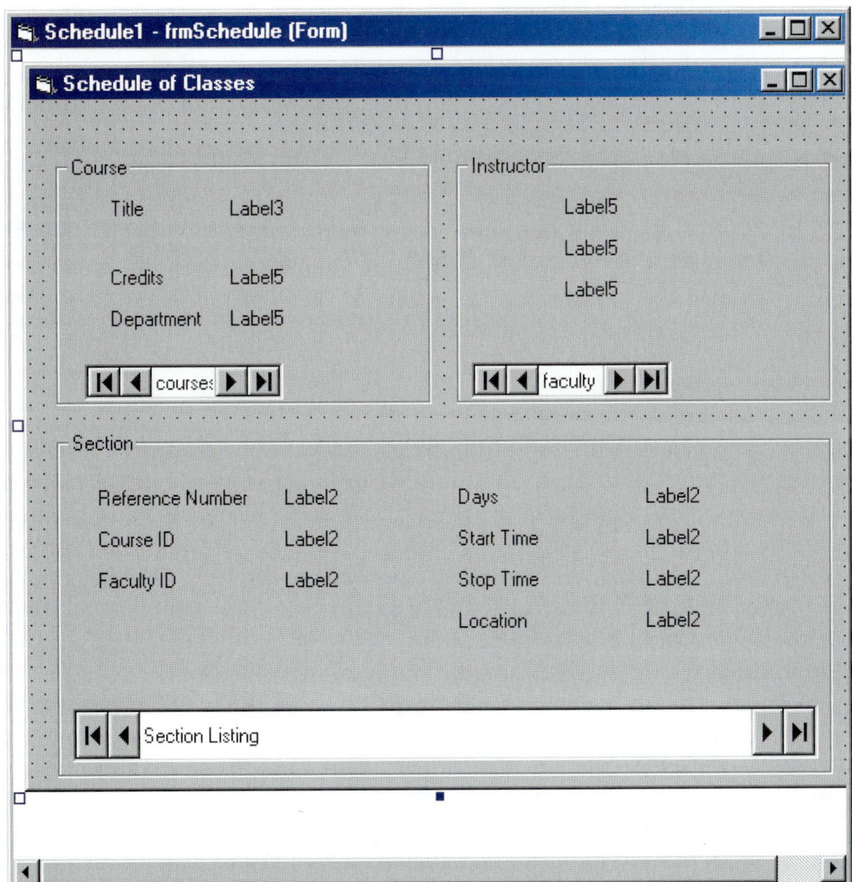

FIGURE 10.16 *frmSchedule at design time*

user scrolls through the Sections table, and the program is supposed to automatically display the corresponding course information. Labels in fraCourse are bound to the course Title, Credits, and Department fields of the Courses table.

- In fraFaculty, the RecordSource for dbFaculty is the Faculty table, and again the Data control is invisible. Labels are bound to the faculty member's Rank, FirstName, and LastName fields.

Go ahead and build the GUI as described here.

Reposition Event and Refresh Method

To cause the current record in dbCourse.Recordset to match the CourseID of the current record in dbSection.Recordset, you will need to program the Reposition event for dbSection. The **Reposition event** for a Data control fires whenever the current record changes, either through user-initiated action (such as clicking the MoveNext arrow on the Data control) or through program code (such as a MoveNext method invoked in code). When dbSection's current record changes, we want to use the FindFirst method to locate the corresponding course information in the Courses table; ditto with the Faculty table.

Also, in the event that the CourseID in the Sections table has no matching record in the Courses table, we want to avoid accidentally displaying the wrong course data. Therefore, after the FindFirst method is invoked, if NoMatch is True, we will make fraCourse invisible. Exactly the same logic will be applied for the Faculty table and fraFaculty.

Based on this brief description, try writing the code for the Reposition event, and then run the program. Even if you code it correctly, you may get an error message within the Reposition event: "Object variable not set." This error is generated because of the order in which VB initializes the three Data controls. Essentially, when dbSection's Reposition event fires for the first time, the other two Data controls must already exist. We can force this to occur by invoking the **Refresh** method in the Form_Load event for all three Data controls, making sure that dbSection is refreshed last. Since the Form_Load event occurs before the form is painted on the screen, the Refresh method opens the Data control and creates the Recordset.

App (Application) Object

The only other programming wrinkle in this application derives from the fact that a programmer or user is apt to move a completed project and its associated database to a different computer or disk drive or folder from its original location. When this happens, unfortunately, the Data control's DatabaseName property does not get automatically updated. In other words, if you create a folder on your hard drive for building this program and you place the College.mdb file as well as your frmSchedule1.frm into that folder, and then you copy the completed program to your A:\ drive and try to run the program on another computer, you will encounter an error message because the Data control will still try to find the College.mdb file on that computer's hard drive. The code for Schedule1.exe addresses this problem by always looking for the College.mdb file in the same disk drive and folder where the program is located. (A more flexible solution to this problem is introduced in the next chapter.)

At runtime, the location of the running program is given by the App object and its Path property. The **App object** refers to the current application, and the **Path property** of the App object is the folder in which the current application resides. Therefore, we might expect the following code to correctly assign the DatabaseName property of dbSection:

```
dbSection.DatabaseName = App.Path & "\College.mdb"
```

Right Function and IIf (Immediate If) Function

Before we can use App.Path in assigning the DatabaseName property of the Data controls at run time, we have to deal with one small problem: App.Path may or may not end in a backslash. If it does (which will occur if the Database happens to be loaded in the root directory of a disk, say, "A:\"), then the desired string is App.Path & "College.mdb". But if App.Path does not end in a backslash, then a backslash must be inserted in between, so the desired string is App.Path & "\College.mdb".

In code, we can isolate the last character of a string by the **Right function:**

```
Right(string, n)
```

returns the last *n* bytes of *string*. So in this case we want to test whether

```
Right(App.Path,1) = "\"
```

In the code below, dbSection.DatabaseName is assigned the return value from a call to the Immediate If function. The **IIf function** has three arguments:

1. a condition to be tested,
2. the value to be returned if the condition is True, and
3. the value to be returned if the condition is False.

The complete statement would look like this:

```
dbSecton.DatabaseName = IIf(Right(App.Path,1) = "\", _
    App.Path & "College.mdb", App.Path & "\College.mdb")
```

The Immediate If function is useful in shortening code that, without it, would be a bit cumbersome. In the present case, we obtain in one IIf-assisted assignment statement what would otherwise require much longer wording, such as:

```
If Right(App.Path,1) = "\" Then
    dbSection.DatabaseName = App.Path & "college.mdb"
Else
    dbSection.DatabaseName = App.Path & "\College.mdb"
End If
```

STEP 3. Develop Your Logic. / STEP 5. Write the VB Code.

See the Hierarchy Table (Figure 10.17) and the pseudocode (Figure 10.18). This program has very little actual code:

```
Option Explicit
Private Sub dbSection_Reposition()
    Dim strCriteria As String
    strCriteria = "CourseID = '" & lblCourseID & "'"
    dbCourse.Recordset.FindFirst strCriteria
    If dbCourse.Recordset.NoMatch Then
        fraCourse.Visible = False
    Else
        fraCourse.Visible = True
    End If
```

SPLASH.FRM, the Startup form, should display your name, program title, and date. Also include an image that flashes on and off. After 5 seconds, show DISPLAY.FRM and unload SPLASH.FRM.

DISPLAY.FRM should contain two frames (initially invisible) and a Menu control. Menu selections:

E&xit

&View

——&Courses

——&Find a Course

——&Sections

&About Display

The Courses Frame should contain

- a Data control for the Courses Table;
- bound Label controls to display all of the fields in the Courses Table;
- a TextBox control for the user to enter the Course ID of one course;
- a Command Button that finds the record in the Courses Table whose Course ID matches the Course ID in the TextBox. Display an error message if no match is found.

The Sections Frame should contain

- a Data control for the Sections Table;
- bound Label controls to display all of the fields in the Sections Table.

Menu funtionality:

- Exit should end the program.
- View | Courses should toggle the visibility of the Courses Frame.
- View | Sections should toggle the visibility of the Sections Frame.
- About Display should Show the Splash form again.

Publishers Display

This program uses the BIBLIO.MDB database supplied with Visual Basic. Start by copying this file into a new directory created for this project. (But note that BIBLIO.MDB will not fit on one floppy—it is 3.5MB in size.)

Create a Visual Basic project with two forms, frmStart and frmPubs. Frm-Start, the Startup form, should display your name, program title, and date. Include two alternating images that flash on and off. After five seconds, show frm-Pubs and unload frmStart.

frmPubs contains a menu with these items:

E&xit

&View Publishers

——&Browse

——&Find

&Flash

frmPubs contains two Frame controls (initially disabled), captioned "Browse Publishers" and "Find Publisher". The "Browse Publishers" Frame contains a Data control for the Publishers Table and bound Label controls to display all of the fields in the Publishers Table. The "Find Publisher" Frame contains a Label captioned "Enter a Publisher ID", an empty TextBox (where the user will type in a PubID), and a Command Button captioned "Find." When the user clicks the "Find" button, the program finds the record in the Publishers Table whose PubID matches the PubID in the TextBox. (Hint: PubID is a Long Integer, not a string, and so the search argument cannot be enclosed in single quotes.) Display an error message if no match is found.
Menu functionality:

- "Exit" ends the program.
- "View | Browse" is a toggle switch. When clicked once, it enables the "Browse Publishers" Frame and places a checkmark before the "Browse" item in the menu. When clicked again, it disables the "Browse Publishers" Frame and unchecks the "Browse" menu item.
- "View | Find" is a similar toggle switch. When first clicked, enable the "Find Publisher" Frame and check the "Find" menu item; when clicked again, disable the "Find Publisher" Frame and uncheck the "Find" menu item.
- "Flash" shows frmStart again.

CHAPTER ELEVEN

DATA CONTROL (UPDATABLE)

Application: Class Scheduling (Version 2)

LEARNING OBJECTIVES

Upon completion of Chapter Eleven, you will be able to:

- Use a Data control and bound controls and associated events and methods to edit, add, and delete records in a table of a database, including data security considerations.
- Use the CheckBox control and apply it to a Boolean (logical) variable in a database.
- Use a List Box control to display a list of items and to select one item from the list. Also use the related Combo control.
- Use the Data-Bound List controls (DBList and DBCombo).
- Use the Common Dialog control for opening and saving files, and for choosing colors, printers, fonts, and help files.
- Control and respond to changes in focus through the GotFocus and LostFocus events and the SetFocus method

Keywords

AddItem method
AddNew method
BOF property
Bookmark property
CancelUpdate method
CheckBox control (prefix: chk)
Clear method
Color property
Combo Box control (prefix: cbo)
Common Dialog control (prefix: dlg)
Count property
DataChanged property
DBCombo control (prefix: dbcbo)
DBList control (prefix: dblst)
DefaultExt property
Delete method
DropdownCombo style
DropdownList style
Edit method
EditMode property
EOF property
Fields collection
FileName property
Filter property
FilterIndex property
Flags property
ForeColor property
GotFocus event

HelpCommand property
HelpFile property
InitDir property
LastModified property
List Box control (prefix: lst)
List property
ListCount property
ListField property
ListIndex property
LostFocus event
MS Flex Grid control (prefix: msfg)
ReadOnly property
RemoveItem method
RowSource property
SetFocus method
ShowColor method
ShowFont method
ShowHelp method
ShowOpen method
ShowPrinter method
ShowSave method
SimpleCombo style
Sorted property
Style property (cbo control)
Update method
Validate event

INTERMEDIATE-LEVEL VISUAL BASIC PROGRAMMING

By now you have become an intermediate-level Visual Basic computer programmer. You have learned a substantial portion of the Visual Basic package: You are thoroughly familiar with VB's Integrated Development Environment; you can use the on-line Help facility to research new features and to analyze programming problems; you can use the Debugger to isolate and fix runtime errors; you recognize most of the VB objects (Forms and Controls, Data Access, Screen, Debug, and Printer objects); you can design a rather sophisticated GUI; you have been exposed to most of VB's Properties, Events, and Methods; you have written applications involving multiple forms and MDI forms; and you have used a significant percentage of the VB programming language (syntactical constructs, statements, and functions).

You have also learned a lot about the discipline of structured computer programming: You know the steps in computer programming and the importance of following them in a linear, step-by-step fashion; you have practiced consistent naming conventions for all words invented by the programmer, from objects to variables; you have implemented the three principal control structures (sequence, selection, iteration); you have experimented with both simple and more complex programs; and you have interfaced an application with an external database.

You have become sufficiently knowledgeable about Visual Basic programming so that you no longer need the kind of detailed, step-by-step guidance provided in earlier chapters of this text. Accordingly, beginning with this chapter, each remaining chapter concentrates on a summary of the syntax relevant to a particular topic, followed by a complete program that demonstrates that syntax. You will find fewer of the meticulous examples offered earlier; rather, the focus will be on showing you the code in relatively more sophisticated programs, and offering brief additional explanations and tips only where necessary.

INTRODUCING VERSION 2 OF THE CLASS SCHEDULING APPLICATION

STEP 1. Understand the Problem.

Run FACULTY2.EXE, the next Class Scheduling Database application using VB's Data control. The menu now offers the additional selections File | Open and Window | Modify.

If you develop and distribute a commercial application, and if your application includes a user-controlled database, a real issue arises concerning the name and location of the database on disk. The programmer has no way of knowing ahead of time where the user is going to store his data files. Version 2 of the Class Scheduling application shows you how the user can determine the database location at run time through the Common Dialog control.

When running the Faculty2 application, start by opening the database, COLLEGE.MDB, located in the Chap10 folder of the student executables. You do this by selecting File | Open (Figure 11.01) from the application's menu, which causes an Open File Dialog Box to appear. This dialog box is one of six common dialogs accessible through VB's Common Dialog control. In this case, the Open File dialog has been told to display only Microsoft Access files (those with the filename extension .mdb), and to start by displaying the folder in which the Faculty2 application is running.

Window | Find has been improved in this version: To find a particular faculty member's record, a DBCombo control contains only the last names of faculty; when one name in the DBCombo's drop-down list is selected, the program repositions the Data control to point to that faculty member's record. The DBCombo control is one of a number of related controls discussed in this chapter.

Like the Faculty1 application in Chapter 10, Faculty2 allows the user to scroll through the Faculty Table using the Data control (Figure 11.02). Unlike version 1, this version also allows the user to add, delete, or edit records in the Faculty Table. Select Window | Modify, and try adding a new record, editing (changing) a record, and deleting a record. All changes to the database were prevented in version 1 by using Labels rather than TextBoxes for all of the bound controls. But in version 2, we want the user to be able to make changes some of the time, so we did use TextBoxes; but we took a few other simple steps to try to help the user avoid inadvertent modifications to the database.

When the user clicks on the Add Command Button, a blank record is added at the end of the Recordset. After the user fills in the TextBoxes with the values for the new record, the user clicks either the Save Changes Command Button or the Cancel Command Button. If Save Changes is clicked, the program records the new information in this new record, and then physically adds the new record to the underlying table in the database. If Cancel is clicked, the Add operation is aborted before any changes to the underlying table are made. While the Add operation is pending, all other operations (Browse, Find, Add, Edit, and Delete) are unavailable.

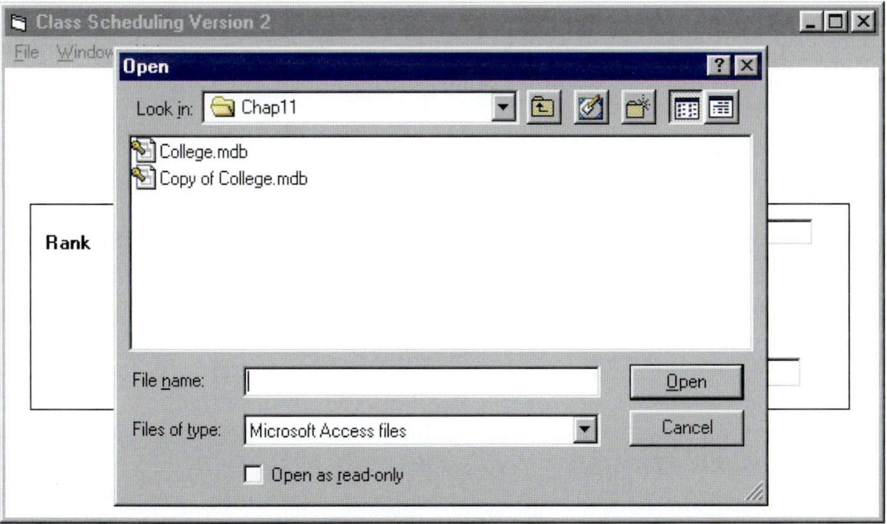

FIGURE 11.01 *Faculty2, opening the database file*

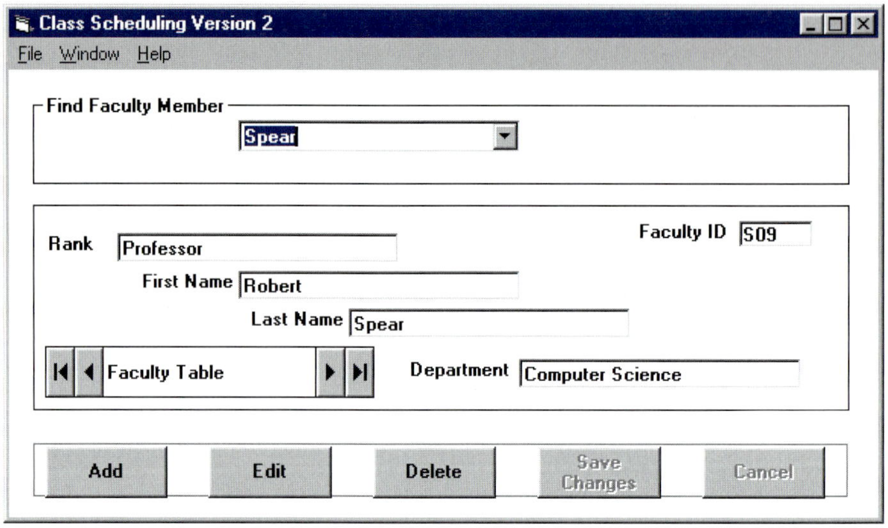

FIGURE 11.02 *Faculty2, displaying the browse, find, and modify options*

Similarly, the Edit Command Button allows the user to make any desired changes to the current record. After all changes to the current record have been typed in, the user again can decide to Save Changes or Cancel the transaction.

The Delete Command Button removes the current record from the Recordset and from the underlying database, and then recreates the Recordset. (The Data control ends up pointing to the first record.)

By the way, don't worry about messing up your only copy of College.mdb while you experiment with this program. Not only can you download the database again from the Web, but also note that the Website's student executables includes College.mdb and Copy of College.mdb. If needed, use Windows Explorer to a) delete College.mdb; b) copy "Copy of College.mdb" to the Clipboard; c) paste "Copy of College.mdb" into your current folder; and d) rename "Copy of Copy of College.mdb" as College.mdb.

STEP 2. Design a Solution.

We now must cover the new controls, methods, and events needed for the design of Version 2 of the Class Scheduling Application. This includes features related to database access and maintenance, as well as a few more VB GUI items.

Review of Data Access Objects Terminology

The Add, Edit, and Delete operations introduced in this chapter require the programmer to take special care concerning the state of the underlying database Table, the Recordset object, and the current record. First, we will review the definitions of these interrelated terms.

- A Table consists of a set of data organized into rows (records) and columns (fields), and is part of a database, defined as a collection of one or more Tables. A Table may be specified as the RecordSource property of a Data control.
- A Recordset is a collection of database-type records, again organized into rows and columns. The Recordset object is created by the VB Data control when it opens the database at run time and whenever its Refresh method is invoked.

The Data control's RecordsetType property determines which type of Recordset is created: Table-type, Dynaset-type, or Snapshot-type.

- A Dynaset-type Recordset is a dynamically updatable collection of records. It could be the functional equivalent of a database Table, created by opening a Data control whose DatabaseName property is the name of a database and whose RecordSource property is the name of a single table. This is the type of Recordset created in the Class Scheduling application. However, you should know that a Dynaset-type Recordset could be composed as the result of a QueryDef stored as part of a database. Since query definitions may cull information from two or more Tables, the resulting Recordset might not be the equivalent of any Table.
- Essentially, when a form containing a Data control is loaded, the Data control opens a database (based on its DatabaseName property) and creates a Recordset object (based on its RecordSource property—which must be either the name of a Table or the name of a QueryDef stored within the database).
- A Data control always points to one record in the Recordset, called the current record. When the Data control creates the Recordset or when the Refresh method is invoked, the current record is the first record in the Recordset, order being set by the primary index of the Recordset (usually the primary index of the underlying Table).

Modifying a Table with AddNew, Edit, and Update Methods

The **AddNew method** creates a new, empty record in a Table and Recordset. The **Edit method** prepares the current record to accept changes. When an AddNew or Edit operation is pending, the **Update method** confirms the new/changed record and saves this record in the Table and Recordset; the **CancelUpdate method,** as the name implies, cancels the pending AddNew or Edit.

The AddNew, Edit, Update, and CancelUpdate methods, available to the Recordset property of a Data control, all use a temporary memory area called the copy buffer. The copy buffer can hold one record of a Table:

- When the AddNew method is executed, the fields in the copy buffer are all set to nulls, and the copy buffer is made the current record. While the AddNew operation is pending, all bound controls are temporarily released from the Recordset and are bound instead to the fields in the copy buffer. The user is then expected to enter data in those fields.
- When the Update method is executed after an AddNew method, the contents of the copy buffer are copied to both the Table and the Recordset. The new record is placed in its proper position in the Database Table, but it is stored temporarily at the end of the Recordset. To make it available in its correct location, use the Refresh method. Also following an AddNew/Update sequence, the current record is the one that was the current record before AddNew was invoked. To make the new record the current record, you can set the Recordset's **Bookmark property** to the value of the Recordset's **LastModified property.** Alternatively, before invoking the Update method you can save the primary key of the new record in a variable, and then use the FindFirst method to locate that new record. When the Update operation is completed, the copy buffer is released, and all bound controls are again bound to the current record within the Recordset.
- When the Edit method is executed, the current record is copied to the copy buffer, and the copy buffer is made the current record. During the time that an

Edit operation is pending, all bound controls are temporarily released from the Recordset and are bound instead to the record in the copy buffer.

- Following an Edit method and then Update method, the updated record replaces the previous contents of that record in both the Recordset and the underlying table. Following an Edit/Update sequence, the current record is still the one that was in the copy buffer. Again, when the Update operation is completed, the copy buffer is released, and all bound controls are again bound to the current record within the Recordset.

Delete Method

The **Delete method** removes the current record from the underlying Table, and it sets the current record to Null in the Recordset. The deleted current record is still the current record, but any reference to it causes a runtime error. Therefore, after invoking the Delete method, it is important to move to another record. This can be accomplished by the MoveFirst method.

If you would rather move to the adjacent record, then use MoveNext. But then test to see if **EOF (end of file)** is True, which will be the case if the deleted record was the last record in the Recordset. If indeed EOF is True, then use MovePrevious to reposition the Data control to the previous (now the last) active record.

Similarly, by using MovePrevious you could move instead to the record preceding the deleted record. But in this case too, you could have a problem if the deleted record was the first record in the Recordset. So if you invoke MovePrevious, then this should be followed by a test to see if **BOF (beginning of file)** is True, which, if it is, then you should invoke MoveNext to get to the next (now the new first) record in the Recordset.

ToggleAddEdit

Run the Faculty2 program again, and notice the behavior of the five command buttons when the Window | Modify menu item has been selected. Essentially, when an Add or an Edit operation has been initiated, the Add, Edit, and Delete buttons, the Find frame, and the dbFaculty Data control are all disabled; and at the same time, the Save Changes and Cancel buttons (initially disabled) are enabled. Also note that, when the pending Add or Edit operation is completed (by clicking either the Save Changes or the Cancel button), these enabled properties are all reversed: the Add, Edit, and Delete buttons are enabled, as are the Find frame and the Data control, while the Save Changes and Cancel buttons are again disabled. Since the same actions are called for (that is, reversing the Enabled property of all of these controls) whenever the user selects Add, Edit, Save Changes, or Cancel, it makes sense to write the code just once, and to call for it whenever it is needed. Accordingly, a general procedure called ToggleAddEdit was written, as follows:

```
Public Sub ToggleAddEdit()
   fraFind.Enabled = Not fraFind.Enabled
   dbFaculty.Enabled = Not dbFaculty.Enabled
   cmdAdd.Enabled = Not cmdAdd.Enabled
   cmdEdit.Enabled = Not cmdEdit.Enabled
   cmdDelete.Enabled = Not cmdDelete.Enabled
   cmdSaveChanges.Enabled = Not cmdSaveChanges.Enabled
   cmdCancel.Enabled = Not cmdCancel.Enabled
End Sub
```

This procedure reverses the Enabled property of all five Command Buttons, the Find frame, and the Data control. It is called when the user clicks any of these four Command Buttons: Add, Edit, Save Changes, or Cancel. Of course, clicking the Add button also invokes the AddNew method; the Edit button also executes the Edit method; the Save Changes button, the Update method; and the Cancel button, the CancelUpdate method.

DataChanged and EditMode Properties

The ToggleAddEdit procedure works well enough if the user selects Window | Modify and then clicks the Add or the Edit button to initiate a new record or to change an existing record. A problem occurs, however, if the user simply clicks on a textbox and begins typing in a new value. Such an action does initiate a change to the record, and if the user subsequently moves to a different record, any such changes will be made permanent. Further, if the user decides not to retain such changes, it's very difficult to avoid having them become permanent——one radical method would be to turn the computer off before moving to another record (this technique is not recommended!). To solve this problem, we used the DataChanged and the EditMode properties. Again, the objective here is to prevent *inadvertent* changes to the database. The user can make the changes, but the user should be aware that such changes are in fact being made, and the user should have the opportunity to reverse the process.

Data bound controls have a **DataChanged property,** unavailable at design time and read-only at runtime, which indicates whether or not the value displayed in that control has been changed from the current record as retrieved from the Recordset. In the Faculty2 Application, we built a control array of Text Boxes called txtFields to contain a faculty member's rank, first name, last name, and department. If DataChanged for one of these TextBoxes is True, then that means that the user has typed in a new value for that Text Box since the last time the current record was retrieved from the Recordset.

A Recordset has an **EditMode property,** whose value indicates whether an edit or add is in progress. The three possible values of this property are defined in the DAO Library: 0 (dbEditNone) means that no edit or add is pending; 1 (dbEditInProgress) means that an Edit method has been invoked and the current record is in the copy buffer; 2 (dbEditAdd) means that an AddNew method has been invoked, and the current record in the copy buffer is a new record not yet saved in the database.

We can use these properties to our advantage in the present case: If the EditMode for the Recordset is 0 while DataChanged for a Text Box is true, then this means that the user has started changing the value of a Text Box without having clicked the Edit button. Therefore, we will click the Edit button on behalf of the user. This code is placed in the Change event for the txtFields control array, so the procedure is executed every time the user presses any key while the blinking cursor is inside any of the Text Boxes. However, the Modify frame is made visible and cmdEdit_Click is called only when both conditions obtain:

```
Private Sub txtFields_Change(Index As Integer)
   If dbFaculty.Recordset.EditMode = dbEditNone And _
      txtFields(Index).DataChanged Then
         fraModify.Visible = True
         mnuWindowModify.Checked = True
         Call cmdEdit_Click
   End If
End Sub
```

constants, and the meaning of each are as shown below. To cancel an operation, the program can set the Action equal to vbDataActionCancel.

```
 0 vbDataActionCancel           Cancel the operation.
 1 vbDataActionMoveFirst        MoveFirst method.
 2 vbDataActionMovePrevious     MovePrevious method.
 3 vbDataActionMoveNext         MoveNext method.
 4 vbDataActionMoveLast         MoveLast method.
 5 vbDataActionAddNew           AddNew method.
 6 vbDataActionUpdate           Update method.
 7 vbDataActionDelete           Delete method.
 8 vbDataActionFind             Find method.
 9 vbDataActionBookmark         Bookmark property was set.
10 vbDataActionClose            Close method.
11 vbDataActionUnload           The form is being unloaded.
```

4. Snapshots—You can create a Snapshot-type rather than a Dynaset-type Recordset. A Snapshot, which takes far fewer machine resources to create and maintain, permits no changes to the underlying database.

Summary Comments Concerning Database Access

Chapters Ten and Eleven cover a lot of territory dealing with Database access. You will need to study this code carefully to follow what is going on. Also, you should read liberally in the Microsoft Developers Network (MSDN) Library and in the on-line library concerning the many Data Access related topics. You can spend a long winter weekend just reading about Data Access in the Help screens and trying out some of the code for yourself.

Beyond the few techniques introduced in this text, Visual Basic provides much more functionality in the area of Database-related Objects. VB programs can create Databases, Tables, and Query Definitions; declare object variables of any of these types (Databases, tables, TableDefs, Snapshots, and QueryDefs); use a series of functions related to Data Access (such as OpenDatabase, RepairDatabase, BeginTrans, CommitTrans, and Rollback); and access any mainframe database that supports the Open Database Connectivity (ODBC) protocol. Earlier versions of Visual Basic featured Data Access Objects (DAO) and Remote Data Objects (RDO), both of which are still supported in VB 6.0 but are considered somewhat passé. The newest contribution from Visual Basic 6.0 is ActiveX Data Objects (ADO) and the ADO Data Control (ADODC), which we will address in Chapter Twelve. Using these more robust facilities of VB, professional programmers create fully functional "front-end" GUIs that carry out all needed database operations, including security features.

Here is one additional tip for learning about Data Access in Visual Basic: Many of the examples in the Help screens refer to Tables in the sample Microsoft Database BIBLIO.MDB, which is distributed as a sample file with Visual Basic. We suggest that you copy this file into a new directory, then write your own practice programs to play around with the Tables in that database. If you happen to corrupt the database in the course of your practice sessions, you can just re-copy it from the original.

Finally, as you become more proficient in Visual Basic's Data control and other Database-related objects and techniques, you will find it increasingly valuable to study Structured Query Language. SQL is beyond the scope of this text, but mastery of SQL will allow your Visual Basic (and other language) programs to access most of the world's popular Database Management Systems. Buy an SQL book and study it.

We will now turn our attention to the other new features introduced in Version 2 of the Class Scheduling Application.

Common Dialog Control

This chapter introduces the Common Dialog control, a most versatile and useful control. The **Common Dialog control** includes a series of six Dialog Boxes, through which your program can obtain user input for these common tasks:

- opening a file—the Common Dialog method for activating this Dialog Box is **ShowOpen;**
- saving a file under a new filename or in a new folder (Save File As . . .)—**ShowSave;**
- selecting a color—**ShowColor;**
- selecting a font and various font characteristics—**ShowFont;**
- selecting characteristics concerning the document to be printed—**ShowPrinter;**
- opening a Windows Help file—**ShowHelp.**

You will probably recognize most of the Dialog Boxes and the functions they support. The project DLG.VBP demonstrates the six different Dialog Boxes. Load and run this project.

To try these features yourself, start a new project, and put an array of six Command Buttons (named cmd) and a Common Dialog control on the form (Figure 11.03). If the icon for the Common Dialog control does not appear in the Toolbox, then you must add it to the Toolbox. Select Project | Components | Controls tab, check the checkbox for Microsoft Common Dialog Control 6.0, and click OK.

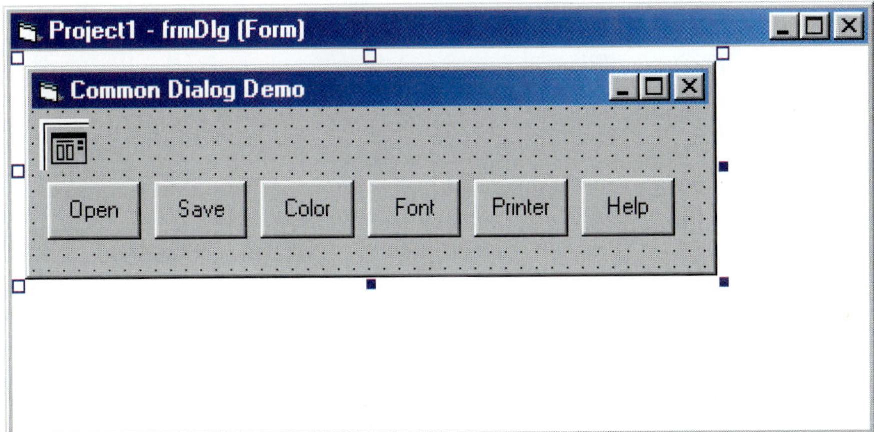

FIGURE 11.03 *frmDlg at design time*

Caption the Command Buttons as shown, name the Common Dialog control dlg, and insert the following code:

```
Private Sub cmd_Click(Index As Integer)
    Select Case Index
        Case 0, 1
            dlg.DefaultExt = "txt"
            dlg.InitDir = App.Path
            dlg.Filter = "Microsoft Data Base|*.mdb|"_
            & "Text files|*.txt|All files|*.*"
            dlg.FilterIndex = 1
            If Index Then dlg.ShowSave Else
            dlg.ShowOpen
            Print dlg.filename
        Case 2
            dlg.ShowColor
            BackColor = dlg.Color
        Case 3
            dlg.Flags = cdlCFScreenFonts
            dlg.ShowFont
            FontBold = dlg.FontBold
            FontItalic = dlg.FontItalic
            FontName = dlg.FontName
            FontSize = dlg.FontSize
            FontStrikethru = dlg.FontStrikethru
            FontUnderline = dlg.FontUnderline
            Cls
            Print "This is my selected font"
        Case 4: dlg.ShowPrinter
        Case 5
            dlg.HelpFile = "c:\windows\help\VBcmn96.hlp"
            dlg.HelpCommand = &HB
            dlg.ShowHelp
        End Select
End Sub
```

Figures 11.04 through 11.09 are the Dialogs resulting from clicking the six Command Buttons in DLG.VBP. A few explanations of the code follow.

- Case 0, 1—The Open File and Save File As Dialogs share the same properties. Significant properties include these:
  DefaultExt—if the user does not type in the filename extension, then the filename extension entered into this property will be appended to the filename.
  InitDir—determines the initial drive and directory for the Drive ListBox and the Directory ListBox.
  Filter—provides a list of filters for the File ListBox. Each filter consists of the filter text to be printed in the "List files of type" Dropdown list, then a pipe symbol (|), and then the actual filter. Another pipe precedes the next filter text.
  FilterIndex—determines which of the filters will be in effect when the Dialog Box opens. The first filter listed is FilterIndex 1.
  Flags—A long list of possible flags can restrict the user's choices in many ways. For example, the selected file may have to already exist, or may not be allowed to already exist. Or a caution may be displayed if the user selects a file

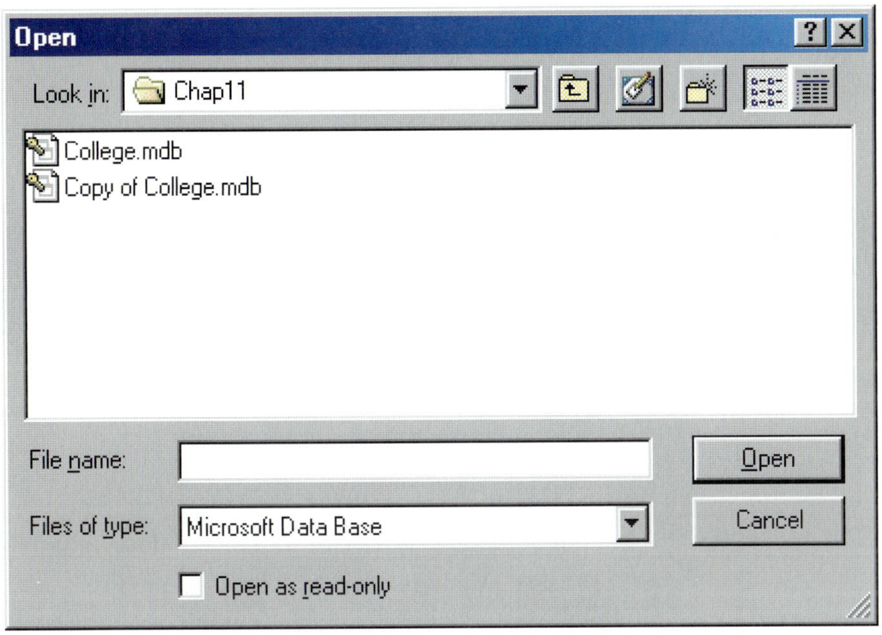

FIGURE 11.04 *ShowOpen method*

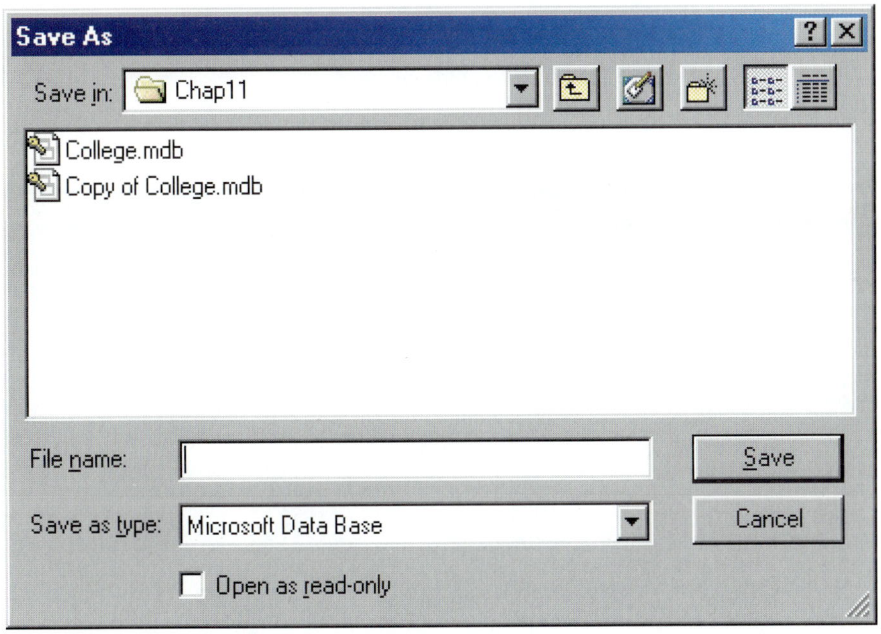

FIGURE 11.05 *ShowSave method*

whose extension does not match the one in the DefaultExt property. There are many other flags, all listed in the VB Help files for the Flags property.

Filename—When the user leaves the Dialog Box, the Filename property contains the complete drive, path, and filename of the selected file. Use the Filename property in your program to open or save a user-selected file. In the Class Scheduling Application version 3, the ShowOpen method lets the user select the proper location of COLLEGE.MDB, after which the Filename property of the Common Dialog control is assigned to the DatabaseName property of all of the Data controls used in the application.

FIGURE 11.06 *ShowColor method*

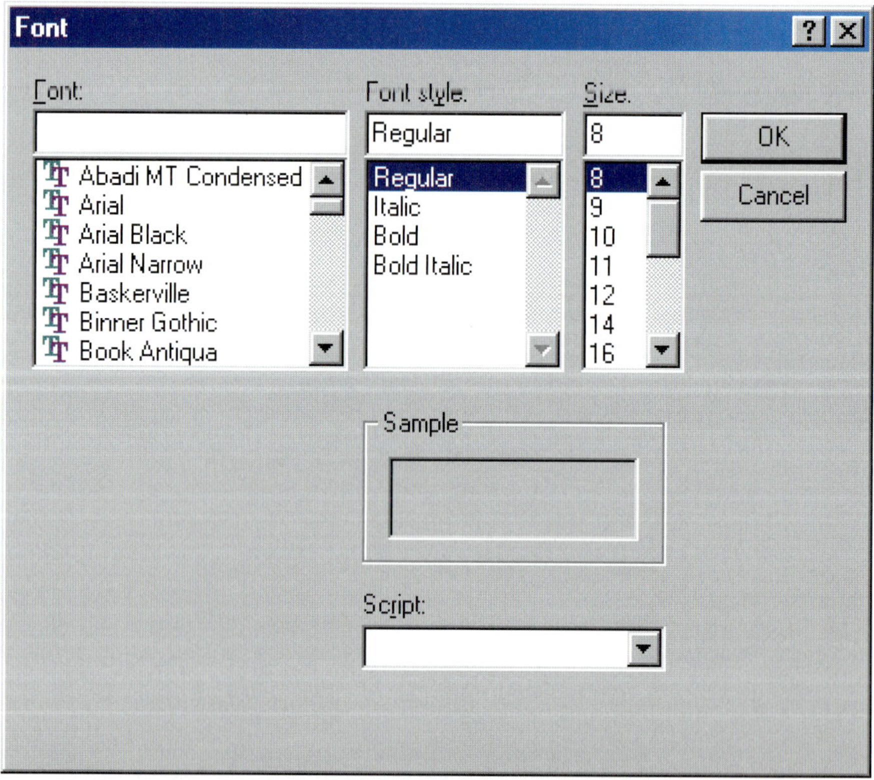

FIGURE 11.07 *ShowFont method*

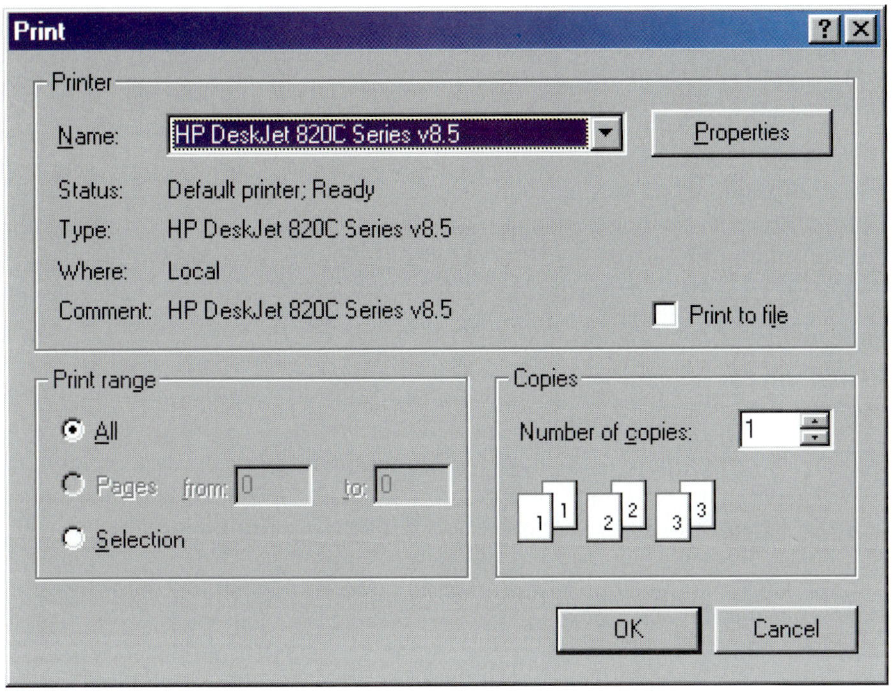

FIGURE 11.08 *ShowPrinter method*

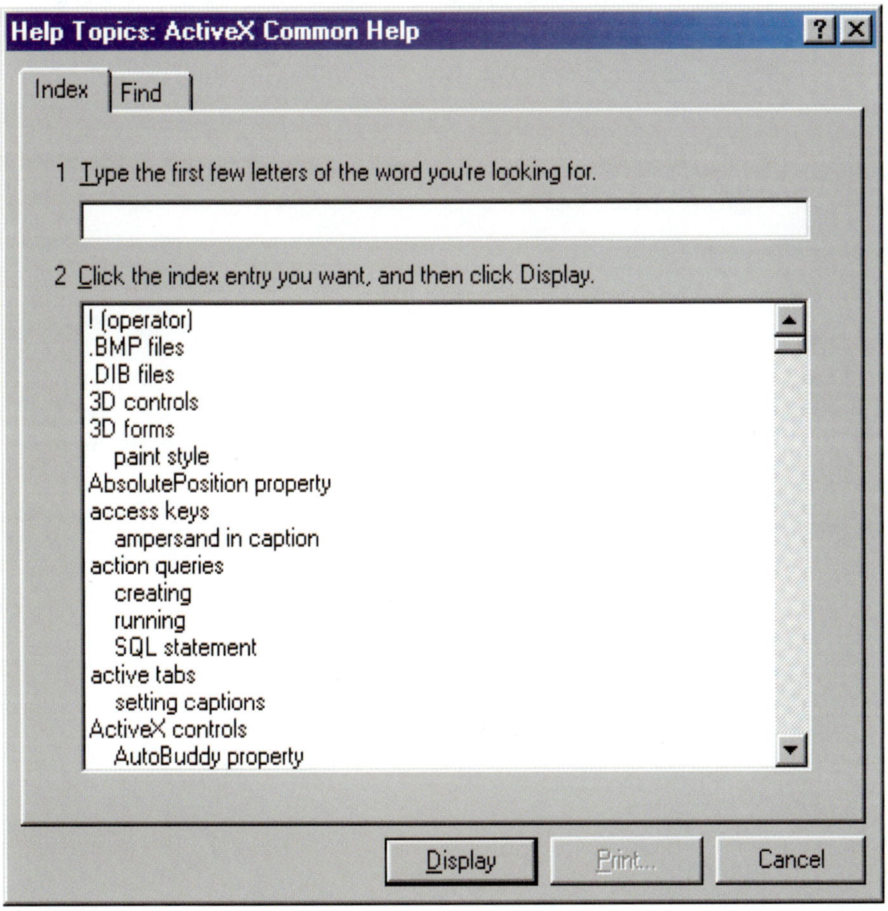

FIGURE 11.09 *ShowHelp method*

- Case 2—Use the **Color** Dialog to let the user select any color; then assign that color as needed by your program. In the Class Scheduling Application version 3, we used it twice—once to select the BackColor of the Courses form, and once to select the **ForeColor property** for the ComboBox control on the Faculty form.
- Case 3—Before you can use the ShowFont method, you must set the Flags property of the Common Dialog control to one of three settings: cdlCFBoth, cdlCFScreenFonts, or cdlCFPrinterFonts. This flag determines which set of fonts installed on your system will be displayed. In the College3 application, we used the ShowFont method to let the user pick the font for the **Combo Box** on the Faculty form.
- Case 4—ShowPrinter allows the user to select characteristics of the current document for purposes of printing.
- Case 5—Before you can use ShowHelp, you must assign a value to the HelpFile and HelpCommand properties. The **HelpFile property** must be the name (plus path, if needed) of a Windows-type help file (.hlp filename extension). The **HelpCommand property** identifies which type of help will be displayed—look up the HelpCommand property in VB Help to see the many possible settings. The ShowHelp method is the only one of these Common Dialog methods that results in something other than a familiar, modal Dialog Box. Rather, the user is presented with a help screen, which the user can then read, search, or close as needed.

ListBox, ComboBox, DBList, DBCombo, and MS Flex Grid Controls

The Faculty2 Application uses a **Data-Bound Combo control** (DBCombo), one of a family of controls that we will introduce here.

List Box Control

The **List Box control** allows you to provide a list of items for the user to observe and select from at runtime. The user may not make additions or changes to a List Box, but the user can select an item from the list. If the List Box is not large enough to display all of the items in the list, a vertical scroll bar is automatically created to allow the user to scroll through all of the items in the list.

The three methods available to change the contents of a List Box in Visual Basic are **AddItem, RemoveItem,** and **Clear.** Our next example demonstrates these methods.

Start a new project, and double-click the icon for the List Box control in order to put a small List Box control on Form1. Then put this code into the Form_Load event procedure:

```
Private Sub Form_Load ()
    List1.AddItem "Clubs"
    List1.AddItem "Diamonds"
    List1.AddItem "Hearts"
    List1.AddItem "Spades"
End Sub
```

and write this List1_Click procedure:

```
Private Sub List1_Click ()
    Dim i As Integer
    i = List1.ListIndex
    Print i, List1.Text, List1.List(i)
End Sub
```

Now run this little project (Figure 11.10). Use the scroll bar to scroll through the four items in the List Box. (If no scroll bar appears, then your List Box is large enough to accommodate all four items in the list.) When you click on one of the items (not on the scroll bar), the click event causes the ListIndex property to be printed on the form, along with two copies of the selected item itself.

- The **ListIndex property** has a value of –1 before any item in the list is selected. The first item in the list has a corresponding ListIndex value of 0, the second has a value of 1, and so on. Therefore, after an item in the list has been selected, ListIndex indicates the position of the selected item in the list.
- The Text property of a List Box is an empty string before any item in the list is selected. After an item is selected, the Text property contains the selected item.
- The **List property** of a List Box is a string array containing all of the items that are in the list. Thus, List1.List(0) is the first item in the list, List1.List(3) is the fourth item in the list, and List1.List(ListIndex) is the selected item in the list. List1.List(ListIndex) is the same as List1.Text.
- The **ListCount property** of a List Box (not available at design time; read-only at runtime) indicates how many items are in a list. Since the first item in a list is always number 0, the last item in the list is always number ListCount –1.

Add a control array of four Command Buttons to your form, with the captions "Add Jokers," "Remove Item," "Clear List," and "Reload List". Insert the following procedure.

```
Private Sub Command1_Click(Index As Integer)
    Select Case Index
        Case 0: List1.AddItem "Jokers", 1
        Case 1: List1.RemoveItem List1.ListIndex
        Case 2: List1.Clear
        Case 3: Call Form_Load
    End Select
End Sub
```

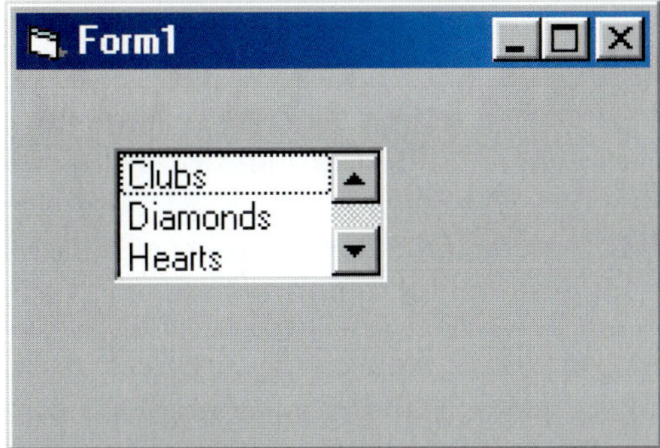

FIGURE 11.10 *Example of a ListBox control*

You have this program under the name LISTSAMP.EXE. It's easy to see how the List Box control works; it's also easy to make the program blow up. For example, if you clear the list and then try to add jokers, you will get an illegal function call error, because the list is empty and the next item to be added must fill position 0, not position 1. If you try to remove an item when no item is selected, you will also abort the program.

Try these variations:

- Make your List Box taller in design mode. Then run the program and press repeatedly on the Command Button to reload the list. When the ever-lengthening list gets too long to fit in the list box, a vertical scrollbar automatically appears.
- Set the List Box's **Sorted property** to true in design mode. VB now maintains the list in sorted order, except when you tell it to add an item at a particular place in the list. If you remove ", 1" from the AddItem method in Command1_Click, then Jokers will be added in the correct place, and if you reload the list, all of the items will be sorted correctly. However, if you leave ", 1" in the AddItem method while setting the Sorted property to True, then VB gets confused. Try it, and reload the list several times while also adding Jokers several times. The list is partially sorted but partially not sorted, because you have given Visual Basic conflicting directions. In general, if you set the Sorted property to True, then don't tell Visual Basic exactly where to place a new item in the list.

ComboBox Control

This versatile control combines the features of a ListBox and a TextBox. Therefore, you are already familiar with almost all of the long list of properties applicable to this control. The principal exception to this statement is the **Style property,** which determines in which of three forms the ComboBox will appear and how it will behave:

- Style 0 **Dropdown Combo**—The Text portion has a drop-down arrow on the right. When this arrow is clicked at runtime, a Dropdown List appears. The user can select from the Dropdown List or type an entry in the TextBox portion of the control. The Text property can have an initial value.
- Style 1 **Simple Combo**—The Text portion and the List portion always appear (that is, the List does not drop down). Again, the user can select an item from the List or type an entry in the TextBox. The Text property can have an initial value.
- Style 2 **Dropdown List**—The Text portion has a drop-down arrow on the right. When this arrow is clicked at run time, a Dropdown List appears. The user can only select from the Dropdown List. The Text property cannot have an initial value and is Read-only at runtime.

In all three styles, the Text portion of the control contains the user-selected (or typed-in) entry, and the Text property contains this same value. The List, ListCount, and ListIndex properties, and the AddItem, RemoveItem, and Clear methods work the same as they do in a ListBox control.

Data-Bound List (DBList), Data-Bound ComboBox (DBCombo), and MS Flex Grid Controls

The DBList, DBCombo, and MS Flex Grid controls can be used in conjunction with one or more Data controls to simplify greatly the coding needed to display an entire column of a table, to look up records in an associated table, or to display all of the columns and rows of a table.

DBList Control

The **DBList control** displays an entire column from a table. Additionally, it can be associated with a second Data control to facilitate table lookups. The **RowSource property** identifies the Data control which will provide the data items to fill the list. The **ListField property** identifies the field within RowSource whose values will populate the list. Thus, RowSource and ListField work like the DataSource and DataField properties of a TextBox. In the DBList control, the DataSource and DataField properties identify an associated Data control which is automatically updated when a selection is made from the list at runtime.

DBCombo Control

The DBCombo control differs from the DBList control in the same way that the ComboBox control differs from the ListBox control: Namely, DBCombo includes a TextBox area in which the user can type an entry, and three combo styles are available.

MS Flex Grid Control

The **MS Flex Grid control,** in conjunction with a Data control, can display all of the fields of all of the records in a Table, with no need for further controls or coding. Simply set the DataSource property to point to the Data control.

The MS Flex Grid control is an example of a third-party control that Microsoft has included in the Visual Basic package. Many such controls exist. Although these controls add much functionality and flexibility to VB, in the past they have also been somewhat of a problem when a new release of VB comes out: In some cases, the third-party controls are not updated to work correctly with the new release of VB.

To demonstrate all three of these data-aware controls, start a new project, and place a Data control on the form (Figure 11.11). You now need to make the three new controls available to your project. Select Project | Components . . . , and click the Checkboxes for Microsoft Data Bound List Controls 6.0 and Microsoft Flex Grid Control 6.0. This will add the controls to your Toolbox. Now add a DBList control, DBCombo control, and MS Flex Grid control to your project. Make the MS Flex Grid control wide enough to display all of the columns in the Courses Table. Set these properties:

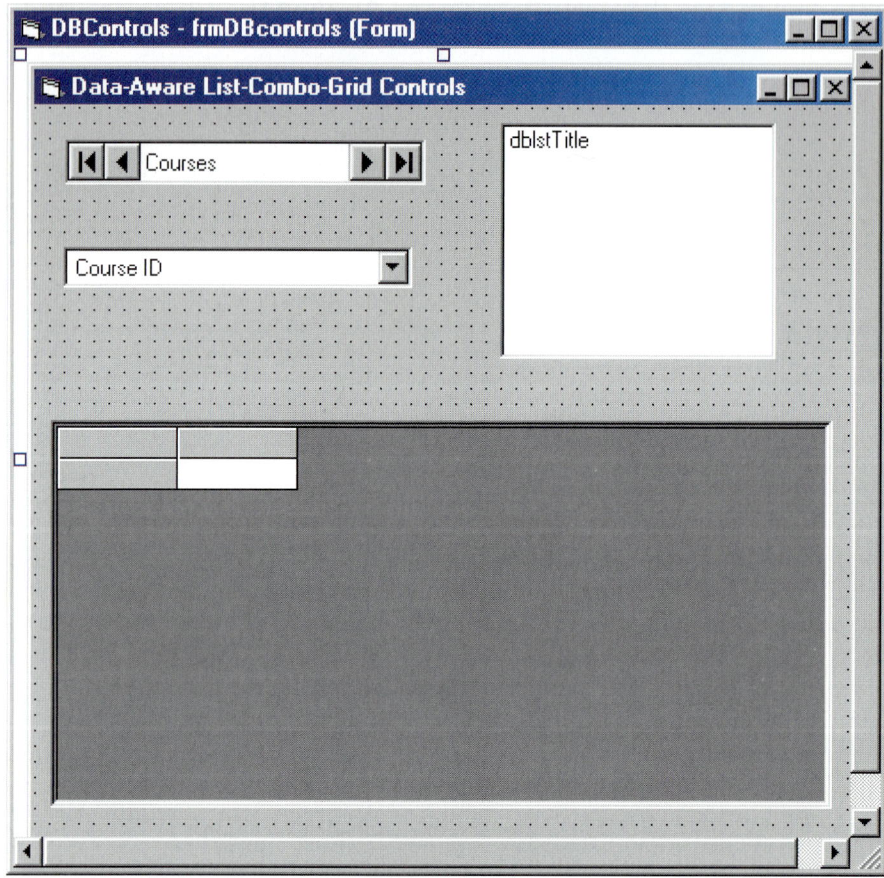

FIGURE 11.11 *frmDBControls at design time*

OBJECT	PROPERTY	SETTING
Form	Name	FrmDBControls
	Caption	Data-Aware List-Combo-Grid Controls
Data control	Name	DbCourses
	DatabaseName	College.mdb (wherever you have loaded it)
	RecordSource	Courses
	Caption	Courses
DBList control	Name	DblstTitle
	RowSource	DbCourses
	ListField	Title
DBCombo control	Name	DbcboCourseID
	RowSource	DbCourses
	ListField	CourseID
	Text	Course ID
MSFlexGrid control	Name	MsfgCourses
	DataSource	DbCourses

Run this program, which you have under the name DBControls.exe (Figure 11.12). Like a spreadsheet, you can select an entire row or column of data in the grid at run time and do something with it in code. If you select a particular cell, the Row and Col properties reflect which cell was selected—the left-hand column is Col 1, the column headers are in Row 0, and the first row of data is Row 1.

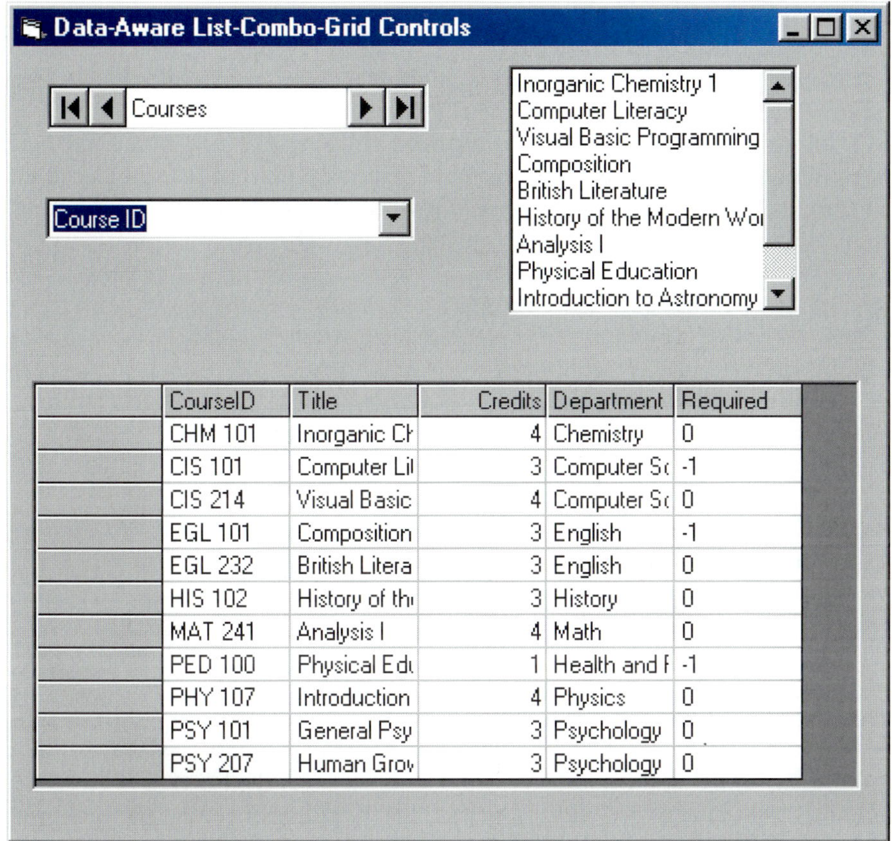

FIGURE 11.12 *DBControls.exe, executing*

Focus and TabIndex

When you run your own implementation of Faculty2.vbp, and when you select the Add or the Edit command buttons, you may or may not see the blinking cursor where it belongs—namely, in the first TextBox at the top of the appropriate Frame. And subsequently, when entering data into a new or revised record and tabbing from field to field, you may or may not see the cursor advance appropriately to the next field on the screen. And finally, you may want to notify the user about certain restrictions or options when the user begins to edit a certain field, or you may want to validate a field immediately when the user tabs to the following field. These programming requirements are handled by a combination of the TabIndex property, the GotFocus and LostFocus events, and the SetFocus method.

The TabIndex property controls the order of the controls that receive focus, starting with 0. If pressing the tab key does not move the blinking cursor to the correct control, then change the TabIndex property of the control that should (but does not) receive focus. Assign it the TabIndex equal to the previous control's TabIndex + 1. Subsequent controls' TabIndex properties will be adjusted by VB automatically.

By employing the **SetFocus method,** the programmer can also assign in code which control has focus when a particular event occurs. For example, when the user clicks the Add button in Faculty2, we want the user to supply a new FacultyID for this new record, and then we want the cursor to jump automatically to the Rank field. Easy. In the click event procedure for the Add button, enter the statement

```
TxtFields(0).SetFocus
```

In the **GotFocus event** procedure, you can give guidance for current input. Similarly, in the **LostFocus event** procedure, you can react to previous user input. For example, a horseracing application might respond to the GotFocus event for txtAmountOfWager, notifying the bettor that bets may be placed for $2, $5, or $10. After the horseplayer enters the Amount of Wager and moves on to the next field, the LostFocus event procedure could make sure that the bet was placed for a legitimate amount, and then return to that TextBox if the horseplayer entered an invalid number.

```
Private Sub txtAmountOfWager_GotFocus()
   MsgBox "Bet $2, $5, or $10. Enter 2, 5, or 10."
End Sub
Private Sub txtAmountOfWager_LostFocus()
   Select Case txtAmountOfWager
      Case 2, 5, 10
      Case Else
         MsgBox txtAmountOfWager & " is invalid"
         txtAmountOfWager = ""
         txtAmountOfWager.SetFocus
   End Select
End Sub
```

We used exactly the same logic in Faculty2 for the Rank field. Try, for example, entering the rank "Bozo the Clown" for a new faculty member. Not only is that a rather rank rank, but the computer will not accept it! In the LostFocus event, we examined the value of txtFields(0), that is, the TextBox containing the rank, and we ensured that it contained a valid entry. If the entry is not valid, the entry is rejected, and focus returns to that field.

CheckBox Control

Although Faculty2.exe does not demonstrate a CheckBox control, we did include it in Schedule2.exe, the second version of the Schedule of Classes display.

A **CheckBox control,** like an Option Button, displays a Boolean value, that is, True (Checked) or False (Unchecked).

The essential difference between a CheckBox and an Option Button is that only one Option Button within a container can be True at any point in time, while any number of CheckBox controls within a container can be True simultaneously. In Figure 11.13, for example, only one option within the Class Standing Frame can be True for a given student, while a student may select any number of the CheckBox optional services.

At design time or in code, the programmer can assign to a CheckBox control a third value besides Checked and Unchecked, namely, Grayed. This could be used to suggest that a particular CheckBox is unavailable or irrelevant in a certain situation. However, unlike the Enabled property when set to False, the Grayed value of a CheckBox does not prevent the user from clicking it.

The CheckBox control has special applicability to a database, because it is employed as a bound control to display the value of a Boolean field. Run Schedule2.exe, for example, and notice the Required field as you scroll through the Courses Table. Courses required for all students (Computer Literacy, Composition, and Physical Education) are checked, while other courses are not. In the underlying Table, "Required" is a Boolean field, which is marked True only for the aforementioned courses.

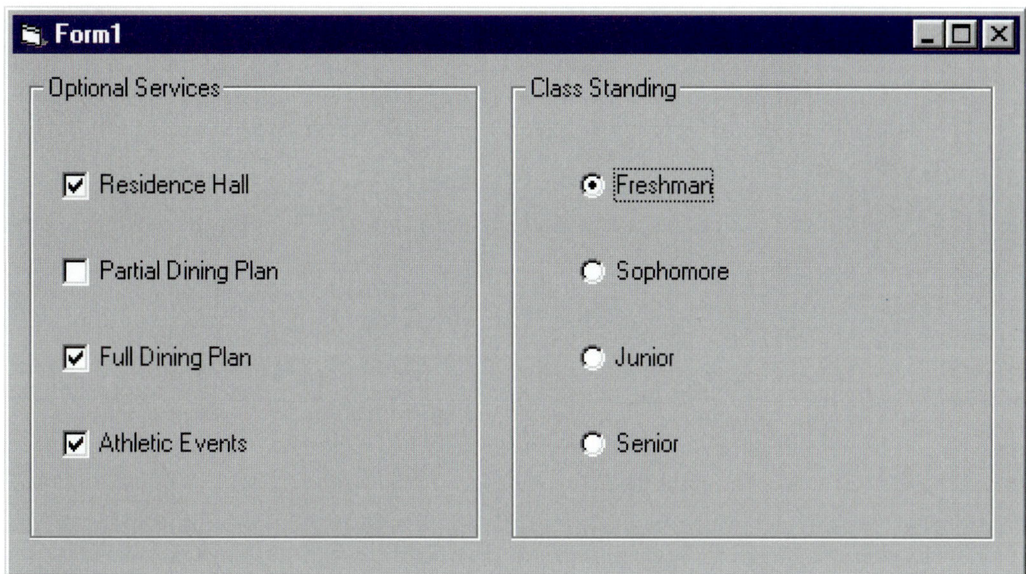

FIGURE 11.13 *Check Boxes Versus Option Buttons*

STEP 3. Develop Your Logic.

By this point on your Visual Basic learning curve, you should be able to follow the logic within each procedure in the program listings, without the necessity of detailed pseudocode. We will continue to include the Hierarchy Table for each of the remaining projects, because the Hierarchy Table provides a good overall view of the entire application (Figure 11.14).

```
HIERARCHY TABLE-CLASS SCHEDULING VERSION 2

Project:  Faculty2 (Faculty2.vbp)
Form:     frmFaculty2 (frmFaculty2.frm)
          General procedure:
             Sub ToggleAddEdit
          Click event procedures:
             cmdAdd
             cmdCancel
             cmdDelete
             cmdEdit
             cmdSaveChanges
             cmdFileExit
             mnuFileExit
             mnuFileOpen
             mnuHelp
             mnuWindowBrowse
             mnuWindowFind
             mnuWindowModify
          Other event procedures
             txtFields_Change(Index As Integer)
             txtFields_LostFocus(Index As Integer)
             dbcboLastName_Click(Area As Integer)
```

FIGURE 11.14 *Hierarchy Table—Class Scheduling Version 2*

STEP 4. Build Your GUI.

Use Windows Explorer to make copies of Faculty1.vbp and frmFaculty1.frm, then rename the copies as Faculty2.vbp and frmFaculty2.frm. (You accomplish this in Windows Explorer by selecting one of these files, holding down the Control key while clicking the other file, and then clicking the Copy icon followed by the Paste icon. After Windows Explorer makes the copies, right-mouse-click on one of the copied files, select Rename, and type the new name; then rename the other one.)

Now open the project Faculty2.vbp. Change the internal name of the form to frmFaculty2 and the caption to "Class Scheduling Version 2".

From the Project menu, select Faculty1 properties. On the General tab, change the Project Name textbox to Faculty2. Make sure the Startup Object appears as frmFaculty2. On the Make tab, in the Application frame, change the Title to Faculty2. Click Ok, and then save the project.

Modify the menu for frmFaculty2. The revised menu should contain the following:

```
&File          mnuFile
---- &Open     mnuFileOpen
---- -         mnuFileSep
---- E&xit     mnuFileExit
&Window        mnuWindow
---- &Browse   mnuWindowBrowse
---- &Find     mnuWindowFind
---- &Modify   mnuWindowModify
&Help          mnuHelp
```

Unlock the controls so that you can modify them.

This project requires two controls that are not automatically included in the Toolbox when you start a new standard project: the Common Dialog control and the Data Bound Combo control. To make these controls appear in your Toolbox, select Project | Components. On the Controls tab, which displays an alphabetical listing of additional controls available in Visual Basic, check the checkbox for Microsoft Common Dialog Control 6.0 and for Microsoft Data Bound List Controls 6.0, and click OK. [While you're at it, notice the many controls available in VB, as well as the Designers and Insertable Objects.]

Delete the controls inside fraFind. Insert instead a DBCombo control, and set these properties. Set the RowSource property before the ListField property, and use the dropdown arrow in the settings box to select the Data control (dbFaculty) and field name (LastName) respectively:

Name	DbcboLastName
RowSource	DbFaculty
ListField	LastName
Text	Faculty Last Names

Add a new frame to your project, named fraModify with a blank caption, as shown in Figure 11.15, and set the frame's Visible property to False. Place five command buttons inside this frame. (To make sure your command buttons are really inside the frame, run the project: Since the frame is not visible, the command buttons should be invisible as well.) Caption the command buttons as shown, and name them as we are wont. cmdSaveChanges and cmdCancel should be initially disabled. If your new command buttons are not all the same size, you can select all of them and then click Format | Make Same Size | Both. If your new command buttons are not evenly spaced within the frame, position the leftmost and rightmost command buttons correctly, and then click Format | Horizontal Spacing | Make Equal.

STEP 5. Write the VB Code.

```
Option Explicit

Private Sub cmdAdd_Click()
   Call ToggleAddEdit
   dbFaculty.Recordset.AddNew
   lblFacultyID = InputBox("Enter the Faculty ID (e.g., A01)")
End Sub

Private Sub cmdCancel_Click()
   Call ToggleAddEdit
   dbFaculty.Recordset.CancelUpdate
End Sub

Private Sub cmdDelete_Click()
   If MsgBox("Are you sure?", vbYesNo + vbCritical) = vbYes Then
   dbFaculty.Recordset.Delete
   dbFaculty.Recordset.MoveNext
   If dbFaculty.Recordset.EOF Then dbFaculty.Recordset.MoveLast
   End If
End Sub

Private Sub cmdEdit_Click()
   Call ToggleAddEdit
   dbFaculty.Recordset.Edit
End Sub
```

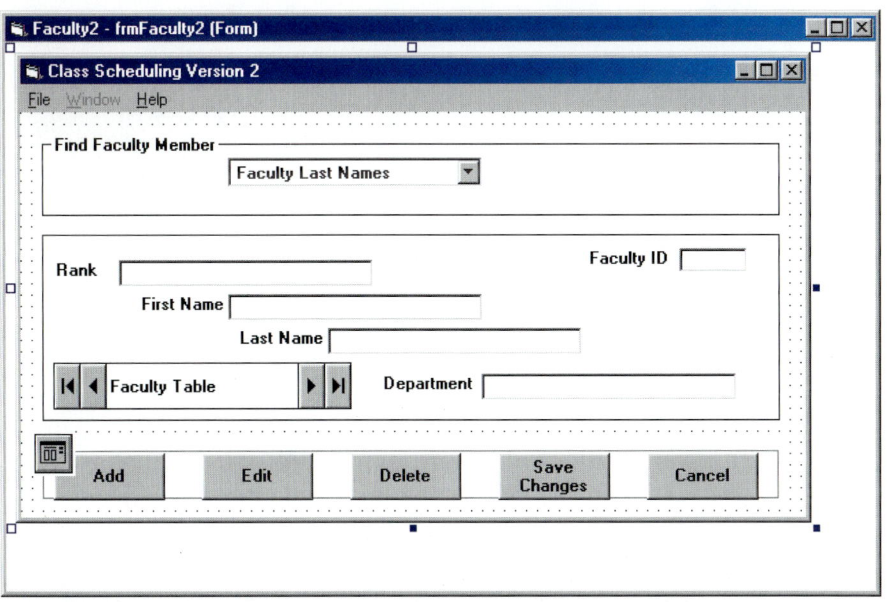

FIGURE 11.15 *frmFaculty2 at design time—no caption on fraModify*

```
Private Sub cmdSaveChanges_Click()
   Call ToggleAddEdit
   dbFaculty.Recordset.Update
End Sub

Private Sub dbcboLastName_Click(Area As Integer)
   dbFaculty.Refresh
   dbFaculty.Recordset.FindFirst "LastName = '" & dbcboLastName.Text & "'"
End Sub

Private Sub mnuFileExit_Click()
   End
End Sub

Private Sub mnuFileOpen_Click()
   dlg.InitDir = App.Path
   dlg.ShowOpen
   dbFaculty.DatabaseName = dlg.FileName
   dbFaculty.Refresh
   mnuWindow.Enabled = True
End Sub

Private Sub mnuHelp_Click()
   MsgBox "Under File, click Open to open the " _
   & "College database. Under Window, choose " & _
   "Browse to scroll through all of the records, " _
   & "Find to search for a Faculty member, " _
   & "or Modify to add, delete, or edit a record"
End Sub

Private Sub mnuWindowBrowse_Click()
   dbFaculty.Visible = Not dbFaculty.Visible
   mnuWindowBrowse.Checked = Not mnuWindowBrowse.Checked
End Sub

Private Sub mnuWindowFind_Click()
   mnuWindowFind.Checked = Not mnuWindowFind.Checked
   fraFind.Visible = Not fraFind.Visible
End Sub

Private Sub mnuWindowModify_Click()
   If dbFaculty.Recordset.EditMode = 0 Then
   mnuWindowModify.Checked = Not mnuWindowModify.Checked
   fraModify.Visible = Not fraModify.Visible
   End If
End Sub

Public Sub ToggleAddEdit()
   fraFind.Enabled = Not fraFind.Enabled
   dbFaculty.Enabled = Not dbFaculty.Enabled
   cmdAdd.Enabled = Not cmdAdd.Enabled
   cmdEdit.Enabled = Not cmdEdit.Enabled
   cmdDelete.Enabled = Not cmdDelete.Enabled
   cmdSaveChanges.Enabled = Not cmdSaveChanges.Enabled
   cmdCancel.Enabled = Not cmdCancel.Enabled
End Sub
```

```
Private Sub txtFields_Change(Index As Integer)
    If dbFaculty.Recordset.EditMode = 0 And _
    txtFields(Index).DataChanged Then
    fraModify.Visible = True
    mnuWindowModify.Checked = True
    Call cmdEdit_Click
    End If
End Sub

Private Sub txtFields_LostFocus(Index As Integer)
    If Index = 0 Then
    Select Case txtFields(0)
    Case Is = "Instructor", "Assistant Professor"
    Case Is = "Associate Professor", "Professor"
    Case Else
    MsgBox "Invalid rank"
    txtFields(0).SetFocus
    End Select
    End If
End Sub
```

STEP 6. Test and Debug Your Program.

When you write programs that use the Data control, a number of new error messages may enter your VB world.

The Add procedure in our sample program is still lacking one important edit check. Namely, we do not prevent the user from attempting to add a record whose primary key matches an existing record. The database software will not permit a duplicate record. If the user tries to add a record that already exists, a runtime error will ensue. "Can't have duplicate key; index changes were unsuccessful" is the error message. A special case of this error occurs if your program does not prevent the user from adding a blank record to a Table. In this case, when the user enters a second blank record, you now have a duplicate, and an error is generated. After you understand the procedure in its present form, we suggest that you improve on the model by handling this situation without allowing the program to blow up. One technique is to search (using FindFirst) for the record key in the Table before allowing the Update method to be completed (put this code in the **Validate event** procedure). If the Recordset's NoMatch property is True, then this is a new record key and the Add/Update operation can continue; otherwise, notify the user that a duplicate key is not permitted and cancel the Add/Update operation.

If you load a form containing a Data control whose DatabaseName property contains an invalid path\filename, the "File not found" error occurs.

If you attempt the AddNew, Edit, or Update methods on the Recordset of a Data control that is set to ReadOnly, an "Operation is illegal" error occurs.

If you attempt a MoveNext when you are already positioned at EOF (end of file) or a MovePrevious when you are already positioned at BOF (beginning of file), a "No current record" error is generated. (When the last record in a Recordset is the current record and MoveNext is executed, the current record becomes a null record and EOF becomes True; when the first record in a Recordset is the current record and MovePrevious is executed, the current record becomes a null record and BOF becomes True.)

In a shared environment, if you try to access a record while the Table or page is locked by another user, the "Permission denied" error interrupts execution of your program.

If you attempt any operation on a Recordset before the Data control containing that Recordset has been created, an "Object variable not set" error message occurs. This is really the most difficult of the Data control-related error messages to debug. It can occur for very un-obvious reasons. For instance, when developing the last chapter's Class Scheduling Application, we assigned the DatabaseName property of each of the three Data controls at design time. When the Data control for the Sections Table is loaded at run time, the controls bound to it are initialized with the contents of the first record. This event fires the Reposition event, which searches for corresponding records in the Courses and Faculty Tables. But if when this first occurs the Courses Table or the Faculty Table has not yet been loaded, the "Object variable not set" error occurs and your program is aborted. The solution to this problem is to assign the DatabaseName property and then execute the Refresh method for all three Data controls in code, with the Sections Table referenced last. These actions ensure that the Faculty Table and the Courses Table are open when the Sections Data control is opened.

Sometimes you will encounter enormous frustration in trying to determine the order of events that triggered an error, especially that pesky "Object variable not set" error. It may be helpful to use the Step-Into (single-step) or Step-Over (procedure-step) mode of operation to isolate the error. With Quick Watch, examine the value of variables. In the Immediate Window, print the value of key program elements.

For all of these errors, you can program error traps to handle them without aborting your program. One good technique is as follows:

1. Write a general error-handling procedure. Name this procedure ErrorProc (ByVal vintReason As Integer). This procedure, using a Select Case statement, would examine the cause of the error (vintReason) and initiate appropriate action. If the error is not one of those anticipated by the error routine, the program should generate a fatal error and abort.
2. Insert an "On Error Goto ErrorTrap" statement at the beginning of all other procedures.
3. At the bottom of all other procedures, insert this code:

```
Exit Sub
ErrorTrap:
    Call ErrorProc(Err)
    Exit Sub
```

STEP 7. Complete the Program Documentation.

As should be familiar by now, complete all relevant program documentation.

SUMMARY

Viewing, editing, adding, and updating of database records are controlled with the **ReadOnly, EditMode,** and **DataChanged** properties; the **AddNew, Edit, Update, Refresh,** and **Delete** methods; and the **Validate** and **Reposition** events.

The **Common Dialog** control provides six dialog boxes often needed in Windows applications. These are activated through the **ShowOpen, ShowSave, ShowColor, ShowFont, ShowPrinter,** and **ShowHelp** methods. The programmer can control the operation of the common dialogs through manipulation of the control's properties, especially **DefaultExt, InitDir, Flags, Filter, FilterIndex, Filename, Color, Font, HelpFile,** and **HelpCommand.**

The **List Box** control allows the programmer to display a list of items, whose contents are manipulated through the **AddItem, RemoveItem,** and **Clear** methods; and the **List, ListCount,** and **ListIndex** properties. A **Combo Box** control combines the features of a **List Box** with a Text Box. The Combo control's **Style** property determines whether the control appears as a **Simple Combo,** a **Dropdown List,** or a **Dropdown Combo.**

Focus can be moved to a particular control by the **SetFocus** method. An application can also respond to a **GotFocus** or **LostFocus** event. A **CheckBox** control may be used to display the value of a Boolean variable in a table.

PROGRAMMING ASSIGNMENTS

Bookstore Database

This program uses the BIBLIO.MDB database supplied with Visual Basic.

The project has one maximized form containing two Frames. The top Frame, captioned "Titles", contains a Data control to access the Titles Table and bound TextBox controls for all of the fields in the Titles Table. These TextBoxes are initially disabled. The lower Frame, captioned "Publisher", contains an invisible Data control to access the Publishers Table and bound Label controls for all of the fields in the Publishers Table.

Initially, the user is able to scroll through all of the records in the Titles Table. As each Title appears, the program searches for and then displays the corresponding record from the Publishers Table (that is, the record in the Publishers Table whose PubID matches the PubID in the Titles Table). (Hint: PubID is a Long Integer, not a string, and so the search argument cannot be enclosed in single quotes.) If a match is found, make the "Publishers" Frame visible; if no match is found, make the "Publisher" frame invisible.

At the bottom of the form, place a row of Command Buttons, captioned "New Title", "Edit Title", "Delete Title", "Update", "Cancel", "Find ISBN", and "Find Title". Clicking these Command Buttons causes the following to occur:

- "Add Title"—Invoke the AddNew method for the Titles Table. Enable the TextBoxes so the user can input new information in them. Disable the Data control for the Titles Table. Hide the "Publisher" Frame. Disable all of the Command Buttons except for "Update".
- "Edit Title"—Invoke the Edit method for the Titles Table. Enable the TextBoxes so the user can input new information in them. Disable the Data control for the Titles Table. Hide the "Publisher" Frame. Disable all of the Command Buttons except for "Update".
- "Delete Title"—Invoke the Delete method for the Titles Table.
- "Update"—Invoke the Update method for the Titles Table. Disable all of the TextBoxes. Enable the Data control for the Titles Table. Enable all of the Command Buttons.
- "Cancel"—Invoke the CancelUpdate method for the Titles Table. Disable all of the TextBoxes. Enable the Data control for the Titles Table. Enable all of the Command Buttons.
- "Find ISBN"—Use the InputBox function to ask the user for an ISBN. Then find the corresponding record in the Titles Table.
- "Find Title"—Use the InputBox function to ask the user for a Title. Then find the corresponding record in the Titles Table.

Save the completed project as BOOKS.VBP.

College Database—Updating the Schedule of Classes

Write an MDI application to allow users to update the College database. Include a main menu and four child forms: one for each of the three tables, and one for the combined Schedule of Classes.

The form for each table should have buttons to add, delete, edit, browse, update, cancel, and find. Model each form on frmFaculty2. (In fact, you can build frmFaculty2 as described herein, and then make it one of your child forms.) Use appropriate edits and validation routines to prevent these errors:

- Adding a record with a duplicate primary key (FacultyID in the Faculty table, CourseID in the Courses table, RefNum in the Sections table).
- Adding a section for a non-existent course or for a non-existent faculty member.

The child form for displaying the schedule of classes should be modeled on frmSchedule2. This form and code are the same as that for Schedule1 in Chapter 10, except that the fields "Required" and "Department offering the course" in the Courses table are also displayed. Note that the "Required" field is a Boolean element in the database and is therefore displayed by a CheckBox control.

CHAPTER TWELVE

ADVANCED CONCEPTS

Applications: Class Scheduling (Versions 3 & 4) and Cool Visuals

LEARNING OBJECTIVES

Upon completion of Chapter Twelve, you will be able to:

- Create an application by using the Visual Data Manager.
- Create an application with the ActiveX Data Object Data Control.
- Use the VB Application Wizard to generate a database-related application.
- Write standard modules (.BAS files).
- Create a user-defined data type.
- Draw directly on a form with graphic methods.
- Use the OLE control to embed an object in a VB application.
- Incorporate Windows API calls in a Visual Basic program.
- Write a Class module for defining a new object class.
- Run another program via the Shell function.
- Use the Package and Deployment Wizard to generate distribution disks for installing a VB application on another computer.

Keywords

ActiveX Data Object (ADO)
ActiveX Data Object Data Control (prefix: adodc)
Add-In Manager
Add-Ins Toolbar
Application Wizard
AutoRedraw property
Circle method
Class module (.CLS file)
Clear (Clipboard) method
Clipboard object
ConnectionString property
Controls collection
Cos function
CurrentX property
CurrentY property

Data Form Wizard
Data Project
Declare statement
DoEvents statement
DrawStyle property
DrawWidth property
GetData method
GetText method
Horizontal Scroll bar control (prefix: hsc)
LargeChange property
Line Control (prefix: lne)
Line method
ListView control (prefix: lv)
Max property
Min property
MoveComplete event
OLE control (prefix: ole)
Package and Deployment Wizard
Paint event
Private declaration
Property procedures
PropertyPage window
PSet method
Public declaration
Scroll event
ScrollBars property
SetData method
SetText method
Shell function
Sin function
SmallChange property
Standard module (.BAS file)
Tag property
TreeView control (prefix: tv)
Type/End Type statements
Value property (scrollbars)
Vertical Scrollbar control (prefix: vsc)
WillChangeRecord event

ADVANCED CONCEPTS

This chapter provides a brief introduction to some of the intermediate level programming techniques and advanced language features available in Visual Basic. The objective here is more to pique your curiosity than to expect you to master these concepts at any great depth. In accordance with this notion, we have included the source code for this chapter's sample applications at the student Web site: We invite you to download the source files and examine them as we discuss the various features.

Chapter 12 presents five separate VB applications in order to demonstrate the entire collection of new ideas:

- The first project, Faculty3, is our third version of the program that displays and maintains records in the Faculty table of the College database. We created this program entirely by using the built-in facility of the Visual Data Manager and its Data Form Designer.
- The second project, Faculty4, looks just like Faculty3, but uses the more powerful **ActiveX Data Object Data Control** (ADODC), rather than the intrinsic Data control. We created Faculty4.vbp by using the automated features of the Add-In tool called the VB 6.0 **Data Form Wizard.** The application is incomplete: You need to add your own code to make it completely functional.
- The third project in this chapter, Schedule3, presents another method of displaying and maintaining all of the information in the three tables of the College database. However, in this case we constructed the application by using VB's **Application Wizard,** with only a small amount of additional coding. The Schedule3 project uses the more sophisticated ActiveX Data Objects (ADO) rather than ADODC or the intrinsic Data control, and also demonstrates a standard module and a class module. Thus all three of these Class Scheduling projects were created largely by using built-in "Wizards".
- The fourth project, Cool Visuals, introduces the notions of a user-defined data type, Windows API calls, object linking and embedding, and calling another program from within a VB program. This program, alone among this chapter's applications, was written from scratch, that is, without the help of any of VB's wizards or templates. You may consider the coding techniques too complex for a beginning programmer's textbook; but again the objective is to show you what

is possible and to stimulate your interest in further study of Visual Basic. We trust you will learn something by studying this program, even if you do not understand all of it. Cool Visuals also displays some cool visual effects.

- Finally, at the end of the chapter, the VB Package and Deployment Wizard demonstrates how you can create a set of installation diskettes for distribution of a Visual Basic application.

INTRODUCING THE VISUAL DATA MANAGER AND THE FACULTY3.VBP PROJECT

Visual Basic contains a subset of the Microsoft Access "Jet Database Engine" called the Visual Data Manager. VB's Visual Data Manager is a design time tool through which you can design a database in Access, dBase, Foxpro, or Paradox; a database based on the Open Database Connectivity Protocol (ODBC); or a database based on a preformatted or delimited text file, such as a text file exported from Excel. The Visual Data Manager can modify the structure of tables within that database, fields and indexes for each table, and Structured Query Language (SQL) statements (queries). Within the Visual Data Manager, you can open a database created either by the Data Manager or by another database management system, in order to add, delete, or change records in the database. Finally, the Visual Data Manager contains a tool (or "wizard") for creating a simple VB program that includes a Data control bound to a specified Record Source, Labels that identify each field in the Recordset, Text Boxes bound to those fields, and Command Buttons for the common tasks of adding, deleting, and updating a record; refreshing the database; and closing the application.

In this brief example, we will use the Visual Data Manager to create the Faculty table of the College.mdb Access database; and then we will employ the Visual Data Manager to create the MyFaculty3 application. Start by examining the Faculty table again and by loading and running Faculty3.vbp (the source code can be downloaded from our Website). After you are familiar with Faculty3.vbp, start a new VB project, so that you can see how to build this application.

Using the Visual Data Manager to Create a Table, an Index, and Records

Creating a New Table

Create a new folder on your disk for the Class Scheduling Application Version 3. You will place into this folder all of the files associated with this project, including the database that we are about to design now. In Visual Basic, select Add-Ins | Visual Data Manager from the VB Menu Bar to load VB's Visual Data Manager, which is actually a separate program delivered along with VB.

- From the Visual Data Manager's main menu, select File | New Database | Microsoft Access | Access 7.0.
- Select the drive and folder that you have created for this project.
- Insert COLLEGE.MDB as the name of the Database, and press OK (Figure 12.01).
- Right-mouse-click inside the Database Window and select New Table.
- In the Table Structure window, insert Faculty as the Table name and then click Add Field.
- The Add Field dialog box allows you to define one field at a time. In the Field Name TextBox, type FacultyID (that is, Faculty Identification Code) as the field name.

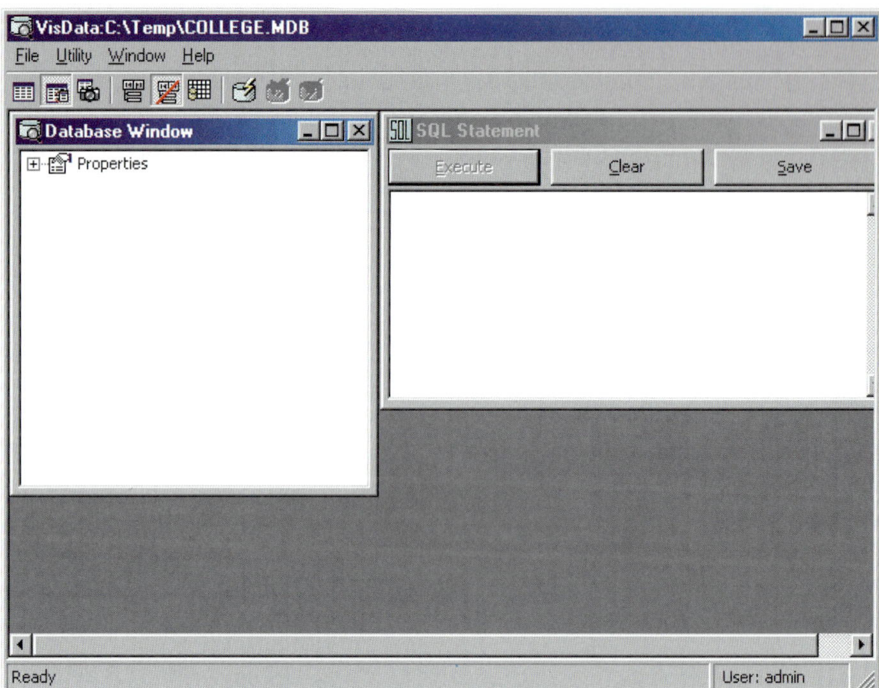

FIGURE 12.01 *Creating College.mdb in VB's Visual Data Manager*

- From the Data Type drop-down list, note the different data types supported by Microsoft Access. Every field in an Access table must be assigned one of these data types. Select Text as the field type for the FacultyID.
- Enter 3 as the Field size. For this application, we will assume that all FacultyIDs are three characters long. Also click the Required textbox, since FacultyID will be the primary key of this table and is a required entry for each record in the table. The Add Field Window should now appear as it does in Figure 12.02. Then click OK.

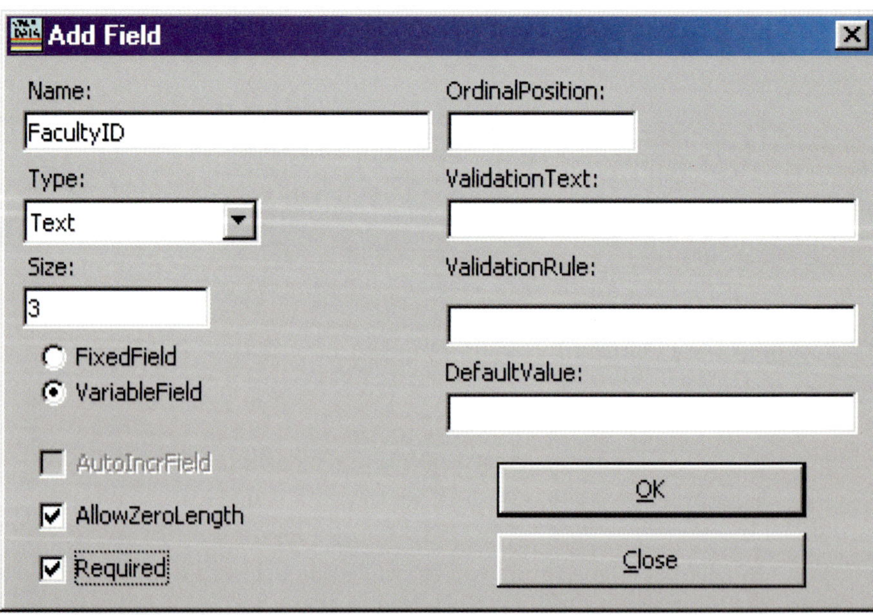

FIGURE 12.02 *Adding the FacultyID field*

When designing databases, you will often be faced with the choice of assigning a field type as Text (what we would call String in VB) or one of the numeric types (Single, Double, Integer, or Long Integer). Follow this rule of thumb: Use only a numeric data type for something subject to computation, such as a quiz score, a temperature, a counter, or an accumulator. When a number serves simply as a label or identifier, then store that data as Text (String). Examples of numbers properly stored as Text are a Social Security number, a ZIP Code, or a UPC.

- In similar fashion, add the second field, LastName, to the Faculty Table. This is a Text field 20 bytes long, and it is also a required field.
- Then add the third field, FirstName; the fourth field, Department; and the fifth field, Rank. All of these are Text fields 20 bytes long.
- After all of the field names have been entered for the Faculty Table, click Close (the Add Field window).
- If you make a mistake when adding fields (misspell a field name, assign the wrong type or length), simply highlight that field in the ListBox and click the Remove Field button to remove it; then re-enter it from scratch.
- The Table Structure window should now look like Figure 12.03. Click Build the Table, which completes the creation of this Table and adds it to the College database.

Creating an Index for a Table

We may wish to modify the design of a table after its initial creation, accomplished by right-mouse-clicking the table name in the Database Window and then clicking Design. In this case, we want to add an Index to the Faculty Table.

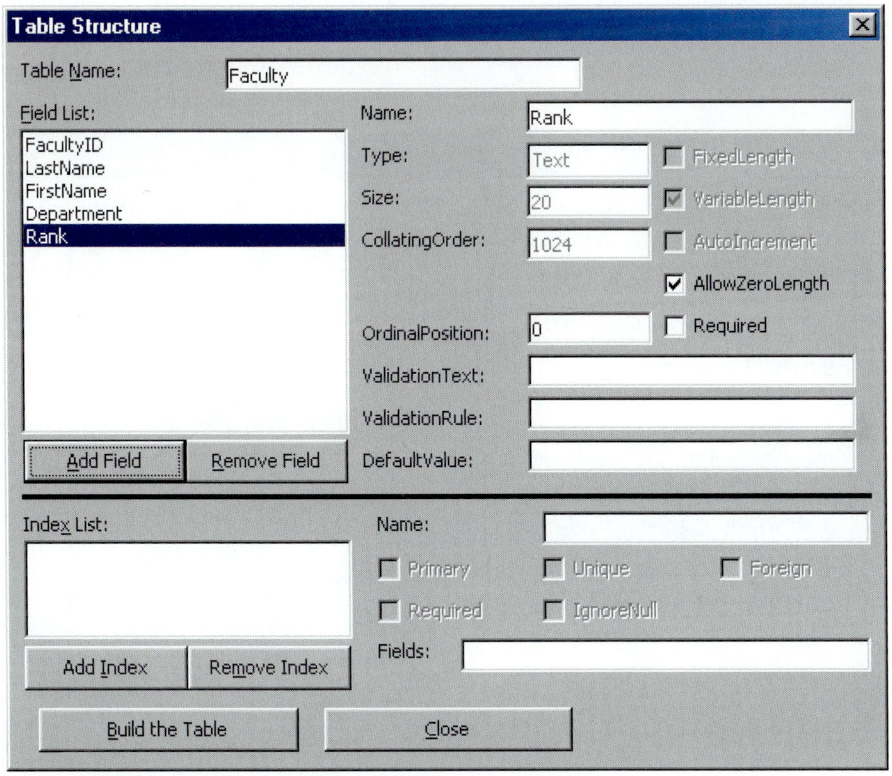

FIGURE 12.03 *The Table Structure window*

- Right-mouse-click the Faculty Table in the Database Window, and then click Design, which opens the Table Structure window again.
- Click Add Index, which opens the Add Index to Faculty window.
- Enter the name FacultyIDIndex in the Name TextBox.
- Select FacultyID from the Available Fields ListBox.
- A checkmark should appear in the Primary and Unique CheckBoxes, to make this the primary Index for this table.
- The completed Add Index to Faculty window appears as in Figure 12.04. Click OK, which creates this index and adds it to the College database. Then click Close, since this is the only index we need to create.
- Click Close in the Table Structure window.

In similar fashion, you could create the other Tables in the College Database: Courses and Sections.

Adding/Deleting/Modifying Records

To add, delete, or modify the records in a table using the Visual Data Manager, right-mouse-click the name of the table in the Database Window and select Open. The operation of the Command Buttons (Add, Update, Delete, Find, Refresh, Close) are intuitive for the most part, so we won't belabor them here beyond the following few notes:

- If you make a mistake by entering the same FacultyID twice, entering data too long to fit in a field, or entering text data where only numeric data is acceptable, the Visual Data Manager will prevent you from thus corrupting your database. If you make a mistake while entering a new record, you can click Cancel to cancel the Add operation.
- If you make a mistake by mistyping a data value that is nevertheless acceptable to the Visual Data Manager, you can go back to that record later, make the

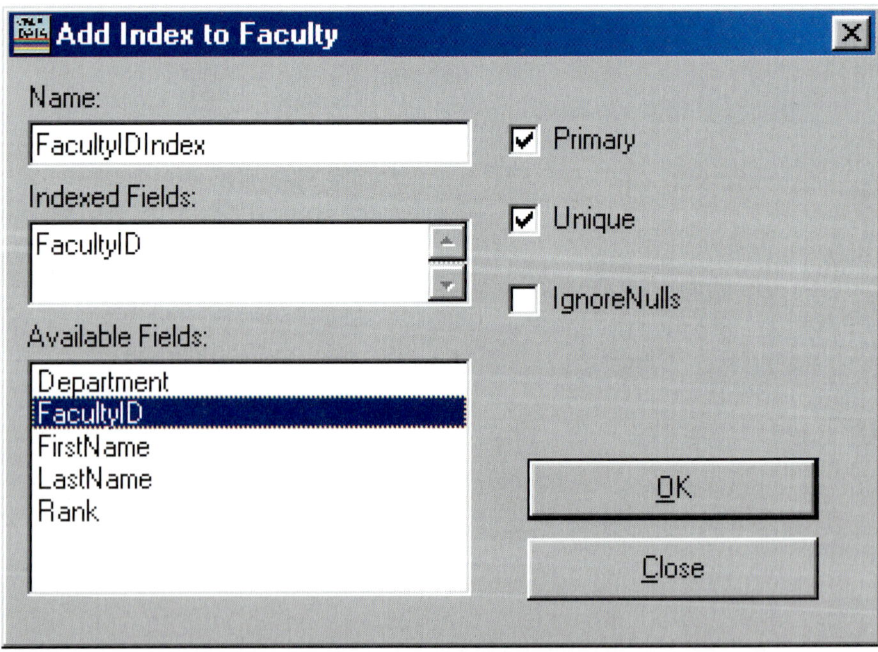

FIGURE 12.04 *Add Index to Faculty window*

appropriate changes, and click Update to record those changes. Alternatively, you can select the errant record and then click the Delete button.

- You can put the records into the database in any order; Visual Data Manager will keep them sorted by each table's Primary Index.
- You can move from record to record in the table by clicking the arrow keys at the bottom of the screen. These arrows correspond to those on VB's Data control.
- Use the Find button to locate a particular record. In the Enter Search Expression Dialog Box, enter Department = 'Comp Sci' and press OK. The first record in which Comp Sci is the Department will become the current record.

Using the Visual Data Manager to Create a Database Application

The Faculty3.vbp application was created entirely by the Visual Data Manager. Follow these steps to create this application yourself:

- Start a new Visual Basic project. Load the Visual Data Manager by selecting Add-Ins | Visual Data Manager from the VB Menu Bar.
- Select Utility | Data Form Designer from the Visual Data Manager's Menu Bar. This opens the Data Form Designer window.
- In the TextBox for Form Name (without extension), enter frmFaculty3.
- In the ComboBox for RecordSource, click the down arrow and select Faculty. The fields in the Faculty Table will appear in the Available Fields ListBox.
- Click >> (the double right arrow) so that all of the fields in the Available Fields ListBox move to the Included Fields ListBox. The Data Form Designer window should appear as in Figure 12.05.
- Click Build the Form. It will take the Visual Data Manager several minutes to build the form. When this process is finished, you will see another blank Data Form Designer window. Click Close.
- Close the Visual Data Manager.
- You are now back in Visual Basic Design mode. In the Project Explorer window, select Form1. Then select Project | Remove Form1.

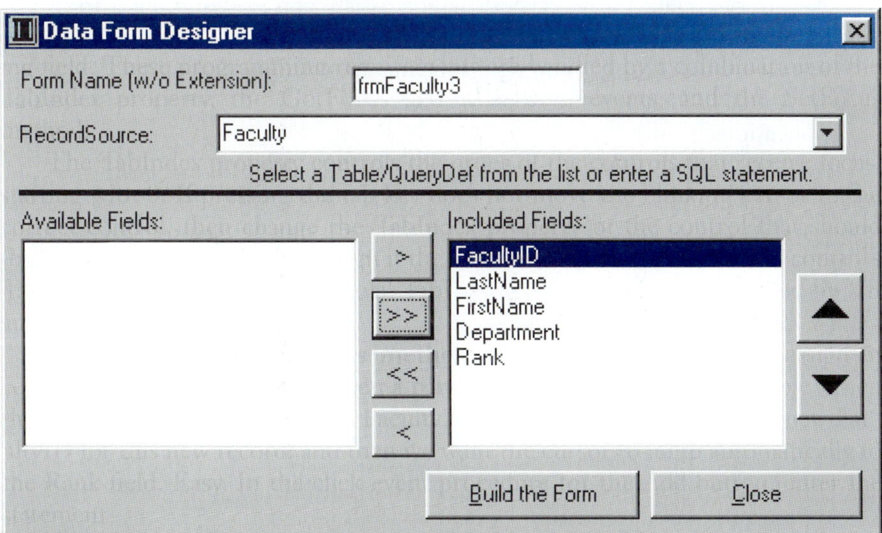

FIGURE 12.05 *Data Form Designer window—include all fields*

- Select Project | Project1 Properties.
- In the Project Properties window, change the Project Name to Faculty3; select frmFaculty3 as the Startup Object; click OK.
- Save the form as MyFrmFaculty3.frm and the project as MyFaculty3.vbp.

Now examine the form. Quite obviously, this is an easy way to create a database application with a standard Data control. Also take a look at the code which the Visual Data Manager created. Examine especially the Data1_Error, Data1_Reposition, and Data1_Validate event procedures. For a complete application, you would want to code for errors in the Data1_Error event procedure, and you would want to examine pending changes to the database before they are finalized by coding the Data1_Validate event procedure. The Data1_Reposition procedure displays the record number inside the Data control.

Put yourself in the mind-set of your user. What data entry errors might your user make? Does your program trap those errors and deal with them? You must cultivate the concept of "defensive programming"—like defensive driving, the intent is to anticipate an error on the other guy's part, compensate for that error, and keep the application running normally, or, if the error is unrecoverable, terminate the program but set the user down gently.

Put yourself in the mind-set of your user. What questions might your user have? What problems might your user encounter? For commercial programming, Help screens, context-sensitive help, online help, and technical support emergency phone numbers are all needed.

Implementation note: for the version of Faculty3.vbp at the Website, we programmed the Form_Load event to look for College.mdb in the folder where the project itself resides.

INTRODUCING THE DATA FORM WIZARD AND THE FACULTY4.VBP PROJECT

While the Visual Data Manager can help you build a database-related application using the intrinsic Data control, Visual Basic also includes more powerful tools for accessing a database and manipulating database records. One of those tools is the ActiveX Data Object Data Control (ADODC), introduced in this project. VB 6.0 also offers a Data Form Wizard, which assists you in designing a form and writing the initial code for an application using the ADODC. We also decided to demonstrate the DataGrid control, displaying all of the records in the Recordset at once in a table format rather than one record at a time as we have done in earlier applications.

Start by loading and running the Faculty4.vbp project. Again, the source code can be downloaded from our Website. The power of the ADODC is its ability to access more kinds of databases using more sophisticated connections, including databases resident on the World Wide Web, and to accomplish these tasks more efficiently than Microsoft's earlier tools. Since we are still using the College.mdb database, still a Microsoft Access database resident on your local computer, the application does not demonstrate the increased power of the ADODC over VB's intrinsic Data control, but you can see the ADODC's properties, events, and methods, and thereby you can compare the two techniques from an implementation standpoint.

[Note: You may have heard of some of the earlier tools for data access in Visual Basic: Besides the intrinsic Data control (still being used for relatively simple database applications), the tools included Data Access Objects (DAO) and Remote Data Objects (RDO). Microsoft recommends that these older technologies, while still supported in VB 6 for purposes of backward compatibility, not be used for new applications development. We have determined that DAO and RDO are no longer important enough to include in an introductory text.]

You may have noticed that the VB Menu Bar's Add-Ins menu includes a menu selection called **Add-In Manager.** Select the Add-In Manager now, which allows you to add certain VB capabilities to your VB design environment. Click on VB 6 Data Form Wizard, and in the Load Behavior frame, click on Load/Unload, causing the word Loaded to appear to the right of VB 6 Data Form Wizard. Then click OK. [Note: Also clicking Load on Startup causes the Data Form Wizard to be loaded automatically whenever VB is launched in the future.] Follow this by selecting Add-Ins | Data Form Wizard (which opens the Data Form Wizard, Figure 12.06), and follow these steps:

- On the Data Form Wizard—Introduction window, just click Next.
- On the Data Form Wizard—Database Type window, the ListBox lists DBMSs registered on the local system and also provides for an Open Database Connectivity (ODBC) Protocol connection to a remote database. [To satisfy your curiosity about an ODBC connection, click Remote (ODBC) instead of Access, and click Next to see the Data Form Wizard—Connection window. Then click Back to return to the Database Type window.] Since College.mdb is an Access database, select Access, and click Next.
- On the Data Form Wizard—Database window, click Browse, and locate the College.mdb database on the local machine. Then click Next.
- The Data Form Wizard is designed to work with the most up-to-date set of Microsoft data objects: the ActiveX Data Object Data Control, ActiveX Data Objects (created in code without using any graphical control), and Class objects. In this case, we have chosen to use the ADODC. We have also chosen to display all of the records in the recordset in a single table format, that is, Grid (Datasheet), rather than the single record form layout we used in earlier examples.

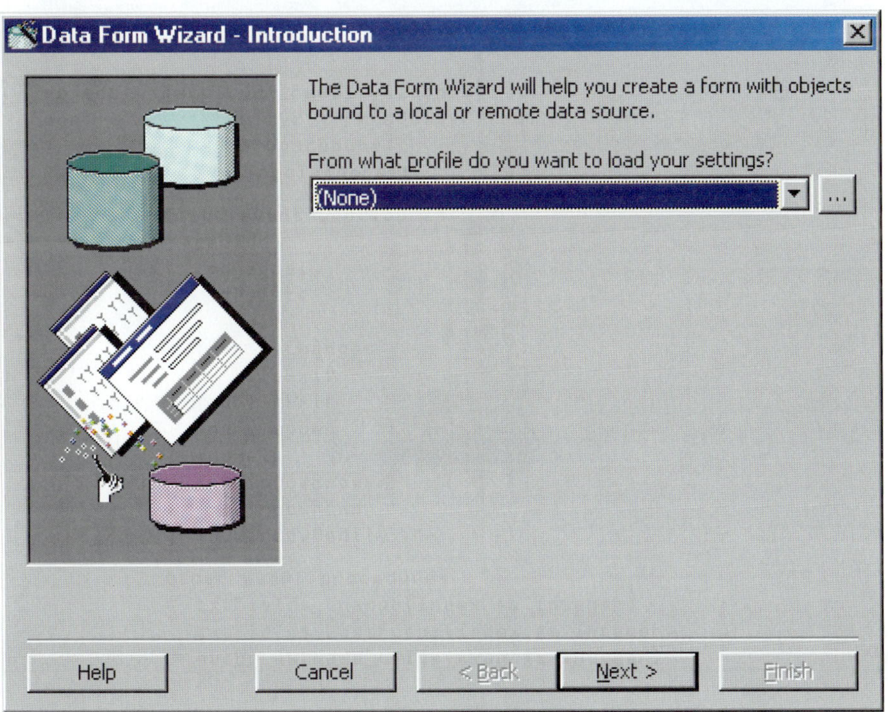

FIGURE 12.06 *Data Form Wizard—opening screen*

Therefore, on the Data Form Wizard—Form window, type frmFaculty4 as the Form Name, select Grid (Datasheet) as the Form Layout, and select ADO Data Control as the Binding Type (see Figure 12.07). Then click Next.

- On the Data Form Wizard—Record Source window, click the down arrow and select Faculty from the DropDown List, then click the >> (double arrow) to move all of the fields from the Available Fields ListBox to the Selected Fields ListBox, and select FacultyID as the Column to Sort By (Figure 12.08). Then click Next.
- On the Data Form Wizard—Control Selection window, click Next. This will mean that all of the indicated Command Buttons (Add, Update, Delete, Refresh, and Close) will appear on the completed form, as will the ADO Data control itself.
- On the Data Form Wizard—Finished window, if you wish to save all of the Data Form Wizard selections you have just made, you can enter the name of a profile to store them under. Whether or not you choose to save the settings in a profile, click Finish. The Data Form Wizard will now build the form. After the form has been created, the Data Form Wizard will disappear, and the VB design environment returns to the foreground.

The remaining steps are the same as they were when using the Visual Data Manager's Data Form Designer facility in the Faculty3.vbp project:

- You are now back in Visual Basic Design mode. In the Project Explorer window, select Form1. Then select Project | Remove Form1.
- Select Project | Project1 Properties.
- In the Project Properties window, change the Project Name to Faculty4; select frmFaculty4 as the Startup Object; click OK.

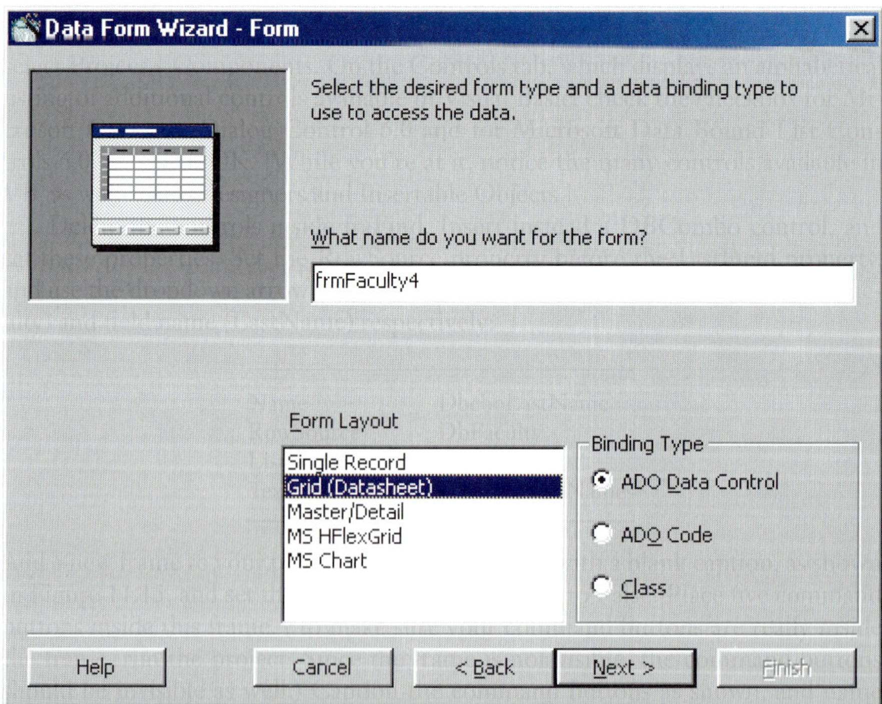

FIGURE 12.07 *Data Form Wizard—Form window*

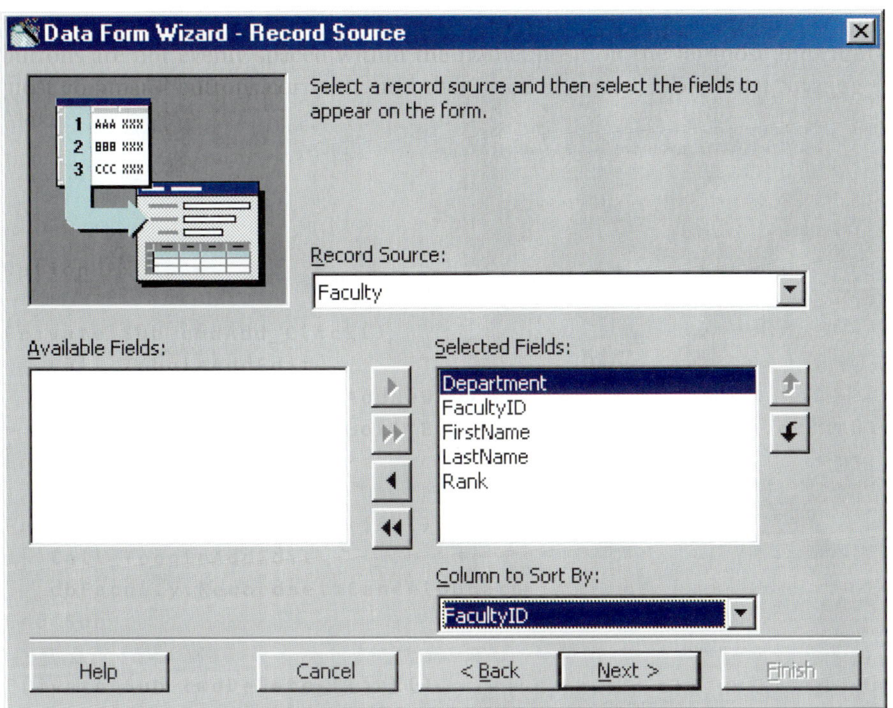

FIGURE 12.08 *Data Form Wizard—Record Source window*

- Save the form as MyFrmFaculty4.frm and the project as MyFaculty4.vbp.

Run your completed program (to make sure that it works and that you haven't made any mistakes while creating it).

To learn a little more from this exercise, compare the properties of the intrinsic Data control in Faculty3.vbp with those of the ADODC in Faculty4.vbp, especially the **ConnectionString property** of the ADODC (replacing the DatabaseName property plus the Connection property of the intrinsic Data control), and the RecordSource property, which now always appears as an SQL statement in the ADODC. Also compare the code generated by the Data Form Designer in Faculty3.vbp with that generated by the Data Form Wizard in Faculty4.vbp: the ADODC's **MoveComplete event** replaces the intrinsic Data control's Reposition event, and the **WillChangeRecord event** replaces the Validate event.

The Data Form Wizard is only one of many Add-Ins, mostly wizards and templates, available in Visual Basic. If you would like to experiment with more of them, a convenient method is to put the **Add-Ins Toolbar** on your screen. You can accomplish this by clicking Add-Ins | Add-In Manager, then select the VB 6 Add-In Toolbar, click Loaded/Unloaded and (optionally) Load on Startup in the Load Behavior frame, and click OK. This will load a new toolbar with only one item on it, called Add/Remove Toolbar Items. Click this icon, and then click all of the option buttons in the ensuing list (Figure 12.09). This will give you a complete Add-Ins Toolbar. You can then click on any of them to see what they do. (One of these Add-Ins, the VB Application Wizard, is the subject of our next project in this chapter.)

Implementation note: as was the case with Faculty3.vbp, for the version of Faculty4.vbp at the Website, we programmed the Form_Load event to look for College.mdb in the folder where the project itself resides.

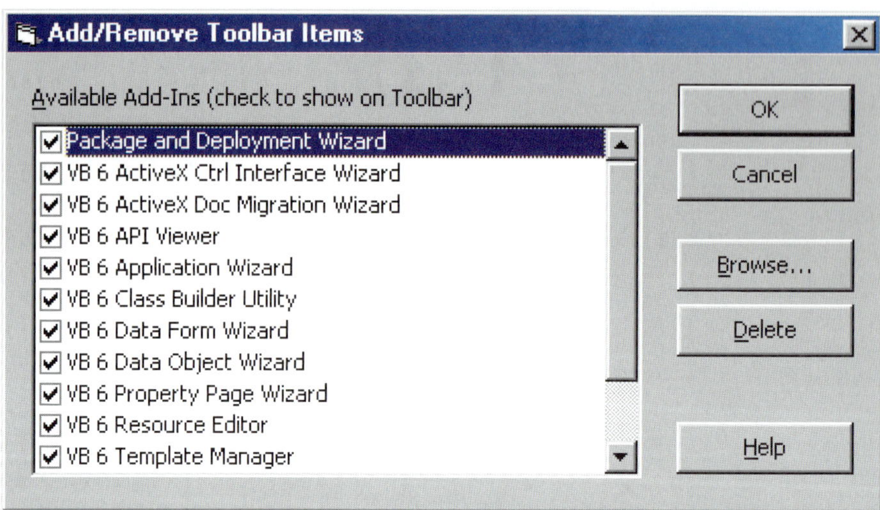

FIGURE 12.09 *The Add/Remove Toolbar items list from the Add-In Manager*

INTRODUCING THE VB APPLICATION WIZARD AND THE SCHEDULE3.VBP PROJECT

Class Scheduling Application (Version 3)

You can use the VB Application Wizard to develop a complete, though skeleton, application. Although the wizard includes multiple options, we will demonstrate only the database-related application for displaying the schedule of classes and for maintaining the three tables of the College.mdb database.

First try loading and running Schedule3.vbp. The source code and the executable can be downloaded from our Website.

Although this project may seem to include a great deal of new techniques, the actual implementation involves only a few new objects and program code. First we will describe the new coding features in this project. Then we will demonstrate how to use the Application Wizard itself. The new features include standard modules, public variables, class modules, the TreeView control, and the ListView control.

Standard Modules and Public Variables

We have encountered a number of VB applications containing several forms. In fact a commercial VB application may have dozens of forms. Visual Basic also allows the programmer to create another type of component called a **standard module,** which consists only of declarations and code (that is, no form or GUI). A standard module offers two principal advantages over a form: 1) Procedures and variables may be declared **Public,** making them visible and available throughout an application with no further need to reference the name of the module whence they came, and 2) standard modules lend themselves readily to the notion of reuse, since other forms and event procedures need not worry about conflicting object references in a standard module. Commercial applications with multiple forms will also typically contain one or more standard modules, containing code that is shared by all of the forms.

To see this feature in operation, start a new project and insert a new standard module into the application. This is accomplished either by selecting Project | Add Module or by clicking the new module icon from the drop-down list of new objects (second icon on the left on the Standard Toolbar).

The (General) object is the only object in a standard module. Declarations, as you might expect, will appear in the (Declarations) portion of the (General) object, while procedures will appear in the procedures drop-down list.

In the (Declarations), declare a global integer variable and then write a procedure to initialize this variable:

```
Option Explicit
Public gintSample As Integer
Public Sub InitializeSample()
    gintSample = 100
End Sub
```

Then return to Form1, and put the following code into the Form_Click event procedure:

```
Private Form_Click()
    Call InitializeSample
    Print gintSample
End Sub
```

Run the program and click the form—the value 100 will be printed on the form.

When you save a standard module, VB assigns the filetype BAS. As with form and project names, we recommend that you change the default filename from Module1, but keep the default filetype.

Class Module

A Class module allows the programmer to declare a new object class.

A Visual Basic Class module defines the properties and methods of a new class, but this class has no visual interface. The built-in properties of a Class module are Instancing, Name, and Public. The Instancing and Public properties determine whether instances of the class are creatable by an external project. Instances of the class are always creatable within the project in which the Class module exists. The Name property, as always, defines the name of the object class. The two built-in methods of an object class are Initialize, which fires when an instance of the class is created, and Terminate, which fires when an instance of the class ceases to exist (that is, all references to this instance are set to Nothing or fall out of scope). The programmer can define additional properties and methods for an object class.

The easiest way to establish a property for an object class is to declare a public variable in the general object of a Class module. However, you can also define and assign properties in Property Procedures: Property Get, Property Let, and Property Set. These property procedures will be executed whenever the property is read or written. Property procedures can also be written to create additional user-defined properties for a form. Methods are defined in Sub or Function Procedures of a Class module.

TreeView and ListView Controls

In Windows Explorer, the left side of the window consists of a **TreeView control,** in which items are displayed in a hierarchical fashion, connected by lines, with each "child" item indented under its "parent" item. The right side of the Windows Explorer window consists of a **ListView control,** whose contents are always the list of items contained within the selected item on the TreeView control.

The TreeView and ListView controls are available within VB. Although we will incorporate these two new controls automatically through the VB Application Wizard in the current project, you can also make them available to any application by putting these controls into your Toolbox. To see how, start a new project, and look at the contents of the Toolbox. Then click Project | Components | Controls tab | Microsoft Windows Common Controls 6.0. When you click OK, nine new controls are added to the Toolbox: TabStrip, Toolbar, StatusBar, ProgressBar, TreeView, ListView, ImageList, Slider, and ImageCombo.

VB Application Wizard

We will use the VB Application Wizard to generate most of the forms and code for this project. Start by creating a new folder called MyAppWizard to store all of the project components, and copy the College.mdb database into that folder. Then load Visual Basic, or start a new VB project, and choose the VB Application Wizard rather than Standard.exe. The first screen you will see is the Application Wizard—Introduction, Figure 12.10. You do not have a previously stored profile for the wizard to use, so click Next.

On the Application Wizard–Interface Type window, click Explorer Style, and enter MySchedule3 as the Project Name (see Figure 12.11). The Explorer Style means that the main form for this application will contain a TreeView control on the left and a ListView control on the right, much like Windows Explorer. Then click Next.

The Application Wizard–Menus window lets you customize the main form's Menu Bar. For the moment, just click Next. The Application Wizard–Customize Toolbars window lets you customize the main form's Toolbar. For the moment, just click Next. The Application Wizard–Resources File lets you identify a file containing translations of menu commands into a foreign language, should you intend to distribute your application to a non-English-speaking audience. Just click Next.

The next screen, the Application Wizard Standard Forms window, Figure 12.12, lets you include certain standard or common forms in your new application. Select the splash screen and the About Box, and then click Next.

The Application Wizard–Data Access Forms window allows you to identify a table whose records and maintenance will be the subject of a form. Click Create

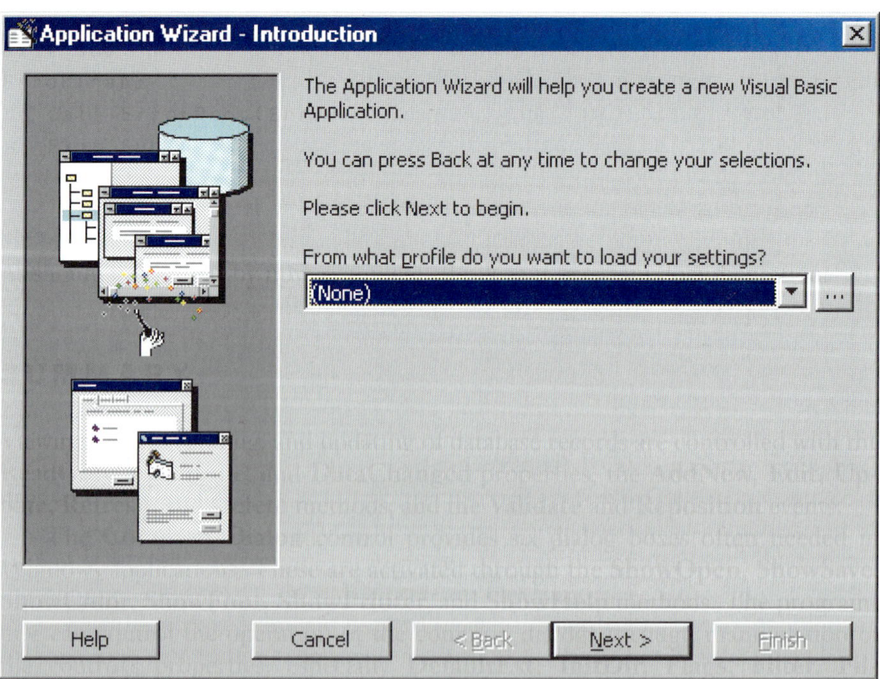

FIGURE 12.10 *VB's Application Wizard—opening screen*

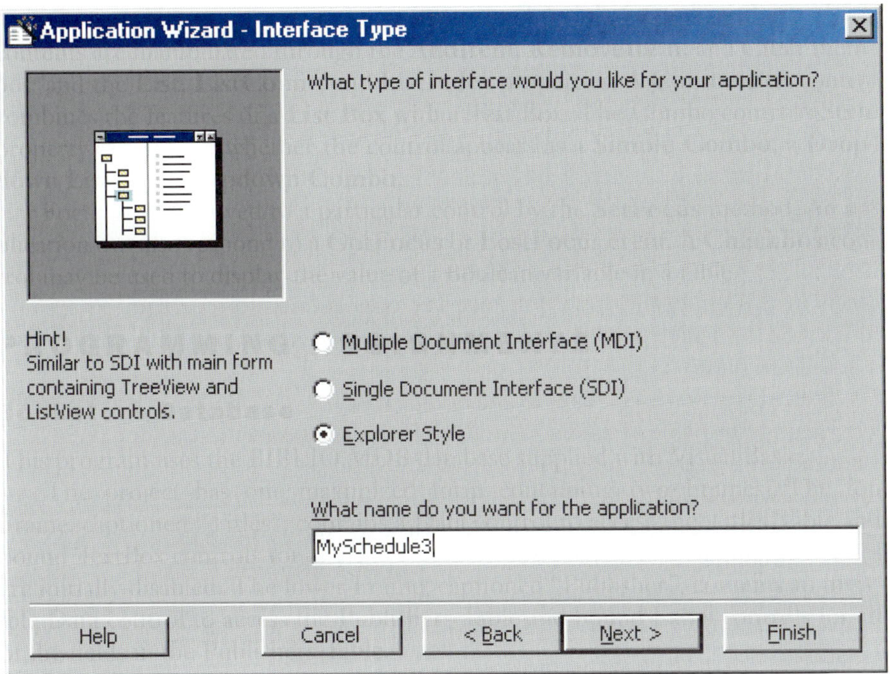

FIGURE 12.11 *Application Wizard—Interface Type window*

New Form. Then, in the Data Form Wizard–Introduction window, click Next (since you have not yet stored any profile). In the Data Form Wizard–Database Type window, select Access and then click Next.

In the Data Form Wizard–Database window, click Browse . . . and locate your new folder with College.mdb. Select College.mdb, then click Next.

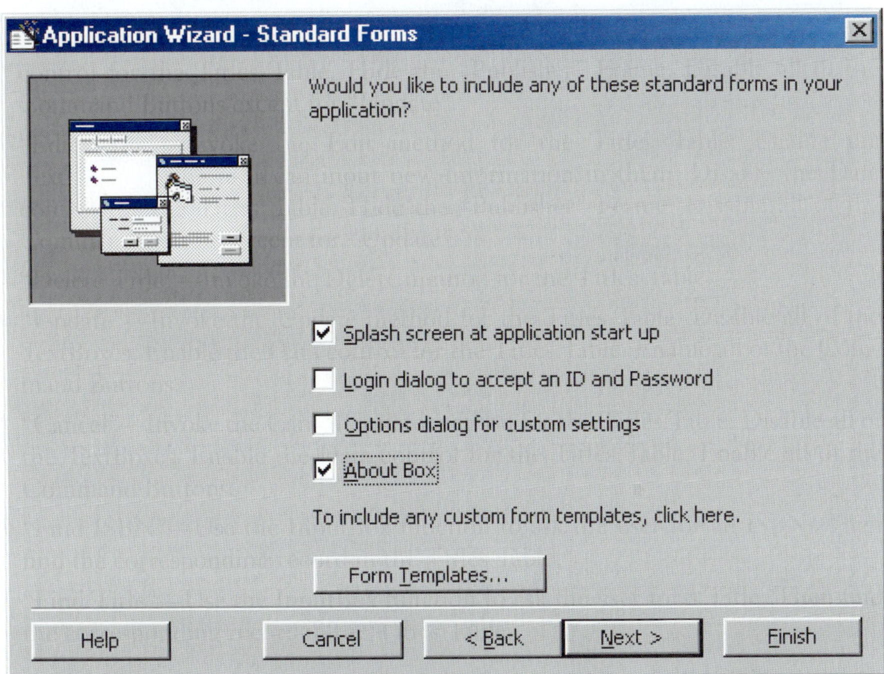

FIGURE 12.12 *Application Wizard—Standard Forms window*

In the Data Form Wizard–Form window, type Faculty into the Form Name TextBox. Now look at the Form Layout ListBox, and click on each of the options one at a time. You will see a thumbnail sketch of the appearance of the resulting form in the upper left corner of this window as you click on Single Record, Grid (Datasheet), Master/Detail, MS FlexGrid, and MS Chart. Each of these options is most appropriate in certain applications. For our purposes here, we want to use the Single Record Form Layout. The Binding Type frame offers three methods of binding controls on the form to the underlying database table: the ADO Data Control, ADO Code, and Class. Since we are going to create three different data forms in this application, we will take the opportunity to see all three binding types. For the Faculty form, select the ADO Data Control as the Binding Type. Then Click Next.

In the Data Form Wizard–Record Source window, click the down arrow and select Faculty (the name of the Faculty table in the College database). After a moment, all of the fields in the Faculty table will appear. Click >> (the double-right-arrow) so that all of these fields move from the Available Fields ListBox to the Selected Fields ListBox. In the Column to Sort By field, click the down arrow and choose FacultyID. The completed window appears as in Figure 12.13. Choose Next.

In the Data Form Wizard–Control Selection window, the default (selecting all available controls) is correct. Click Next. In the Data Form Wizard–Finished! Window, select Finish. The Data Form Wizard will now create the Faculty form.

A dialog box asks whether you wish to create any more data forms. The answer is Yes, since you need to create a data form for the Courses table and for the Sections table. Therefore, you must now repeat the process using the Data Form Wizard two more times. Follow the same steps above, but with these changes:

- For the Courses form: In the Data Form Wizard—Form window, type Courses into the Form Name TextBox, and select ADO Code in the Binding Type. Then click Next. Obviously, in the Data Form Wizard–Record Source window,

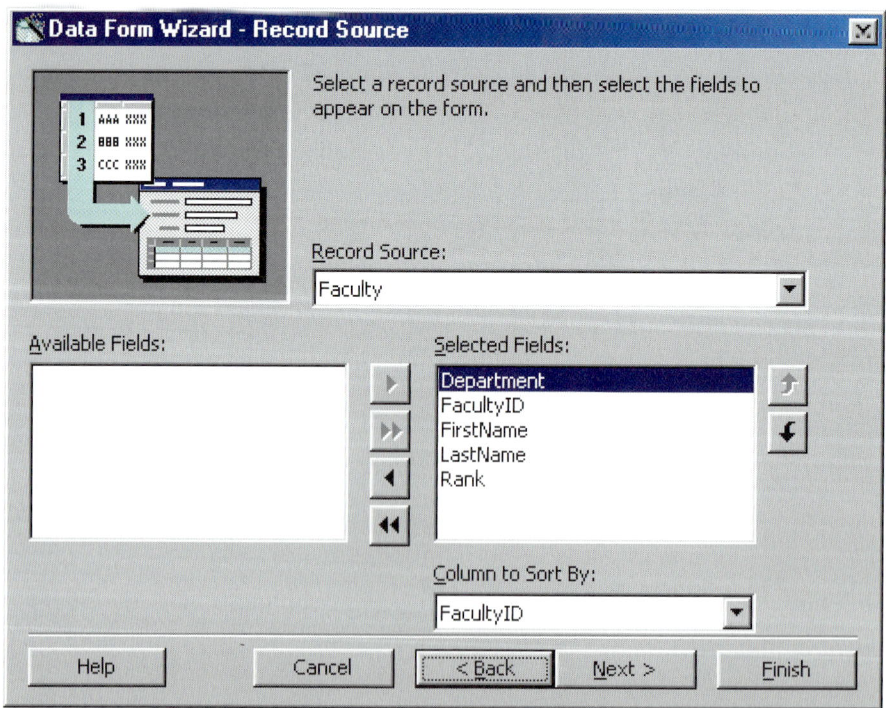

FIGURE 12.13 *Data Form Wizard—Record Source window*

click the down arrow and select Courses, and in the Column to Sort By field, click the down arrow and choose CourseID.

- For the Sections form: In the Data Form Wizard–Form window, type Sections into the Form Name TextBox, and select Class in the Binding Type. Then click Next. Obviously, in the Data Form Wizard–Record Source window, click the down arrow and select Sections, and in the Column to Sort By field, click the down arrow and choose CourseID.

After all three data forms have been specified, answer the question about creating more data forms in the negative. This returns you to the Application Wizard–Data Access Forms window, which appears as in Figure 12.14. Click Next.

In the Application Wizard—Finished window, you may choose to save all of the selections and settings you have chosen for this application, just in case you need to replicate the process at a later time. If you wish to do so, click the ellipsis, and save your Application Wizard selections in an appropriately named file. Click View Report to see a brief description of the application the Wizard has created, as well as instructions for how you can use this skeleton or framework application to further develop and refine your own app. Then click Finish. The Application Wizard creates all of the forms and code, then exits. Save all of the forms, standard module, and class module in your MyAppWizard folder, and save the project as MySchedule3.vbp.

Now try running your semi-complete application. As you can see, the app starts with a splash screen (Figure 12.15), and then the Main form appears (Figure 12.16). The TreeView and ListView controls are not populated with anything. Most of the menu and toolbar selections do not do anything yet—you would have to program them if you want them to become functional. The only preprogrammed menu items are these:

- In the File menu, File | Open activates a Common Dialog control and prompts the user to select a file to be opened; but the program includes no code to actually open or process the user-selected file.

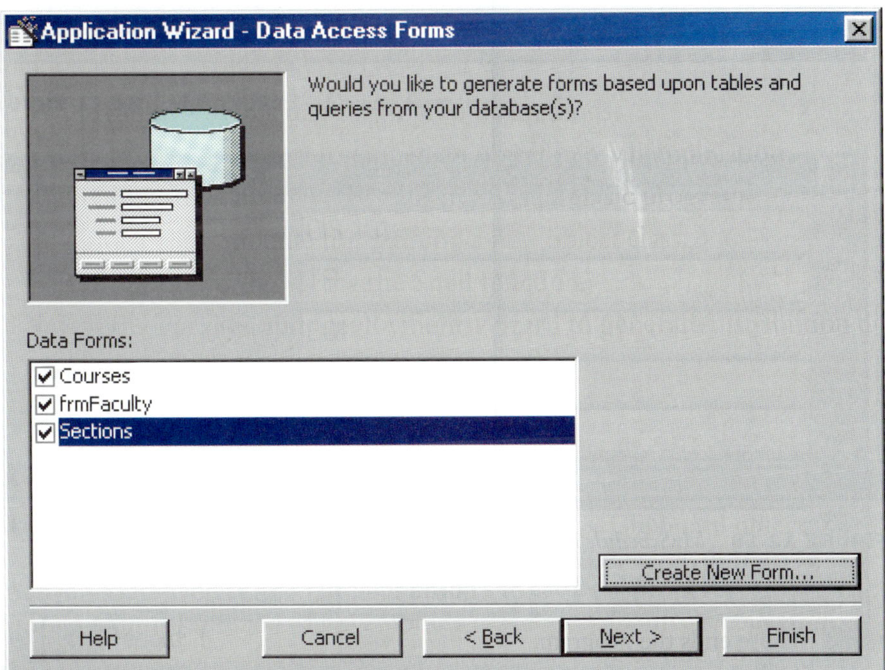

FIGURE 12.14 *Application Wizard—Data Access Forms window*

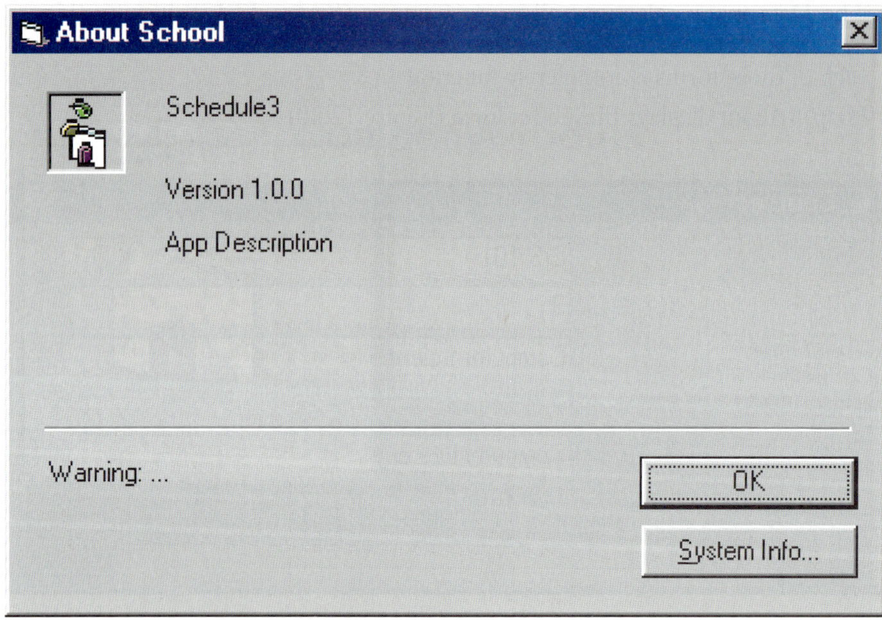

FIGURE 12.20 *MySchedule3—About form*

Compare and contrast the results of selecting the three different binding types:

- The Faculty form contains the ADO Data control (named datPrimaryRS) and code, which is familiar from the Faculty4.vbp project above.
- On the Courses form and the Sections form, the Application Wizard created a Data control "look-alike" by piecing together a label and four Command Buttons.
- The Courses form uses ActiveX Data Object (ADO) code to build a Recordset from the Courses table. Study this code and read about ADO in the MSDN library.
- The Sections form references an object class called clsSections, which is defined in the class module clsSections.cls. Again, if you want further explanations of this code, read about object classes and class modules in the MSDN library.

Some of these techniques, controls, and coding are beyond the scope of an introductory text, but we think it may be instructive for you to get a glimpse of what is possible.

Windows API Calls

The Windows Application Programming Interface consists of many hundreds of standardized library routines which are part of Windows itself but which are also available to Windows applications programs through calls to built-in Windows libraries. To use an API call, you must include the function declaration in the general object of your form or module, and then call the function in your code. In the Schedule3.vbp project, the VB Application Wizard inserted one Windows API call, which doesn't actually do anything, but you might want to take note of its existence.

The function declaration for OSWinHelp occurs in frmMain in the general object. Then, in the mnuHelpContents_Click and the mnuHelpSearchForHelpOn_Click procedures, the OSWinHelp API function is called. This code would only get executed if the programmer created and designated a Help File for this application.

Finishing the Schedule3.vbp project

The application that you have created so far is nearly complete, but it lacks several items: We need to populate the TreeView and ListView controls, and we need to automatically locate the database within the folder in which the application is executing at runtime. The splash screen and the About forms should be customized to reflect your own authorship. Finally, error trapping could usefully be added to the code on all three data forms. The splash screen, About form, and error trapping have been discussed elsewhere in this text.

Populating the tvTreeView control is accomplished at the time the Main form is loaded. To see how this is done, save your project and load our Schedule3.vbp again. Examine the code in Sub Form_Load (which includes the statement "Call LoadTree"), Sub LoadTree (which initializes the tree, and calls LoadDeptNodes for each separate department), Sub LoadDeptNodes (which initializes a department node, and then calls AddNode for each faculty member in the department and for each course offered by that department), and Sub AddNode (which actually puts each node into tvTreeView). These procedures create several Recordsets, based on a database class object called DBInfoClass, defined in the class module of the same name.

Populating the lvListView control is accomplished in the tvTreeView_Click event procedure.

By the way, in our Schedule3.vbp, we used ADO Code instead of the ADODC for the Faculty table. Through DBInfoClass, it is easier to assign the location of College.mdb at runtime using ADO code rather than ADODC.

Lots of luck in completing this project on your own! Like the first 500-piece puzzle you attacked as a youngster, this project and infinite variations on it can give you hours of fun.

INTRODUCING THE COOL VISUALS PROJECT

We thought you might enjoy looking at one more application in this chapter, which demonstrates a few additional graphical and programming features. We won't spend much time explaining how it works—we leave that for you to figure out for yourself. But we have posted both the source code and the executable on our Website, so you can play with it as you wish.

Run CoolVisuals.exe, or load CoolVisuals.vbp and run the program from the design environment. When you load the vbp file, you will note right away that this project is considerably more complex than any of the other projects in this book. Just the number of components is indicative of this complexity: an MDI form, five child forms, four standard modules, and one class module. Although the application itself is not serious, this programming complexity is serious: The Cool Visuals Application does begin to approach the type of complexity you can expect to find in everyday commercial programming.

From the Main Menu or the Toolbar, select OLE Paint (Figure 12.21). The child form displays a hand-drawn picture in an **OLE control.** Now double-click the picture, which activates MSPAINT.EXE, the application used to create the picture (Figure 12.22). You can use the Paint program to edit or completely replace the drawing; when you exit MSPAINT, the modified picture is saved in the VB application. This small example demonstrates Object Linking and Embedding (OLE), the technology that allows you to incorporate into your VB application an object created by another application, in this case Mspaint; and, further, to

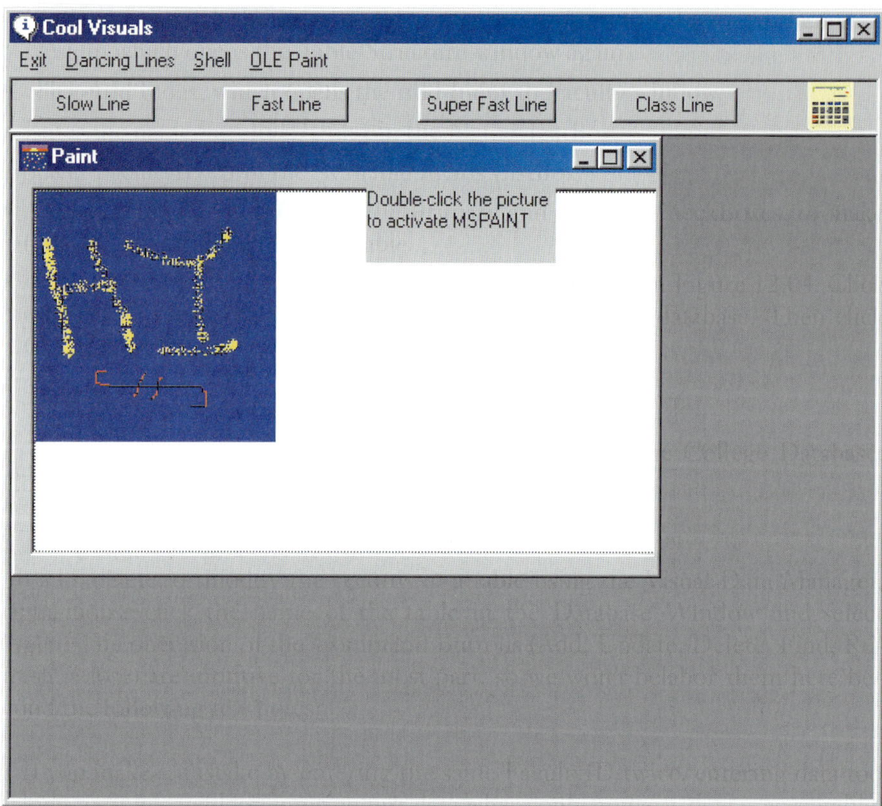

FIGURE 12.21 *Cool Visuals—OLE Paint selected*

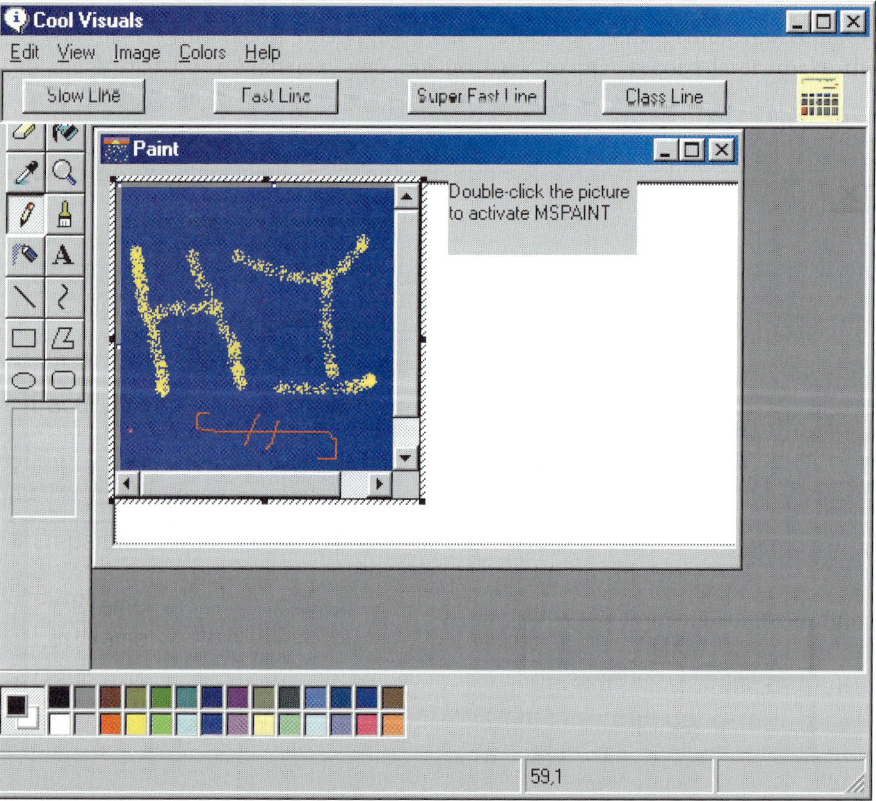

FIGURE 12.22 *Cool Visuals—modifying the picture in MSPaint*

activate the original application that created the object in order to modify or replace the object.

Dancing Lines offers four selections that draw a series of lines on the screen in slow, fast, or super fast mode (Figures 12.23, 12.24, and 12.25), or using a new object class (Figure 12.26). Each mode is accomplished through a separate child form.

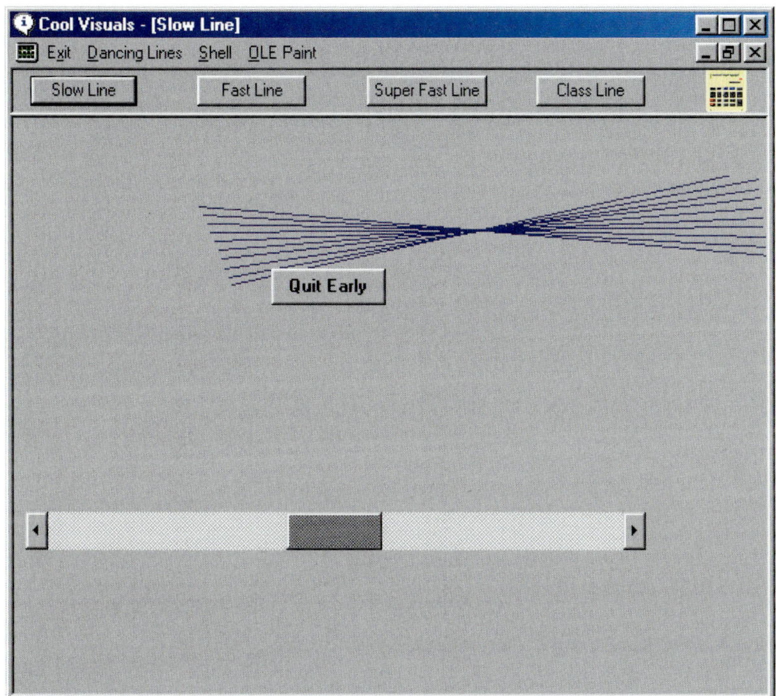

FIGURE 12.23 *Cool Visuals—slow Dancing Lines*

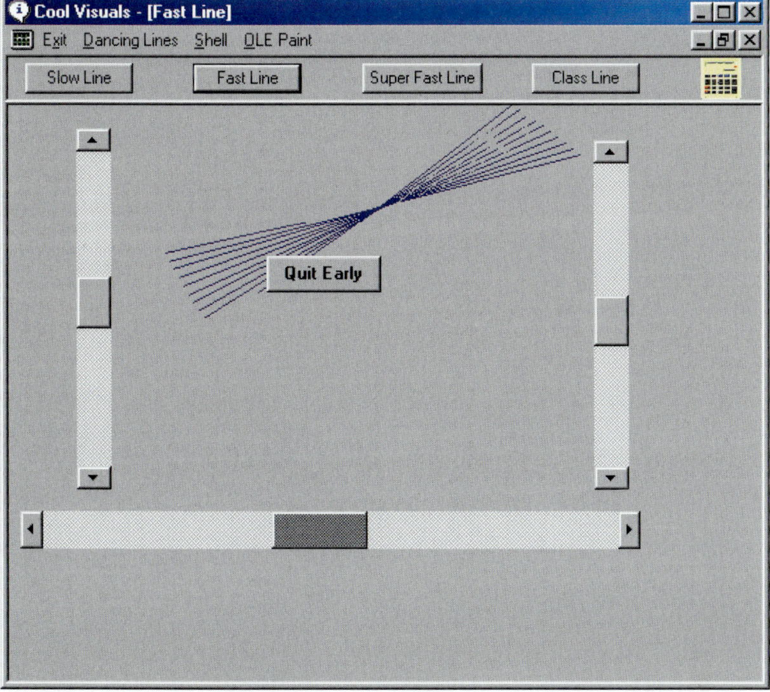

FIGURE 12.24 *Cool Visuals—fast Dancing Lines*

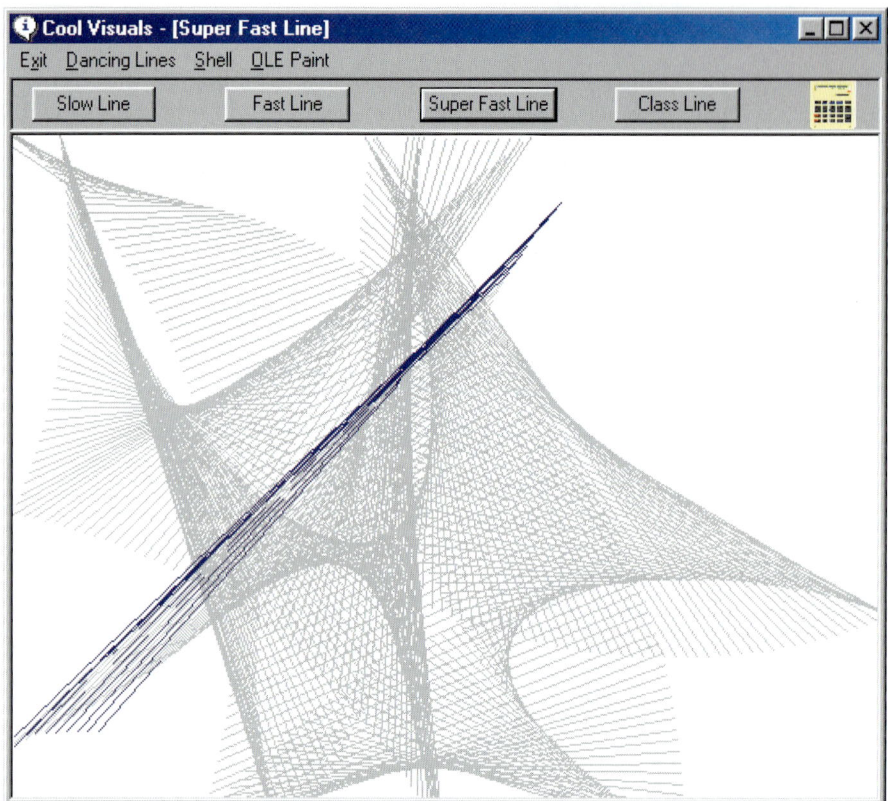

FIGURE 12.25 *Cool Visuals—superfast Dancing Lines*

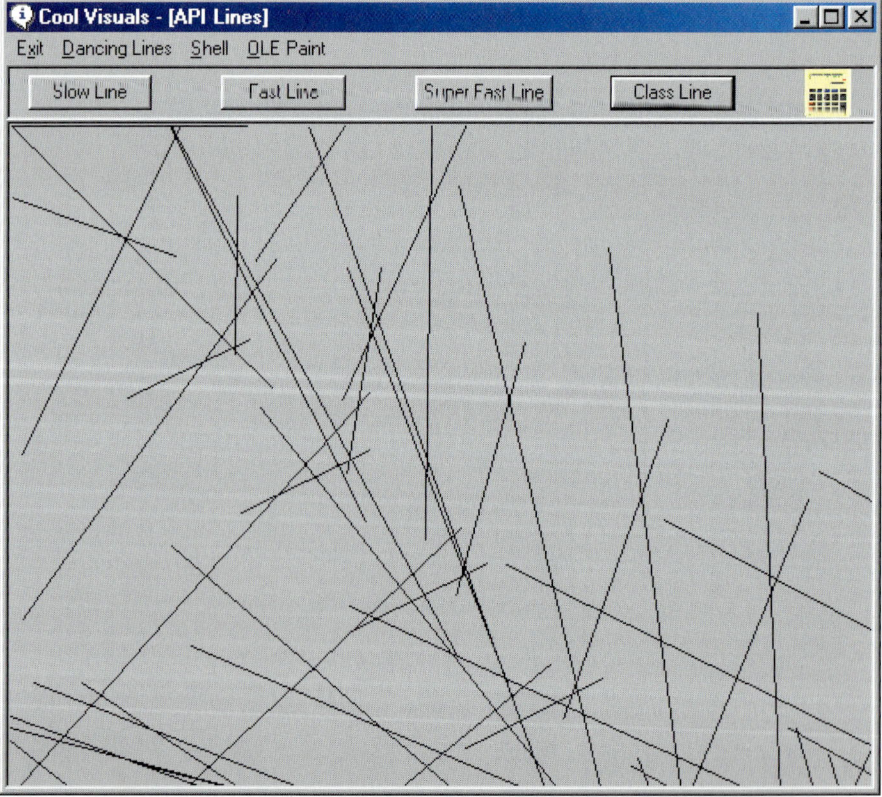

FIGURE 12.26 *Cool Visuals—Dancing Lines via a new object class*

The Shell window allows the user to run the Calculator accessory from within a running Visual Basic program.

Cool Visuals Learning Objectives

The Cool Visuals Project has four principal learning objectives. The first is to complete your repertoire of graphic design tools. This will include Scrollbar controls and graphic methods, plus a little high school trigonometry. The second objective of the Cool Visuals Project is to demonstrate Object Linking and Embedding (OLE), one of the primary technologies for sharing functionality among Windows-based applications. The third objective is to provide another example of a VB Class module, defined earlier in this chapter. And the last objective is to demonstrate the Windows Applications Programming Interface, which provides the VB programmer with access to myriad underlying Windows functions.

Note that the MousePointer changes to crosshairs when it is pointing to the Toolbar and to an hourglass when it is pointing to the Super Fast Lines child form while it is executing. The shape of the MousePointer for an object (form or control) is set by the object's MousePointer property.

Object Linking and Embedding (OLE) is a technology which allows applications to share each other's functionality. In Visual Basic, OLE is implemented principally through the OLE control. Linking allows a client application to display a data object created by a server application, and to be updated by the server when the data in that application changes. Embedding is a technique in which an object in a VB application (the client) is tied to the software (the server) which created that object. By double-clicking the object in the VB application (in this case, the hand-drawn greeting), the server software is activated (in this case, Microsoft Paint). You can edit or replace the drawing (provided, of course, that MSPAINT is installed on your computer).

The Dancing Lines selections (Slow Line, Fast Line, Super Fast Line, and Class Line) demonstrate **Scrollbars,** the **Line control, graphic methods,** and a Class module. Try them out. Each of the first three Windows, if allowed to run to conclusion, paints the same number of lines on the screen, namely, 500 sets of 10 lines each. Slow Line employs an array of ten Line controls and one **Horizontal Scrollbar.** (You can Quit Early if the display is putting you to sleep.) Fast Line uses the **Line method,** obviously much faster than the Line control, but the overall speed is retarded by the need to constantly update three Scrollbar controls. Super Fast Line uses the Line method alone, unimpeded by other controls. In each case, a series of ten blue lines appears on the Window. With the Line control array, each of the lines is repositioned. With the Line method, the leading line is painted in blue, and the trailing line is subsequently repainted in gray. (The gray lines blend into the gray background in the Fast Mode, but appear as shadows over a white background in SuperFast mode.) Because it runs so quickly, you may not be able to see the leading blue lines in SuperFast Mode. Class Line, the last of the Dancing Lines menu selections, demonstrates both the notion of a Class module and the incorporation of Windows API calls.

Finally, the Shell menu selection demonstrates how the **Shell function** can be used to run another executable program from a Visual Basic program.

Cool Visuals—New Code, Graphics, and Controls

User-defined Data Types

Visual Basic provides the fundamental data types we have been using throughout this book—Integer, Long, Single, Double, Currency, String, Boolean, Byte, Date, and Variant. And VB allows us to declare multiple occurrences of such fundamental data types in arrays. Often, however, we would like to combine several fundamental data types, including arrays, into one user-defined data structure.

For example, consider a program dealing with many different kinds of bubble gum. For each kind of gum, the program includes the brand name, color, flavor, size, and price. The program might have any number of modules, forms, and procedures that need the elements of information about each kind of gum. Of course, it would be possible to use only the fundamental data types and pass to each procedure the gum's brand name, color, flavor, size, and price. But that quickly becomes tedious. It would be far better to put all of those elements together into one package, give the whole package a name, and then pass the package back and forth among the procedures of the program. A user-defined data type provides the means of accomplishing this goal.

A user-defined data type is declared in a standard module (see above), where, by default, it is Public, even without the keyword Public. By Public, we mean that this declaration is visible and available to all of the forms and modules throughout an application.

We also like to use the word Type as the last word of a type declaration. For our bubble-gum example, here would be the type declaration:

```
Type BubbleGumType
   strBrandName As String * 20
   strColor As String * 10
   strFlavor As String * 20
   sngSize As Single 'in ounces
   curPrice As Currency
End Type
```

Note that BubbleGumType is not a variable. Rather, it is a new type of data. After this declaration has been made, variables of this data type can be declared. The prefix udt indicates that a variable is a user-defined type. For example:

```
Public gudtBubbleGum As BubbleGumType 'global
'variable
Dim mudtMyGum As BubbleGumType 'module level
'variable
ReDim audtAllGums(100) As BubbleGumType 'local array
```

You can also construct a user-defined type from other previously declared user-defined types and from arrays. For example, we might want to have a data type that could store information about as many as 20 types of gum sold at one supermarket. That might lead us to declare:

```
Type GumStoreType
   strStoreName As String * 30
   strStoreLocation As String * 50
   udtaGums(20) As BubbleGumType
End Type
Public gudtGumStore As GumStoreType
```

After a variable of a user-defined type has been declared, assignments can be made, but to avoid a Type Mismatch error, only equivalent data types can be assigned to each other. For example, using the bubble gum-related declarations above, the following are all legal:

```
mudtMyGum = gudtBubbleGum
audtAllGums(3) = mudtMyGum
mudtMyGum.strFlavor = "Cherry"
audtAllGums(5).curPrice = gudtBubbleGum.curPrice
gudtGumStore.strStoreName = "Frank's Pretty Good _
```

```
    Grocery"
gudtGumStore.udtaGums(1).strColor = mudtMyGum.strColor
```

User-Defined Data Types Representing a Record Layout

A VB programmer can create a new type of data structure consisting of any number of fundamental variable types. In many cases, a user-defined data type corresponds to the notion of a record in a file, which is made up in turn of some number of data elements. For example, the following declaration could define a data structure for a personnel record:

```
Type PersonnelType
    strSSN As String * 9
    strLastName As String * 20
    strFirstName As String * 20
    dteDOB As Date
    strTitle As String * 30
    curSalary As Currency
    intDependents as Integer
End Type
```

Note that declaring PersonnelType does not actually reserve any storage space. We do not have a new variable named PersonnelType. Rather, we have a new variable type, and we can declare variables to be of that type just as we can declare variables to be of type Integer or Single or String. Following the declaration of PersonnelType, we might want to use any of these statements to declare variables of type PersonnelType:

```
'to declare a global record (g=global, _
    udt=user-defined-type):
Public gudtPersonnelRec As PersonnelType
Public gudtMyPersonnelRec As PersonnelType
'to declare a global array of 10 records:
Public gaudtPersonnelTable(1 To 10) As PersonnelType
'to declare a module level personnel record:
Dim mudtPersonnelRec As PersonnelType
'to declare a procedure level array of 100
    'records:
Dim audtPersonnelTable(100) As PersonnelType
```

To reference a particular element of a user-defined data type, you must use the variable name, a period, and then the element name. With this syntax, all of the operations defined for an elementary data type are available for an element of a user-defined data type. Some examples:

```
mudtPersonnelRec.strLastName = "Smith"
strMyLastName = audtPersonnelTable(10).strLastName
intTotalDependents = intTotalDependents + _
    gaudtPersonnelTable(i).intDependents
```

Very few operations are defined for a user-defined data type as a whole. The most important defined operation is assignment. Given the declarations above, these following statements are valid.

```
gudtPersonnelRec = gudtMyPersonnelRec
gudtPersonnelRec = gaudtPersonnelTable(i)
```

If you try to assign an elementary data type to a user-defined data type, or vice versa, as in these two invalid examples,

```
gudtPersonnelRec = ""                'invalid
Dim MyString As String
MyString = gaudtPersonnelTable(3) 'invalid
```

a Type Mismatch error will occur.

For the most part, input/output operations on user-defined data types are not supported, but i/o operations on the fundamental data types that make up a user-defined data type are fine. This means that the statement

```
Print gudtPersonnelRec
```

will not work, although

```
Print gudtPersonnelRec.strLastName
```

will work just fine, since gudtPersonnelRec.strLastName is a string, and the Print method is defined for strings.

Graphics Methods versus Graphical Controls

This project introduces the graphic methods (Line, Circle, Pset) and also contrasts them with the graphic controls (Line, Shape). The **Line method** draws a line or box on the form, and can fill or draw it with color. The **Circle method** draws a circle, ellipse, pie slice, or arc on a form. **PSet** colors a point on a form. In each case, the settings of the form's **DrawWidth, DrawMode, DrawStyle, ForeColor, FillColor,** and **FillStyle** properties can affect the results of the method. Listed below is a typical implementation:

```
Line (1000, 1500) - (5000, 3000), vbBlue
```

Draws a blue line diagonally on the form, from X1 = 1000 and Y1 = 1500 to X2 = 5000 and Y2 = 3000, where X1 and Y1 are the horizontal and vertical coordinates of the starting point of the line, and X2 and Y2 are the coordinates of the ending point of the line.

```
Circle (2000, 3000), 1500
```

Draws a circle whose locus is at the coordinates 2000 and 3000 and whose radius is 1500. Since color is not specified, the form's ForeColor is used. FillColor and FillStyle determine the color and style inside the circle.

```
PSet Step (600, 5000), vbMagenta
```

CurrentX and CurrentY are the coordinates of the most recent spot on the form painted by any graphics method (line, circle, or PSet). The Step option identifies new coordinates as an offset to CurrentX/CurrentY. Therefore, in this statement, the color of the point at coordinates 600 to the right of **CurrentX** and 5000 below **CurrentY** is set to magenta. The size of the colored point is determined by the form's DrawWidth property. CoolVisuals.vbp includes the Line method in frmFast and in frmSuperFast.

Though not relevant to the CoolVisuals applications, the **AutoRedraw property,** the **Paint event,** and the **Refresh method** are important for the proper use of graphic methods in many applications. The form's AutoRedraw property indicates whether graphic methods will be repainted on a form which has been resized or which is newly exposed (because some other window had been partially or completely covering it). When the repainting takes place, the Paint event fires. If AutoRedraw is False (the default value), the Refresh method can be used to force the occurrence of a Paint event.

All three forms use a Timer event, entered once and then disabled, to draw the dancing lines on the form. The Timer event procedure in all three Dancing Lines forms calls a common procedure (Sub SetPos in LINE.BAS) to position the beginning point and then the ending point of the next new line to be drawn on the form. LINE.BAS also includes the definitions of the user-defined data types LINE_TYPE and POINT_TYPE. In the atLinePos array (declared in the Timer event procedure), each line is defined by two sets of X-Y coordinates, by the direction (expressed in degrees, from 0° to 359°) that each line tip is moving, and by the line color. The degrees are like those on a compass: due north is 0°, due east is 90°, due south is 180°, and so on. The initial direction is selected randomly, and it is reset randomly every time one of the tips of a line bumps into a window border.

The cosine of an angle (which measures the ratio of the length of the adjacent leg divided by the hypotenuse) is used for calculating a new X, which makes intuitive sense since X provides the horizontal coordinate. And the sine (which measures the ratio of the opposite leg divided by the hypotenuse) is used for calculating a new Y, which also makes intuitive sense since Y gives the vertical coordinate. In both cases, the mathematical function requires an argument expressed in radians. Since the Direction in our project is stated in degrees, this value must be converted to radians, which is given by the formula.

$$\text{radians} = \text{degrees} * \pi / 180$$

The return value from both the **cos (cosine)** and the **sin (sine) functions** is a real number in the range of −1 to +1.

In Sub SetPos, rtPoint is passed to the procedure by reference. Since rtPoint is a POINT_TYPE parameter, it has X, Y, and Direction components. To construct a new line, first the direction is incremented. Then, the cosine of the direction (converted to radians) is multiplied by vnMove (a multiplication factor, set in this program to 100), and the resulting value is added to the previous X. In the same fashion, the sine of the direction is multiplied by vnMove, and the resulting value is added to Y. If the new value of X or Y would place that coordinate outside the border of the window, then the coordinate is set exactly at the border and a new direction (from 0° to 359°) is chosen randomly.

Now back to the Timer event procedures in each of the three Dancing Lines child forms:

After the initial contents of the atLinePos array are set (representing the coordinates and direction of only the very first line, atLinePos(0)), a loop is entered, which will be repeated 500 times. Each iteration of this loop determines the coordinates and directions for one new line, then repositions all of the lines in the Line control array (in frmSlowLine) or draws the leading blue line and redraws the trailing gray line (in frmFastLine and frmSuperFastLine).

After the coordinates and direction of the beginning point and of the end point of the new line (stored in atLinePos(0)) have been determined through two calls to Sub SetPos, new lines are drawn on the form. In the case of frmSlowLine, all of the lines in the Line control array are redrawn in blue, as the coordinates for lne(ictr) are taken from atLinePos(ictr). In the case of frmFastLine and frmSuperFastLine, a line method draws the new line in blue (coordinates extracted from atLinePos(0)) and another line method redraws the last blue line in gray (coordinates extracted from atLinePos(MAX_LINES)). In all three procedures, after the lines have been drawn/redrawn on the form, the contents of the atLinePos array are reassigned:

```
For iCtr = MAX_LINES To 1 Step -1
    atLinePos(iCtr) = atLinePos(iCtr - 1)
Next
```

which makes atLinePos(10) contain the values that had been in atLinePos(9), atLinePos(9) contain what had been atLinePos(8), and so on, down to atLinePos(1) containing what had been at atLinePos(0).

At this juncture, a DoEvents statement is executed. The **DoEvents statement** releases control of the screen to Windows so that any pending Windows messages can be handled by other processes. After pending messages have been dealt with, control returns to the next statement in the Timer event procedure, which is the bottom of the main loop.

Horizontal and Vertical Scrollbars

frmSlowLine and frmFastLine both include **Horizontal Scrollbar controls,** and frmFastLine also includes **Vertical Scrollbar controls.** The relevant properties are **Min, Max, Value, SmallChange,** and **LargeChange.**

Windows API Calls

As mentioned in passing in the Schedule3.vbp project, the Windows Application Programming Interface (API) consists of many hundreds of standardized library routines that can be inserted or called into a VB program. In the CoolVisuals application, we included six Win API calls, all declared and called in the WinAPI.bas module:

- MessageBeep
- GetDC
- ReleaseDC
- MoveTo
- MoveToEx
- LineTo

The WinAPI.bas module includes the SmartQuestion procedure, which calls the MessageBeep API Sub, and the PaintLine procedure, which includes calls to all of the API Functions.

The discussion above has given you a thumbnail sketch of a number of important, advanced VB programming topics: Class modules, Property procedures, user-defined properties and methods for forms and for classes, and Windows API calls. To delve into these topics completely would require an entire book.

"Class Lines"—Class Modules and Standard Modules

In the CoolVisuals applications, the Class Lines menu selection paints groups of lines on the screen. The number of lines in each group is user-selected. The functionality is created by these modules:

- APILines.frm (frmAPILines)
- APILine.cls (APILine Class module)
- APILines.bas (APILines Standard module)
- Line.bas (Line Standard module)
- WinAPI.bas (WinAPI Standard module)

The APILine object class is defined in the Class module. The APILines Standard module asks the user for the number of lines to be drawn, and assigns this value to the user-defined NumLines property of frmAPILines (note that this property is defined in frmAPILines with a PropertyLet procedure, which assigns to mnNumLines the value of NumLines less one). The APILines Standard module then calls the Public Init procedure in frmAPILines. (A Public procedure inside a form is actually referred to as a user-defined method for the form.) The Init procedure creates NumLines instances of the object class APILine and assigns these new objects to maoLine(), a module-level array of objects. (Because of the **PropertyLet** procedure, the statement "For i = 0 to mnNumLine" iterates NumLines times.) In the Class module, the Initialize event procedure fires every time an instance of the class is created. This Initialize procedure (through calls to the SetPos procedure in Line.bas) sets the initial coordinates for each APILine object. The APILines Standard module then executes frmAPILines.Show.

In the Timer event procedure of frmAPILines, the Class object's DrawTheLine method draws each object in the array on the screen. The DrawTheLine method includes a call to PaintLine, a procedure in WinAPI.bas, which is explained below.

Although the use of so many components (form, class module, and standard modules) may seem unnecessarily complex for such a relatively simple task, the CoolVisuals applications does demonstrate the fundamental architecture used by professional Visual Basic programmers when they have a large project that must include many instantiations of many user-defined objects.

Object Linking and Embedding (OLE)

Object Linking and Embedding is a rather sophisticated tool for sharing data and applications. Visual Basic's OLE control is a straightforward means of implementing OLE in a Visual Basic program.

Under OLE Automation, an object created by a foreign (non-VB) application resides inside a Visual Basic application. That is, both the data object and the application which created it are "embedded" in a VB application. To manipulate the data object, the user can execute the foreign application by double-clicking the OLE object. Many applications can be linked to an object. When the object is changed and saved, it is changed in all of the applications to which it is linked. Visual Basic maintains a reference to the object's data and properties in the foreign application, and creates a **metafile**-type image of the data for purposes of displaying the object in VB.

Embedding involves the placing of an object created by a foreign application into a Visual Basic program, along with information which allows the VB program to access the foreign application for purposes of editing the object. The object's data and properties are maintained according to the foreign application, but are stored inside the VB program.

Visual Basic's OLE control allows us to demonstrate OLE automation without writing any code at all, much like the simplest form of access to a database can be achieved through the Data control and bound controls but without any code. We have used this technique to demonstrate the OLE control in the Cool Visuals Project. Just double-click the drawing in frmPaint. As you can see, the Microsoft Paint program is entered; you can edit this picture and then return to CoolVisuals.exe. This functionality is achieved merely by placing the OLE control on the form and then, in the Insert Object Dialog Box, selecting the PaintbrushPicture and drawing your own picture, or by choosing an existing object from a file.

Beyond this simple example, OLE can be a large subject for your own self-study, but detailed treatment is beyond the scope of an introductory programming textbook. Furthermore, the use of OLE depends on what other applications which support OLE automation happen to be installed on your computer. The OLE control has 28 unique properties. Through the Object property, you can also invoke all of the properties and methods of the linked or embedded object in the application that created it. You can experiment with these and entertain yourself for much longer than one lazy summer afternoon. (If you develop some good OLE applications, send us a note; maybe we could write another book!) Enjoy!

Clipboard object

Another simpler method of exchanging data among two applications is by using the Windows Clipboard, which provides temporary storage locations for text or graphics. Visual Basic offers the **Clipboard object,** whose methods allow you to copy and paste data through the operating environment's Clipboard:

- **Clear**—clears the contents of the Clipboard:
  Clipboard.Clear
- **SetText**—puts text data into the Clipboard, for example:
  Clipboard.SetText Text1
- **SetData**—puts a picture into the Clipboard, for example:
  Clipboard.SetData Image1.Picture
- **GetText**—retrieves text from the Clipboard, for example:
  Clipboard.GetText Label2
- **GetData**—retrieves a picture from the Clipboard, for example:
  Clipboard.GetData Picture1.Picture

Tag Property

The **Tag property** is a convenient place to store any additional identifying data related to a form or control. VB does not use the Tag property for anything, so the programmer can use it freely for any purpose whatsoever. The Tag property contains string data.

For example, on a splash screen, you might want to cause a whole bunch of controls to flash on and off. Perhaps this includes some image controls, shapes, lines, and labels. Other controls on the splash screen are not supposed to flash on and off. The Tag property and the form's **Controls collection** can be combined to perform this task quite easily.

Try this out: Start a new project, and put a dozen or so graphical controls on the form. Set the Tag property to 1 on about half of these controls. Then put a Timer control on the form, with an Interval of 500 milliseconds. In the Timer event, type in this code, and run the project to see how it works:

```
Dim I as Integer
For I = 0 to Me.Controls.Count-1
   If Me.Controls(I).Tag = "1" Then
      Me.Controls(I).Visible = Not Me.Controls(I).Visible
   End If
Next I
```

Now that you see how this can be done, tailor this splash screen to serve for the Cool Visuals Application, save the form in the folder that contains Cool Visuals, and then add the form to the Cool Visuals Application. Make your splash screen the Startup Form. Put another Timer on the splash screen form to display the MDI form and unload the splash screen after three or four seconds.

Once again, have fun with the Cool Visuals application. You can use it as a basis for many additional Visual Basic projects of your own imagination!

PACKAGE AND DEPLOYMENT WIZARD

The last wizard we wish to demonstrate for you in this chapter is not a new project, but rather something you use after your application development is complete. The **Package and Deployment Wizard** gives you the capability of distributing VB applications to your customers. Starting with a completed Visual Basic application, the Package and Deployment Wizard leads you through the process of identifying all necessary components (VB design time components, like forms and modules, plus databases, text files, help files, dynamic link libraries, fonts, system files, and so on). The wizard then compresses these files and creates an installation utility. Finally, the completed application setup utility is saved in one large "cabinet" (.cab) file on a hard disk (for network installation or an Internet download facility, for example) or on as many floppy disks as are necessary. The user installs the application by inserting disk #1 and typing the familiar a:\setup.

In this example, we will use the Package and Deployment Wizard to create an installation diskette for the Faculty3 application from the beginning of this chapter. Follow these simple steps:

- From the Windows Start Menu, choose Programs | Microsoft Visual Basic 6.0 | Microsoft Visual Basic 6.0 Tools | Package and Deployment Wizard.
- In the opening window of the Package and Deployment Wizard, browse to locate Faculty3.exe in the Select Project TextBox (Figure 12.27). Then click the Package icon.
- After the wizard examines Faculty3.exe, you will see the Package and Deployment Wizard–Packaging Script window. No script exists yet for this application, so "none" should appear in the Packaging Script ComboBox. Click Next.
- In the Package and Deployment Wizard–Package Type window, select Standard Setup Package, and click Next.

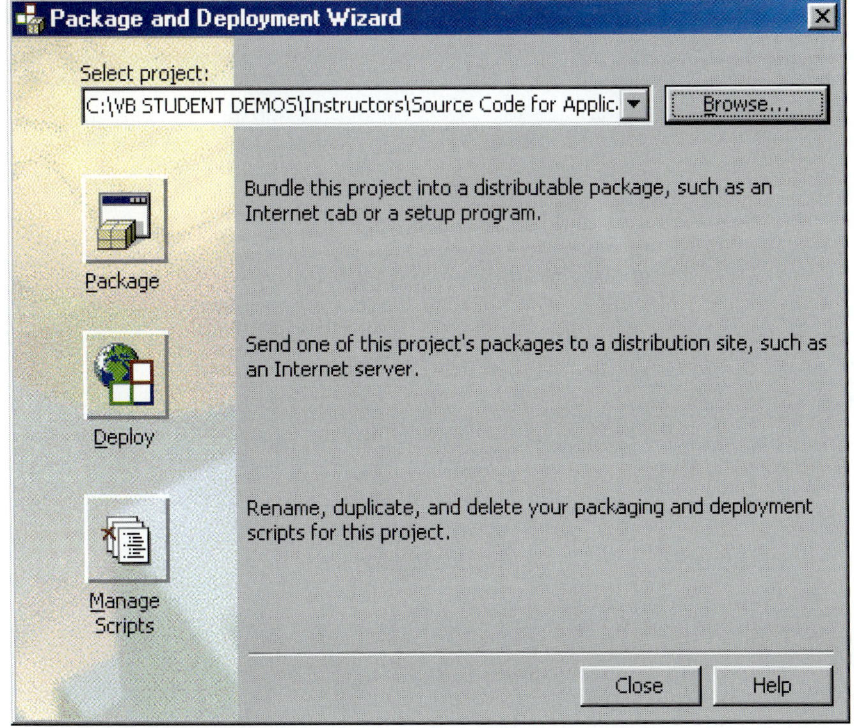

FIGURE 12.27 *Package and Deployment Wizard—opening screen*

- In the Package and Deployment Wizard–Package Folder window, select the folder where you want the wizard to assemble the completed package.
- In the Package and Deployment Wizard–DAO Drivers window, just click Next.
- In the Package and Deployment Wizard–Included Files window, there appears a list of files needed directly or indirectly by the Faculty3.exe application. Point the mouse at any of the listed files, and a pop-up message explains why that file was included. However, the wizard does not know how to identify data files (such as databases, text files, or random access files). So in this case we have to tell the wizard to include College.mdb. Click Add . . . , and in the Add File window, locate and select the College.mdb database. The Included Files window now looks like Figure 12.28. Then click Next.
- In the Package and Deployment Wizard–Cab Options window, click Single cab if you want the entire package to be placed in one large "cabinet" file. This would be the case if you plan on distributing the application electronically, across a local or wide area network, by download from the Web, or on a CD. Click Multiple cabs if you plan on distributing the application on floppy disks. (We chose the Multiple cabinets option.) Then click Next.
- In the Package and Deployment Wizard–Installation Title window, type Faculty3 into the TextBox. Then click Next.
- In the Package and Deployment Wizard–Start Menu Items window, just click Next.
- In the Package and Deployment Wizard–Install Locations window, just click Next.
- In the Package and Deployment Wizard–Shared Files window, just click Next.
- In the Package and Deployment Wizard–Finished window, type Faculty3 Setup Package into the Script Name TextBox. Then click Finish. The wizard will now create the installation package, which takes several minutes.

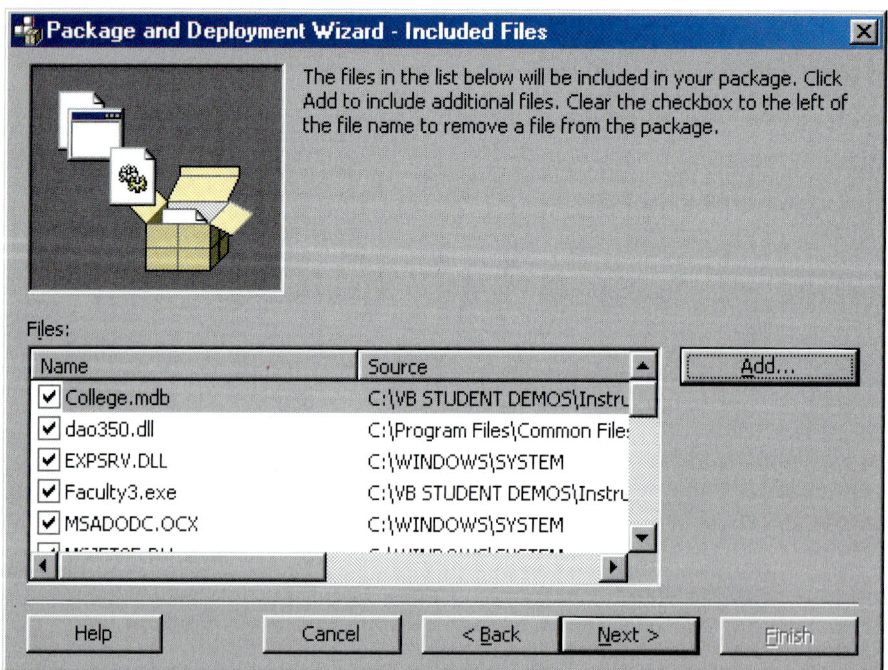

FIGURE 12.28 *Package and Deployment Wizard—Included Files window*

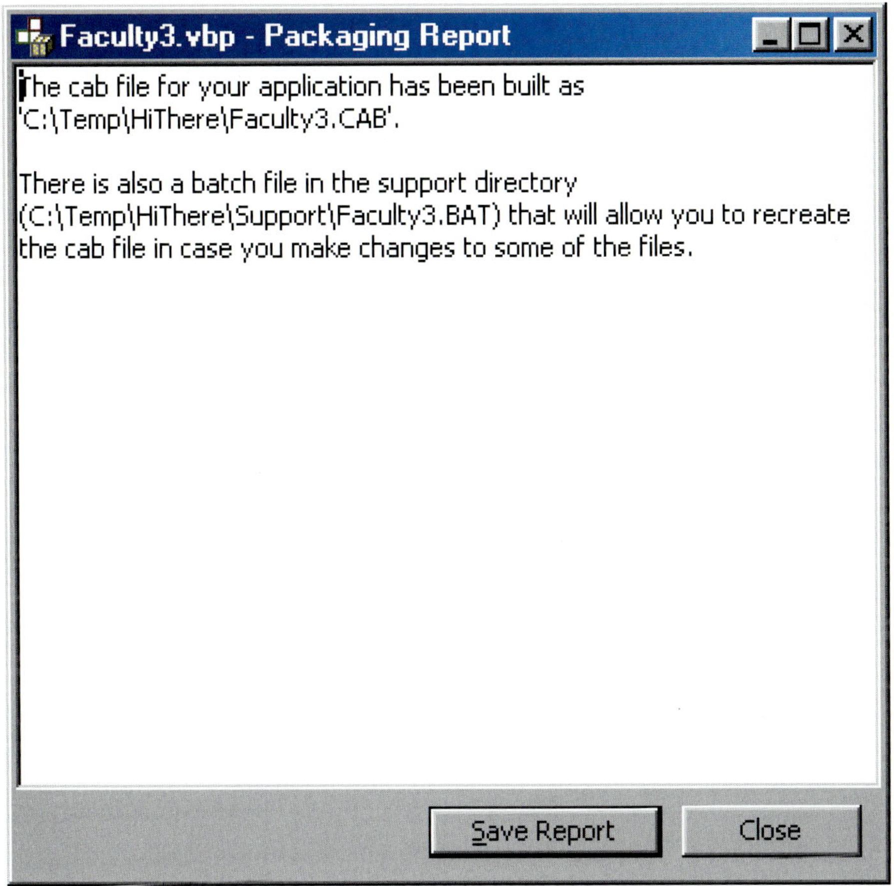

FIGURE 12.29 *Package and Deployment Wizard—Packaging Report*

- When the package has been created, the Package and Deployment Wizard–Packaging Report window (Figure 12.29) gives you some useful information about its use. Save or close this window; then close the Package and Deployment Wizard itself.

Open Windows Explorer to see the files created by the Package and Deployment Wizard. In our example, installation requires Setup.exe, Setup.lst, and three cabinet files (Facult1.cab, Facult2.cab, and Facult3.cab). To distribute the application, copy the two Setup.* files and Facult1.cab onto a floppy disk and label this disk #1. Then copy Facult2.cab onto disk #2, and Facult3.cab onto disk #3. Try doing this yourself. Then use these three disks to install the application on a different computer—one that also does not have Visual Basic.

SUMMARY

The **Visual Data Manager** is a VB **Add-In** tool which facilitates the creation and direct manipulation of a database, tables, records, and queries. From Visual Data Manager, the **Data Form Designer** can be used to create a new form containing a Data control, bound fields to a table of a database, and all of the normal table maintenance functions.

VB's **Add-In Manager** allows the user to add certain advanced functions into the VB design environment, including the VB 6.0 **Data Form Wizard.** The Data

Form Wizard provides an easy way to create a form for database access or maintenance. Using the Data Form Wizard, the programmer can choose one of three Binding Types: ADODC, ADO Code, or Class.

The **ActiveX Data Object Data control** (ADODC) is a more capable replacement for VB's intrinsic Data control. Its **ConnectionString property** identifies a data source, which can be nearly any type of database, spreadsheet, or text file. The ConnectionString can be constructed at design time using the **PropertyPage window. ActiveX Data Objects** (ADO) code can also be used to access an external database.

A **Standard module** contains only code (that is, no form). A Standard module is often used to declare Public variables and Public procedures (accessible throughout the project).

A **Class module** allows the programmer to define a new object class. User-defined properties and methods can be defined for both Class modules and forms. **Property procedures** (Property Get, Property Let, and Property Set) can be used to create and assign values to user-defined properties.

The **TreeView control** and the **ListView control** provide a means for displaying related data values—the TreeView control displays items in root-and-branch format, while the ListView control is similar to a multi-column table.

The VB **Application Wizard** assists in the development of an entire VB application. The main form for the application can be one of three types: Single Document, Multiple Document, or Explorer Style. The Application Wizard also accesses the **Data Form Wizard** to create as many different data forms as the application requires. Other forms developed through the wizard include a splash screen, logon form, customize screen, and about form. The output of the Application Wizard is a skeleton application with all of its forms, modules, and code.

A **user-defined data type** is declared with the **Type/End Type statements.** Standard modules (.BAS files) contain declarations and procedures unattached to any particular form, and these are often used to declare user-defined data types.

This chapter completes your repertoire of graphical design tools. **Horizontal** and **Vertical ScrollBars** provide an analog, visual measurement tool. The **Line control,** like the **Shape control,** draws a fixed object on the screen and is easy to use, although it consumes considerable Windows resources if it must be constantly refreshed. The **Line, Circle,** and **Pset methods** draw directly on a form and are faster than the Line and Shape controls. Simple trigonometric functions, such as **Sin** and **Cos,** can be employed to assist in drawing lines and shapes on a form. If **AutoRedraw** is set to True, results of the graphic methods are stored in a screen memory map and can be repainted if a window is resized or uncovered. The **Paint event** fires when a window is partially or wholly repainted. The **Refresh method** causes repainting of the entire screen and invokes the Paint event.

With the **Clipboard object, SetText** and **SetData** temporarily store text or graphic data, **GetText** and **GetData** retrieve text or data previously stored, and **Clear** clears the Clipboard. **Object Linking and Embedding (OLE)** provides a more recent innovation in data sharing: with this technology, objects can be linked to or embedded in a VB application. The Visual Basic program can then edit the object in the application which created it.

The **Tag property** can be used to store additional data concerning a form or control.

Hundreds of Windows library routines are available to the VB programmer through the Application Program Interface (API). The **"Declare <function-name> Lib–<libname>" statement** makes an API library routine available. The actual API call appears the same as any other function call. Many Windows API calls require very careful coding, especially for the long parameter lists.

PROGRAMMING ASSIGNMENTS

Completed Class Scheduling Application (Version 4)

Start with SCHEDULE3.VBP. Copy the whole project with all of its components to a new directory. Save the project as SCHEDULE4.VBP. Then proceed as follows.

- Customize the splash screen and the About Form to make this your project.
- Insert appropriate code for all useful and needed menu selections and toolbar icons; delete all other menu selections and toolbar icons.
- Insert error-handling procedures in the Courses, Sections, and Faculty forms. Prevent the addition of records with duplicate primary keys. In the Sections form, prevent the addition or modification of a record with a non-existent course or a non-existent faculty member.

Wine Inventory Valuation

The program graphically displays the year, number of bottles of wine left in inventory, price per bottle, and total inventory value. The operation of the program is under control of a timer, so that user input is not needed at all. The only optional user actions are to pause the display and then to continue the display thereafter.

Delete the Control Box, Max Button, and Min Button from the Wine Inventory Valuation Form (Figure 12.30).

Controls:

- The Year scrollbar starts on the left with the current year and continues to the current year + 10.

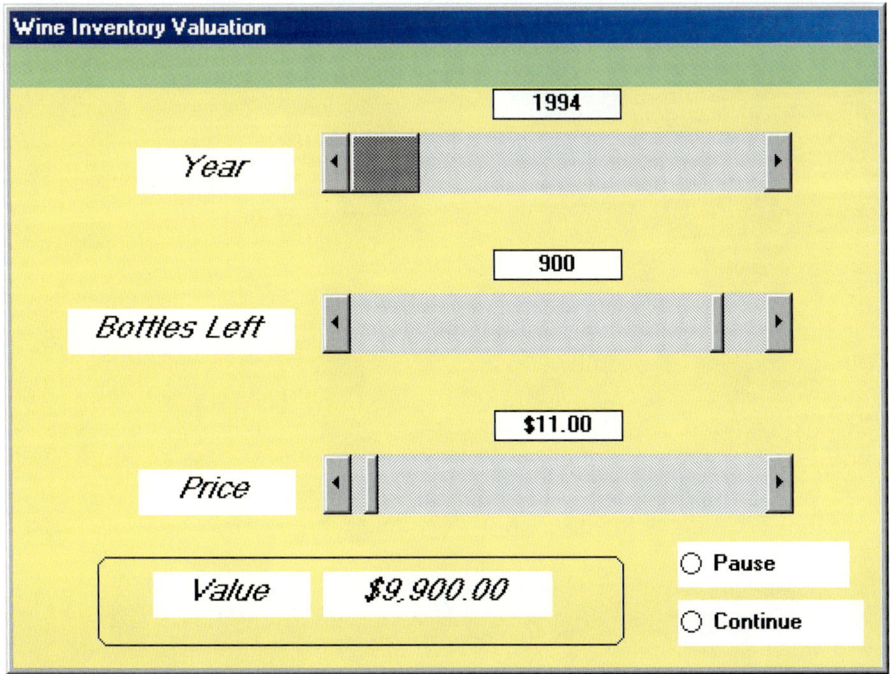

FIGURE 12.30 *Wine valuation, running*

- The Bottles Left scrollbar starts at 1000 on the right and decreases toward 0 on the left.
- The Price scrollbar starts at 1000 (meaning $10) on the left and increases toward 4500 (meaning $45) on the right.
- There are 8 Labels. Note that the three Labels above the scrollbars have borders, and that the two Labels at the bottom are placed inside a rounded-rectangle shape control.
- Two option buttons. The Pause button should disable the timer, while the Continue button enables the timer.
- Initially, the timer should be set to an interval of 5 seconds, so that the opening screen displays for five seconds before it starts changing.

Within the timer click event:

- set the timer interval to two seconds
- toggle the form's background color between light green and light yellow.
- increment the Year scrollbar
- decrease the value of the Bottles Left scrollbar by 10 percent, since you drank 10 percent of the remaining wine last year
- increase the value of the Price scrollbar by 15 percent, since the value of each bottle goes up each year
- calculate the value of the Inventory Value label, that is, the total dollar value of the Bottles Left scrollbar * the value of the Price scrollbar. Note that all numeric figures are integers, since a scrollbar's value is an integer by definition.
- update all of the numeric labels (Year, Bottles Left, Price, and Inventory Value).
- Note that Price and Inventory Value are displayed in currency format.

CHAPTER THIRTEEN

TRADITIONAL FILES

Application: State Information

LEARNING OBJECTIVES

Upon completion of Chapter Thirteen, you will be able to:

- Create and use a sequential data file in input, output, and append filemodes.
- Create a user-defined data type to represent the record layout of a file.
- Load a sequential data file into a table of user-defined data structures.
- Bracket a series of statements referencing an object or data structure with the With/End With statements.
- Sort records in a table.
- Use the properties, events, and methods related to mouse movements.
- Become familiar with the concepts and Visual Basic statements related to random data files.

Keywords

Append filemode
Close statement
DragDrop event
DragIcon property
Drag method
DragMode property
DragOver event
EOF function
Filenumber
FreeFile function
Get statement
Input # statement
Input filemode
Input function
Kill statement
Line Input # statement
MouseDown event
MouseMove event
MouseUp event
Open statement
Output filemode
Put statement
Random data file
Sequential data file
With/End With statements
Write # statement

INTRODUCING THE STATE INFORMATION PROJECT

STEP 1. Understand the Problem.

When you first run STATES.EXE (Figure 13.01), a List Box appears containing an alphabetized list of the states of the United States, along with the state abbreviation, state capital, the year the state was admitted to the Union, and the state population according to the 1990 census. The Help menu item displays a Message Box, which explains the program's functionality. You can choose a different sort order by selecting from the Combo Box's drop-down list (Figure 13.02); you can change a state's population by clicking the state information line in the List Box; and you can save the updated state information by clicking the Save button.

One note about the display: As designed, the ListBox control uses a nonproportional font (Courier) so that the list of items appears in neat columns. However, if this font is not installed on your computer, the system-assigned substitute font may be proportional instead, in which case the data display will not be properly aligned.

The central new coding feature in this chapter is the use of a sequential data file for storing information provided by the user during program execution. The data file used by this application, STATES.DAT (Figure 13.03), is a text file that you can view or modify with any text editor or word processor. (Don't modify STATES.DAT, if you want STATES.EXE to run correctly! If you do accidentally

State Name	Abbrev.	Capital	Year in US	Population
alabama	al	montgomery	1789	1,099,999
alaska	ak	juneau	1959	550,000
arizona	az	phoenix	1912	2,450,000
arkansas	ar	little rock	1830	1,678,000
california	ca	sacramento	1866	34,000,000
colorado	co	denver	1878	2,789,000
connecticut	ct	hartford	1792	3,890,000
delaware	de	dover	1789	1,500,000
florida	fl	tallahassee	1838	12,000,000
georgia	ga	atlanta	1789	2,500,000
hawaii	ha	honolulu	1962	2,000,000
idaho	id	boise	1880	1,245,333
illinois	il	springfield	1818	10,000,000

FIGURE 13.01 *State Information—opening screen*

State Name	Abbrev.	Capital	Year in US	Population
alabama	al	montgomery	1789	1,099,999
alaska	ak	juneau	1959	550,000
arizona	az	phoenix	1912	2,450,000
arkansas	ar	little rock	1830	1,678,000
california	ca	sacramento	1866	34,000,000
colorado	co	denver	1878	2,789,000
connecticut	ct	hartford	1792	3,890,000
delaware	de	dover	1789	1,500,000
florida	fl	tallahassee	1838	12,000,000
georgia	ga	atlanta	1789	2,500,000
hawaii	ha	honolulu	1962	2,000,000
idaho	id	boise	1880	1,245,333
illinois	il	springfield	1818	10,000,000

FIGURE 13.02 *State Information—sort order dropdown list*

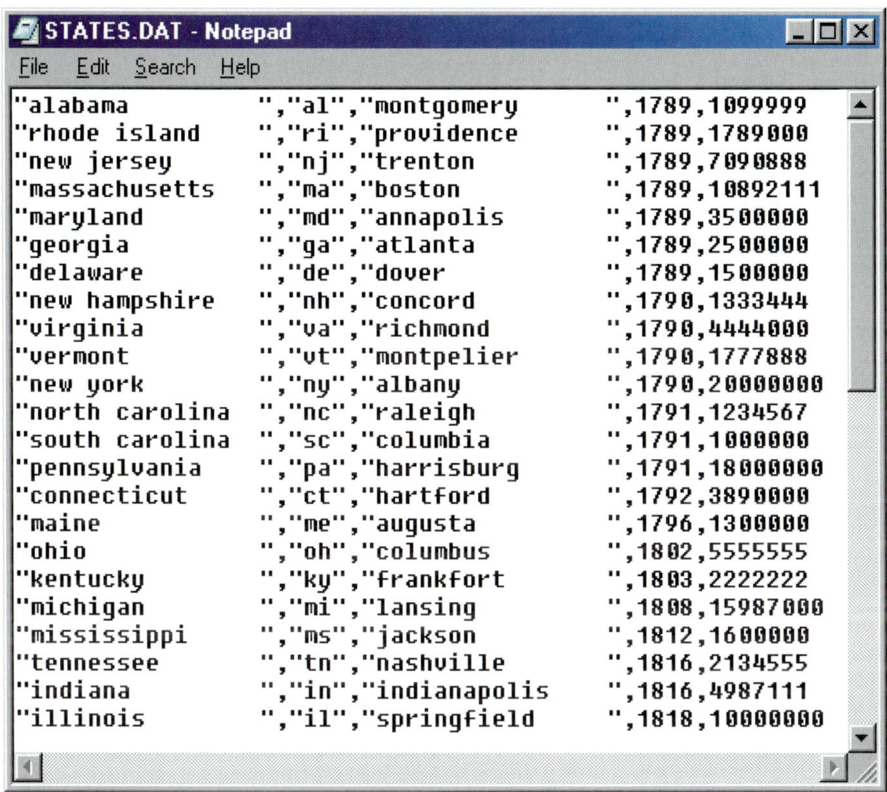

STATES.DAT - Notepad

File Edit Search Help

```
"alabama        ","al","montgomery     ",1789,1099999
"rhode island   ","ri","providence     ",1789,1789000
"new jersey     ","nj","trenton        ",1789,7090888
"massachusetts  ","ma","boston         ",1789,10892111
"maryland       ","md","annapolis      ",1789,3500000
"georgia        ","ga","atlanta        ",1789,2500000
"delaware       ","de","dover          ",1789,1500000
"new hampshire  ","nh","concord        ",1790,1333444
"virginia       ","va","richmond       ",1790,4444000
"vermont        ","vt","montpelier     ",1790,1777888
"new york       ","ny","albany         ",1790,20000000
"north carolina ","nc","raleigh        ",1791,1234567
"south carolina ","sc","columbia       ",1791,1000000
"pennsylvania   ","pa","harrisburg     ",1791,18000000
"connecticut    ","ct","hartford       ",1792,3890000
"maine          ","me","augusta        ",1796,1300000
"ohio           ","oh","columbus       ",1802,5555555
"kentucky       ","ky","frankfort      ",1803,2222222
"michigan       ","mi","lansing        ",1808,15987000
"mississippi    ","ms","jackson        ",1812,1600000
"tennessee      ","tn","nashville      ",1816,2134555
"indiana        ","in","indianapolis   ",1816,4987111
"illinois       ","il","springfield    ",1818,10000000
```

FIGURE 13.03 *Contents of States.dat data file*

damage STATES.DAT, you have also been given a backup copy, called STATES.BAK.) To view the STATES.DAT file, open it in Notepad or any text editor or word processor.

STEP 2. Design a Solution.

Sequential Data Files

In terms of their internal file organization, data files can appear in a number of different file formats. Ever since Chapter Ten, we have been using data stored in a Database Management System. While many such DBMSs exist, sometimes a Visual Basic programmer, for a variety of reasons, may choose to use one of the earlier, simpler file organization schemes. In this chapter, we present the simplest of these schemes, a sequential data file; at the end of the chapter, we also look briefly at a random data file. A sequential data file consists of records that are stored in a serial or sequential fashion from beginning to end, and that must be retrieved from the file in exactly the same order in which they were written to the file. Thus if you open a sequential data file that contains the feeding habits of all the animals in the zoo in alphabetical order, and you are most interested in reading about zebras, there is no way to go directly to the record concerning zebras—you must read through the records pertaining to aardvarks, baboons, chimpanzees, . . . , and yellow-bellied sapsuckers before arriving at the record for zebras. Such files are typically stored as flat ASCII files, also called text files. That is, the data are stored as individual characters coded according to the American Standard Code for Information Interchange (ASCII).

Like a table in a DBMS, a sequential file is usually made up of records, and each record is subdivided into fields. To distinguish where fields begin and end within a record, one can use either fixed-length fields or a specific delimiter (a comma, a space, or quotation marks) to separate the fields. Our sample State Information Project is comma-delimited. Additionally, since string information sometimes includes internal commas (such as the name "John Jones, Jr."), string data are also enclosed in quotation marks.

Visual Basic's statements and functions dealing with sequential data files include the following:

- Open statement
- Close statement
- Kill statement
- Write # statement
- Input # statement
- Input() function
- Line Input # statement
- EOF() function

Open Statement

The first step in using a sequential data file is to Open the file, which makes it available for processing. The **Open statement** is in the form

```
Open <filename> For <filemode> As #<filenumber>
```

where

filename is the name of the file, including its complete path if the file is stored on a disk drive or in a directory different from the VB application.

filemode is either Input, Output, or Append:

Input—if the file already exists and your program will read (input) data from this file to use in processing,

Output—if your program will create this data file and write data out to it, or

Append—if the file already exists but your program will add data to it, writing (appending) new data at the end of the existing file.

filenumber is an integer that is assigned to a data file in the Open statement and is then used by all of the other file-related statements and functions. The filenumber is not part of the file, nor is it stored on the disk. It is only used within a VB program that uses a data file. The filenumber remains associated with the data file for only so long as the file remains open.

Write # Statement

The **Write # statement** writes data out to a file that has been opened in Output or Append filemode. The format is

```
Write #<filenumber>, <expressionlist>
```

where

filenumber is the integer assigned to the file in the Open statement, and *expressionlist* is a list of one or more expressions, separated by commas.

The values in the expression list will be copied to the file, separated by commas. String values will be enclosed in quotation marks. A carriage return/newline will be written to the file following the last expression in the Write # statement.

Input # Statement

The **Input # statement** is used to retrieve data from a file that has been opened in Input filemode. The format is

```
Input #<filenumber>, <variablelist>
```

where *variablelist* is a list of one or more variables, separated by commas. Data values will be retrieved from the data file and assigned to the variables in the variable list in sequence.

Close Statement

The **Close statement,** the complement to the Open statement, is used to end the processing of data in a file. The Close statement releases the filenumber; subsequently, the same file can be opened with the same or a different filenumber, or the same filenumber could be used to open a different file. If the file was opened in Output or Append mode, the Close statement also writes an end-of-file (EOF) mark after the last record in the file. Its simple form is

```
Close #<filenumber>
```

Kill Statement

When you are through using a file forever and wish to erase it rather than just Close it, the **Kill statement** accomplishes this purpose. However, the file must not be open by Visual Basic when you Kill (erase) it:

```
Kill <filename>
```

To try out these file-related statements, start up a new project, and insert this code into the Form_Click event procedure:

```
Private Sub Form_Click ()
Dim i As Integer, j As Integer, x As String
Open "MYDATA" For Output As #1
For i = 1 To 5
   Write #1, i, "Message number"
Next i
Close #1
Open "MYDATA" For Input As #2
For i = 6 to 10
   Input #2, j, x
   Print x; j
Next i
   Close #2
End Sub
```

Then run the project and click the form (Figure 13.04).

EOF() Function

In many real-world programming situations, the programmer cannot know how many data values or records are in a sequential file. Accordingly, you cannot usually employ a For/Next loop to read through all of the data in the input file.

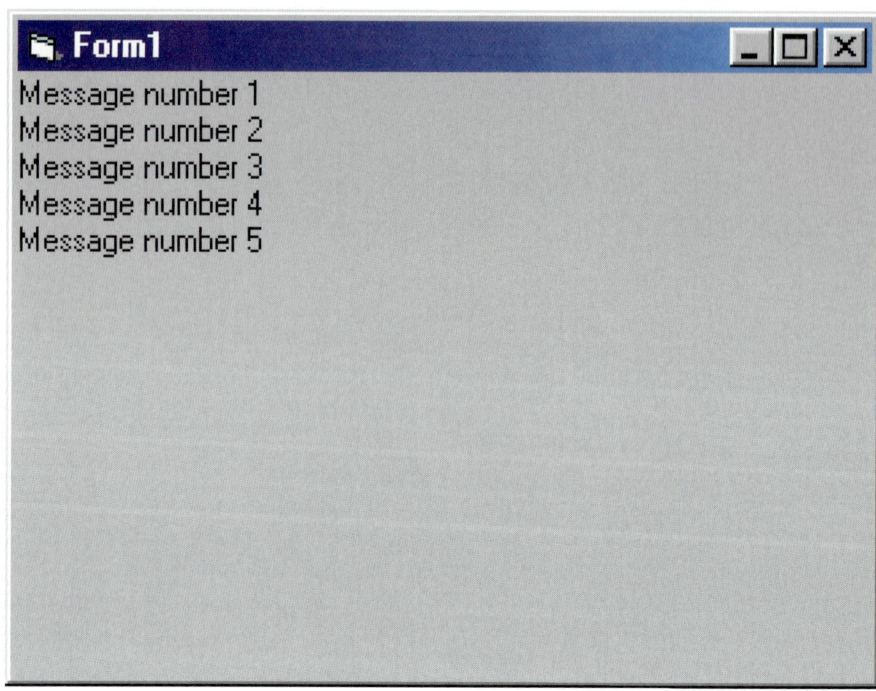

FIGURE 13.04 *Creating and then reading a sequential data file*

Rather, you need to check before each Input # statement to find out whether you have reached the EOF mark on the file. VB has a built-in **EOF() function** that tests for the end-of-file mark. The function's form is

```
EOF(filenumber)
```

and it returns True if the data pointer into the file is currently pointing at the EOF mark. Normally, the input of an unknown number of records is accomplished by building a "Do Until EOF(filenumber)" loop, with statements inside the loop which input the data from the file and then process that data. Hence, you can rewrite the Form_Click event procedure as follows:

```
Private Sub Form_Click ()
    Dim i As Integer, j As Integer, x As String
    Open "MYDATA" For Output As #1
    For i = 1 To 5
        Write #1, i, "Message number"
    Next i
    Close #1
    Open "MYDATA" For Input As #8
    Do Until EOF(8)
        Input #8, j, x
        Print x; j
    Loop
    Close #8
End Sub
```

Line Input # Statement and Input() Function

The Input # statement accepts input from the file, beginning with the byte (character) to which the data pointer is currently pointing, and up to an end-of-data-value byte (which could be a comma, a carriage return/newline, or a close quotation marks if the data value started with an open quotation marks). In some situations, such as reading data in a text file, commas are placed in the middle of lines, and the portion of a line delimited by a comma does not match the requisite logic of a program. Accordingly, programmers may need an input statement that accepts an entire line from a data file as one data value, without respect to any internal punctuation—commas, quotation marks, or anything else. The **Line Input # statement** handles this situation. In our sample program, we could substitute a Line Input # statement. Note that the entire line of input is assigned to the string variable x, and that only x is printed.

```
Do Until EOF(1)
    Line Input #1, x
    Print x
Loop
```

The result is that the entire line (including the quotation marks and comma, which are really stored as part of the data file) is assigned to x and then printed to the screen. Of course, if you want to process the data contained within the String x, then you will have to incorporate the logic to parse that string into its component pieces.

A most handy use of the record type occurs when we need to sort the records into one of four sort orders (by state name, by capital, by year, or by population). Table sorting is discussed in the next section.

Sometimes a VB program needs to read the data in a free-form input file, without regard to the type of data present in the file. A good technique for accomplishing that is the **Input(1,#n) function,** which reads and returns one byte from filenumber n.

```
Dim x As String * 1
x = Input(1, #2) - assumes filenumber 1
```

User-Defined Type (UDT) to Represent a Record

A fairly common method of manipulating records from a sequential data file in a computer program is to declare a user-defined data structure that represents the layout of one record in the sequential file. If the data file is small enough, the entire file can be loaded into an array of the user-defined type. The State Information Project is a good candidate for this technique because 1) each record in the data file is in the same format, and 2) the application requires that all of the records be displayed in the ListBox in four different sequences (sorted by state name, by state capital, by year of admission to the Union, and by population). This requirement is most easily satisfied by loading all of the records into an array, and then sorting the array as needed. Here are the necessary declarations, which must be placed in a Standard Module (.BAS file):

```
Type StateInfoType
    strStateName As String * 16
    strAbbreviation As String * 2
    strCapital As String * 16
    intYear As Integer 'admission to the Union
    lngPopulation As Long '1990 census
End Type
'g=global, udt=user-defined type, a=array
Global gudtStateRec As StateInfoType
Global gaudtStatesTable(60) As StateInfoType
```

Unfortunately, the Basic language has not defined a record-level input/output operation for a sequential data file, so the individual elements within the file must be read into the program one at a time. In this case, we chose to load the individual elements of each record into the elements of a UDT variable (gudtStateRec). Then, after the record has been retrieved from the data file, we assign the record to an element of a UDT array (gaudtStatesTable):

```
Open "C:\VBStudent Demos\Chap13\States.dat" For Input As #1
Do Until EOF(1)
   Input #1, gudtStateRec.strStateName, _
      gudtStateRec.strAbbreviation, _
      gudtStateRec.strCapital, _
      gudtStateRec.intYear, _
      gudtStateRec.lngPopulation
   i = i + 1
   gaudtStatesTable(i) = gudtStateRec
   Loop
Close #1
mintNumRecs = i
```

With/End With Statements

When you need to reference a particular object or user-defined data structure repeatedly, your code can be shortened and simplified by incorporating the With and End With statements. The **With statement** identifies an object or data structure that will be referenced in the block of subsequent code; the **End With statement** marks the end of that block.

For example, a procedure might be needed to position an Image control (Image1) in the middle of the form, half as wide/tall as the form itself. The first code segment below accomplishes this task without With; the second code segment accomplishes the same task with With.

```
'Code segment 1
Image1.Width = Me.Width / 2
Image1.Height = Me.Height / 2
Image1.Left = (Me.Width - Image1.Width) / 2
Image1.Top = (Me.Height - Image1.Height) / 2

'Code segment 2
With Image1
   .Width = Me.Width / 2
   .Height = Me.Height / 2
   .Left = (Me.Width - .Width) / 2
   .Top = (Me.Height - .Height) / 2
End With
```

Exactly the same efficiency can be achieved with a user-defined structure. The code for retrieving data from the States data file could be rewritten as follows:

```
Open "C:\VBStudent Demos\Chap13\States.dat" For Input As #1
With gudtStateRec
   Do Until EOF(1)
      Input #1, .strStateName, .strAbbreviation, _
      .strCapital, .intYear, .lngPopulation
```

```
        i = i + 1
        gaudtStatesTable(i) = gudtStateRec
    Loop
End With
Close #1
mintNumRecs = i
```

In similar fashion, the code for rewriting the States data file could be revised as follows:

```
Open "C:\VBStudent Demos\Chap13\States.dat" For Output As #1
For i = 1 To mintNumRecs
    With gaudtStatesTable(i)
        Write #1, .strStateName, .strAbbreviation, _
        .strCapital, .intYear, .lngPopulation
    End With
Next i
Close #1
```

Sorting a Table

Because computers spend such a large percentage of their processing cycles sorting data for one purpose or another, computer scientists have devoted an enormous amount of energy coming up with better ways of doing it. A table-sorting algorithm that is both perfectly simple to understand and to code and perfectly efficient in its execution has yet to be developed. Rather, we have about a dozen popular schemes, which vary from highly inefficient but easy to implement on the one hand, to highly efficient but hard to understand or implement on the other hand. The scheme we present here is among the least efficient, but it is pretty easy to understand. Further, you are only sorting at most 60 records in the State Information Project, and you are using a fairly fast processor since you are running Windows 95 to begin with. Therefore, this sorting routine is adequate for the task at hand (it takes less than a second on an old Intel-486–equipped laptop).

We wanted to write a single sort routine to handle all four sorting situations: sorting the table by state name, by capital, by year, and by population. For that reason, we begin the sort routine by copying the key sort field (called the sortkey) to an array called vntSortKey, created to be of the exact size as the active records in our table. The ReDim statement declares vntSortKey to be of type Variant, because the sortkey itself could be a string (strStatename or strCapital), an integer (intYear), or a long integer (lngPopulation). In this way, the variant array vntSortKey can accept any kind of elementary data. We use a Select Case statement to put the correct sortkey field from gaudtStatesTable into the vntSortKey table:

```
ReDim vntSortKey(mintNumRecs)
Dim i As Integer
For i = 1 To mintNumRecs
    Select Case cbo.Text
        Case "State Name"
            vntSortKey(i) = gandtStatesTable(i).strStateName
        Case "Capital"
            vntSortKey(i) = gandtStatesTable(i).strCapital
        Case "Year"
```

```
            vntSortKey(i) = gaudtStatesTable(i).intYear
        Case "Population"
            vntSortKey(i) = gaudtStatesTable(i). _
            lngPopulation
    End Select
Next i
```

Next, as to the sorting algorithm itself, this sort routine belongs to the class of simple sorts known as exchange sorts. All sort routines depend on successive comparisons between two elements in the table. In an exchange sort, if two compared elements are not properly sequenced in the table with respect to each other, then their positions in the table are reversed. That is to say, we compare sortkey(i) with sortkey(j); if these two values are not properly positioned with respect to each other, then the value stored in sortkey(j) is placed in sortkey(i), and the value in sortkey(i) is placed in sortkey(j). To do this requires an additional storage location, which will temporarily hold the value of sortkey(i) while sortkey(j) is assigned to sortkey(i), after which the temporary variable's value is assigned to sortkey(j):

```
If vntSortKey(i) > vntSortKey(j) Then
    Dim vntSortHold
    vntSortHold = vntSortKey(i)
    vntSortKey(i) = vntSortKey(j)
    vntSortKey(j) = vntSortHold
```

The vntSortKey table is only a copy of the key field in the table to be sorted, so reversing the contents of two elements in vntSortKey does not automatically reverse the contents of the records in the original table. Therefore, we need the following coding as well.

```
    gudtStateRec = gaudtStatesTable(i)
    gaudtStatesTable(i) = gaudtStatesTable(j)
    gaudtStatesTable(j) = gudtStateRec
End If
```

In this particular version of the exchange sort (there are many versions), the algorithm works like this (see the table below):

- Consider a table of five records. For any table of n records, we will pass through the table n – 1 times. Therefore, we will pass through this table four times.
- On the first pass, each element of sortkey from element 1 to 4 (which we will call sortkey(i)) is compared with element 5 (which we will call sortkey(j)); since we are sorting in ascending order, whenever sortkey(i) > sortkey(j), the elements need to be reversed.
- When the first pass is completed, element 5 must contain the highest value in the table, so we need not consider this element again. On the second pass through the table, elements 1 through 3 are compared with element 4, again reversing the contents whenever sortkey (i) > sortkey (j). At the end of this pass, element 4 contains the second-highest value in the table.
- On the third pass, we compare elements 1 through 2 with element 3; similarly, this guarantees that element 3 contains the correct value.
- On the fourth pass, we compare element 1 with element 2; this places the correct value in element 2, and, since all of the positions save the first position are occupied correctly, element 1 must contain the least value in the table.

ORIGINAL TABLE	FIRST PASS	SECOND PASS	THIRD PASS	FOURTH PASS	FINAL TABLE
SAM	GEORGE	ANN	ANN	ANN	ANN
BILL	BILL	BILL	BILL	BILL	BILL
MARY	MARY	GEORGE	GEORGE		GEORGE
ANN	ANN	MARY			MARY
GEORGE	SAM				SAM

The following code implements this logic in the State Information Project.

```
For j = mintNumRecs To 2 Step -1
    For i = 1 To (j - 1)
        If vntSortKey(i) > vntSortKey(j) Then
            vntSortHold = vntSortKey(i)
            vntSortKey(i) = vntSortKey(j)
            vntSortKey(j) = vntSortHold
            gudtStateRec = gaudtStatesTable(i)
            gaudtStatesTable(i) = _
             gaudtStatesTable(j)
            gaudtStatesTable(j) = gudtStateRec
        End If
    Next i
Next j
```

Mouse Movements

Visual Basic applications can be visually enhanced through creative use of mouse-related properties, events, and methods. We have seen the MousePointer property, whose settings determine the icon representing the mouse on the screen.

The following keywords relate to mouse movements and events but are not needed directly for this sample project. (You can, of course, include them in your code to create an improved project.) To obtain a more complete understanding of mouse-related keywords, you should read about these topics in the Visual Basic Help screens and experiment with them.

- **Drag method**—Use this method to pick up and drag a control to a new position.
- **DragDrop event**—At the end of an automatic or manual drag operation, when the mouse button is released, the DragDrop event takes place.
- **DragIcon property**—This property determines the icon that represents an object during a drag operation.
- **DragMode property**—This property determines whether drag operations are automatic (initiated by the user with a mouse click). If this setting is manual, then drag operations can only be initiated with the Drag method.
- **DragOver event**—This event occurs when a drag-and-drop operation is in progress.
- **MouseDown event**—This event occurs once when a mouse button is pressed.
- **MouseMove event**—This event takes place continually as the user moves the mouse. Parameters passed to the procedure indicate whether the left, middle, or right mouse button is currently pressed, whether the shift, control, or alt key is currently pressed, and the X-Y coordinates of the current mouse position.
- **MouseUp event**—This event occurs once when a mouse button is released.

Mouse movement and status events occur for an object when the mouse is within its borders, unless the event is trapped by another object. For example, the

MousePointer property on the form is in effect whenever the mouse is pointing inside that form; but if a control in that form also has a non-default MousePointer property setting, then the control's MousePointer takes precedence whenever the mouse is within the control's borders. You can use this characteristic to trap only the events you wish to trap. For example, you could program the DragOver event for an object to do something during a drag-and-drop operation only when the mouse is pointing to a valid DragDrop location.

STEP 3. Develop an Algorithm.

See the Hierarchy Table in Figure 13.05.

```
HIERARCHY TABLE-STATE INFORMATION

Project:   States (States.vbp)
Form:      frmStates (States.frm)
           Form level variable:
              mintNumRecs-assigned to the number of records in States.dat
           General procedure:
              Sub SortTable
           Click event procedures:
              cbo
              cmdQuit
              cmdSave
              lst
              mnuHelp
           Other event procedures:
              Form_Load
Standard Module: States 1 (States.bas)
           Public declarations:
              Type StateInfoType
              Public gudtStateRec As StateInfoType
              Public gaudtStatesTable(60) As StateInfoType
```

FIGURE 13.05 *Hierarchy Table—State Information*

STEP 4. Build Your GUI.

OBJECT	PROPERTY	SETTING
Form	Name	FrmStates
	Caption	State Information
CommandButton	Name	CmdQuit
	Caption	Quit
CommandButton	Name	CmdSave
	Caption	Save
ComboBox	Name	Cbo
	Text	State Name
ListBox	Name	Lst
Label	Name	LblHeaders
	Caption	State Name Abbrev Capital Year in U.S. Population
Label	Name	Label1
	Alignment	Center
	Caption	Sort Order
Menu	Name	MnuHelp
	Caption	&Help

STEP 5. Write the VB Code.

```
frmStates (States.frm)
States.BAS (Standard Module)
Option Explicit

Type StateInfoType
   strStateName As String * 16
   strAbbreviation As String * 2
   strCapital As String * 16
   intYear As Integer 'admission to the Union
   lngPopulation As Long '1990 census
End Type
'g=global, udt=user-defined type, a=array
Global gudtStateRec As StateInfoType
Global gaudtStatesTable(60) As StateInfoType

Option Explicit
Dim mintNumRecs As Integer
Private Sub cbo_Click()
   Call SortTable
End Sub

Private Sub cmdQuit_Click()
   End
End Sub

Private Sub cmdSave_Click()
   Dim strStateFile As String
   Dim i As Integer
   If Right$(App.Path, 1) = "\" Then
      strStateFile = App.Path & "STATES.DAT"
   Else
      strStateFile = App.Path & "\STATES.DAT"
   End If
   Open strStateFile For Output As #1
   For i = 1 To mintNumRecs
      With gaudtStatesTable(i)
         Write #1, .strStateName, _
         .strAbbreviation, .strCapital, .intYear, _
         .lngPopulation
      End With
   Next i
   Close #1
End Sub

Private Sub Form_Load()
   Dim strStateFile As String
   Dim i As Integer
   If Right$(App.Path, 1) = "\" Then
      strStateFile = App.Path & "STATES.DAT"
   Else
      strStateFile = App.Path & "\STATES.DAT"
   End If
   Open strStateFile For Input As #1
   With gudtStateRec
```

```
      Do Until EOF(1)
         Input #1, .strStateName, .strAbbreviation, .strCapital
         Input #1, .intYear, .lngPopulation
         i = i + 1
         gaudtStatesTable(i) = gudtStateRec
      Loop
   End With
   Close #1
   mintNumRecs = i
   cbo.AddItem "State Name"
   cbo.AddItem "Capital"
   cbo.AddItem "Year"
   cbo.AddItem "Population"
   Call SortTable
End Sub

Private Sub lst_Click()
   Dim i As Integer
   i = lst.ListIndex + 1
   gaudtStatesTable(i).lngPopulation = _
      Val(InputBox("Enter the population", _
      , Format(gaudtStatesTable(i).lngPopulation)))
   Call SortTable
End Sub

Private Sub mnuHelp_Click()
   Const MB_ICONINFORMATION = 64
   Dim msg As String
   Dim strNL As String
   strNL = Chr(13) & Chr(13)
   msg = "To change the sort order, click the down" & _
   "arrow under Sort Order and click the desired order."
   msg = msg & strNL & "To update a state's" & _
   "population, click the line containing that" & _
   "state's information."
   msg = msg & strNL & "To rewrite the file with" & _
   "the updated data, click the Save button."
   msg = msg & strNL & "To exit the program, click" & _
   "the Quit button."
   MsgBox msg, MB_ICONINFORMATION, "State" & _
   "Information -- Help"
End Sub

Private Sub SortTable()
   ReDim vntSortKey(mintNumRecs)
   Dim vntSortHold
   Dim i As Integer, j As Integer
   Dim strListRec As String
   For i = 1 To mintNumRecs
      Select Case cbo.Text
      Case "State Name"
         vntSortKey(i) = gaudtStatesTable(i).strStateName
      Case "Capital"
         vntSortKey(i) = gaudtStatesTable(i).strCapital
      Case "Year"
         vntSortKey(i) = gaudtStatesTable(i).intYear
```

```
        Case "Population"
            vntSortKey(i) = gaudtStatesTable(i).lngPopulation
    End Select
Next i
For j = mintNumRecs To 2 Step -1
    For i = 1 To j - 1
        If vntSortKey(i) > vntSortKey(j) Then
            vntSortHold = vntSortKey(i)
            vntSortKey(i) = vntSortKey(j)
            vntSortKey(j) = vntSortHold
                gudtStateRec = gaudtStatesTable(i)
                gaudtStatesTable(i) = gaudtStatesTable(j)
                gaudtStatesTable(j) = gudtStateRec
            End If
        Next i
    Next j
    lst.Clear
    For i = 1 To mintNumRecs
        With gaudtStatesTable(i)
            strListRec = .strStateName & .strAbbreviation _
            & "   " & .strCapital & _
            Str$(.intYear) & Right$(Space$(10) & _
            Format$(.lngPopulation, "#,#"), 13)
        End With
        lst.AddItem strListRec
    Next i
End Sub
```

STEP 6. Test and Debug.

One of the additional things you might do here to test your program is to open your data file in Notepad after running your program and saving a new set of data. See whether the data match your expected format.

STEP 7. Complete the Program Documentation.

INTRODUCING RANDOM DATA FILES

In additional to sequential data files, another traditional type of file organization is called a "random data file." The term *random* means not that the data itself are random or that the data are placed randomly on the disk; rather, it means that the order of processing of records in the file is random. Many modern computer applications would be inconceivable without some kind of random file processing. For example, an ATM device must retrieve the record for a particular customer. If we only had a sequential file to work with, customers would have to form a queue at the automated teller machine in checking account number sequence!

Visual Basic supports random data files consisting of fixed-length records. In the typical implementation, the programmer defines a record layout with the Type statement. The programmer then declares a record (a variable name) to be of the user-defined type. The difference for random files (as opposed to sequential files) is that this record can be directly written to or retrieved from the random data file, which makes input/output operations much less cumbersome, especially if the record layout is complex.

Records in the random data file are numbered consecutively, starting with record number 1. In the Open statement, the programmer declares the length of each record. Subsequent references to the file always specify a record number. The operating system identifies the location of that particular record on the disk as an offset to the location of the beginning of the file. For example, if the file starts at disk location 450, and if the record length is 100 bytes, then record number 3 is found at (3–1) * 100 = 450 + address 650.

The Get and the Put statements are used to read and to write records, respectively. Here is the syntax and a very simple example of a program that creates and then reads a random data file containing five records:

```
'RANDOM.BAS
Option Explicit
Type SampleType
   strStudentName As String * 30
   sngGPA As Single
End Type
Public gudtSampleRec As SampleType
Sub CreateRecords()
   Dim i As Integer
   ' in the next statement, Len=Len(gudtSampleRec)
   'means "The length of one record is equal _
   'to the length of gudtSampleRec."
   Open "MyFile" For Random As #1 Len=Len _
   (gudtSampleRec)
   For i = 1 To 5
      gudtSampleRec.strStudentName = InputBox("Enter Name of Student")
      gudtSampleRec.sngGPA = Val(InputBox("Enter GPA"))
      Put #1, i, gudtSampleRec 'write the record
   Next i
   Close #1
End Sub
Sub ReadRecord()
   Dim i As Integer
   Open "MyFile" For Random As #1 Len=Len _
      (gudtSampleRec)
   i = InputBox("Enter record number (1-5)")
   Get #1, i, gudtSampleRec  'randomly read a 'record
   Close #1
   Debug.Print "Record Number:"; i,
   Debug.Print gudtSampleRec.strStudentName,
   Debug.Print gudtSampleRec.sngGPA
End Sub
Sub Main()
   Call CreateRecords
   Call ReadRecord
   Call ReadRecord
End Sub
```

By the way, the above code works as a complete program. You do not need to have a form in a Visual Basic application. Instead, you can have a standard module that contains Sub Main, which will become the first procedure executed. Just select Sub Main as the Startup Form.

FreeFile Function

In many applications, users can cause multiple files to be open at the same time. To ensure that duplicate filenumbers are avoided, the filenumber used in an Open statement can be assigned with the help of the **FreeFile function,** which returns the next available (unused) filenumber.

For example, to Open MyFile in this way, you would use this model:

```
Dim n As Integer
n = FreeFile
Open "MyFile" For Random As #n Len=Len _
    (gudtSampleRec)
```

SUMMARY

A **sequential data file** contains a series of data values that can be accessed only in the same order in which they were created. The **Open statement** opens the file in **Input, Output,** or **Append modes.** A **filenumber** is assigned in the Open statement and remains associated with the file as long as it remains open. The **Write # statement** is used to add data values to a file opened in the Output or Append filemodes. The **Input # statement** reads data values from a sequential data file that was opened in **Input filemode.** The **Line Input # statement** reads an entire record from a sequential data file. The **Input(n,#m) function** reads n bytes from filenumber m. The **EOF function** tests for an end-of-file condition on a file opened for Input. The **Close statement** terminates file access and releases the assigned filenumber. The **Kill statement** erases a file from disk.

A common implementation involves the use of a sequential data file, a record layout for that file declared in a **user-defined data type,** and a table that holds all of the records in that file in memory during processing. If the file is sufficiently small, this technique affords rapid access to all of the data in the file. Further, the records in the file can be sorted in a table quite readily. A series of statements referencing a user-defined data type can be significantly shortened with the **With/End With statement.**

Mouse-related properties, events, and methods include **Drag, DragMode, DragIcon, DragDrop, DragOver, MouseDown, MouseUp, MouseMove,** and **MousePointer.**

Visual Basic supports random data files. Opening a file in Random filemode makes a random data file available for processing. The record layout of a random data file is always declared in a Type statement. The **FreeFile function** returns the next unused filenumber. The **Put statement** writes a record into a **random data file,** and the **Get statement** retrieves a record from a random data file.

Programming Assignments

Flags

Use Windows Explorer to copy these Visual Basic icon files (in the ICONS\FLAGS folder) to your floppy disk:

FLGASTRL.ICO	(the flag of Australia)
FLGAUSTA.ICO	(the flag of Austria)
FLGBRAZL.ICO	(the flag of Brazil)
FLGCAN.ICO	(the flag of Canada)
FLGDEN.ICO	(the flag of Denmark)
FLGFIN.ICO	(the flag of Finland)

Use Notepad to create the file A:\FLAGS.DAT, and type this text into it:

A:\FLGASTRL.ICO
A:\FLGAUSTA.ICO
A:\FLGBRAZL.ICO
A:\FLGCAN.ICO
A:\FLGDEN.ICO
A:\FLGFIN.ICO

(Because you may accidentally corrupt your FLAGS.DAT file while working on this project, use Windows Explorer to copy FLAGS.DAT to FLAGS.BAK, so that you never need to retype it.)

Put these controls on frmFlags (Figure 13.06):

A large vertical picture box down the right side of the form.

A control array (IMAGE1) of six image controls inside the picture box.

A vertical scroll bar next to the picture box (set max and value properties to 5).

A list box in the top middle of the form, large enough to hold FLAGS.DAT.

A fairly large image control (IMAGE2) under the list box.

Five command buttons, arranged vertically down the left side of the form. Note the captions, "File," "Go," "Stop," "Color," and "Exit." Initially, the "Go" button must be disabled.

Two shape controls towards the bottom and left of the form. Make one of them a yellow oval; make the other a blue circle.

A timer control, Interval set to 1000, and initially disabled.

Processing

When the "File" command button is clicked:

Open FLAGS.DAT

For each of the six records in FLAGS.DAT

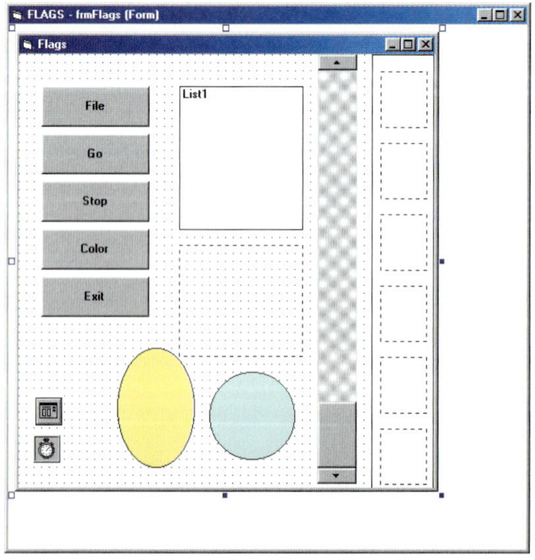

FIGURE 13.06 *frmFlags at design time*

input the record as a string.

add this string to List1.

use the LoadPicture method to load this string into the IMAGE1 array.

Enable the "Go" command button.

When the "Go" command button is clicked, enable the timer.
When the "Stop" command button is clicked, disable the timer.
When the "Color" command button is clicked:
Activate the common dialog button in color mode.
Change the background color of List1 to the user-selected color.
When the "Exit" command button is clicked, end the program.
When the timer event fires:
Increment the value of the scroll bar, but use the MOD function so that the value never reaches 6. That is, the value should cycle 0-1-2-3-4-5-0-1-2-3-4-5-0-1-2-3-4-5 forever.
Set the ListIndex property of List1 to the value of the scroll bar.
Set the picture property of IMAGE2 to the picture property of the IMAGE1 array element corresponding to the value of the scroll bar.

Basketball

(Note: We hail from Maryland, and so naturally we root for the University of Maryland's athletic teams to win over all of its rivals in the Atlantic Coast Conference. Feel free to adapt this design as you see fit.)

First, use Notepad to create a sequential data file called "TEAMS.DAT" and save it on your diskette. Place the following strings in this file (one per line) (these are the University of Maryland's opponents in the Atlantic Coast Conference):

Duke

North Carolina

North Carolina State

Wake Forest

Florida State

Virginia

Georgia Tech

Create a Visual Basic form that looks like Figure 13.07.

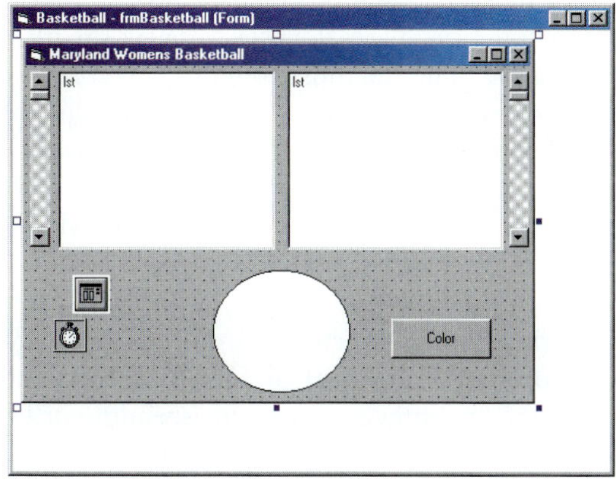

FIGURE 13.07 *frmBasketball at design time*

Set the Form Caption to "Maryland Women's Basketball." For each List Box, set the MousePointer property to an icon, and designate which icon it is with the DragIcon property; use a different icon for each List Box. The oval is a Shape Control; note the FillColor and FillStyle properties. Set the Timer Interval to 1 second. Both Scroll Bars have a minimum value of 0 and a maximum value of 100.

Write the Visual Basic code to accomplish these functions:

Open TEAMS.DAT at Form Load

When the Timer Event occurs:

input the next string from TEAMS.DAT and assign this value to mstrTeam.

using the RND function, randomly generate an integer between 50 and 100; this random number is Maryland's score.

using the RND function, randomly generate an integer between 40 and 90; this random number is mstrTeam's score.

the higher score is the winner. Put the winning score and the name of the winning school in List1; put the losing score and the name of the losing school in List2.

set the value of the left scroll bar equal to the winning score; set the value of the right scroll bar equal to the losing score.

disable the timer when you reach the end of the data file (test this with the EOF() function).

When the user clicks on the "Color" command button:

set the timer interval to 0.

using the Common Dialog control, allow the user to select a color.

fill the oval with the user-selected color.

set the timer interval to 1 second.

Paradigm for a Random Data File

Your program will have one form, the layout of which is up to you. Include a menu with four items entitled Create, Display One, Display All, and Exit. Listed below are the functions to be performed when each menu item is selected by the user.

Create. Create a random data file from these specifications:

a. The record layout (a user-defined data type) consists of one alphabetic character followed by five integers.
b. With the InputBox function, allow the user to select the filename.
c. Then build the data file. The file must contain 26 records, one for each letter in the alphabet. Each record contains a letter of the alphabet (A for the first record, B for the second record, . . . , Z for the last record) and five randomly generated integers in the range of 0 to 99.
d. Inform the user when the file creation is completed. While the file is being created, change the mousepointer to an hourglass.

Display One. Retrieve a user-selected record number. Display the alphabetic portion of the record in a Label control. Display the five integers in a Simple Combo Box, with the five integers sorted in ascending order.

Display All. Retrieve all of the records and display them in a List Box.

Exit. End the program.

Personnel

Create a VB application using a random data file (PERS.DAT). This application supports personnel functions for a small company.

The file is laid out as follows:

Employee ID number—integer in the range of 1 to 99

Last name

First name

Year of birth

Year of employment

Year of retirement eligibility

Year of actual separation

Starting pay (that is, first year's gross income)

Annual gross income (table of values for up to 50 years). Table includes

- Year
- Gross income

At the time that an employee record is created, the year of retirement eligibility is computed (the earlier of age 60 or 30 years' service). Also, the table of annual gross income is computed. By company policy, employees are given a 10 percent raise for each of the first 10 years of service, 5percent for each of the next 10 years of service, and 2percent for each year thereafter. However, no salary increase is given after age 70.

To compute retirement pay:

At the time of retirement, the employee must have worked for the company for at least five years. Otherwise, retirement pay = 0.

Retirement pay = (2% * years of service) * average annual gross income for the last three years of service.

The application should allow the user to

- add an employee;
- separate an employee;
- display, for a given employee, the annual pay for any given year, the year of retirement eligibility, and the retirement pay; and
- display the total retirement pay liability for the current year, assuming that all the employees would retire today. Include a detailed list of employees and each of their retirement pays, as well as a total.

Build records for 20 employees who have come to work for the firm during the last decade. Include five who separated with more than five years of service, one who separated with less than five years of service, and 14 of various ages and lengths of service who are still employed.

APPENDIX A
ASCII Codes

DEC	HEX	ASCII	DEC	HEX	ASCII	DEC	HEX	ASCII	DEC	HEX	ASCII
0	0		32	20	space	64	40	@	96	60	`
1	1		33	21	!	65	41	A	97	61	a
2	2		34	22	“	66	42	B	98	62	b
3	3		35	23	#	67	43	C	99	63	c
4	4		36	24	$	68	44	D	100	64	d
5	5		37	25	%	69	45	E	101	65	e
6	6		38	26	&	70	46	F	102	66	f
7	7		39	27	‘	71	47	G	103	67	g
8	8		40	28	(	72	48	H	104	68	h
9	9		41	29	)	73	49	I	105	69	I
10	A	linefeed	42	2A	*	74	4A	J	106	6A	j
11	B		43	2B	+	75	4B	K	107	6B	k
12	C		44	2C	‘	76	4C	L	108	6C	l
13	D	carriage ret	45	2D	-	77	4D	M	109	6D	m
14	E		46	2E	.	78	4E	N	110	6E	n
15	F		47	2F	/	79	4F	O	111	6F	o
16	10		48	30	0	80	50	P	112	70	p
17	11		49	31	1	81	51	Q	113	71	q
18	12		50	32	2	82	52	R	114	72	r
19	13		51	33	3	83	53	S	115	73	s
20	14		52	34	4	84	54	T	116	74	t
21	15		53	35	5	85	55	U	117	75	u
22	16		54	36	6	86	56	V	118	76	v
23	17		55	37	7	87	57	W	119	77	w
24	18		56	38	8	88	58	X	120	78	x
25	19		57	39	9	89	59	Y	121	79	y
26	1A		58	3A	:	90	5A	Z	122	7A	z
27	1B	escape	59	3B	;	91	5B	[	123	7B	{
28	1C		60	3C	<	92	5C	\	124	7C	|
29	1D		61	3D	=	93	5D	]	125	7D	}
30	1E		62	3E	>	94	5E	^	126	7E	~
31	1F		63	3F	?	95	5F	–	127	7F	

GLOSSARY

ActiveX Data Object (ADO)
Microsoft's current technology for managing local or remote databases. It replaces the earlier Data Access Objects (DAO) and Remote Data Objects (RDO) technologies.

ActiveX Data Object Data Control (prefix: adodc)
Represents an ActiveX Data Object. Provides access to a local or remote database.

Actual parameter
The variable, value, or expression used in a procedure or function call:

```
Call Sample(actual parameter)
```

Add watch
On the Tools Menu, opens a Window for designating an expression to be monitored in the Debug Window during execution.

AddItem method
In a ListBox or ComboBox control, adds an item to the list:

```
List1.AddItem item
```

AddNew method
In a Data control, adds a new empty record to the end of the Recordset, and makes that new record the current record:

```
Data1.Recordset.AddNew
```

Align property
Determines whether a control can appear anywhere on a form, or whether it is aligned with one border of the form (top, bottom, left, or right).

Alignment property
For a TextBox or Label control, indicates whether text is left aligned, right aligned, or centered. For an OptionButton or CheckBox control, indicates whether text appears to the left or to the right of the control.

App object
A global object which refers to the currently running application.

Append filemode
In an Open statement, the Append filemode indicates that data will be added to the end of an existing sequential data file:

```
Open sMyFile for Append As #1
```

Application
A use for computers; a computer program or project.

Application Wizard
A program that takes the programmer through a series of predefined steps to generate a shell or skeleton VB application.

Argument
Parameters passed to a function:

```
sngX = Sqr(argument)
```

Arithmetic expression
One or more constants and/or variables, separated by arithmetic operators, which is resolved at run time into a single numeric value.

Arithmetic operator
An operator which causes arithmetic to be performed between two operands in an arithmetic expression. The operators are + (addition), – (subtraction or negation), * (multiplication), / (floating point division), \ (integer division), ^ (exponentiation), and Mod (remainder operator).

Arrange Icons arrangement
On an MDI Form, using the Arrange method, groups all minimized child form icons at the bottom of the MDI Window:

```
MDIForm1.Arrange vbArrangeIcons
```

Arrange method
On an MDI Form, groups open child forms according to arrangement:

```
MDIForm1.Arrange arrangement
```

Asc function
Returns the ASCII code which represents the first character of the string argument:

```
intX = Asc("A") ' returns 65
```

ASCII codes
The 7-bit or 8-bit codes (usually expressed in decimal form) which represent characters. For example, the upper case alphabet is represented in ASCII by the codes 65 through 90.

Assembler
A program which translates a source program written in assembly language into an object program in machine language.

Assembly language
A machine-oriented, low-level programming language tied closely to the machine language for a processor or a family of processors.

Assignment statement
The most common type of statement in Visual Basic; assigns a value to a target:

```
curSalesTax = curTotalCost * SALESTAXRATE
```

Atn function
A function which returns the arctangent of a number in radians:

```
Print Atn(60)  'the result is 1.554131
```

AutoRedraw property
Causes a form to be automatically redrawn from memory as needed.

BackColor property
Establishes the background color of an object:

```
Me.BackColor = vbYellow
```

BackStyle property
For a Label or Shape control, indicates whether the backcolor is transparent or opaque.

BOF property
For a Data control, indicates whether the record pointer is currently pointing to the Beginning of the File (BOF):

```
If Data1.Recordset.BOF Then
Data1.Recordset.MoveNext
End If
```

Bookmark property
Uniquely identifies a record within a Recordset. Used to mark and subsequently locate a record. First, to mark the record, assign the bookmark to a Variant:

```
vntMyBookmark = db.Recordset.Bookmark
```

Later, to return to that record, assign the variable to the bookmark:

```
db.Recordset.Bookmark = vntMyBookmark
```

Boolean data type (prefix: bln)
A two-byte data type whose only possible values are True and False.

BorderColor property
For a Shape control, determines the color of the border. For a Line control, determines the color of the Line.

BorderStyle property
Determines the border style for an object—fixed position or sizable, single or double line, dots or dashes, or no border.

BorderWidth property
Width of the border.

Break time
The time during which a running program is suspended: when a program is running within the VB Development Environment, break time occurs if the user selects Run | Break, if a Breakpoint is encountered, or if an error occurs.

Breakpoint
A line designated by the programmer where a break will automatically occur.

Bug
A mistake in a program.

Byte data type (prefix: byt)
A one-byte data type, storing an unsigned binary value from 0 to 255.

ByVal parameter
Indicates that an argument is passed By Value:

```
Private Function TwiceMe(ByVal vsngInput As
  Single) As Single
```

Call statement
Calls (executes) a procedure. Arguments appear in parentheses after the procedure name. If the word Call is omitted, then the parentheses are omitted; however, the code executes more slowly. These two examples are the same:

```
Call MySub(Arg1, Arg2)
MySub Arg1, Arg2
```

Caption property
Determines the text displayed in or next to a control, or in the Title Bar of a Form.

Cascade arrangement
Within an MDI Form, cascades all open but non-minimized child forms.

Case construct
A multiple-selection structure which allows for the selection of one group of statements among many groups of statements, depending on the evaluation of an expression. Implemented in Visual Basic by the Select Case statement (viz.).

CCur function
Returns a currency value from a numeric argument:

```
Dim curCash As Currency
Dim sngFloat As Single
sngFloat = 1132.3456213
curCash = sngFloat
Debug.Print curCash, sngFloat
'result is: 1132.3456   1132.346
```

Change event
Fires when the contents of a control have changed. The specifics of what constitutes a change depends on the control. Applies to ComboBox, DirListBox, DriveListBox, HScrollBar, VScrollBar, Label, PictureBox, and TextBox.

Check Box control (prefix: chk)
Used to display a Yes/No or Boolean value. An X appears inside a tiny square when the value is selected or True; the X disappears when the value is non-selected or False.

Checked property
Determines whether a menu item has a checkmark which appears in front of it.

Choose function
Returns one value from a list of arguments. The selected choice depends on *Index*:

```
strName = Choose(Index, "Sam", "Alice",
  "Barbara", "Bill")
'if Index was 1, then "Sam" is returned; if
  Index was 2, then "Alice" is returned.
```

Chr function
Returns the character represented by the ASCII value of the argument. For example, the number 65 in ASCII represents a capital A:

```
Print Chr(65) 'prints "A"
```

Circle method
Draws a circle, ellipse, or arc on an object.

Clear method
Clears the contents of a ListBox, ComboBox, or the System Clipboard:

```
lst.Clear
cbo.Clear
Clipboard.Clear
```

Click event
Fires when the user presses and releases a mouse button while it is pointing to an object. Can also occur when the value of a control has changed.

Clipboard object
Provides access to the System Clipboard. SetData and SetText place information on the Clipboard, while GetData and GetText retrieve information previously placed onto the Clipboard:

```
Clipboard.SetText "New Information is at hand"
```

Close statement
For a file previously opened with an Open statement, ends input/output processing of that file and releases its filenumber.

Cls method
Clears graphics and text from a Form or PictureBox.

Col property
At run time only, returns or sets the column of a DBGrid control (used with the Row property for identifying or designating the Active Cell).

Color property
Returns or sets the selected color in a Common Dialog control using the ShowColor method.

ComboBox control (prefix: cbo)
A control which combines the features of a TextBox with a ListBox. The TextBox can contain an entry selected from the List or an entry typed in by the user. The List portion of the control can be a drop-down list or can be always visible.

Command Button control (prefix: cmd)
Used to start or end some process in code, usually by means of the Click event.

Common Dialog control (prefix: dlg)
Provides a set of six standard Dialog Boxes, activated through these methods: ShowColor, ShowFont, ShowHelp, ShowOpen, ShowPrinter, and ShowSave.

Compiler
Software which converts a program written in a higher level language (such as Visual Basic) into an object program, ready for linking and later execution.

ConnectionString property
Provides detailed information needed to establish a connection to a data source.

Const declaration
Declares a constant. By convention, constants are usually written in capital letters:

```
Const TAX_RATE = 0.125
```

Context-sensitive Help (F1)
Provides a relevant help screen to the programmer whenever the F1 key is depressed.

Control array
An array of controls, all identified by the same name, and sharing certain properties and procedures, and distinguished from each other by a unique Index value.

Control object
One of the graphical objects which can be placed on a Form.

Control structures
The way in which code statements control the sequence of execution of other statements. In structured programming, the permissible code structures are sequence, selection, and iteration.

Controls collection
The collection of all of the controls on a Form.

Copy
From the Edit Menu, copies the selected object or text to the System Clipboard.

Cos function
Returns the cosine of an angle, measured in radians. When a right triangle is formed including this angle, the cosine is defined as the adjacent side divided by the hypotenuse.

Count property
Determines the number of members in a Collection.

Currency data type (prefix: cur)
A currency-type (dollars and cents) value, stored as a 19-digit scaled integer in 8 bytes. Provides 15 digits to the left of the fixed-position decimal point, and 4 digits to the right of the decimal.

CurrentX property
At run time only, determines or sets the horizontal coordinate for the next printing or drawing method.

CurrentY property
At run time only, determines or sets the vertical coordinate for the next printing or drawing method.

Cut
From the Edit Menu, copies the selected object or text to the Clipboard, and removes the selected object or text from the current program.

Data control (prefix: db)
A control which provides access to a table of a Database. The control opens the Database and creates a Recordset of all of the records specified by the control's RecordSource property (which can specify a Table, a QueryDef, or an SQL-like query statement). Values in the current record are passed to bound controls. The Data control allows the user to scroll through the records in the Recordset.

Data Form Wizard
A program that takes the programmer through a series of predefined steps to generate a form that uses ActiveX Data Objects.

Data Project
A VB application that includes access to a database.

Database
A collection of one or more Tables, which in turn is used for storing and manipulating data.

Database object
An object that references a database within a VB application.

DatabaseName property
For a Data control, determines the path and name of the Database from which the RecordSource property specifies a Recordset.

DataChanged property
A Boolean value which indicates whether the data value in a bound control differs from the data in the current record.

DataField property
For a bound control, indicates the field in the Recordset to which the control is bound.

DataSource property
For a bound control, identifies the Data control to which the control is bound.

Date data type (prefix: dtm)
Stores the date and time in 8 bytes.

DateValue function
From a string argument in the format of a recognizable date, returns the numeric equivalent of that date as a variant.

DBCombo control (prefix: dbcbo)
A special ComboBox control bound to a Data control; automatically fills with a field from all of the records in the

Recordset to which it is bound. Also includes a Text box, for user entry of a value.

DBGrid control (prefix: dbgrd)
A control bound to a Data control; automatically fills with all of the fields in all of the records of the Recordset to which it is bound. Data are displayed in rows (representing records) and columns (representing fields), in a manner similar to a spreadsheet.

DBList control (prefix: dblst)
A control bound to a Data control; automatically fills with a field from all of the records in the Recordset to which it is bound.

DDB function
Returns the depreciation for the specified year of an asset, calculated according to the double-declining balance (DDB) method:

```
curDepreciation = DDB(curCostOfAsset,
  curSalvageValue, _
intAssetLifeInYears, intSpecifiedYear)
```

Debug object
The Debug object sends output to the Debug window at run time:

```
Debug.Print fMyValue
```

Declare statement
Specifies an external function, such as an Application Programming Interface (API) call.

DefaultExt property
For the CommonDialog control, sets the default filetype (filename extension):

```
dlg.DefaultExt = "TXT"
```

Delete method
For the Recordset of a Data control, deletes the current record:

```
dbMyDatabase.Recordset.Delete
```

Derivative math functions
Trigonometric functions that are derived from intrinsic functions.

Design time
The time during which the programmer is creating or modifying a Visual Basic application within the Visual Basic Development Environment.

Dim statement
Declares (dimensions) a local or module-level variable or a module-level array:

```
Dim sngTaxRate As Single 'local variable
Dim msngTaxRate As Single 'module level
  variable
Dim msngTaxTable(5) As Single 'module level
  array
```

Dimension
See Dim statement.

Directory List Box control (prefix: dir)
Displays directories and paths at run time, and allows the user to select a directory.

Do. . .Loop statement
An iteration control structure which executes a loop repetitively until a specified condition exists or while a specified condition is true. Both pre- and post-test conditions are supported:

```
Do
n = InputBox("Enter a number from 1 to 10")
Loop Until n > 0 And n < 11
```

DoEvents statement
Passes control to Windows so that pending Windows events can be processed.

Double data type (prefix: dbl)
An 8-byte data type for large or minuscule floating-point values. Supports about 15 digits of precision, and over 300 decimal places or trailing zeros.

Drag method
Used to control dragging of a control (begin, cancel, or end the dragging operation).

DragDrop event
Occurs at the end of a drag-and-drop operation.

DragIcon property
During a drag-and-drop operation, determines which mousepointer icon will be displayed.

DragMode property
Determines whether the user can initiate a drag-and-drop operation automatically by clicking the object, or whether the Drag method must be invoked from code.

DragOver event
During a drag-and-drop operation, used to determine when the Mousepointer points to an object, and to respond accordingly.

DrawMode
Determines the appearance of a Shape or Line control.

DrawStyle property
Determines the appearance of output from graphics methods (such as Line or Circle).

DrawWidth property
Determines the width of a line drawn by a graphics method.

Drive List Box control (prefix: drv)
A control which permits the user to select a disk drive at run time.

Drive property
For a Drive List Box, determines the selected drive.

DropdownCombo style
For a ComboBox control, provides both a dropdown list and an edit area.

DropdownList style
For a ComboBox control, provides only a dropdown list for user selection.

Duplicates allowed
When a new record is added to a Table, a record whose record key matches an existing record will be allowed.

Dynamic Link Library
An external file which contains procedures which can be called from within a VB program.

Dynaset recordsettype
An updatable set of records created from a Table, QueryDef, or SQL-like statement.

Edit Field
Synonym for a TextBox.

Edit method
Copies the current record to the copy buffer for editing:
```
db.Recordset.Edit
```

Edit Watch command
On the Tools Menu, opens a Window for modifying a Watch expression.

EditMode property
For a Data control, indicates the current state of editing:
```
Select Case db.EditMode
Case 0: Print "No edit in progress"
Case 1: Print "Edit pending"
Case 2: Print "AddNew pending"
End Select
```

Enabled property
A Boolean property; determines whether a control is available.

End Function statement
Must be the last statement in a Function procedure.

End Select statement
Completes the Select Case construct.

End statement
Stops execution of a program (terminates processing).

End Sub statement
Must be the last statement in a Sub procedure.

EOF (End Of File) function
When reading data from a sequential data file, indicates whether the next value in the file is the end-of-file mark.

EOF (End Of File) property
A Boolean property; indicates whether the current record position is after the last record in a Recordset.

Err function
Following a run time error, returns an error code which identifies the type of error.

Err object
Provides information about run time errors, including error number, description, and source.

Event
Something which occurs during run time and which can be trapped by VB code. VB objects are associated with trappable events. For example, the CommandButton control has a Click event.

Executable program
A computer program which can be run (executed) directly from Windows.

Exit For statement
Provides premature exit from a For loop:
```
For i = 1 to intNumCustomers
   If strSelectName = strCustomerName(i) Then
      intWinningNumber = mintCustomerNumber(i)
      Exit For
   End If
Next i
```

Exit Sub statement
Provides premature exit from a procedure. Used especially when a procedure has an error trap.

Exp function
Returns the natural logarithm e raised to the power of the argument. You can use Exp to see the value of e:
```
Print Exp(1)
```

Expression
Consists of one or more literals, constants, and variables, separated by operators:
```
strFirstName & " " & strLastName 'string
  expression
curSubtotal * (TAX_RATE + 1)    'numeric
  expression
```

Fields collection
The collection of all Fields in a Recordset object.

File List Box control (prefix: fil)
A control which lists all of the files in a specified directory and allows the user to select a file.

Filemode
Part of the Open statement for a traditional data file; identifies whether a file is being opened for Input, Output, Append, or Random:
```
Open "Sample" for Input As #2
```

FileName property
For a CommonDialog control or a File List Box control, indicates the path and filename of the user-selected file:
```
strFile = dlg.FileName
```

FillColor property
Determines the color used to fill in a Shape control, or a circle or box created with the Circle or Line graphics methods. If FillStyle is transparent, FillColor is ignored. This example draws a circle containing horizontal red lines on the form:
```
Me.FillColor = vbRed
Me.FillStyle = 2 'horizontal lines
Me.Circle (500,500), 400
```

FillStyle property
Determines the pattern which fills a Shape control, or a circle or box created with the Circle or Line graphics methods. (See FillColor above for an example.)

Filter property
For the CommonDialog control, identifies the filters which appear in the "List files of type..." ListBox. For example, the following statement sets the filters to text files or to all files:
```
CMDialog1.Filter = _
"Text files |*.txt|All files |*.*"
```

FilterIndex property
Specifies which filter is in use when the CommonDialog control first opens. Using the Filter property example above, the following sets the initial filter to "Text files":
```
CMDialog1.FilterIndex = 1
```

FindFirst, FindLast, FindNext, and FindPrevious methods
For a Data control, looks for the first (last, next, previous) record in the Recordset matching the specified criteria, and makes that record the current record:
```
db.Recordset.FindFirst "LastName = '" & _
  sSearchName & "'"
```

Flags property
For the CommonDialog control, sets a series of options. Different sets of Flag definitions apply to each type of Dialog Box.

Focus
The form or control which can receive mouse clicks and keyboard input "has the focus." Only one object has the focus at any one time.

Font object
Describes the FontName, FontSize, and other attributes of a display or printer font.

FontSize property
Determines the size of text displayed on a form or control.

For/Next loop
A looping control structure, in which a loop control variable (lcv) is incremented after each iteration of the loop until a limit value is exceeded:

```
For lcv = 1 To 10
Sum - Sum + lcv
Next lcv
Print lcv, Sum   'prints 11  55
```

ForeColor property
Determines the foreground color for the form or control:

```
txt.ForeColor = vbBlue 'text will appear in
  blue
```

Form object
The window or basic object for development of a graphical user interface.

Formal parameter
A parameter which appears in the heading and body of a Sub or Function procedure, and which serves as a stand-in for the actual parameter passed to the procedure at the time of the Sub or Function call.

Format function
Returns a formatted expression for screen display or printing, based on a value and a specified format:

```
Print Format(5.6, "Currency") 'prints $5.60
```

Frame control (prefix: fra)
A control which serves as a container for other controls. May also be used merely to draw a border around a group of controls.

FreeFile function
Returns the next available file number for a sequential or random data file.

Function
Performs a specific task and returns a value. A built-in function is part of the Visual Basic language. A Function procedure is a user-defined function whose definition constitutes a section of code in a VB project.

Function statement
Declares the name and arguments of a Function procedure. In this example, the Function MyFunc is Private, has a single integer argument which is passed by value, and returns a string:

```
Private Function MyFunc(ByVal vintArg As
  Integer) _
As String
```

FV function
The Future Value function returns the future value of an investment, based on a constant payment at a fixed interest rate for a specified period:

```
curFutureValue = FV(sngAnnualRate/12, intYears
  * 12, _
-curMonthlyPayment, curPresentValue, 0)
```

General object
The object in a form or module which contains module-level declarations and general procedures.

Get statement
For a random data file, retrieves record number intRecNum from random data file intFileNum and places that record in strPlace:

```
Get #intFileNum, intRecNum, strPlace
```

GetData method
Retrieves a picture from the Clipboard.

GetText method
Retrieves text from the Clipboard.

Global variable
Also called a Public variable; a variable which is accessible throughout a project.

GotFocus event
Occurs when the object receives the focus.

Graphical User Interface (GUI)
What the user sees while a Windows-based program is running.

Handles
Tiny squares at the corners and along the sides of a selected control during design time. Click and drag to resize the control.

Height property
Determines the height of an object.

HelpCommand property
Specifies the command to be displayed when the ShowHelp method is invoked in the Common Dialog control.

HelpFile property
Specifies the help file to be searched when the ShowHelp method is invoked in the Common Dialog control.

Hex function
A function which returns the hexadecimal equivalent of its decimal argument:

```
Print Hex(26)   'prints 1A
```

Hide method
Removes a form from the visible screen but leaves it in memory:

```
Me.Hide
```

Hierarchy Table
A table that lists all of the components in an application and displays their functional interrelationships.

Higher-level language
A computer programming language whose syntax is closer to the domain for which it was written rather than to the machine, and which usually contains many macros. Basic is a higher-level language.

Horizontal Scroll Bar control (prefix: hsc)
A horizontal, analog graphical device for representing integer values within a specified range.

Hungarian notation
A system for identifying the class of an object and the scope and type of a variable through an organized protocol of name prefixes.

Hypertext
Text which is linked to related text in another location and is visually identifiable. Clicking the hypertext item causes the related text to become visible.

Icon
A small pictorial representation (32 _ 32 pixels).

Icon property
Determines the bitmap which will serve as the icon for an object.

If/Then
A selection structure which determines whether or not an action or block of actions will be executed:

```
If A = 9 Then B = 5 'single-line-If statement
If A = 9 Then 'beginning of a block-If
  statement
B = 5   'first statement in block
C = 14  'second statement in block
End If  'end of a block-If statement
```

If/Then/Else
A selection structure which forces a choice between two actions or blocks of actions:

```
If A = 9 Then B = 5 Else C = 14 'single-line If
If A = 9 Then 'beginning of block-If
B = 5
Else
C = 14
End If   'end of block-If
```

IIF function
The Immediate If function is a functional selection structure with three arguments: the condition to be tested, the return value if the condition is true, and the return value if the condition is false. In this example, the message which appears depends on the value of the Boolean bGameWon:

```
MsgBox IIf(bGameWon, "Hooray!", "Too bad")
```

Image control (prefix: img)
Used to display a picture.

Immediate window
At break time, a window in which commands can be immediately executed.

Index
Specifies one control in a control array.

Infinite loop
See Loop, Infinite

Information hiding
The practice of hiding from higher-level modules the internal details of lower-level operations.

InitDir property
For a CommonDialog control, identifies the directory which will be used initially to list the files:

```
dlg.InitDir = "C:\Document\CompLit"
```

Input # statement
Retrieves data from a sequential data file. This example retrieves a number and a string from a file which was opened as file number 2:

```
Input #2, sngNumber, strString
```

Input function
Returns a specified number of bytes from the specified filenumber. This example retrieves one byte from file number 2:

```
strMyByte = Input(1, #2)
```

Input filemode
In an Open statement, specifies that a sequential data file will be used as input to a program.

InputBox function
Creates a dialog box containing a prompt, and returns the user-entered string:

```
intAge = Val(InputBox("Enter your age"))
```

Instantiation
Declaration or creation of one instance of a class:

```
Public gudtMyRec As MyRecType
```

Integer data type (prefix: int)
A two-byte whole number. Contains values in the range –32768 to 32767.

Interpreter
A systems software program which translates a single source language statement into machine language and immediately executes it, then goes on to interpret the next source language statement.

Interval property
For a Timer control, determines the number of milliseconds between Timer events.

ItemData property
For a ListBox or ComboBox control, an array of long integer values associated with the list items. In this example, a ListBox control's List property is loaded with employee last names for all active records in a 1000-record random data file; the corresponding record numbers are loaded into the ItemData property. NewIndex is used because the ListBox's Sorted property is True:

```
For intRecNum = 1 to 1000
  Get #1, intRecNum, gudtEmployeeRec
  If gudtEmployeeRec.blnActiveRec Then
    List1.AddItem gudtEmployeeRec.strLastName
    List1.ItemData(List1.NewIndex) = intRecNum
  End If
Next intRecNum
```

Iteration control structure
Any control structure which provides for looping. VB supports both internally controlled (For/Next) and externally controlled (Do) loops.

Jump
Any kind of transfer of control, such as GoTo, Call, or Hypertext links.

KeyAscii value
The ASCII value of a key on the keyboard.

KeyPress event
Occurs when a key is pressed on the keyboard.

KeyPreview property
Allows a form to trap KeyPress events before they are trapped by the control which has focus.

Kill statement
Erases a file.

Label control (prefix: lbl)
Used to display text on a form, which text cannot be changed by the user.

LargeChange property
The amount by which the Value property of a Scrollbar is changed when the Scrollbar area is clicked in between the Scrollbox and either arrow at the ends of the Scrollbar.

LastModified property
In a Data control, used to make the most recently modified record the current record. Contains the Bookmark of the most recently added or changed record:

```
db.Recordset.Bookmark =
  db.Recordset.LastModified
```

Left function
Returns the left portion of a string for n bytes:

```
strResult = Left("Robert", 3) 'strResult gets
  "Rob"
```

Left property
Determines the distance between the left edge of an object and the left edge of its container. This code, for example, aligns a form along the left edge of the screen:

```
Me.Left = 0
```

Len function
Returns the length of a string; specifies the length of one record in a random data file:

```
n = Len(strMyString)
Open strMyRandomFile For Random As #1 Len = 34
```

Line continuation character
An underscore preceded by a space at the end of a line of code; causes the statement to continue on the next line.

Line control (prefix: lne)
Used to draw a line on a form. The line's position is set by its X1, Y1, X2, and Y2 properties.

Line Input # statement
Retrieves an entire line from a sequential data file, regardless of internal punctuation:

```
Line Input #2, strLineOfText
```

Line method
Draws a line or box on a form. This example draws a red box (B) also filled (F) with the same color. The coordinates of the opposite corners are 200, 500 and 1000, 1500:

```
Line (200, 500) - (1000, 1500), vbRed, BF
```

Linker program
A systems software program which links an object module with predefined input/output routines in a dynamic link library (DLL file) in order to produce an executable program (EXE file).

List property
A string array of all of the items in a control's list portion. List(index) specifies one entry in a ListBox, ComboBox, DBList, or DBCombo control.

ListBox control (prefix: lst)
Used to display a list of data values, from which the user can select.

ListCount property
Identifies the number of items in a control's list portion.

ListField property
Identifies the source of data for these data-bound controls: Data Combo, Data List, DBCombo, and DBList.

ListIndex property
Contains the index of the selected item in a control's list portion.

ListView control (prefix: lv)
A control that provides a graphical view of a list of files or other items, similar to the right panel in Windows Explorer.

Load statement
Loads a form or control into memory:

```
Load MyForm
```

LoadPicture function
Loads a bitmap or other picture file into a form, PictureBox, or Image control:

```
img.Picture = LoadPicture("cars.bmp")
```

Local variable
A variable declared and only visible within a procedure:

```
Sub MyProc()
  Dim intLocVar As Integer 'dynamic local
    variable
  Static strLocArr(5) As String 'static local
    array
```

Log function
Returns the natural log of its argument:

```
X = Log(10) 'returns 2.302585
```

Logic error
A programming error which causes incorrect results (as opposed to a syntax error, which is a violation of the rules of the language, and a run time error, which causes a running program to abort).

Logical inch
The visual screen equivalent to a physical inch as it would appear on paper.

Long data type (prefix: lng)
A 4-byte numeric field which can hold whole numbers up to about +/−2 billion.

Loop, Infinite
See Infinite loop

LostFocus event
Occurs when an object which had the focus no longer has it.

Machine language
The binary language which the computer processor understands.

Macro
A statement in a programming language which stands for and is translated into many machine language statements.

Make <Project> command
Compiles a VB project into a pseudo-executable (or p-coded) file.

Max property
For a Horizontal or Vertical Scrollbar control, determines the maximum value of the Value property.

MDIChildForm property
Determines whether a form is an MDI Child Form.

MDIForm object (prefix: mdi)
A form which serves as a container for other forms (called MDI Child Forms).

Me object reference
The form in which the reference occurs:

```
Me.Height = Screen.Height
```

Menu control (prefix: mnu)
Creates a set of pull-down menus under the title bar of a form.

Menu Editor
The Window for creating a menu.

Method
An action which operates upon an object or which an object can perform.

Microsoft Flex Grid Control (prefix: msfg)
A control for displaying tabular data, such as a table of a database.

Min property
For a Horizontal or Vertical Scrollbar control, determines the minimum value of the Value property.

Mod operator
The "remainder" operator: determines the remainder of integer division:

```
Print 23 Mod 7  'prints 2
```

Module
A portion of a program. In VB, code which exists independent of any form. It may exist as a Standard Module, Class Module, or Property Module.

MouseDown event
Occurs when the user presses a mouse button while it is positioned over the object.

MouseMove event
Occurs when the user moves the mouse while it is positioned over the object.

MousePointer property
The shape of the icon which betrays the position of the mouse on the screen.

MouseUp event
Occurs when the user releases a mouse button which had been pressed while the mouse was positioned over the object.

MoveFirst, MoveLast, MoveNext, and MovePrevious methods
For a Data control, moves to the first (last, next, previous) record in the Recordset:

```
db.Recordset.MoveFirst
```

MsgBox function and statement
Displays a message in a Dialog Box and waits for the user to click a button. The MsgBox function also returns a value indicating which button the user clicked:

```
If MsgBox("Pick yes or no", vbYesNo) = vbYes
  Then
Print "You picked Yes"
Else Print "You picked No"
End If
```

MultiLine property
A Boolean property; determines whether text exceeding the width of a TextBox will be displayed on multiple lines or simply hidden beyond the border of the control.

Name property
Contains the name of an object.

NewIndex property
Contains the Index value of the most recently added item in a control's list portion.

Next sequential instruction
The feature of digital computers which causes the next instruction after the current instruction to be automatically executed as soon as the current instruction finishes executing.

NoMatch property
Following a Find operation on a Data control's Recordset, NoMatch is True if the Find operation failed; otherwise, NoMatch is False:

```
If db.Recordset.NoMatch Then Print "No match"
```

Object data type (prefix: obj)
Using the Set statement, a variable declared as type Object can be made to reference any VB object.

Object Browser (F2 key)
A Window in the VB Development Environment which lists all components in an application and all objects associated with the selected component.

Object program
The machine language program created by an assembler or compiler from a source (as written) program.

Object-Oriented Programming
A model of computer programming involving the manipulation of complex, functional objects rather than simpler forms of data.

OLE control (prefix: ole)
Used to make the capabilities of a foreign application available within a VB program.

On Error Goto statement
Establishes an error trap within a procedure.

Open statement
Opens a traditional (sequential or random) data file:

```
Open "MyFile" For Input As #1
```

Option Button control (prefix: opt)
Used to allow the user to select one of several options. Usually used in related sets. Only one Option Button within a container can be True at any one time, so selecting one as True sets all others to False.

Output filemode
Part of the Open statement, opens an empty sequential file so that data can be written to it.

```
Open "C:\Document\Out.dat" For Output As #3
```

Package and Deployment Wizard
A program which creates a set of distribution disks for a completed Visual Basic application.

Paint event
Occurs when part or all of a form becomes visible because another window which was hiding it is no longer in the way.

Paste
In the VB Development Environment, copies the contents of the Clipboard into the code window at the cursor position for text, or into the active container for a graphical object.

Path property
For the App object, Directory ListBox control, or File ListBox control, identifies the complete absolute path and drive name. In this example, the Directory and File ListBox paths are initialized to start with the application's path:

```
Dir1.Path = App.Path
File1.Path = App.Path
```

PathChange event
Occurs when the Path changes by setting the Path or Filename properties in code.

Pattern property
Determines the format of the filenames listed in a File ListBox:

```
File1.Pattern = "*.com; *.bat; *.exe"
```

PatternChange event
Occurs when the pattern of files listed in a File ListBox changes because the FileName or Pattern property is changed in code.

Picture Box control (prefix: pic)
Used to display a picture or to serve as a container for other controls.

Picture property
Determines which picture is displayed in a form, Image control, or PictureBox control.

Pixel (measurement scale)
One picture element.

Pmt function
Returns the monthly payment, given the monthly interest rate, number of months for the loan, and principal amount of the loan. This example gives the monthly payment on a 3-year, $9000 loan, at 13% interest:

```
Print Pmt(.13/12, 36, -9000, 0, 0) 'prints
  303.25
```

Point (measurement scale)
1/72 of a logical inch.

Point method
Returns the RGB color of a point on a form. If a form is red, then this prints the value 255:

```
Print Point (1,1)
```

Print method
Prints text on an object (form, Printer, or Debug Window):

```
Debug.Print "Sum = "; sngSum, "Count = ";
  intCount
```

Private statement
Limits the scope of a Sub or Function procedure or variable to the module in which it occurs.

Procedure
A block of code executed together.

Procedure step
During break time, executes one statement. If that one statement calls a procedure, then the entire procedure is executed.

Project Explorer window
In the VB Development Environment, lists all of the files which are contained in the current VB Project.

Properties window
Displays the properties (characteristics) of the currently selected graphical object.

Property
A characteristic of an object.

PSet method
Sets a specified point on an object to a given color. This example sets the point at the top left corner of the form to red:

```
Pset (0,0), vbRed
```

Pseudocode
Step-by-step representation of the logic inside a program or procedure, rendered in outline form. Also called structured English.

Public statement
Makes a declaration public or globally accessible throughout a project.

Put statement
Writes a record to a random data file:

```
Put #1, intRecNum, gudtEmployeeRec
```

QBColor function
From an integer argument in the range 0 to 15, returns the RGB color code.

Quick Watch command
At break time, displays the current value of the selected expression.

Randomize statement
Reseeds the random number generator. Use this statement so that a new sequence of random numbers is generated by the Rnd function every time the program runs.

ReadOnly property
Causes a Data control to open a Database in ReadOnly mode.

Recordset object
The set of records created when a Data control is opened.

RecordsetType property
Identifies the type of Recordset which a Data control creates: a Dynaset, a Table, or a Snapshot.

RecordSource property
Identifies the Table, QueryDef, or SQL-like statement which defines the source of records for the Recordset created by a Data control.

ReDim statement
Declares a dynamic array within a procedure:

```
ReDim intMyArray(10) As Integer
```

Refresh method
Re-creates a Data control's Recordset. Repaints a form or control:

```
db.Refresh
```

Relational expression
An expression that can be evaluated as True or False.

```
nNumberOfDependents > 0
cmdMath.Enabled
True
```

Relational operator
=, <, >, <=, >=, <>

RemoveItem method
For a ListBox or ComboBox control, removes a selected item from the list:

```
cbo.RemoveItem cbo.ListIndex
```

Reposition event
For a Data control, occurs after a record becomes the current record.

Resume statement
After an error has been trapped, resumes execution of the program or cancels error trapping.

RGB color scheme
The color coding scheme used by Visual Basic. The scheme consists of 3 hexadecimal values representing (on a scale from 00 to FF) the amount of blue, then green, and then red which make up a given color.

RGB function
Returns a long integer representing a color using the RGB color scheme. Given that the presence of all three colors in full intensity is white, the following makes the form's background color white:

```
Me.BackColor = RGB(255, 255, 255)
```

Right function
Returns the final *n* characters in a string:

```
Right("Robert", 4) 'returns "bert"
```

Rnd function
Returns a random fraction >=0 and <1. To generate a random number from 1 to 10 and assign it to intX:

```
intX = Int(Rnd * 10) + 1
```

Row property
At runtime, returns or sets the row of a DBGrid control (used with the Col property for identifying or designating the Active Cell).

RowSource property
In a DataCombo or DataList control, identifies the Data control that is the source for the data displayed in the bound control.

Runtime
The period during which a program is executing.

Runtime error
An error which interrupts execution, essentially directing the computer to do something it cannot do, such as divide by zero, open a file on a floppy with the disk drive door open, read past the end of a file, or reference an out-of-range subscript.

ScaleHeight, ScaleWidth properties
Sets a custom measurement scale for the vertical or the horizontal interior measurements of a container.

ScaleMode property
Sets the measurement scale to be used for internal measurements of a container.

Scope
The range of visibility and accessibility for a procedure, constant, or variable. Scope may be local to a procedure, form or module level, or global to the entire project. (See Dim, ReDim, Static, Private, and Public.)

Screen object
Used to access certain screen properties at runtime, especially height and width.

Scroll event
For a Vertical or Horizontal Scrollbar control, occurs when the user drags the scrollbox along the scrollbar.

ScrollBars property
For an MDIForm or TextBox control, specifies the presence or absence of scrollbars.

Select Case statement
A multiple selection structure. (See Case for a complete example.)

Selection control structure
A structure which permits the program to choose among alternative courses of action. In VB, the selection control structures are: If/Then, If/Then/Else, Select Case, and IIF (Immediate If).

Sequence control structure
The natural control structure, in which instructions are executed in the order in which they appear in a procedure.

Set statement
Assigns an object reference to an object variable. In this example, MyForm is declared as an object variable:

```
Dim MyForm As Form
Set MyForm = New Form1
MyForm.Caption = "see new form called MyForm"
MyForm.Show
```

SetData method
Copies a graphical object to the Clipboard:

```
Clipboard.SetData Image1
```

SetFocus method
Gives the focus to an object:

```
Text1.SetFocus
```

SetText method
Copies text to the Clipboard:

```
Clipboard.SetText "This goes in the Clipboard"
```

Sgn function
Returns the sign of its argument: 1 for a positive argument, 0 for a 0 argument, and –1 for a negative argument.

Shape control (prefix: shp)
Used to place a shape (rectangle, square, circle, oval, rounded square, or rounded rectangle) on a form.

Shape property
Determines which shape appears in a Shape control: rectangle, square, circle, oval, rounded square, or rounded rectangle.

Shell function
Executes a program:

```
intX = Shell("Notepad.exe",1) '1=normal window
```

Shortcut keys
Assigned to an item in a Menu control, a shortcut key provides a keyboard shortcut to using the menu drop-down list in order to select a menu item.

Show method
Displays a form.
```
frmAbout.Show
```

ShowColor method
For the Common Dialog control, displays the Color Dialog Box.

ShowFont method
For the Common Dialog control, displays the Font Dialog Box.

ShowHelp method
For the Common Dialog control, displays the Help File Dialog Box.

ShowOpen method
For the Common Dialog control, displays the Open File Dialog Box.

ShowPrinter method
For the Common Dialog control, displays the Printers Dialog Box.

ShowSave method
For the Common Dialog control, displays the Save File As Dialog Box.

SimpleCombo style
For a ComboBox control's Style property, displays the TextBox portion and List portion in a fixed size box (rather than as a drop-down list). The user can type in the edit area or make a selection from the list.

Sin function
Returns the sine of an angle measured in radians. The sine of a 45° angle:
```
Const PI = 3.141593
Print Sin(45 * (PI / 180)) 'prints .707106
```

Single data type (prefix: sng)
A four-byte data field containing a single precision floating point number. A Single provides approximately 7 digits of precision with up to 38 trailing zeros or preceding decimal places.

Single step
During break mode, executes one statement.

SizeMode property
Determines the display size of an image in an OLE container control.

SLN function
Determines the depreciation for one period using the straight-line method.
```
curDepreciation = SLN(curCostOfAsset,
  curSalvageValue, _
intAssetLifeInYears)
```

SmallChange property
For a Horizontal or Vertical Scrollbar control, determines the amount by which the control's Value property changes each time the arrow at either end of the scrollbar is clicked.

Snapshot recordsettype
For a Data control, specifies that a non-updatable Recordset will be created by taking a "snapshot" of the underlying records at the time of Recordset creation.

Sorted property
For a ListBox or ComboBox control, determines whether the items added to the list will be maintained in sorted order or not.

Source program
The program as written by the programmer.

SQL
Structured Query Language, the de facto standard programming language for manipulation of Database Tables within a DBMS.

Sqr function
Returns the square root of its argument:
```
sngX = Sqr(100)  'sngX is assigned 10
```

Standard module (.BAS file)
A module containing only declarations and procedures, that is, no GUI.

Start Up form
The form which VB loads and displays when a program begins execution.

Static statement
Causes a variable declared within a procedure to remain in existence and retain its value between procedure calls.

Str function
Returns a string from its numeric argument.

Stretch property
For an Image control, a Boolean property which determines whether the Image control will be sized to fit the picture loaded into it, or whether the picture will be sized (stretched) to fit the dimensions of the Image control.

String data type (prefix: str)
A data field which contains characters (a string). Maximum string length is about 65,000 characters.

Style property (cbo control)
For the ComboBox control, determines whether the style is 0-Dropdown Combo, 1-Simple Combo, or 2-Dropdown List.

Sub Main() procedure
A procedure in a Standard module, which may serve as the StartUp form for an application.

Sub/End Sub statement
Marks the beginning and end of all procedures except Function procedures.

SYD function
Returns the depreciation for a specified period, calculated by the sum-of-years-digits method.
```
curDepreciation = SYD(curCostOfAsset,
  curSalvageValue, _
intAssetLifeInYears, intSpecifiedYear)
```

Syntax
Grammar rules. The syntax of a VB statement/function is a prototype or model for its proper use.

Syntax error
A violation of the rules of Visual Basic.

TabIndex property
Determines the tab order of controls on a form.

Table object
Within a Database, a facility for storing data in rows and columns.

Table recordsettype
For a Data control, a limited type of Recordset created from a single Table.

Tag property
For any form or control, an extra string field for programmer use.

Tan function
Used in wintertime to simulate the effects of summer. In Visual Basic, returns the tangent of an angle measured in radians. This prints the tangent of a 45° angle (which should be 1, if π is sufficiently accurate):

```
Const PI = 3.141593
Print Tan(45 * (PI / 180))
```

TextBox control (prefix: txt)
Used to display text and to obtain text input from the user.

Tile Horizontal arrangement
In the Arrange method, causes open, non-minimized child forms to be displayed horizontally within the MDIForm:

```
MDIForm1.Arrange vbTileHorizontal
```

Tile Vertical arrangement
In the Arrange method, causes open, non-minimized child forms to be displayed vertically within the MDIForm,:

```
MDIForm1.Arrange vbTileVertical
```

Timer control (prefix: tmr)
Used to schedule the execution of procedures at a fixed Interval.

Toggle Breakpoint (F9)
Sets or removes a breakpoint. During execution, when a line of code containing a breakpoint is encountered, execution halts and the program enters break mode.

Toolbar
The row of icons underneath VB's Menu Bar.

Toolbox
The set of icons along the left side of the VB Development Environment, containing icons which represent controls.

Top property
Determines the distance from the top border of an object to the top border of its container.

TreeView control (prefix: tv)
A control that provides a graphical view of a list of folders or other items, similar to the left panel in Windows Explorer.

Trim function
Returns the string argument, but without leading or trailing spaces:

```
strTrimmed = Trim("  Start  ") 'strTrimmed =
  "Start"
```

Type declaration character
A character appended to a variable name which denotes its data type.

Type/End Type statements
Creates a user-defined data type:

```
Type MyType
bytMyByte As Byte
blnMyBoolean As Boolean
strMyAlpha As String
End Type
```

UCase function
Returns the same string as the argument, but with all lower case letters converted to upper case:

```
Loop While UCase(sAnswer) = "YES"
```

Unique Index
In the Data Manager, designating a Unique Index for a Table guarantees that duplicate record keys will not be permitted by the Microsoft Jet.

Unload statement
Unloads a form's graphic image from memory (code remains in memory):

```
Unload frmCollege
```

Until conditional
In a Do loop, provides a test condition which allows the loop to continue until the condition is True:

```
Do
Loop Until InputBox("cry 'Uncle'") = "Uncle"
```

Update method
For a Data control, following an Edit or an AddNew method, records pending changes in the Recordset and in the underlying Tables:

```
db.Recordset.Update
```

Val function
Returns a numeric from a string argument, from left to right, up to the first non-numeric character:

```
Print Val("123 Main Street") 'prints 123
```

Validate event
For a Data control, occurs before the current record changes to a different record, before the Update method executes, and before a Database closes. Used to cancel pending changes to a record which are not desired.

Variable
A symbolic reference to an address (or a block of addresses) in memory. A variable is defined by its name, data type, scope, and (in the case of an array) number of elements.

Variable declaration
A Dim, Static, ReDim, Private, or Public statement which declares a variable.

Variable name
The name assigned to a variable.

Variant data type
A type of data which can contain any kind of value:

```
Dim vntX As Variant
vntX = "Bob" 'vntX will now be treated as a
  string
vntX = 4.567 'vntX will now be treated as a
  single
```

Vertical Scroll Bar control (prefix: vsc)
A vertical, analog graphical device for representing integer values within a specified range.

View Code (F7) command
Opens the Code Window for the currently selected object.

View Properties (F4) command
Opens the Properties Window for the currently selected object.

Visible property
A Boolean property which determines whether a graphical object is visible.

Visual Data Manager
A subset of the Microsoft Jet Database engine, the Visual Data Manager allows the user to create a Microsoft Database or to add, delete, or modify records in Tables created in most popular PC-based Database Management Systems (DBMS).

Watch variable or expression
A designated variable or expression which is monitored while a program is running within the VB Development Environment. Breaks can be triggered automatically when the value of the Watch expression changes or becomes True.

While conditional
Part of a Do loop; causes the loop to continue executing as long as (that is, While) the specified condition exists:

```
Do
Loop While intCounter < intMaxCount
```

While/Wend statements
Alternative syntax for a Do…Loop.

Width property
Determines the width of an object.

Window
A rectangular box on the screen.

WindowList property
When set for a menu item, causes a list of all open child forms to be displayed at the bottom of the menu drop-down list for that menu item.

WindowState property
Determines which state a window is in: normal, maximized (filling the whole screen), or minimized (reduced to)

With/End With statements
When a series of statements reference components of a recordname, With/End With can shorten and simplify the code:

```
With gudtEmployeeRec
strStatus = "I"
intEmpNum = 0
strLastName = ""
End With
Put #1, intRecNum, gudtEmployeeRec
```

Write # statement
Writes data to a sequential data file:

```
Write #1, strLastName, intNumber, curPrice
```

X1, Y1, X2, Y2 properties
Line coordinates for a Line control.

INDEX

A

Access DBMS 224–229, 231f, 283
Active window 15
ActiveX Data Objects (ADO) technology 278, 312
ActiveX Data Object Data Control 278, 284–287
Actual parameter 156–159, 169
Add Procedure command 168
Add Watch command 112
Add-In Manager 285, 287, 311
Add-Ins toolbar 287
AddItem method 266ff
AddNew method 255, 278
ALGOL language 7
Algorithm 58
Align Property 209f
Alignment property 36, 45, 62, 73
API calls 278, 296, 306, 312
App object 240f, 243
Append filemode 318, 331
Application 22
Application Programming Interface 278, 296, 306, 312
Application Wizard 278, 288, 290–297, 312
Argument 68
Arithmetic expression 52f
Arithmetic operator 52
Arrange Icons arrangement 194, 203–206
Arrange method 203–206, 215
Array of variables 126, 129f, 145
Asc function 179
ASCII codes 53, 88
Assembler 4
Assembly language 4f, 7
Assignment statement 41f, 45, 51, 73
Atn function 179
AutoRedraw property 304, 312

B

BackColor property 28, 31f, 41, 45
BackStyle property 120
Backus, Jim 5
BASIC language 5ff, 22
Bell Labs 7
BOF property 252, 256, 273
Bookmark property 251
Boolean data type 53f, 54, 73
Boolean variables and expressions 126, 135f, 145
BorderColor property 120
BorderStyle property 73
BorderWidth property 120
Borland International 7
Bound control 229, 231f
Breakpoint 111
Bug 64
Byte data type 53f, 73
ByVal parameter 157–158

C

C language 5, 7f
C++ language 5, 7ff
Call statement 156–161, 171
CancelUpdate method 251–
Caption property 10, 28, 30, 32, 45
Cascade arrangement 194, 203–206
Case structure 151, 151f, 169
Change event 100, 148
Check Box control 268, 279
Checked property 199
Child form 200–204, 215
Choose function 174, 181–182, 188
Chr function 88
Circle method 304, 312
Class 8, 31
Class module (.CLS file) 289, 306, 312
Clear (Clipboard) method 308, 312
Clear (List Box) method 262, 275
Click event procedure 31, 45, 67
Clipboard object 62, 308, 312
Close statement 319, 331
Cls method 41, 45
COBOL language 5f, 58
Codd, E.J. 224
Code reuse 148, 191, 292
Color property 260, 262, 274
Combo Box control 264, 266, 274
Command Button control 10, 28, 31ff, 45
Common Dialog control 249, 257–262, 274
Compiler 5
Computer program 4
Concatenation 57
ConnectionString property 287, 312
Const declaration 38ff, 45
Constant 38, 50
Containers: see Form, MDI Form, Picture Box control, Frame control
Context-sensitive Help 81, 92
Control 10, 15, 17, 22
Control array 85, 90, 92, 148
Control object 45
Control structures 59, 73, 86
Controls collection 308
Copy buffer 251
Copy command 62, 67
Corel 9
Cos function 305, 312
Count property 254, 312
Currency data type 53f, 73
Current record 228, 232, 251
CurrentX property 304
CurrentY property 304
Cut command 62

D

Dartmouth BASIC 6
Data Access Objects (DAO) technology 256, 284–285
Data control 225, 227–244, 251, 255
Data Definition Language 224
Data Form Designer window 278, 283, 311
Data Form Wizard 278, 284–287, 312
Data Grid control 284
Data Manipulation Language 224
Data types 53f, 73
Database Management System 224, 238, 243
Database object 227–244
DatabaseName property 228, 240, 243
Databases 220–224
DataChanged property 253, 274
DataField property 228–229, 231, 265
DataSource property 228–229, 231, 265
Date data type 53f, 73
DBase DBMS 224–225, 283
DBCombo control 249, 262, 265
DBList control 262, 265
DBMS 224, 238, 243
DDB function 128, 138
DDL 224
Debug object 111–115, 119
Declarations 38, 44, 63, 312
Declare statement 312
Default object 43
Default value 17
DefaultExt property 258, 274
Delete method 252, 274
Derivative math functions 179
Design time 17
Dijkstra, Edsgar 59
Dim statement 50, 65
Dimension 50
DML 224
Do...Loop statement 126, 133–135, 145
DoEvents statement 306
Double data type 53f, 73
Drag method 325, 331
DragDrop event 325, 331
DragIcon property 325, 331
DragMode property 325, 331
DragOver event 325, 331
DrawMode property 304
DrawStyle property 304
DrawWidth property 304
DropdownCombo style 264, 275
DropdownList style 264, 279

Dynamic Link Library 309
Dynaset RecordsetType 232, 251

E

Edit method 251, 274
Edit Watch command 112
Editions 9
EditMode property 253, 274
Embedded SQL 238
Enabled property 28, 31, 42, 45
End Function statement 180, 188
End Select statement 153
End Sub statement 41f
End Type statement 305–309
End With statement 322
Enddoc method 87
Enterprise Edition 9
EOF function 319–320, 331
EOF property 252
Err object 112, 165f, 171
Error traps 148, 160–168, 169
Event 8, 22, 40, 45
Event procedure 16
Excel 231, 279
Executable program 4f
Exit command 15
Exit Function statement 191
Exit Sub statement 160–163
Exp function 179
Expression 51–53, 73

F

Fibonacci sequence 172–174, 186
Fields collection 254f
File Menu 13
Filemode 318, 331
FileName property 259, 274
Filenumber 318, 331
FillColor property 98
FillStyle property 98
Filter property 258, 274
FilterIndex property 258, 274
Financial functions 125–
FindFirst method 232f, 243
FindLast method 232, 243
FindNext method 232, 243
FindPrevious method 232, 243
Flags property 258, 262, 274
Flashing icons 209
Flowchart 58
Focus 99f, 267
Font object 36, 274
Font.Size property 31, 45
FontBold property 260
FontItalic property 260
FontName property 260
FontSize property 260
FontStrikethru property 262
FontUnderline property 262
For/Next loop 83, 86–92
ForeColor property 262
ForeColor property 79, 262
Foreign key 225, 247
Form 10, 15f, 22
Form Editor toolbar 234
Form location on the screen 107
Form object 28, 45
Form properties 16
Form/module level variable 65
Form_Click event procedure 87
Form_Load event procedure
Formal parameter 156–159, 169
Format function 137, 138f
FORTRAN language 5ff, 58
Foxpro 228, 279
Frame control 125–126, 130, 147
FreeFile function 330
FRM filetype 13f
Function 7, 55, 68
Function procedure 172, 180, 183, 188, 191
Function/End Function statement 180, 188
FV function 128, 140

G

GE (General Electric) 6
General object 38, 44, 63
General procedure 147, 155–160, 166, 169
Get statement 330
GetData method 308, 312
GetText method 308, 312
Global variable 7
GotFocus event 268, 271f, 275, 279
Graphical User Interface (GUI) 12, 16, 22
Graphics methods 301

H

Handles 33f, 62
Height property 97f, 104
Help Menu 19, 78f
Help system 77–83
HelpCommand property 262, 274
HelpFile property 262, 274
Hexadecimal color codes 32, 38ff, 84, 91
Hide method 97
Hierarchy Table 55, 58f, 73, 89
Higher-level language 5, 7
History of Visual Basic 4–9
Hopper, Grace 5
Horizontal Scroll Bar control 301, 306, 312
Hungarian notation 56, 66f, 73

I

IBM (International Business Machines) 5, 9, 224, 238
Icon 8
Icon property 207, 215
If/Then 60f, 69–73
If/Then/Else 60f, 71–73
IIf function 241
Image control 205ff, 215f
Immediate If (IIf) function 241
Immediate Window 21, 22
Index property 85, 88, 91f
Infinite Loop: see Loop, Infinite
Infix notation 55
Information hiding 7, 228
InitDir property 258, 279
Input # statement 318, 331
Input filemode 322, 335
Input function 322, 324f, 335
InputBox function 126, 133, 145
Instantiation 8
Integer data type 53f, 73
Integrated Development Environment 10, 12–19, 22
Internally controlled loop 86, 92
Interpreter 5
Interval property 118f
I-P-O Chart 58
Iteration control structure 59f, 73, 86

J

Java language 9
Jumps 79ff

K

Kemeny, John 6f
Kernighan, Brian 7
KeyAscii value 88, 92
KeyPress event 88, 92, 145
KeyPreview property 88, 92
Keyword 51, 78
Kill statement 319f, 335
Kurz, Thomas 6f

L

Label control 28, 36, 45
LargeChange property 306
LastModified property 251
Learning Edition 9
Left property 97f, 104
Line continuation character 69
Line control 301, 306
Line Input # statement 318, 320, 331
Line method 301, 312
Linker program 4f
List Box control 262ff, 275
List property 263, 275
ListCount property 263, 275
ListField property 265
ListIndex property 263, 275
ListView control 289, 297, 312
Literal 50
Load statement 97
LoadPicture function 207ff, 217
Local variable 7

Locating a form on the screen 107
Lock Controls command 234
Log function 179
Logic error 110, 120
Logical inch 97
Long data type 53f, 73
Loop control variable 86, 92
Loop, Infinite: see Infinite Loop
Looping (iteration) 86
LostFocus event 267f, 275

M

Machine language 4f
Macro 5
Make <Project Name> EXE File command 15, 217f
Max property 307
MDIChild property 199–203, 215
MDIForm object 192, 194, 199–206, 215
Me object reference 84, 91
Menu Bar 13, 22, 116f
Menu control 194–199, 215
Menu Editor 194–199; shortcut keys 199
Metafile 307
Method 8, 22, 41, 45
Microsoft 4, 7ff, 11
Midlevel language 7
Min property 306
Mod operator 126, 135, 145
Module 7
Module level variable 65
MouseDown event 325f, 331
MouseMove event 325f, 331
MousePointer property 208, 216
MouseUp event 325f, 331
MoveComplete event 287
MoveFirst method 232, 243
MoveLast method 232, 243
MoveNext method 232, 243
MovePrevious method 232, 243
MS Flex Grid control 262, 265ff
MsgBox statement 43, 45
MultiLine property 126, 140
Multiple forms 96f, 101–104

N

Name property 30, 32, 45
Naming conventions 168
New Project command 13, 32
Next sequential instruction 59f
NoMatch property 233, 243

O

Object 8, 10, 22, 41
Object Browser 137, 185
Object data type 53f, 73
Object linking and embedding 278, 297, 301, 308, 312
Object name 30f
Object program 4f
Object-Oriented Programming (OOP) 7f
ODBC 225, 227, 283
OLE control 297, 307, 312
On Error Goto statement 160–164, 167
Open Database Connectivity Protocol 225, 226, 279
Open Project command 13
Open statement 318, 330
Option Button control 128, 130, 132f, 145
Option Explicit declaration 39, 63
Options command 18
Oracle DBMS 9
Output filemode 318, 331

P

Package and Deployment Wizard 309–312
Paint event 305, 312
Paradox DBMS 227, 279
Parallel array 153–154
Parameter passing 148, 156–159, 169
Pascal 5, 7, 22, 58
Paste command 62, 67
Path property 240
Picture Box control 207f, 215
Picture property 205ff, 215
Pixel (measurement scale) 98
Pmt function 126, 140
Point (measurement scale) 97f
Primary key 224, 243, 251
Prime number 172, 185–188
Print command 15
Print method 31, 41f, 45
Printer object 87
Private declaration 41, 65
Procedure 7
Procedure calls 154–160
Professional Edition 9, 17
Program 4, 22
Project 13
Project Explorer Window 20, 22, 102
Properties Window 16f, 22, 32
Property 8, 16f, 22, 45
Property Page window 312
Property procedures 309, 312
Prototyping 9
PSet method 304, 312
Pseudocode 55, 58, 73, 89
Public declaration 64, 169, 288, 312
Put statement 334f

Q

QBColor function 83f, 88, 91f
QueryDef 237, 251
Quick Watch command 114
QuickBASIC language 7

R

Raise method 112, 164
Random data file 329ff
Random number 172, 174–178, 184, 188
Randomize statement 176–177, 188
Rapid Application Development (RAD) 9
ReadOnly property 254, 274
Recordset object 225, 227–244, 250f
RecordsetType property 232
RecordSource property 228, 237
Referential integrity 255
Refresh method 238, 240, 243, 250, 274, 305, 312
Relational expression 69–72
Relational model 225f
Relational operator 70–72
Remote Data Objects (RDO) technology 256, 284f
RemoveItem method 262ff, 275
Reposition event 240, 243, 278
Require Variable Declarations command 32, 39
Resume statement 162, 169
Reusable code 148, 188, 288
RGB color scheme 84, 91f
Right function 241
Ritchie, Dennis 7
Rnd function 106f, 175–178, 188
RowSource property 265
Runtime 34, 74, 76, 252
Runtime error 108f, 120

S

Save <Filename> As command 14
Save <Filename> command 14
Save Project As command 14
Save Project command 14, 36
ScaleMode property 98, 104
Scope 64f, 73, 100f, 149, 155
Screen object 107, 120
Scrollbar controls 305
Select Case statement 148, 151ff
Selection control structure 59f, 73
Sequential data file 317–321, 331
Set Next Statement command 115
SetData method 308, 312
SetFocus method 267f, 275
SetText method 308, 312
Sgn function 179
Shape control 96, 98f, 120
Shape property 99
Shell function 301
Shortcut keys 116f, 201
Show method 97
Show Next Statement command 115
ShowColor method 257f, 260, 262, 275
ShowFont method 257f, 260, 262, 275
ShowHelp method 257f, 261f, 275
ShowOpen method 257, 275
ShowPrinter method 257f, 261f, 279
ShowSave method 257f, 275
SimpleCombo style

Simulation 177f, 188
Sin function 305, 312
Single data type 53f, 73
SLN function 128, 138f
SmallChange property 306
Snapshot RecordsetType 232, 256
Sorted property 264
Sorting a table 327ff
Source program 4
Splash screen 192, 207, 216
SQL 224, 238f, 243, 279
Sqr function 179, 184
Standard module (.BAS file) 288f, 306f, 312
Startup form 96, 104, 218
Static declaration 149ff, 169
Step Into command 115
Step Over command 115
Step To Cursor command 115
Steps in computer programming 29
Str function 55, 69, 72
Stretch property 205f, 215
String data type 53f, 73
Stroustroup, Bjarne 7
Structure Chart 58
Structured programming 7, 59, 73, 86
Structured Query Language 224, 238f, 243, 279
Style property (cbo control) 264, 275
Sub/End Sub statement 41f
Subprogram 7
SYD function 128, 138f
Symbolic code 4
Symbolic constants 44f, 136, 255f
Syntax 5
Syntax error 108, 120
Syntax error 5

T

Tab Width command 32
TabIndex property 99f, 267f
Table 221–224, 250f
Table join 238
Table RecordsetType 232
Tag property 308, 312
Tan function 179
TextBox control 96, 99f
Tile Horizontal arrangement 194, 202–205
Tile Vertical arrangement 194, 202–205
Timer control 118ff, 215
Timer event 118f
Title Bar 12
Toggle Breakpoint 111
Toggle switches 201
Toolbar (inside a VB app) 209f
Toolbar 18, 22, 115–116f
Toolbox 17, 22
Tools Menu 18
Top property 98f, 104
TreeView control 289f, 297, 312
True BASIC language 7
Turbo BASIC language 7
Twips measurement scale 97f, 120
Type declaration character 53f
Type/End Type statements 305–309, 316, 325f

U

Unix 7
Unload statement 97
Until conditional 134f
Update method 251–256, 274
User-defined data type 278, 301–305, 312, 321f, 331

V

Val function 55, 68f
Validate event 255f, 274
Value property 130, 132f, 268, 306
Variable 4, 50f, 73
Variable array 126, 129f, 145
Variable declaration 7, 50
Variable name 50f, 168
Variant data type 53f, 73
VBP filetype 13f
Vertical Scroll Bar control 301, 309, 312
View Code command 15f, 20
View Menu 15–18
View Object Browser 137, 185
View Object command 15f
View Properties 15ff
Visible property 28, 31, 34, 42, 45
Visual Basic for Applications (VBA) 9
Visual Basic history 7ff
Visual Data Manager 227, 228, 279–284, 315

W

Warnier-Orr diagram 58
Watch 112, 120
While conditional 134f
Width property 98f, 104
WillChangeRecord event 291
WindowList property 194, 202–205, 215
Windows 8, 10, 17f
Windows API calls 278, 301, 306, 312
Windows Explorer 10
WindowState property 181, 215
Wirth, Nicholas 7
With/End With statements 322f, 331
Write # statement 318f, 331